THE COLD WAR AS RHETORIC

PRAEGER SERIES IN POLITICAL COMMUNICATION
Robert E. Denton, Jr., *General Editor*

THE COLD WAR AS RHETORIC

The Beginnings, 1945–1950

LYNN BOYD HINDS
THEODORE OTTO WINDT, JR.

Praeger Series in Political Communication

New York
Westport, Connecticut
London

Library of Congress Cataloging-in-Publication Data

Hinds, Lynn Boyd.
　　The cold war as rhetoric : the beginnings, 1945–1950 / Lynn Boyd
Hinds, Theodore Otto Windt, Jr.
　　　　p.　　cm. — (Praeger series in political communication)
　　Includes bibliographical references and index.
　　ISBN 0–275–93578–7 (alk. paper)
　　1. Cold War.　2. World politics—1945–　　I. Windt, Theodore.
II. Title.　III. Series.
　　D1053.H525　　　1991
　　327′.09′045—dc20　　　　　91–445

British Library Cataloguing in Publication Data is available.

Library of Congress Catalog Card Number: 91–445
ISBN: 0–275–93578–7

First published in 1991

Praeger Publishers, One Madison Avenue, New York, NY 10010
An imprint of Greenwood Publishing Group, Inc.

Printed in the United States of America

The paper used in this book complies with the
Permanent Paper Standard issued by the National
Information Standards Organization (Z39.48–1984).

10 9 8 7 6 5 4 3 2 1

For our families
Cindy, Shelley, Jeff, and Rob;
and Beth, Ted III, and Thad

Contents

CONTENTS

About the Series

Those of us from the discipline of communication studies have long believed that communication is prior to all other fields of inquiry. In several other forums I have argued that the essence of politics is "talk" or human interaction.[1] Such interaction may be formal or informal, verbal or nonverbal, public or private but always persuasive, forcing us consciously or subconsciously to interpret, to evaluate, and to act. Communication is the vehicle for human action.

From this perspective, it is not surprising that Aristotle recognized the natural kinship of politics and communication in his writings of *Politics* and *Rhetoric*. In the former, he establishes that humans are "political beings [who] alone of the animals [are] furnished with the faculty of language."[2] And in the latter, he begins his systematic analysis of discourse by proclaiming that "rhetorical study, in its strict sense, is concerned with the modes of persuasion."[3] Thus, it was recognized over two thousand years ago that politics and communication go hand in hand because they are essential parts of human nature.

Back in 1981, Dan Nimmo and Keith Sanders proclaimed that political communication was an emerging field.[4] Although its origin, as noted, dates back centuries, a "self-consciously cross-disciplinary" focus began in the late 1950s. Thousands of books and articles later, colleges and universities offer a variety of graduate and undergraduate coursework in the area in such diverse departments as communication, mass communication, journalism, political science, and sociology.[5] In Nimmo and Sanders's early assessment, the "key areas of inquiry" included rhetor-

ical analysis, propaganda analysis, attitude change studies, voting studies, government and the news media, functional and systems analyses,
technological changes, media technologies, campaign techniques, and
research techniques.[6] In a survey of the state of field in 1983 by the same
authors and Lynda Kaid, they found additional, more specific areas of
concerns such as the presidency, political polls, public opinion, debates,
and advertising to name a few.[7] Since the first study, they also noted a
shift away from the rather strict behavioral approach.

Today, Dan Nimmo and David Swanson assert that "political communication has developed some identity as a more or less distinct domain of scholarly work."[8] The scope and concerns of the area have
further expanded to include critical theories and cultural studies. While
there is no precise definition, method, or disciplinary home of the area
of inquiry, its primary domain is the role, processes, and effects of
communication within the context of politics broadly defined.

In 1985, the editors of *Political Communication Yearbook: 1984* noted that
"more things are happening in the study, teaching, and practice of
political communication than can be captured within the space limitations of the relatively few publications available."[9] In addition, they
argued that the backgrounds of "those involved in the field [are] so
varied and plurist in outlook and approach, . . . it [is] a mistake to adhere
slavishly to any set format in shaping the content."[10] And more recently,
Swanson and Nimmo call for "ways of overcoming the unhappy consequences of fragmentation within a framework that respects, encourages, and benefits from diverse scholarly commitments, agendas, and
approaches."[11]

In agreement with these assessments of the area and with gentle
encouragement, Praeger established in 1988 the series entitled Praeger
Studies in Political Communication. The series is open to all qualitative
and quantitative methodologies as well as contemporary and historical
studies. The key to characterizing the studies in the series is the focus
on communication variables or activities within a political context or
dimension. Scholars from the disciplines of communication, history,
political science, and sociology have participated in the series.

I am, without shame or modesty, a fan of the series. The joy of serving
as its editor is in participating in the dialogue of the field of political
communication and in reading the contributors' works. I invite you to
join me.

Robert E. Denton, Jr.

NOTES

1. See Robert E. Denton, Jr., *The Symbolic Dimensions of the American Presidency*
(Prospect Heights, IL: Waveland Press, 1982); Robert E. Denton, Jr., and Gary

Woodward, *Political Communication in America* (New York: Praeger, 1985; 2d ed., 1990); Robert E. Denton, Jr., and Dan Hahn, *Presidential Communication* (New York: Praeger, 1986); and Robert E. Denton, Jr., *The Primetime Presidency of Ronald Reagan* (New York: Praeger, 1988).

2. Aristotle, *The Politics of Aristotle*, trans. Ernest Barker (New York: Oxford University Press, 1979), p. 5.

3. Aristotle, *Rhetoric*, trans. Rhys Roberts (New York: The Modern Library, 1954), p. 22.

4. Dan Nimmo and Keith Sanders, "Introduction: The Emergence of Political Communication as a Field," in *Handbook of Political Communication*, ed. Dan Nimmo and Keith Sanders (Beverly Hills, CA: Sage, 1981), pp. 11–36.

5. Ibid., p. 15.

6. Ibid., pp. 17–27.

7. Keith Sanders, Lynda Kaid, and Dan Nimmo, eds., *Political Communication Yearbook: 1984* (Carbondale, IL: Southern Illinois University: 1985), pp. 283–308.

8. Dan Nimmo and David Swanson, "The Field of Political Communication: Beyond the Voter Persuasion Paradigm" in *New Directions in Political Communication*, ed. David Swanson and Dan Nimmo (Beverly Hills, CA: Sage, 1990), p. 8.

9. Sanders, Kaid, and Nimmo, *Political Communication Yearbook*, p. xiv.

10. Ibid., p. xiv.

11. Nimmo and Swanson, "Field of Political Communication," p. 11.

Series Foreword

Nearly two generations of Americans, if we consider the years of cog-
nitive and political awareness, have grown up under the shadows of
the cold war. For most of us, it was a war of words, not bombs. It was
a war of threats, name-calling, fear, and distrust. At the heart of the
cold war was the fact that the United States and the Soviet Union had
the instantaneous power, and hence control, of life and death. The issue
was not one of absolute power as much as of its arbitrary use.

In traditional studies of international relations, nations are perceived
as actors with specific needs, goals, and rights. Each nation seeks to
preserve its power against encroachments of others; to maximize its
needs, goals, and rights; and to extend its power often at times at the
expense of other states. From an international perspective, politics may
be viewed as the art of facilitating the pursuit of a state's interest broadly
defined.

The cold war, however, was more than a clash of national needs,
goals, and rights. It was an *ideology*, a struggle for the right way of life.
Such a moral imperative feeds prejudice, hate, and general suspicion.
The cold war was portrayed as a struggle between good and evil, freedom versus communism. From this perspective, perhaps what we have
witnessed in the last fifty years is a shift from an ideological view of
international affairs to a more realistic one. Some may argue the shift
became a political necessity as a result of declining resources and the
lack of national will to serve as "big brother" to every region without
elements of clear self-interest. Others claim it was a maturation process

of realizing the proper role in international affairs of a great superpower. Somehow, we avoided what might have been analogous to the religious wars of the eighteenth century; wars based not on the dispute of territory but on the disputes of social dogmas.

The first shots of the cold war, according to Khrushchev, were fired by Churchill within the borders of the United States (Khrushchev, 1974, p. 202). At Westminister College in Fulton, Missouri, on March 5, 1946, Churchill warned that "an iron curtain has descended across the continent" and called upon Western democracies to stand together "in strict adherence to the principles of the United Nations Charter" to stop the Soviet Union's continued aggression (Churchill, 1965, p. 804). At the time, Truman was not prepared to endorse the tone or intent of Churchill's remarks and even invited Stalin to come to Missouri to deliver a speech presenting the USSR's view of world peace (Truman, 1974, 312). Stalin refused to visit the United States. Years later, Khrushchev remembers that Churchill's speech

was extremely significant that, of all the times and places he could have given that speech, he chose to give it during a visit *to America*. We knew that if there were to be another war, we would find ourselves confronted with a coalition of Western countries led by the United States. Furthermore, the Cold War was sure to profit big American monopolistic capital. Therefore Churchill's choice of an American platform made his speech all the more threatening to us (Khrushchev, 1974, p. 355).

The Cold War as Rhetoric is a wonderful and insightful study of the symbolic creation of the political reality of the cold war. The study carefully documents how, after World War II, the new world order was rhetorically created and perpetuated for decades to come. The study further demonstrates the power of words in shaping not only political actions but also in reflecting a political consciousness and culture. The rhetoric of the cold war made events, motives, and actions reasonable and understandable. The cold war was an evolution and process of interaction that perhaps began with Churchill's metaphor of an iron curtain and became an ideology of anticommunism. The Red Scare was more deadly than the black plague. Our language determined what we saw, what we thought, and what we did.

This book makes several important contributions to the study of political communication. First, it represents another systematic study of the role of public communication in the creation of political reality. Just as political scientists, historians, psychologists, and sociologists offer analyses of various events, communication scholars need to do the same in order to not only better understand the episode under review but also the influence of communication in human life.

Second, the study contributes to our understanding of the development of the cold war. Hinds and Windt challenge the more traditional, historical, and economic explanations of the cold war. By viewing the development of the cold war as a process, the authors avoid the simplistic temptation of placing blame or second-guessing world leaders. If anything, their analysis is more open and less limited than those of other orientations. I am confident that this work will be recognized as an important contribution to the postrevisionist analyses of the cold war.

Finally, this study provides insight into the nature of the development and execution of foreign policy. As a result, this volume should be essential reading for all students and practitioners of foreign affairs. The authors note that the rhetoric surrounding the Iraqi–American conflict follows much of the same pattern of the Soviet–American disputes of the late 1940s.

Words, of course, have consequences. Words play an important part in any war. For those of us in communication, it is not surprising that wars of words last longer than wars of bullets. Their wounds, while never fatal, can last a lifetime. Edward Bulwer-Lytton informed us in 1839 that "the pen is mightier than the sword." But this study holds the lesson perhaps best expressed in the words of Ralph Waldo Emerson that "eloquence a hundred times has turned the scale of war and peace at will."

Robert E. Denton, Jr.

REFERENCES

Churchill, Winston. 1965. "The Sinews of Peace." In Houston Peterson, ed. *A Treasury of the World's Great Speeches* (pp. 803–6). New York: Simon and Schuster.

Khrushchev, Nikita. 1974. *Khrushchev Remembers: The Last Testament*. New York: Little, Brown.

Truman, Margaret. 1974. *Harry S. Truman*. New York: William Morrow.

Preface

The Cold War as Rhetoric is a study of the rhetorical construction of the political reality called the cold war. It might be described as an exercise in political rhetoric as political ontology. We are here concerned with the ways in which a new world order was rhetorically conceived and rhetorically created in the aftermath of World War II, a new universal political reality. We are not saying that rhetoric produced this change in a direct causal way that can be empirically demonstrated, as in "these specific words" caused "that specific action." Rather we are examining the early postwar rhetoric as the originator of a cold war consciousness that, in turn, created the political environment in which the perceptions of threat led to policies to meet that threat. In *Russia's Road to the Cold War: Diplomacy, Warfare, and the Politics of Communism, 1941–1945*, Vojtech Mastny stated the importance of this environment by noting that "political culture . . . does not determine with any finality the kind of decisions that nations and their leaders make. But the collective experience does shape both their perception of the available choices and the manner in which the decisions are reached."[1] We would add that rhetoric is central to shaping both political consciousness and political culture. At the end of World War II American political culture was fluid, containing a variety of general ideas and vague hopes. Some longed for isolationism; others believed that America had to participate fully in international politics. Some pinned their hopes on the United Nations; others on U.S. military superiority symbolized by the atomic bomb. Americans wanted to avoid another war, but above all, they wanted their soldiers home.

It was within these fluid and shifting conditions that a new political culture emerged, one created through public statements that defined its scope, nature, and purposes. By 1950 conditions were no longer fluid but had fossilized into the all-pervasive new consensus of anticommunism.

In the early years of the cold war, American political leaders created an environment that said Americans had no choice but to respond as they did to the "communist threat." At the same time, they contended that the Soviet Union could at any time choose to end the threat by acting like a civilized nation. However, even as this universal rhetoric took hold, both the United States and the Soviet Union acted upon the age-old assumptions of power politics and spheres of influence. In other words, major American leaders supported by influential opinion-makers created the universal ideology of anticommunism, but applied it selectively in foreign affairs and selectively (though often indiscriminately) in domestic affairs. Nonetheless the all-encompassing rhetoric of anti-communism took possession of people's minds and imaginations so that by 1950 Americans found themselves involved in a real war in Korea and on the verge of a reign of terror at home, generically called Mc-Carthyism. Both grew out of the political preoccupations of the early postwar period and both were waged in the name of anticommunism.

Before describing our effort in more detail, we should say what this book is *not*. First, it is not a history of the origins of the cold war. They exist in abundance from a broad sweep of the era to narrow specialized studies, from orthodox interpretations to revisionist interpretations to postrevisionism. On particular topics we have indicated in the notes the historical and critical sources we used. We assume that many of our readers are acquainted with events during this period and therefore we have not gone into great detail about them.

Second, we should stress that we are not attempting to determine "who started the cold war" nor are we attempting to assess who was primarily to blame for it. The cold war was like an acrimonious divorce complete with much finger-pointing, moral posturing, and firm beliefs in the rightness of each aggrieved party. Trying to untangle the various events and statements that originated or placed blame for the cold war on one party to the exclusion of the other is as futile as trying to determine who was really at fault in a contested divorce action. Instead, we are more concerned with the perceptions of U.S. leaders to Soviet actions or statements and the rhetoric they constructed based on those perceptions. What we do insist upon is that there was choice. Here we depart from the orthodox historians and many of the participants who seem to insist that the United States was "forced" into the cold war against its will.[2] These orthodox histories emphasize that U.S. leadership in the postwar world had no choice but to respond as it did. We reject that notion. People always have choices—choices in perceptions, choices in policies, choices in rhetoric. These may be limited by one's background and beliefs, by one's sense of what is appropriate and practical, by one's psychological make-up or mental capacities, by the ways in which one views the world, by political pressures both domestic and foreign or by the constraints of institutions and circumstances. But these only limit the range of choices. They do not eliminate choices. We have tried to show why certain choices were made and on occasion, what other choices were available.

Conversely, we do not subscribe to the economic interpretation of the revisionist school of cold war historians.[3] Such interpretations seem too narrow and place an inordinate burden on the United States for originating the cold war in the dubious pursuit of economic imperialism. This interpretation diminishes the significant influence of public ideas expressed rhetorically in forming the consciousness and perceptions that guide policy. Our analysis is about the development of those public ideas and their influence.

If anything, our interpretation is closer to the postrevisionist analysis of the cold war.[4] However, we disagree with some of these analysts as well. They—along with the orthodox and revisionist historians—limit their interpretations for the most part to Soviet–American affairs attempting to understand who started the cold war. We insist that the cold war was an all-encompassing rhetorical reality that developed out of Soviet–American disputes but eventually transcended them to reach to American perceptions of Asia and to American actions against domestic dissidents. This ideological rhetoric became so embedded in American consciousness that it eventually limited the political choices leaders could make, created grossly distorted views of adversaries, and finally led to the witch-hunts of McCarthyism.

We are not attempting to place the blame for U.S. participation in the cold war on either the Democrats or Republicans. There is enough responsibility to go around. But in this early critical period, Democrats were in control of the White House where decisive policies and rhetorical events were formulated. Since many Republicans—especially those supporters of Senator Vandenberg's bipartisanship in foreign affairs and those who initiated and supported the early inquisitions by the House Committee on UnAmerican Activities in the domestic cold war—were in agreement with the Truman administration, it is idle speculation to suggest things might have been different had the Republicans controlled the presidency. Indeed, one of the central arguments of this book is that there was a national consensus that developed in the early postwar period that transcended political parties to create a bipartisan political reality for Americans toward policies and events, people and motives in this maelstrom we know as cold war.[5]

Finally, we must concern ourselves with these troublesome words, "rhetoric" and "reality." We take "rhetoric" to be those persuasive forms of discourse—whether spoken or written—that give public meaning to events, people, and policies as a basis for belief or action. The word "reality" is more difficult, and we do not wish to plunge into the philosophic debates over the relation of rhetoric to epistemology or ontology that have so occupied recent scholars of rhetoric.[6] To place our position clearly before the reader, political rhetoric creates the arena of political reality from which political thought and action proceed. Such a statement has become commonplace.[7] But even as that is said, troubling questions remain about what is meant by saying political rhetoric creates political reality. In another connection Richard Cherwitz and James Hikins remarked: "The existence of a reality separate from our human efforts to create or destroy it is the linchpin upon which turns the whole system of rhetorical epistemology we have developed."[8] For some time, the question of whether a "reality" exists separate from "human efforts" has been central among rhetorical theorists who deal with rhetorical epistemology and ontology. But framing the fundamental question in this way has led more to speculative theorizing rather than to productive conclusions.

The major problem is the word "reality." Sometimes it is used to refer to object or events, sometimes to the meaning of those objects or events. These two different uses create confusion. To provide greater clarity, we would do better if we used the word "actuality" to refer to events, objects, and people in the external world; and used the word "reality" to refer to the meaning of these events, objects, and people. With this usage we recognize that the external world exists, that things happen, that people and governments act. Such is the nature of the actual world in which we live. But we argue about what events signify, which actions were important, and what understanding of each is more prudent and reasonable. When we begin to argue about meaning, we are engaged in constructing reality. Insofar as people believe these meanings, a reality is created upon which people act. It is in this sense that we believe political rhetoric creates political reality, structures belief systems, and provides the fundamental bases for decisions.

The Cold War as Rhetoric is divided into the following chapters:

Chapter 1, "Political Rhetoric and Political Reality," outlines the theoretical principles that are used in the subsequent analysis. We are eclectic in our use of rhetorical principles drawing from traditional rhetorical theory but also using theoretical insights originated by Kenneth Burke, methods borrowed from metaphoric and narrative analysis, from hermeneutic theory developed in religious studies, and from a variety of other sources. Above all, we are entering the arena of political epistemic attempting to demonstrate that such a rhetorical approach does indeed have a practical application in criticism. This chapter describes our critical categories and explains their uses in analyzing the American cold war rhetoric. We reject the notion that any one critical perspective can account for the fullness of the anticommunist American rhetoric. In taking this position, we depart from those who seek to find in narrative or metaphoric or any other particular perspective the fundamental method of analyzing discourse. We freely admit to using any theoretical insight or concept that will help us illuminate various rhetorical efforts because we believe that is the role of rhetorical theory in the practice of criticism.

Chapter 2, "The Rhetorical Stockpile," traces the development of certain American images of Russia and the Soviet Union from which leaders selected images that would be used in American rhetoric during the cold war. Just as rhetoric creates history by giving meaning to events, so too language and images have histories that speakers and writers draw upon to speak and write about current events, people, and motives. This chapter describes some of the most salient images that later contributed to the postwar perceptions and rhetoric.

Chapter 3, "Prologue to the Cold War," recounts selective developments from the end of World War II to Winston Churchill's Iron Curtain speech. Several rhetorical streams meandered through this early postwar period as American political leaders sought to hold the old war allies together and at the same time sought to adjust to new circumstances that developed in the first year after the war. Two of the most significant rhetorical events of this period were Stalin's election speech of 1946 which led to George F. Kennan's "long telegram." Both are analyzed as a prelude to the rhetorical thrusts of subsequent years.

Chapter 4, "Churchill's 'Iron Curtain' and Beyond," focuses on the decisive address that began the public rhetorical process in the West of dividing the world into two warring camps. This chapter also narrates the events that followed the speech, especially the Clifford-Elsey report, which provided the bases for President Truman's rationale for the need to send aid to Greece and Turkey in 1947.

Chapter 5, "The Truman Doctrine," is an extended analysis of the writing and presentation of President Truman's March 12, 1947 address, a speech that sanctioned an anticommunist grammar for the postwar period and elevated a policy to an ideological struggle between two "ways of life." Although he did not voice a sophisticated ideological analysis of world events, Truman drew upon the division of the world that Churchill had created a year before, converted it to American terms, and set a universal frame of reference that would guide foreign policy through the next four decades.

Chapter 6, "The Truman Doctrine Extended," briefly analyzes the Truman Loyalty Program and the 1947 hearings in Hollywood of the

House Committee on UnAmerican Activities. The central points of the chapter are that the Truman Doctrine being universal had to be extended to containing domestic communism as well as foreign communism and that the president's program gave legitimacy to the Republican search for subversives in U.S. society.

Chapter 7, "Maintenance and Moral Imperative of the New Political Universe: The Marshall Plan and 'X'," concentrates on two major rhetorical events: Secretary of State George Marshall's address originating the European Recovery Act, and George F. Kennan's "The Sources of Soviet Conduct." Each of these in different ways maintained the rhetorical reality of the political universe previously created by Churchill and Truman, and gave a moral imperative to U.S. actions.

Chapter 8, "Critics and Advocates of the New Reality," examines representative critics of the new political reality that had been announced, and analyzes the reasons for why each failed to one degree or another. It also analyzes advocates of the cold war reality who wanted to extend it beyond Europe to Asia or wanted to apply it more extensively in domestic political life.

Chapter 9, "The Final Proofs and Conclusion," is concerned with summarizing the new reality that had been created and with events that gave final "proof" to the "correctness" of the original rhetorical formulations that had created the cold war reality. These final proofs of rhetoric as reality culminated in a complete ideological statement of U.S. foreign policy, NSC–68, and in the U.S. commitment to act upon this ideology by entering the Korean conflict.

The perspective of this book is that rhetoric is not merely ornamental, but intellectual. Rhetorical endeavors contain ideas about people, events, policies, and objectives. It is upon these ideas that policymakers often act. American rhetoric in the early post-World War II era presented an ideological interpretation of the world and America's place and purpose in it. These ideas did not come from paranoid imaginings, but had a rich heritage which policymakers drew from and adapted to current conditions as they perceived them. The ideas presented in these rhetorical efforts became the most influential ideas in American political culture for the next several decades. Even as policies changed, the rhetorical representations remained constant.

Our focus is primarily upon American rhetoric applied to Soviet–American relations and focused on Europe. In so doing we have paid scant attention to the whole rich area of the anticommunist rhetoric applied to Asia. Only part of Chapter 8 focuses on Asia. However, we made this choice to concentrate on Europe because that was the primary concern of the Truman administration and most others in the early years of the cold war. They saw the Soviet Union as the enemy and constructed the cold war rhetoric to deal with what they perceived as belligerent moves in Europe. In addition, when U.S. leaders did turn their attention to Asia as part of the cold war, those who feared the loss of Asia to communism applied the anticommunist rhetoric they had previously used (with significant variations) to Asian events because they saw the communist threat as monolithic and because the anticommunist rhetoric was so entrenched that it was a relatively simple matter to apply it there as well as to Europe. What follows, then, is the process by which the choices in language and rhetoric as justifications for policies became the pervasive political reality of the time, no longer only justifying policies but dictating them as well.

We wish to extend our appreciation to Daniel Foss, who served as research assistant to Dr. Windt and did diligent background work on the Truman Doctrine, the Marshall Plan, and Kennan's "Sources of Soviet Conduct." His assistance was most helpful. We also appreciate the critical reading Dr. Robert P. Newman and Dr. Richard Cottam gave several chapters of the book. However, we alone bear responsibility for the analysis and content of this book.

NOTES

1. Vojtech Mastny, *Russia's Road to the Cold War* (New York: Columbia University Press, 1979), p. 2.

2. As examples of orthodox interpretations, see Herbert Feis, *Churchill, Roosevelt, Stalin: The War They Waged and the Peace They Sought* (Princeton, NJ: Princeton University Press, 1957), *Between War and Peace: The Postdam Conference* (Princeton, NJ: Princeton University Press, 1960), and *From Trust to Terror: The Onset of the Cold War, 1945–1950* (New York: W. W. Norton, 1970); Louis Halle, *The Cold War as History* (New York: Harper & Row, 1967); and a variety of memoirs including President Truman's two volumes *Memoirs: Year of Decisions* and *Years of Trial and Hope* (Garden City, NY: Doubleday, 1955, 1956); Dean Acheson, *Present at the Creation* (New York: W. W. Norton, 1969); Joseph M. Jones, *The Fifteen Weeks* (New York: Viking, 1955). These are only samples of the most prominent orthodox interpretations. There are literally hundreds of others both in book and article form dealing with the whole cold war or with particular aspects of it.

3. As examples of the revisionist interpretation, see D. F. Fleming, *The Cold War and Its Origins*, 2 vols. (New York: Doubleday, 1961); William Appleton Williams, *The Tragedy of American Diplomacy*, 2d ed., rev. and enlarged (New York: Delta, 1962); David Horowitz, *The Free World Colossus: A Critique of American Foreign Policy in the Cold War* (New York: Hill and Wang, 1965); David Horowitz, ed., *Corporations and the Cold War* (New York: Modern Reader, 1969); Gabriel Kolko, *The Politics of War: The World and United States Foreign Policy, 1943–1945* (New York: Random House, 1968); Joyce and Gabriel Kolko, *The Limits of Power, 1945–1954,* (New York: Harper and Row, 1972).

4. As examples of postrevisionism, see John Lewis Gaddis, *The United States and the Origins of the Cold War 1941–1947* (New York: Columbia University Press,

1972) and *Strategies of Containment* (New York: Oxford University Press, 1982); Daniel Yergin, *Shattered Peace: The Origins of the Cold War and the National Security State* (Boston: Houghton Mifflin, 1977). On postrevisionism, see John Lewis Gaddis, "The Emerging Post-Revisionist Synthesis on the Origins of the Cold War," *Diplomatic History* (Summer 1983), pp. 171–90.

5. On the development of this bipartisanship and the controversy surrounding it, see Cecil V. Crabb, Jr., *Bipartisan Foreign Policy: Myth or Reality?* (Evanston, IL: Row, Peterson, 1957).

6. For one summary of many of the issues involved in this debate, see Richard A. Cherwitz and James W. Hikins, *Communication and Knowledge: An Investigation in Rhetorical Epistemology* (Columbia, SC: University of South Carolina Press, 1986). For an update on some of these issues as they relate to criticism, see Barry Brummett, "A Eulogy for Epistemic Rhetoric," *Quarterly Journal of Speech* 76 (February 1990), pp. 69–72; Robert L. Scott, "Epistemic Rhetoric and Criticism: Where Barry Brummett Goes Wrong," *Quarterly Journal of Speech* 76 (November 1990), pp. 300–3.

7. Theodore Otto Windt, Jr., *Presidents and Protesters: Political Rhetoric in the 1960s* (Tuscaloosa, AL: University of Alabama Press, 1990), p. 3. Cf. Murray Edelman, *The Symbolic Uses of Politics* (Urbana, IL: University of Illinois Press, 1964); William E. Connolly, *The Terms of Political Discourse*, 2d ed. (Princeton, NJ: Princeton University Press, 1983); Fred Dallmayr, *Language and Politics* (Notre Dame, IN: University of Notre Dame Press, 1984).

8. Cherwitz and Hikins, *Communication and Knowledge*, p. 116.

THE COLD WAR AS RHETORIC

Chapter One

Political Rhetoric and Political Reality

The cold war between the United States and the Soviet Union is over. It ended as it began with statements from the leaders of the United States and the Soviet Union. But unlike other wars, there was no general armistice, no V-J Day, no signed surrender, no formal claims of victory or concessions of defeat. In fact, we cannot even date the day the cold war ended. During 1989 and 1990 various governments in eastern Europe collapsed, resigned, or were overthrown. The Soviet Union changed radically under the leadership of Mikhail Gorbachev. First it was the journalists declaring the cold war over. That was followed in subsequent months by President Gorbachev and President Bush saying the same thing, usually in casual circumstances. Now, it is part of our political reality that it is finished. One era ended; a new one began. But our purpose is to look back on that old era and attempt to determine how it developed as it did in the United States in the early postwar days.

The Soviet–American cold war was a rhetorical war, one fought with words as weapons. But the cold war was more than threats by one nation hurled against another. The rhetoric created the consensus we call the cold war. When one begins studying its origins, one immediately concentrates on public statements: Stalin's "February Election" address, Churchill's "Iron Curtain" speech, Truman's speech to a joint session of Congress in March 1947, Marshall's commencement address announcing the Marshall Plan, and on and on through major and minor statements by central figures in the rhetorical drama of the beginnings of the cold war. This rhetoric created a complete and pervasive political reality about events, motives, actions, and policies. In the United States, it created a universal worldview of national and international politics where nothing less than the survival of the American way of life seemed to be at stake. The cold war became all encompassing, not merely a rivalry between two great powers, but a Manichaean struggle between the forces of light and the forces of darkness. We may justly ask how this occurred.

The United States emerged from World War II as the most powerful nation in the world. With her allies, the nation had won a decisive military victory. Germany and Japan, who had divided the world into antagonistic camps, had been vanquished, and a new world was in the making. At the end of the war, U.S. casualties had been the lowest among the allies and its territories had been untouched by war. Agriculture was producing at a record high; industrial production was at an all-time peak. The gross national product had grown from $91 billion in 1939 to $212 billion by 1945, fully one half of the entire gross national product of the world.[1] The U.S. military might had never been stronger, and the United States alone had the atomic bomb.

In contrast, the major European powers had suffered heavy losses. England and France had expended much of their treasury—both in money and material—to fight the war. Within eighteen months each country would experience enormous economic problems exacerbated by the bitter winter that engulfed Europe. But the biggest loser among U.S. allies was the Soviet Union. More than 20 million Soviets were dead, a thousand cities and towns had been leveled, industrial production had been cut in half, and the agricultural system, just beginning to recover from the upheaval and purges of the 1930s and the war, was quickly devastated by disastrous drought.

In the first year of peace, the United States stood preeminent in the world. Paradoxically, it also felt the most vulnerable. This paradox, no doubt, was due to the unique experience of seeing a new world in the making and its confusion about its role as the central figure in this emerging world. But America's view of itself would change radically during the next four years. In the course of making specific decisions for particular situations, Americans came to a new understanding of themselves, the world, and their relationship to other nations in the world. By invoking universal principles to justify particular policies, major leaders created a new political reality that caused Americans to make dramatic changes in both foreign and domestic relations.

In foreign affairs the United States discarded its traditional isolationism and became the leader of the "free world." Prior to the war, the nation had no military alliances, no troops stationed in foreign countries, and a small defense budget. By the end of 1950 the United States had extended economic aid to western European countries through the Marshall Plan, had created a great military alliance through NATO, had rearmed not only itself but its former enemy, West Germany, and finally found itself engaged in a land war in Korea to stop the spread of communism in Asia. At home there were crusades to impose "loyalty" upon the population and to purge the country of those who did not conform to its narrowing definition. In 1946 the Progressive Citizens of America (PCA), a new liberal group, could openly accept American communists into its ranks. By the end of the decade the PCA and its most prominent leaders had been discredited, and a rival liberal organization, the staunchly anticommunist Americans for Democratic Action, had replaced it as the principal vehicle for liberal activists. During that time dissent was attacked, unorthodox opinions assailed, and innocent associations became suspect. Professors, entertainers, and government workers were investigated, blacklisted, or fired.[2] In the early 1950s these activities would expand into the full-fledged horror called McCarthyism, but its seeds were planted in the previous decade.

A new political reality developed as Americans—the influential and the ordinary—perceived a threat of monumental proportions sufficient to justify expanding the nation's commitment abroad and stifling dissent at home. The threat was not produced by obvious overt action, such as an attack on a U.S. naval base or the sinking of a U.S. ship by a U-boat. It was created by a new interpretation of the world through rhetoric. The "cold war" summed up this new political reality, and in the words of John Patrick Diggins: "the cold war is not a war at all, but rather a description of the state of affairs."[3] And many people believed that it was the *actual* state of affairs.

In one sense it is strange that the cold war developed. In the images of wartime rhetoric, the Soviet Union had been a brave ally. A diabolical enemy had bound the two nations in common cause to defeat that common enemy and secure a lasting peace. That was the dominant political reality during the war, one that provided the basis for a bipartisan foreign policy and one that was firmly supported by public opinion. It was expected that the two great powers would work together in peacetime as they had during the war. There seemed little reason to question this assumption because "these two great nations had no common land borders to fight over, no ancient heritage of ancient rivalries, no dire economic conflicts, no clashing territorial ambitions."[4] Those who believed conflicts between the two nations might erupt hoped that the new United Nations could mediate and resolve these disputes.

But from another vantage point, it is not strange at all that the cold war developed as it did. Christer Jonsson, in his study of the ideologies of the United States and the Soviet Union, departed from the commonly held notion that the two are "antipodal archetypes" to argue that the two nations are more similar than disparate. Each nation, being dramatically declared into existence by revolution rather than slowly evolving, regarded itself as unique, different from older nations in the established international system. Each acted in two fundamental and apparently contradictory ways: "*withdrawal*—a rejection of the world's complexity; and *globalism*—a wish to end complexity by reforming the world."[5]

From its creation, Americans understood themselves to be a chosen people, God's American Israel,

It was as if, by founding the Republic, Americans had made a new covenant with God. No political reality was ever closer than isolationism to the deep sources of a nation's understanding of its role in the world. That role was not really political. Though it was political in form, it was understood to be a moral role. We were participants in a great moral experiment, the creation of a new kind of political community.[6]

When the United States did decide to intervene in the affairs of the world, the sense of uniqueness and moral superiority manifested itself as a mission to reform the old order. The most prominent instance prior to the cold war was World War I when the official rhetoric proclaimed that America fought to "make the world safe for democracy."

Russians shared this missionary sense of uniqueness and moral superiority. "Going back to the earliest days of Muscovy," Adam Ulam noted "there is the notion of the historical mission of the Russian nation as the representative and defender of eastern Christianity . . . against Catholicism and also . . . against Islam."[7] After the 1917 revolution, as Jonsson pointed out, Soviet leaders secularized this sense of mission but the notions of uniqueness and moral superiority remained. The conflict between withdrawal and globalism erupted in the power struggle following Lenin's death. Leon Trotsky argued for an international communist movement that would engulf the world, a "perpetual revolution." Joseph Stalin took the opposite position, urging that Soviet energy and effort be directed toward securing "socialism in one country."[8] Though Stalin triumphed, the two strains of withdrawal and globalism resided uneasily with each other.

The cold war led each nation to identify the other as a rival and created a mutual animosity that transcended their previously shared contempt for the Old European World. Identifying one another as the primary enemy came gradually, Jonsson observed, through the "frustrated expectations of postwar collaboration" and through analogies and associations drawn from their mutual wartime enemy, Germany.[9] For each nation the enemy became not a state but an ideological conspiracy with each side fighting an "ism" and "inferring the intentions of the adversary not so much from what they *did* as from what they *were* (imperialists/communists)."[10] The boundaries for this warfare became not geographical, as in a traditional war, but ideological, which seemed to know no boundaries either at home or abroad. The Soviets had an ideological rhetoric inherited from the Bolshevik Revolution and case-hardened into a formal stultifying rhetoric under Stalin's reign.[11] To combat the Soviets in the early postwar period Americans developed an ideological rhetoric of anticommunism, America's preeminent ideology and national purpose until the end of the cold war. The question this volume seeks to answer is how Americans who prided themselves on being pragmatic fell prey to a rigid ideology that they applied not only to Soviet–American relations but accepted as the all-encompassing interpretation of political reality in the postwar world, an ideology as strident and stultifying as the communist ideology it sought to overcome. Previous rhetorical scholars have analyzed some of these statements, usually as discrete rhetorical events.[12] Our purpose is to examine them in the process of building upon one another in ways that resulted in the architectonic consensus we call the cold war.

THE COLD WAR AS RHETORIC

The Cold War as Rhetoric is about the rhetorical origins of the cold war in the United States from 1945 to 1950. The primary emphasis is on the critical years of 1946 and 1947 when the rhetorical dimensions and arguments that established the political reality of succeeding years was set. Our other emphasis is on the U.S. side of the cold war. We are concerned with how the American version of the cold war developed, how it was extended to other areas of the world, how it came to be applied to domestic politics as well as foreign affairs. The reason for this emphasis is that we believe the cold war was a rhetorical state of mind rather than a description of Soviet–American relations, a rhetorically constructed ideological reality that was first accepted within the ruling circles of government, then publicly conveyed through major speeches and writings to Americans who generally accepted it as the reality of both foreign and domestic politics. In this sense we are going beyond standard interpretations of the cold war—be they orthodox or revisionist that limit themselves to Soviet–American conflicts—and following the lead of such scholars as Richard M. Freeland who argued in his book, *The Truman Doctrine and the Origins of McCarthyism*, that the rhetoric calling the American version of the cold war into existence was directly linked to the search for domestic subversives. Freeland wrote that the

consistent identification by public officials of support for Cold War foreign policy with loyalty and patriotism, and the explicit labeling by the President among others of opponents of Cold War foreign policy as subversives and communists, tended to create very effective constraints upon political activities of a dissident nature.[13]

Later, this same rhetoric was applied to China so that by 1950 the anticommunist reality had a worldwide meaning.

The primary materials for this examination are the central rhetorical texts that formulated the American cold war consensus in the United States. Our concern is with what Professor Richard Cottam of the University of Pittsburgh has called the "generic moment," a time when perception and rhetoric come together to produce policy, and in the case of the cold war, to produce a universal doctrine. Our theme is taken from Walter Lippmann. In *Public Opinion*, he wrote:

For the most part we do not first see, and then define, we define first and then see. In the great blooming, buzzing confusion of the outer world we pick out what our culture has already defined for us, and we tend to perceive that which we have picked out in the form stereotyped for us by our culture.[14]

If one were to add "political leaders" to "culture," one would have the orientation to what follows in this book. Definitions require language both to conceive of reality and to express it, and the kind of language people use then shapes the ways in which they see the world. Choosing one set of words to define reality rather than another not only orients people, it also creates a grammar that structures reality and then expands into a rhetoric that justifies that reality.

Our thesis is that political rhetoric creates political reality, and in the case of the American cold war, the universal rhetoric created in the aftermath of World War II created a universal reality. Words and arguments chosen to justify policies took on lives of their own which eventually meant—especially in the late 1940s and in the 1950s—that perceptions, opinions, attitudes, policies, and even the way people lived, had to be adjusted more or less (and usually more) to be consistent with this universal rhetoric. No more eloquent example of rhetoric taking on its own life can be found than in the history of George F. Kennan's famous article, "The Sources of Soviet Conduct." Originally written as a private memorandum for James V. Forrestal and based on his private "long telegram," Kennan's article, when published in *Foreign Affairs*, became the living doctrine of containment. Kennan recorded in his *Memoirs* that he watched with great anguish as his term containment "was picked up and elevated, by common agreement of the press, to the status of a 'doctrine', which was then identified with the foreign policy of the administration."[15] He went on to note that he felt "like one who has inadvertently loosened a large boulder from the top of a cliff and now helplessly witnesses its path of destruction in the valley below, shuddering and wincing at each successive glimpse of disaster."[16] Such was the vitality of Kennan's language and rhetoric. And so too were the vitality and life of Churchill's "Iron Curtain," Truman's Doctrine, the Marshall Plan, and a variety of other rhetorical acts that when taken together comprise the American version of the cold war reality.

METHODS OF ANALYSIS

Political rhetoric creates the arena of political reality from which political thought and action proceed. Such a statement has become commonplace.[17] Political language and arguments—in sum, political rhetoric—create political consciousness, define political settings, create national identity, stimulate people to act, and give sense and purpose to these actions.[18] Political reality is a persuasive description of "things as they are," and once situations are so described, certain responses are eliminated and others seem right. Decisions are discussed and debated within the rhetorical description, ever with an eye toward action.

Every society has a need to make sense of things, of its identity as a people or a nation and of the world it inhabits. Government leaders need to provide rationales for their decisions in order to govern. Leaders must convince the public "that the government's decisions are legitimate and good and that its foreign policy is correct."[19] Politics is about power, and political power functions within the context of a perceived political reality. Citizens, likewise, need to make sense of things. Without a sense of political reality, the "way things are," the individual is helpless to understand the myriad of facts and opinions that one is bombarded with daily, especially the things that are far-off and cannot be experienced directly. This need to make sense of the political world evokes a constant outpouring of rhetoric, not only by political leaders but by opinion leaders from all strata of society. In speeches, newspaper editorials, magazine articles, and the like people make rhetorical efforts to argue and describe the "way things are," in short, to understand political reality. Such efforts become intensive and extensive when an old order of political reality changes, as when World War II ended, and a new order is needed to make sense out of the confusion that accompanies the fall of the old. For political rhetoric to function in this fashion, three essential conditions must exist: (1) a "raw" event and/or events or its corollary, confusion about events; (2) a rhetoric that clarifies and assigns meanings to these events; (3) publicity for the rhetoric as others share it at the time. All three of these came together to produce the cold war.

But a study of political rhetoric as political reality is more than that. If we "define and then see," such a concept applies both to decision-makers as well as the general public. The language people use becomes a part of what they see because people cannot have definitions without language. In many respects, we are prepared to see what our language has prepared us to see. We account for the rhetoric used in relation to any event in great part through the preconceptions on which it is based. To a substantial degree the rhetoric that accompanies any event comes from an a priori rhetoric, based on values that have come to be regarded as basic beliefs, on a preexisting language that is always present exerting its influence in shaping our consciousness, on previous interpretations of past events that may or may not be similar to current events. In such ways are we both liberated and imprisoned by language. Government officials and others do not construct a language or a rhetoric out of thin air; they inherit it from the past and modify or adapt it to meet current or future concerns. Robert Funk observed, "Language does not merely stand at our beck and call; it is there before we are, it situates us, it restricts our horizon, it refuses us its total complicity."[20] Even as the language politicians use can be dynamic and changing, it also is dependent on rhetorical traditions created previously. The rhetoric of the cold war grew in large part out of preexisting rhetorics as diverse as Churchill's long-standing antibolshevism and the war language of World War II, to name only a few. This analysis demonstrates that the events that contributed to the cold war after 1945 had a rhetorical climate that preceded them as well as a rhetorical interpretation that accompanied them. The latter grew out of the former, took a particular direction, and molded the meaning of events to the extent that they created an all-pervasive political reality that not only "explained" events but became landmark events in and of themselves, ordering and interpreting future events as they occurred.

Two important points need to be made. First, in the world of practical politics a political rhetoric is often constructed quickly and on an ad hoc basis. George Elsey, a member of President Truman's staff, stated the case for politicians succinctly: "You don't sit down and take time to think through and debate ad nauseam all the points [about an issue]. . . . You don't have time. Later somebody can sit around for days and weeks and figure out how things might have been done differently. This is all very well and very interesting but quite irrelevant."[21] One must add that it is only irrelevant for those who believe that whatever action is taken and whatever rhetoric constructed to justify that action constituted the most prudent action and rhetoric. For the critic reexamination is always required because language has consequences, often creating the first conception of a political reality of an event and then creating a lasting meaning of that event.

Second, the creation of a rhetorical reality is a process, rarely a single event. In the rhetoric of the cold war the reality grew over a period of years before it took hold and became elevated to the level of sacred doctrine, an ideological doctrine whose fundamental principles few dared to challenge and to which almost all had to pay rhetorical respects even when they disagreed about how those principles applied to particular situations. The failures of the architects of the American cold war—Truman, Acheson, and Kennan—to restrict the political reality they had created provide compelling illustrations of the power of their own rhetoric. Before getting to the ways in which this rhetorical process worked to define the nature and scope of the cold war, we need to identify the elements that were crucial to its development.

Names, Metaphors, and Definitions

Thus far we have argued that language is an essential part of reality, not merely a tool to interpret events. Language itself is a creative act, not an added-on interpretation that comes from an act. It is the confluence of act and language that is the first step in creating reality, a "raw" event and the political meaning persuasively expressed that is attached to that event. Language and events cannot be easily separated once they become public currency. Again, we turn to Funk who noted:

Language and understanding arise together, are reciprocal. The common [event or actuality] to which they refer both precedes and follows. It makes them possible, and yet the common reality does not become audible without language and understanding. Language and understanding both arise out of and invoke shared reality.[22]

This process of uniting the two, we call a *language-event*, a unity of political language and actual events that creates political reality both in perception and in expression.

For this analysis of the cold war reality, there are three important ways in which language created that reality: through naming, through metaphor, and through formal definitions.

Kenneth Burke remarked that all language is "magical" or creative because "the mere act of naming an object or situation decrees that it is to be singled out as such-and-such rather than as something-other."[23] In this understanding of language we are not merely *saying* something when we use language, we are *doing* something. When we name an object, it becomes real for us because naming "does not mean inventing a convenient designation, but giving reality to the object, calling it into [meaningful] existence."[24] This conception of language has its roots in antiquity, and although it was once discarded by the modern scientific world as a mythical understanding of reality, its significance has been rediscovered by Burke and the postmodernists. The scientific conception of language came to be associated with its noetic function, that is, a word was thought of as a symbol that only conveys meaning, a tool separate from the thing it described. Louis Halle used this concept of language in describing the changes that American leaders had to make in foreign policy in the postwar period. He argued that the confusions of that period and Soviet expansionism required a new language to express the new "realities" of tensions in the world:

> What was required in the first instance, for the replacement of the projected foreign policy by a policy applicable to the developing circumstances, was a conscious recognition of the realities to which it would have to be applicable. The American Government and the American people . . . would then have to accept the need to re-establish a balance of power by filling the remaining power vacuums and thereby limiting the further expansion of the Russian empire. Such a conceptual change as this, while it might take place more rapidly in the subconscious mind, could hardly be explicitly formulated and adopted as such until after an interval of intellectual confusion and inner conflict, during which some persons would continue to adhere with a sort of blind desperation to the outdated concepts and their attendant language, while others would recognize the increasingly manifest realities without being able to find a coherent intellectual pattern or forms of words into which to fit them.[25]

Clearly, Halle viewed language as a tool of expression, not as a creative rhetorical process. For Halle, the new cold war "reality" existed waiting only to be "recognized." Once recognized, the task for U.S. leaders became an independent search for appropriate concepts and language to express that reality. In the older mythic realm, however, language and the comprehension of reality were more deeply fused. This latter conception of language guides our understanding about rhetoric's role in the political construction of reality.

Following this ancient understanding, Gerhard Von Rad noted that "what happens in language is that the world is given material expression. Objects are only given form and differentiation in the word that names them."[26] Language is more than a way of expressing a comprehension of the world that had been acquired apart from language; it is the means for bringing the world into being. The Hebrew word *dabar* connotes a dynamic element by which an object is both named and created through words. Words, then, not only give identity and meaning to objects and events, they also point to what these objects and events are not and do not mean. Words—the raw materials of language—are exclusive, not inclusive. "Names," Charles Kauffman observed, "create unity from diversity, organizing a complex of contradictory characteristics under a single heading which integrates and gives them meaning" and such names, through the images associated with them, "contain implicit descriptions of our opponents, their motives and likewise provide an account of our own virtues."[27] Kauffman overstates the case by

saying they "contain implicit descriptions." Some do, some do not depending on whether the names have evocative histories. Also, they
contain these only as people attribute such descriptions to them or infer
descriptions from them. Naming, however, may stimulate such associations and images. That process is especially true as old names are
attributed to new circumstances or conditions. When certain meanings
become associated with names by habitual usage, naming then functions
to orient us to situations and people, suggesting appropriate responses
or precluding other orientations and responses. Thus political naming
is the beginning of the rhetorical process to structure a specific view of
the world and to generate support for policies and actions. Naming, as
such, creates a common vocabulary for recognizing the world around
us. The naming of a situation—insofar as it is accepted and widely used—
entitles that situation, and that entitlement suggests appropriate responses in policy and action.

A second way in which reality is rhetorically constructed is through
metaphor. George Lakoff and Mark Johnson spoke of *orientational* metaphors that organize "a whole system of concepts with respect to one
another."[28] During the postwar period politicians created a host of metaphors to make the tensions between the United States and the Soviet
Union understandable. The "iron curtain" emerged as a striking metaphor that divided the world into two hostile camps. A variety of other
metaphors were used to orient people to the administration's view of
dangers in the world and the proper policies to confront them. The "cold
war," of course, was the most prominent and pervasive metaphor of
the entire period, one that became an overarching description of the
"way things actually are" between the United States and communist
countries. We will have much to say about the cold war as metaphor
later, especially in connection with our discussion of Walter Lippmann
who popularized it. But another metaphor was just as prominent. Sometimes it was stated outrightly, sometimes it was implicit in the cold war
rhetoric. Richard Barnet noted that during the cold war "both sides used
the rhetoric [metaphor] of disease to describe the system of the other.
Communism was a virus, a social sickness, a disease of the body politic.
Capitalism, bourgeois culture, was a source of contamination, cancer,
rot."[29] Barnet was correct to call the metaphor a rhetoric because it
conjured up all sorts of associated images and emotions. A disease may
be dangerous and even fatal if not treated immediately. Invisible germs
and viruses spread a disease, and in a time of panic, one looks with
suspicion even on healthy people as potential carriers of the virus or
germ. One deadly germ or one fatal strain of a virus can incapacitate
and eventually kill an entire body. Infected people need to be operated
upon or isolated and confined. Healthy people need to be inoculated
and, in the case of fatal diseases, they need to show proof that they

have been inoculated. Since the germs or viruses are invisible to the naked and untrained eye, expert physicians must be consulted to diagnose symptoms that may indicate certain people have the disease or have been infected. Such experts are trusted as they provide the necessary therapy, painful thought it may be, to cure the disease or contain its spread. The parallels to the search for domestic communists and fellow-travelers are too obvious to be belabored here. Suffice it to say, describing domestic communism as a disease ("the cancer of communism") predisposed ordinary citizens to accept the kinds of inquisitional investigations that began in the late 1940s and reached hysterical heights during the McCarthyite period. It was also implicit in the doctrine of containment that was established to stop the "spread" of communism. In truth, the disease metaphor had a long history in describing communism and therefore had an evocative history. Drawing upon this linguistic tradition the disease metaphor set off a chain reaction of associated thoughts, images, and emotions, or to use the technical term, entailments that, in turn, suggested appropriate ways of responding. To summarize, particular metaphors contribute directly to the structuring of political reality and predispose orientations to that reality in ways that the choice of different metaphors might structure and orient differently.

A third way in which language and rhetoric create reality is through defining situations, issues, and the nature of conflicts. The most obvious way in which this is done is through delineating a series of propositions that define an issue or that characterize a situation. Since the cold war was seen by many as a battle for people's minds, such conceptual definitions played a significant part in the rhetoric, particularly as a battle between "two ways of life." Ofttimes such conceptual definitions are founded on a nation's myths about itself and existing myths about foreign nations. Murray Edelman noted that in the complicated existential world people "hold to a relatively few, simple, archetypal myths, of which the conspiratorial enemy and omnicompetent hero-savior are the central ones."[30]

A less obvious means for defining situations, actions, and people is through narratives told about them. Political narratives help us define the meaning of issues by sorting "through acts, characters, and situations so that a dominant central action or point emerges."[31] Of course, this process is highly selective, especially when used in rhetoric. The speaker or writer selects one narrative stream rather than another from the many available; peoples that stream with characters that represent the point he or she intends to make; and omits those incidents or motives that may contradict the narrative flow or the preconceived conclusion. Just as important the kind of narrative one chooses determines the way in which people respond to the stories. For better or worse, rhetorical narratives—unlike some fictional narratives—tend toward melodrama in which absolute good conflicts with absolute evil and unblemished heroes do battle with unredeemable villains. Among playwrights, melodrama is rivaled only by farce for the dubious distinction as the lowest form of drama, the one that requires little imagination and less artistic endeavor. But in rhetoric it is predominate because it simplifies complex conditions, gives a stereotypical human face to virtue and vice, and attracts human interest through the drama of storytelling.

One result of melodramatic narratives is stereotyping. Once an experience is named or narrated, especially in public or political life, people tend to apply that name or character to what they believe to be other similar experiences or people. A stockpile of images with common names then fits new images into our melodramatic system or are subsumed into it. If every experience were an individual experience we could not explain our experiences effectively to others. Lippmann noted that there "is economy in this. For the attempt to see all things freshly and in detail, rather than as types and generalities, is exhausting, and among busy affairs practically out of the question."[32] Thus, particularly in politics, public figures draw upon a stockpile of stereotyped linguistic and dramatic images to describe current events, people, motives, and actions.

The other side of the coin in politics is stereotyping of antagonists. In fact, that may have an even stronger bonding power as Kenneth Burke observed: "Men who can unite on nothing else can unite on the basis of a foe shared by all."[33] In this respect Gordon Allport argued that until people label an "outgroup" it does not clearly exist in their minds. But once labeled it becomes personified.[34] The more sinister the foe, the more menacing the foe. Thus an even stronger unity is required to withstand the danger. In times of crisis a foreign foe is often described as a diabolical enemy thereby heightening the sense of fear and dread if the government does not act to protect the nation. The enemy is described as both inhuman and superhuman; the first image needed to entitle people to annihilate the enemy (for ordinary people do not hate intensely enough to kill that which they recognize as having some human qualities); the second image necessary to urge greater vigilance (for fear of superior powers encourages greater unity).

Hayden White stated that stories "not only permit us to judge the moral significance of human projects, they also provide the means by which to judge them, even while we pretend to be merely describing them."[35] Above all, narratives are powerful persuasive instruments in creating political reality because they redirect attention from critical examination of the expediency or inexpediency of an issue to the aesthetic examination of whether the stories seem complete and internally consistent and to the moral significance the story contains.[36]

These are only three methods by which language is used to create political reality. They are described here because they are the most prominent in creating the cold war reality. But words alone cannot make the linguistic structure of reality take hold. That puts too much burden solely on language and that brings us to the other characteristics that comprise language-events.

Rhetoric as a Community Event

A second element that assists in creating reality is understanding rhetoric as a community event.[37] For a political rhetoric to become more than a personal view of reality it must be shared, that is, it must be widely talked about and well publicized. That is obvious.

But we mean community event in a larger sense. Human beings live in communities with one another. The archetype of community, both historically and symbolically, is the family. In fact, the family often goes beyond even national identity. So one is not surprised to find images of family as symbols of community groups. Public school teachers are often thought to be acting in loco parentis, and with teachers as surrogate parents, the classroom becomes a kind of extended family. George Washington is still referred to as father of the country, and presidents are often described as fatherly or grandfatherly, or in the more authoritative role, as teacher of the nation.

A basic element uniting the family is a common language. It not only creates the conditions for communication but also creates common ways of knowing about the world. A family unit is united not merely by common experiences but by common naming of those experiences. Common naming of experiences provides a common understanding of the world. Just as a child learns from parents to understand the confusing world he or she encounters through language, so too in times of confusion citizens learn to understand the world in terms of the language presented by authoritative political figures. Having language in common bonds individual members together into a cohesive group capable of believing and acting.

But the notion of community needs to be delineated more sharply. To the concept of community as participants we need to add the concept of audiences, the different listeners and receivers. Political rhetoric does not function fully without audiences because audiences shape the way in which political discourse is organized and made purposeful. In her study of the Committee on the Present Danger, Beth Ingold summarized much of the research on political audiences for foreign policy issues and divided them into three specific kinds: elite, knowledgeable, and mass audiences.[38] Elite audiences are composed of those who are policymakers or would-be policymakers who are influential either by virtue of the offices they hold or through the influence they wield in particular areas. Knowledgeable audiences are those who have an "informed awareness of foreign policy issues and [are] attentive to the opinion of and conflicts between the elite groups."[39] Generally, journalists are one of the most prominent members of this group. Finally, there is the mass audience, the general public. In transmitting information and ideas to this audience, Ingold cited Philip Converse who identified two classes or levels of information: "what goes with what" (that is, what ideas go together) and why one piece of information or one concept goes with another:

Such levels of information logically stand in a scalar relationship to one another, in the sense that one can hardly arrive at an understanding of why two ideas go together without being aware that they are supposed to go together. On the other hand, it is easy to know that two ideas go together without knowing why. For example, we can expect that a very large majority of the American public would somehow have absorbed the notion that "Communists are atheists." What is important is that this perceived correlation would for most people represent nothing more than a fact of existence, with the same status as the fact that oranges are orange and most apples are red. If we were to go and explore with these people their grasp of the "why" of the relationship, we would be surprised if more than a quarter of the population even attempted responses (setting aside such inevitable replies as "those Communists are for everything wicked"), and, among the responses received, we could be sure that the majority would be incoherent or irrelevant.[40]

Such is the nature of mass audiences for foreign policy statements, but so too is the nature of public rhetoric. Aristotle noted that public audiences will not stand for long intricate explanations and arguments, and therefore political discourse must be adjusted to this understanding by mass audiences.

But this division of audiences has import for more than how language and arguments were selected for different audiences. In the development of the American version of the cold war each of these audiences had to be persuaded to accept a new version of political reality in the aftermath of World War II. Policymakers—no less than the general public—entered the new era confused about what the end of the war meant to the nation, uncertain about what action to take. As British Ambassador Halifax reported in the early months of Truman's presidency, "To serious observers it seems pitifully obvious that the man at the helm is no longer the master of the ship."[41] Therefore, in the first two years there were internal disputes among elites about Soviet motives and goals as well as the appropriate U.S. response that occasioned the circulation of private rhetorical efforts to impress different interpretations on policymakers.[42] Once a consensus formed and the perceived need to act occurred, another rhetorical effort was launched to convince influential and knowledgeable journalists to accept the administration's version of reality and policies as preparation for getting the public's acceptance of them. Finally, major public speeches and writings were adapted to values and myths of the American public and presented in a "crisis" atmosphere to convince it that the administration's view of reality was meaningful, its policies correct, and action needed immediately. It was this process combined with the language-building process that contributed greatly to the communal understanding of the cold war.

To summarize, people acquire the language of their community as they learn to speak. Once the communal language is accepted, it creates a grammar and a rhetoric that goes with it, as often subconsciously or unconsciously apprehended as consciously. Through these public grammars and rhetoric they come to an understanding of the world about them. This understanding is the shared reality in which they partake with other members of the community whose language with all its ramifications and reasons they have learned to speak. The language of the community, once learned, is like contact lenses that have been in place so long and are so comfortable that people forget they are there. Yet all they perceive of the world is seen through these linguistic lenses, and these lenses provide the frame of reference for meaning in the political world. While any cohesive group creates the language or rhetoric by which it understands itself and the world outside, so too the language and rhetoric creates the group, gives it cohesion and identity.

Rhetoric and Habit

Once a communal language is established, it must be repeated so that it becomes habitual. In the life of a nation the habit of communal language gives identity to the nation and its citizens, purpose to its actions and goals. New words can be introduced to describe new events or people, but these usually stem from the original language and grammar that has been created and do no great violence to the conceptual bases for the original words. Once the language becomes habitually used it predisposes people to habitual responses.

A second way in which communal language becomes habitual is to use words and concepts already in common usage and apply them to new situations and people. The most prominent examples of this process were the uses of the term "totalitarianism" to describe Soviet socialism. The concept of totalitarianism is central to understanding the original cold war rhetoric. Totalitarianism had a complicated genealogy having been originally coined to describe Mussolini's brand of fascism, but having evolved to describe other enemies during World War II and finally adopted and applied to Stalin's rule in the Soviet Union periodically prior to the war and consistently after the war.[43] Totalitarian was

the way in which the Soviet Union was persistently described, sometimes the term was used in a heavy-handed manner to avoid certain
embarrassing diplomatic consequences of describing the enemy as communist, sometimes it was combined with communism to make a more
emphatic point. But more important, totalitarianism was the way to link
fascism and communism inextricably together as two political species
from the same dictatorial genus. In asserting their common ancestry,
policymakers and others opened a rich rhetorical resource for language,
images, and analogies from which to argue for policies in confronting
the Soviet Union. "Red fascism" as a description of communism was
only one of the many descriptions and arguments that came from this
provocative linkage as was the use of "appeasement" to apply to any
concession to the Soviets, coming as the latter did from Chamberlain's
disastrous negotiations with Hitler at Munich.

The historical analogy forms a third important way in which persuasive language becomes habitual. Politicians are prone to say, "History
teaches." Equally, if not more important, politicians believe they learn
"lessons" from the past.[44] It is a commonplace of decisionmaking and
political rhetoric. The historical analogy operates within this commonplace by giving specificity to particular lessons that can be learned from
history as a guide to action. But again, choice is central. Of all the
dramatic events in history, politicians choose those events that seem
most appropriate to their purposes to clarify current situations and to
give direction and authority to action.

In the American cold war rhetoric, influential people drew upon a
variety of analogies including the Munich analogy and comparisons of
Hitler to Stalin. They had their origin in the linkage of fascism and
communism through the term "totalitarianism" as well as the recent
war Americans had fought. This analogy will be discussed in more detail
in due course. But we turn to a later event—Vietnam—to describe briefly
how influential such analogies can be. Neustadt and May contrast two
historical analogies that decisionmakers could draw from when considering what to do in Vietnam. They could have compared their situation
with that of the French in the 1940s and early 1950s or they could have
drawn a comparison between what they might do in Vietnam to U.S.
action in Korea. The French adventure had been unsuccessful, of course,
but the Korean action had achieved its limited results. Decisionmakers
chose the Korean analogy, but the results did not correspond in Vietnam.[45]

In using historical analogies, politicians find a common trait ("dictatorship") or premise ("totalitarianism") that binds the two political situations together and then project a series of traits or premises commonly
believed to be true about the prior situation onto the current situation.
From that choice of comparisons and the common premise, they are

able to understand the second situation in terms of the first, giving the second an identical personality, set of motives and purposes, and central character traits. From such analogies policymakers can view problems they confront by consulting the past, seeing what worked or did not work then, and devising policies in accordance with the consequences of previous actions taken or forsaken in response to previous analogous situations. In the cold war "totalitarianism" was the central premise and "Munich" the central analogy in binding Soviet actions and motives to Nazi actions and motives. As Kenneth Burke pointed out, the "great danger of analogy is that a *similarity* is taken as evidence of an *identity*."[46] That danger would be ignored in much of the cold war rhetoric.

It is at this point that habitual uses of language and arguments from historical analogy become rhetorically potent. Both are attempts to create continuity and consistency in the messy existential world. James Wharton, the theologian, concluded that a nation "is a product of how and what we selectively remember (or forget) as a basis for decision and action."[47] The significant word here is "selectivity." In the national rhetoric leaders and opinion-shapers choose certain events as definitive events, imbue them with national meaning, and thus create a linguistic guide for understanding the present. To put it another way, the present occasion is linked to the past in such a way as to see the present as a continuation of that past and also as a testing of worthiness for the future. Lincoln's Gettysburg Address illustrates this linkage. Lincoln built his speech on the analogical link with the time of the nation's birth, "four score and seven years ago," to the war that was a "testing" of foundational principles of the nation for the purpose of giving a "new birth of freedom" to this government "of the people, by the people, and for the people." Such an analogical thinking becomes part of a nation's self-consciousness, its self-renewal, and of its place in the world. In American political rhetoric this linkage takes on even more intense meaning as a current trial in national determination to fulfill its Manifest Destiny.[48]

In summary, habitual uses of language and rhetoric create a united understanding of national being, a consistent national identity and purpose. These habitual uses may be augmented by new words used to give meaning to new situations, but they usually do not conflict conceptually with the root words that have created the original political reality without requiring additional explanation. Unity is heightened by arguments from historical analogies that create a sense of continuity with the past, a feeling of "testing" for the present in light of the past, and a guide to the future that extends the past through the present to the future. The ritualistic uses of communal language and arguments bind the individual to political society thus making it appear that one shares a common understanding and participates on an equal footing with others.

Rhetoric and Authority

Although rhetoric is central to creating reality, it rarely becomes pervasively believed without believable authorities to voice it. Aristotle called personal persuasion *ethos*, the perception of qualities that make one person more worthy of belief than another. Reputation, probity, and a thousand other qualities mixed in various ways go into establishing *ethos*. Aristotle considered this mode of persuasion the most potent, more powerful than logic or emotion. The concept, *ethos*, includes much more than authority only, but for our purposes, we are concerned with authority. Political authority is just as central to the creation of political reality as it is to the effective functioning of any civic body. In rhetoric, political authority comes from four different sources: from language itself, from a person assuming a prophetic role, from a person acting in his or her official capacity that allows one to set policy, and from experts.

On the simplest level using language that seems definitive rather than conditional lends authority to statements. That is merely a commonplace of elementary textbooks on grammar.

On a more sophisticated level Berger and Luckmann pointed to the link between naming and authority. A child announces, "I'm going to marry Sally when I grow up," only to be informed that "You can't marry Sally, she's your cousin."[49] Built into the naming process is authority. One does not marry cousins. The very naming carries with it a natural authority. Authority is learned as language is acquired. The process is hardly noticeable.

The authority of the kinship structure is legitimized incipiently along with the transmission of a kinship vocabulary. Deeper levels of legitimization come when the need arises, when the authority inherent in the language system is questioned. "Why can't I marry Sally?" may receive various answers. Answers may vary from the simple statement, "one does not marry cousins," to complex theories that posit genetic damage to offspring with the marriage of cousins. The function of the latter answer is to explain and legitimize values contained in the naming system itself. That naming, with the concomitant values, constitutes one kind of linguistic authority. Once the arguments are accepted and remembered they rarely need to be repeated. The name carries its own authority with it. For anyone to break free from the authority of the naming system one has acquired, one must create new names to reach a new level of consciousness. However, when a naming system is generally shared, a new naming system is difficult to insert into public discussion. Totalitarianism, communism, the cold war—all carried their own authority with them once they became generally accepted.

A second form of authority is more familiar to rhetorical critics: the advocate as prophet. John Locke described prophecy as consisting of three things: "Prediction, singing by the dictate of the Spirit, and understanding and explaining the mysterious hidden sense of Scripture by an immediate Illumination and Motion of the Spirit."[50] We might well transfer Locke's observations about religious prophecy to the secular world and say that political prophecy consists of prediction, exceptional oratorical skills, and the ability to explain confusing situations in such an illuminating way that significant segments of the public are moved to accept the prophet's vision of the world as true. One misconception about prophets should be cleared up. William Carl pointed out that usually *prediction* (by which most mean the ability to foretell events) is usually subordinate to the prophet's moral purpose. In other words, prophets usually concentrated on their vision of the world and said that if that vision were rejected, certain terrible consequences will follow. They demanded their universal view be accepted in order to save and redeem the world. Furthermore, prophets speak from outside existing social, political or religious structures for their aim is often to reconstitute those structures in line with their own vision of the world. Metaphors of death and birth abound in prophetic speech, just as prophets present themselves as persecuted but willing to accept martyrdom for the sake of the truth they possess. James Darsey said of the authority of the prophet: "Considered as biography, the prophetic *ethos* is a kind of legend, from . . . the Latin for stories of the Saints and martyrs. The prophetic life as presented by the prophet and his or her disciples becomes its own rhetoric, and must be judged . . . according to its aspirations and to the sympathies it creates."[51] Right after the end of the war Winston Churchill, who had been voted out of office, spoke often in the prophetic vein, as he had in the prewar years, calling his fellow citizens on either side of the Atlantic to view the postwar world as he viewed it. His "Iron Curtain" speech announced a new division in the world. When it appeared later that the division had actually taken place, Churchill was hailed for being prophetic. Henry Wallace, after he was fired from the Truman cabinet, also took a prophetic stance, but his prophesies were discredited and ignored for two decades.

A third form of explicit political authority comes from the office a person holds, and the most powerful office an individual can hold in the United States is president. As such, presidents can set the terms for argument on an issue.[52] In foreign affairs presidents have even greater power because this is the special province of presidents. They can act ex cathedra and thus statements issued in this context have a more authoritative weight to them than statements about domestic issues.

These ex cathedra statements become ex cathedra realities that at the very least establish the political framework within which others must argue alternative policies. Equally important, presidents can establish official policies that become the legal policies that others carry out. When Congress agrees with the president, such policies become bipartisan and generally beyond effective refutation. Conversely, when presidents enact official policies that coincide with the opposition party's proposals or actions, such policies also become bipartisan and legitimize the opponents. Truman's Loyalty Program, for example, legitimized the Republican search for subversives, a search that had been underway for some time before Truman's announcement of an official policy in this area. The rhetoric used to justify official statements of policy, in other words, creates a powerful rationale for accepting a bipartisan political reality.

A final form of authority is that of the expert. The complexities of the modern world, the rise of science, and the division of intellectual labor contributed to the diminution of the generalist—the intelligent and widely read person of letters—in preference for the expert—the person who has specialized in a restricted area of learning and who has attained what is considered authoritative knowledge.[53] The authority of experts is based on presumed superior knowledge gained from intensive study or extraordinary experiences in the field they lay claim to know.[54] One important characteristic of the expert is the claim to a higher knowledge over and above common sense or experiential knowledge. The expert claims to have a theory about reality that transcends ordinary understanding. Theoretical knowledge, as Derber, Schwartz, and Magrass pointed out, has always had a compelling hold on the minds of people over ordinary thought or knowledge.[55] Theory can be used, in the hands of an expert, to reconcile the contradictions of a series of actual events so as to make them seem logical and consistent. These theoretical explanations give coherence to the messy existential world that most of us inhabit, especially the political world of conflicting actions and uncertain motives. Indeed, the theory can be used to reach beneath surface events or actions to excavate the hidden motives or goals that would be invisible to the ordinary eye. Such expert theorizing is invaluable in politics where decisions must be made with dispatch. The expert's claim to impartiality in developing theory and applying it to events gives the politician a claim to objective knowledge that transcends personal motivations.

A second important characteristic of experts is their facility with language, sometimes writing or speaking in a mystifying jargon that is not accessible to ordinary people but understood easily by other experts.[56] During the cold war, experts, such as George Kennan, often reversed this process by explaining the exoteric language and theories of communism in erudite, but understandable, ways that established their own authority. More often than not, the experts speak or write in a style of disinterestedness that conveys the impression of objectivity instead of partisan involvement.

In the opening period of the cold war experts played an important rhetorical role in validating and expanding the original concepts and premises that comprised the anticommunist world view. It should be noted that in the postwar period there were few Americans with more than a rudimentary knowledge of the Soviet Union. Institutes of Russian studies were a long time in the making, and courses about the Soviet Union were for the most part limited to a few elite Ivy League schools. (The Columbia University Russian Institute matriculated its first graduates in 1948.) Those few who had any intimate knowledge of the Soviet Union had gone to Europe in the prewar days to gain their education.[57] With few to challenge them, such experts could lend unprecedented authority to political statements. George F. Kennan emerged during this early period as preeminent expert on the Soviet Union, and with good reason he remains so even to the present time.

A second kind of expert, who plays only a small role in this volume but who deserves mention anyway, also arose at the outset of the cold war. This type was the self-proclaimed expert. Former members of the Communist Party, of whom Whittaker Chambers became the most celebrated, and ex-communists, especially those who became vehemently anticommunist, gained their authoritative expertise not necessarily through the study of communist or socialist doctrine, but through their "experiences" in party work. Even that was sometimes stretched to include their associations with people they believed to be members of the Communist party. Hardly a public hearing of the House Committee on UnAmerican Activities occurred without the appearance of one of these experts ranging from Louis Budenz to Elizabeth Bentley to Whittaker Chambers to a whole host of others. But there were others who had not been communists who also claimed to be experts, sometimes by the most exotic of self-proclaimed experiences. Adolphe Menjou, for example, claimed under oath before the House Committee on Un-American Activities that he had read more than 150 books on communism and therefore considered himself an expert on communist influence in the movies and American life. The committee accepted him as an expert and questioned him on all manner of things including whether certain people "acted like" communists. This form of expertise was far removed from the expertise exhibited by George F. Kennan, but it was accepted by some as just as legitimate.

Authority in each of its different types was essential to the original acceptance of the rhetoric of the cold war. Raymond Aron observed that every political regime offers opportunities to those who possess the ability to manipulate words and ideas. It is no longer the military man, relying on courage or good luck, who accedes to the throne, but the orator, the man who knows how to convince the crowd or the electorate or parliament, the doctrinaire who has elaborated a system of thought.[58]

In the case of the cold war each side had doctrinaires who elaborated "systems of thought" that dominated and directed their nation's thinking to create a comprehensive and universal rhetorical reality. Therefore, it is finally to the nature of ideological or doctrinaire thought that we now turn.

RHETORIC AND IDEOLOGICAL REALITY

Whenever public figures speak or write on public issues, they invent a rhetorical reality fashioned from perceptions, language, and argument. Usually this reality is limited to a specific issue. If the issue is contentious, other public figures challenge it by offering an alternative reality. Much of democratic politics is animated not only by conflicts on issues, but by conflicts of different rhetorical visions or realities about situations, policies, and consequences. Such conflicts are the vital life force of democratic politics.[59] But in the postwar period a single all-encompassing reality about the international world arose that, when it took hold, admitted no exceptions to its basic premises. Soon it was transferred to domestic political life. It was the cold war reality and it was an ideological reality.

Classic ideologies, as a way of thinking about politics, differ radically from other forms of political thinking.[60] First, ideologies strive for universality, a representation or refraction of a complete political world into an internally consistent and cohesive whole. In this sense it is the counterpart of cosmologies or universal religions to which it bears remarkable similarities. Ideologies resort to appeals to the secularized version of the sacred and employ "god terms" to describe these "sacred" or basic beliefs. Being universal, ideologies demand complete adherence to the basic premises of the ideology. The only areas for dispute are technical arguments within the framework of previously accepted principles or disagreements about the strategy and tactics for implementing the ideology in the actual social or political world. But it is the claim to universality that drives both thought and action.

Second, since ideologies strive for universality, they must be sustained over periods of time. Indeed, ideologues contend their basic premises transcend time and history, even as they call upon a theory of history to confirm their timeless nature. For an ideology to be successfully believed it must be maintained. Habitual uses of language and rhetoric, extension of the ideology to all other aspects of life, and actions taken to confirm the ideology—all these contribute to universe maintenance. This extension and the consistency in rhetoric justifying that extension contribute to the crucial development of a universal political reality that we call "universe maintenance."

Third, ideologies divide the world they rhetorically represent into a bipolar world of protagonists and antagonists, of theses and antitheses, of good and evil. Such a division leaves no room for choice beyond "which side are you on?" The bipolar division demands allegiance. Henri Lefebvre noted, "Adherence to the ideology makes it possible to despise those who do not adhere to it, and . . . leads to their conversion or condemnation."[61] Therefore, a rhetoric of nihilation is applied to those who challenge the fundamental beliefs or premises of the ideology. Opponents must be symbolically destroyed not only because they are a threat to the interests of those who adhere to the ideology and are so defined within the ideology, but also because their rhetoric challenges the all-encompassing rhetoric of ideology. It does not matter whether dissidents have a counter-ideology or only question premises of the prevailing ideology. Either activity is dangerous to the ideologue. A dissenting linguistic challenge cannot be allowed because it subverts the universal rhetoric that creates ideological reality. Therefore, dissenters must be discredited, cast as rhetorical and political aliens in their own land. If such people eventually recant their heresy, they can prove their recantation through a rhetoric of therapy in which they admit past political "sins" and witness to the truth of the prevailing ideology. Those who choose an approach different from the protagonists even if they refuse to become members of the antagonistic group may find themselves characterized as dupes or sympathizers, whether willingly or not, of the antagonist ideology if they stray too far from the basic beliefs of the prevailing ideology.

Fourth, those who embrace ideologies contend that human motives are ideologically determined and can be known. Being known leads to being predictable. In the case of Soviet ideology, it taught that people were motivated by economic interests. American anticommunism preached that communists (be they domestic or foreign) were motivated by the Marxist-Leninist ideology. But since each ideology taught that its antagonists were duplistic, they also taught that overt actions seldom could be taken at face value and instead one had to search for hidden motives.

Finally, ideologues use ideology originally to explain the nature of the world. But being universal—not only explaining all current political reality but the past and future as well—ideologies soon transform from an explanation of a particular incident into the explanation for all incidents, and in that transformation become a deductive way of thinking about the world to which events, people, and policies must be adjusted. The ideology thus further transforms events and people into critical examples of the truth of the ideology rather than events or people to be examined in their complexity so as to be assigned their own meaning. In this fashion, ideologies often become self-fulfilling prophesies.

In sum, ideologies are universal in scope, complete in explanation. They direct understanding through a closed system of belief and adherence. Henri Lefebvre stated, "Only another ideology ... can struggle against an ideology."[62] In the postwar period American policymakers confronted an enigmatic adversary in the Soviet Union, one that had a history of ideological thinking. To combat it, Americans developed a counter-ideology, anticommunism, that became as stultifying and rigid as the ideology they despised.

CONCLUSION

The American anticommunist ideology did not erupt full-blown, but developed in rhetorical fits and starts during the early years of the cold war. In the process it created a universal political reality complete with its own demonology. This rhetorical process of constructing the political reality of the cold war resulted in what Kenneth Burke called a "terministic screen" for seeing and thus understanding the disputes that incited the rhetoric in the first place. Burke described "terministic screens" in this way:

Not only does the nature of our terms affect the nature of our observations, in the sense that the terms [words and language, in general] direct the *attention* to one field rather than to another. Also, *many of the "observations" [we make] are but implications of the particular terminology in terms of which the observations are made.* In brief, much that we take as observations about "reality" may be but the spinning out of possibilities implicit in our particular choice of terms.[63]

We shall have occasion to quote these words again during the course of this book, but for now we cite them because Burke expresses the same perspective that Walter Lippmann used: first, one defines and then one sees. It is in this sense that political rhetoric orders political reality. The linguistic terms or language politicians use may be inherited or created, more often than not, a mixture of the two. Old terms (that is, words and arguments used in a previous context) give continuity; new terms (that is, new terms developed specifically for a contemporary context) give a sense of immediacy. But in laying this stress on language as the most important determinant of reality, we do not mean that the external world does not exist except in language. The *actual* world does exist; language and argument give *meaning* and thus *reality* to that world.

In the case of the cold war, the rhetoric used to justify specific policies took on a life of its own, as language often does when people use it repeatedly, to define an entire worldview, an ideological interpretation of the state of Soviet–American relations, the motives of both nations, the moral imperatives that dominated those motives. In a short period of time this original rhetoric—developed and refined—became an ideological rhetoric that persisted long beyond the events and circumstances that originally brought it forth. The remainder of this book is devoted to examining how that happened.

NOTES

1. David H. Bennett, *The Party of Fear: From Nativist Movements to the New Right in American History* (New York: Vintage, 1990), p. 273.

2. For a thorough examination of these early investigations, see David Chaute, *The Great Fear: The Anti-Communist Purge under Truman and Eisenhower* (New York: Simon and Schuster, 1978). For blacklisting of entertainers and writers, see his Appendix C "The Hollywood Blacklist," pp. 557–60. As an example of investigations within a state, see Vern Countryman, *Un-American Activities in The State of Washington: The Work of the Canwell Committee* (Ithaca, NY: Cornell University Press, 1951). Dean Acheson, who did not share the intense concern about domestic subversives that others had and even said he would not turn his back on Alger Hiss, fired nonetheless 80 members of the State Department whom President Truman's Loyalty Board "certified" as "disloyal."

3. John Patrick Diggins, *The Proud Decades: America in War and Peace, 1941–1960* (New York: W. W. Norton, 1988), p. 54.

4. James MacGregor Burns, *The Crosswinds of Freedom* (New York: Alfred A. Knopf, 1989), p. 220.

5. Christer Jonsson, "The Ideology of Foreign Policy," in *Foreign Policy, USA/USSR*, ed. Charles W. Kegley, Jr., and Pat McGowan (Beverly Hills, CA: Sage, 1982), p. 95.

6. E. Stillman and W. Pfaff, *Power and Impotence: The Failure of America's Foreign Policy* (New York: Random House, 1966), pp. 16–17.

7. Adam Ulam, *Expansion and Coexistence: Soviet Foreign Policy, 1917–1973* (New York: Holt, Rinehart and Winston, 1974), p. 5.

8. Theodore O. Windt, Jr., "The Evolution of Soviet Diplomacy," *Pennsylvania Speech Annual* 23 (September 1966), p. 59. See Leon Trotsky, "Against Socialism in One Country, *The Draft Program of the Communist International—A Criticism of Fundamentals*; and Joseph Stalin, "Socialism in One Country," both in *Masters of Russian Marxism*, ed. Thornton Anderson (New York: 1963), pp. 153–58 and 226–230 respectively.

9. Jonsson, "The Ideology of Foreign Policy," p. 93.

10. Ibid., p. 104.

11. See Theodore O. Windt, Jr., "The Rhetoric of Peaceful Coexistence: A Criticism of Nikita Khrushchev's American Speeches (Ph.D. diss. Ohio State University, 1965), pp. 40–44.

12. See, for examples, Larry G. Ehrlich, "Ambassador in the Yard," *Southern Speech Communication Journal* 38 (Fall 1972), pp. 1–12; Carl Wayne Hensley, "Harry S. Truman: Fundamental Americanism in Foreign Policy Speechmaking, 1945–1946," *Southern Speech Communication Journal* 40 (Winter 1975), pp. 180–90; James W. Hikins, "The Rhetoric of 'Unconditional Surrender' and the Decision to Drop the Atomic Bomb," *Quarterly Journal of Speech* 69 (November 1983), pp. 379–400; Wayne E. Brockriede and Robert L. Scott, *Moments in the Rhetoric of the Cold War* (New York: Random House, 1970). More expansive studies include: Philip Wander, "The Rhetoric of Foreign Policy," *Quarterly Journal of Speech* 70 (November 1984), pp. 339–61; Robert L. Ivie, "Presidential Motives for War," *Quarterly Journal of Speech* 60 (October 1974), pp. 337–45; John F. Cragan, "The Origins and Nature of the Cold War Rhetorical Vision," in *Applied Communication: A Dramatistic Perspective*, ed. John F. Cragan and Donald Shields (Prospect Heights, IL: Waveland, 1981), pp. 47–77.

13. Richard M. Freeland, *The Truman Doctrine and the Origins of McCarthyism* (New York: Alfred A. Knopf, 1972), p. 10.

14. Walter Lippmann, *Public Opinion* (New York: Harcourt, Brace, 1922), p. 81.

15. George F. Kennan, *Memoirs: 1925–1950* (Boston: Atlantic-Little, Brown, 1967), p. 356.

16. Ibid.

17. Theodore Otto Windt, Jr., *Presidents and Protestors: Political Rhetoric in the 1960s* (Tuscaloosa, AL: University of Alabama Press, 1990), p. 3. See Murray Edelman, *The Symbolic Uses of Politics* (Urbana, IL: University of Illinois Press, 1964); William E. Connolly, *The Terms of Political Discourse*, 2d ed. (Princeton, NJ: Princeton University Press, 1983); Fred Dallmayr, *Language and Politics* (Notre Dame, IN: University of Notre Dame Press, 1984).

18. See Robert E. Denton, Jr., and Gary C. Woodward, *Political Communication in America* (New York: Praeger, 1985), pp. 28–73.

19. Jacques Ellul, *Propaganda: The Formation of Men's Attitudes*, trans. Konrad Kellan and Jean Lerner (New York: Alfred A. Knopf, 1965), p. 126.

20. Robert Funk, *Language, Hermeneutic, and the Word of God* (New York: Harper and Row, 1966), p. xiii.

21. Quoted in Margaret Truman, *Harry S. Truman* (New York: Pocket Books, 1974), p. 378.

22. Funk, *Language, Hermeneutic, and the Word of God*, p. 4. Even as Funk deftly describes the rhetorical dimension of creating reality, he too gets caught up in the linguistic confusion between actuality and reality.

23. Kenneth Burke, *Philosophy of Literary Form* (Baton Rouge, LA: Louisiana State University, 1941), p. 4.

24. Funk, *Language, Hermeneutic, and the Word of God*, p. 27.

25. Louis J. Halle, *The Cold War as History* (New York: Harper and Row, 1967), p. 103. In a footnote Halle referred to Henry Wallace as a "tragedy" because he adhered to the "old concepts" and thus had his career end in disgrace.

26. Gerhard Von Rad, *Old Testament Theology*, vol. 2 (New York: Harper and Row, 1965), p. 81.

27. Charles Kauffman, "Names and Weapons," *Communication Monographs* 56 (September 1989), pp. 276–77.

28. George Lakoff and Mark Johnson, *Metaphors We Live By* (Chicago, IL:

University of Chicago Press, 1980), p. 14. See also Michael Leff, "Topical Invention and Metaphoric Interaction," *Southern Speech Communication Journal* 48 (Spring 1983), pp. 214–29.

29. Richard Barnet, *The Giants: Russia and America* (New York: Simon and Schuster, 1977), p. 79.

30. Murray Edelman, *Politics as Symbolic Action* (Chicago: Markam, 1971), p. 83.

31. Sonja K. Foss, *Rhetorical Criticism: Exploration and Practice* (Prospect Heights, IL: Waveland, 1989), p. 229.

32. Lippmann, *Public Opinion*, p. 85.

33. Burke, *The Philosophy of Literary Form*, p. 193.

34. Gordon Allport, *The Nature of Prejudice* (Garden City, NY: Anchor Books, 1958), pp. 174–87.

35. Hayden White, "The Narrativization of Real Events," in *On Narrative*, ed. W.J.T. Mitchell (Chicago, IL: University of Chicago Press, 1981), p. 253.

36. Foss, *Rhetorical Criticism*, p. 230.

37. For one way in which experience is transformed into communal reality through political language, see David E. Procter, "The Dynamic Spectacle: Transforming Experience into Social Forms of Community," *Quarterly Journal of Speech* 76 (May 1990), pp. 117–33.

38. Beth Ingold, "The Committee on the Present Danger: A Study of Elite and Public Influence, 1976–1980" (Ph.D. diss. University of Pittsburgh, 1989), pp. 14–59.

39. Ibid., p. 29.

40. Quoted in Ingold, "The Committee on the Present Danger," p. 34.

41. Quoted in Arthur M. Schlesinger, Jr., *The Cycles of American History* (Boston: Houghton Mifflin, 1986), p. 213.

42. See Robert L. Messer, "Paths Not Taken: The United States Department of State and Alternatives to Containment, 1945–1946," *Diplomatic History* 1 (Fall 1977), pp. 297–319.

43. The most exhaustive and invaluable study of the genealogy and uses of the term "totalitarianism," especially for students of the cold war is Thomas E. Lifka's *The Concept "Totalitarianism" and American Foreign Policy, 1933–1949*, 2 vols. (New York: Garland Publishing, 1988).

44. See Ernest R. May, *"Lessons" of the Past: The Use and Misuse of History in American Foreign Policy* (New York: Oxford University Press, 1973), especially pp. 19–86.

45. Richard E. Neustadt and Ernest R. May, *Thinking in Time: The Uses of History for Decision Makers* (New York: Free Press, 1986), pp. 75–90. The authors also outline a useful set of categories that should be used to evaluate analogies politicians and citizens draw from historical events.

46. Burke, *Permanance and Change*, p. 97.

47. James A. Wharton, "The Occasion of the Word of God," *Austin Seminary Bulletin* (September 1968), p. 22.

48. See Henry Butterfield Ryan, Jr., "The American Intellectual Tradition Reflected in the Truman Doctrine," *American Scholar* 42 (Spring 1973), pp. 294–307.

49. Peter L. Berger and Thomas Luckmann, *The Social Construction of Reality* (New York: Anchor Books, 1967), p. 94.

50. Quoted in William Joseph Carl III, "Old Testament Prophecy and the Question of Prophetic Preaching: A Perspective on Ecclesiaastical Protest to the Vietnam War and the Participation of William Sloane Coffin, Jr." (Ph.D. diss., University of Pittsburgh, 1977), p. 34. See also W. Sibley Towner, "On Calling People 'Prophets' in 1970," *Interpretation* 24 (October 1970), pp. 134–51.

51. James Darcy, "The Legend of Eugene Debs: Prophetic *Ethos* as Radical Argument, *Quarterly Journal of Speech* 74 (November 1988), pp. 434–52.

52. George Reedy, *The Twilight of the Presidency* (New York: World, 1977), pp. 41–42.

53. On the rise of the expert, see Richard F. Hofstadter, *Anti-Intellectualism in American Life* (New York: Alfred A. Knopf, 1963), pp. 197–229.

54. On the limitation of experts, see Harold J. Laski, "The Limitations of Experts," in *The Intellectuals: A Controversial Portrait*, ed. George B. de Huszar (Glencoe, IL: Free Press, 1960), pp. 167–75. For an entertaining compendium of authoritative misinformation by experts, see Christopher Cerf and Victor Navasky, *The Experts Speak* (New York: Pantheon, 1984).

55. Charles Derber, William A. Schwartz, and Yale Magrass, *Power in the Highest Degree: Professionals and the Rise of a New Mandarin Order* (New York: Oxford University Press, 1990), pp. 54–55. For a full discussion of experts, theory, and professionalism in contrast to personal knowledge, see pp. 27–78.

56. See, for example, G. Thomas Goodnight, "The Personal, Technical, and Public Spheres of Argument: A Speculative Inquiry into the Art of Public Deliberation," *Journal of the American Forensic Association* 18 (Spring 1982), pp. 214–17; John Lyne and Henry F. Howe, "The Rhetoric of Expertise: E. O. Wilson and Sociobiology," *Quarterly Journal of Speech* 76 (May 1990), pp. 134–51.

57. Two of the most prominent were George F. Kennan and Charles E. Bohlen. For their educational experiences, see Kennan, *Memoirs: 1925–1950*, pp. 24–57; and Bohlen, *Witness to History: 1929–1969* (New York: Norton, 1973), pp. 8–13.

58. Raymond Aron, "Historical and Recent Types," in *The Intellectuals*, ed. George B. de Huszar (Glencoe, IL: Free Press, 1960), p. 164.

59. As an example of rhetorical visions in conflict, see Craig Allen Smith, "Leadership, Orientation, and Rhetorical Vision: Jimmy Carter, The 'New Right,' and the Panama Canal," in *Essays in Presidential Rhetoric*, ed. Theodore Windt and Beth Ingold (Dubuque, IA: Kendall/Hunt, 1987), pp. 364–76.

60. On a distinction between "procedural" and "ideological" politics, see Windt, *Presidents and Protesters*, pp. 139–59..

61. Henri Lefebvre, *The Sociology of Marx*, trans. Norbert Guterman (New York: Pantheon, 1968), p. 81.

62. Ibid., p. 77.

63. Kenneth Burke, *Language as Symbolic Action: Essays on Life, Literature, and Method* (Berkeley, CA: University of California Press, 1966), p. 46.

Chapter Two

The Rhetorical Stockpile

From the beginning Americans have viewed Russia through the window of self-identity and self-interest. "The American world," James Oliver Robertson wrote, "is a world looked at through American perceptions, explained in American ways, discussed and rationalized in the American language, told about and understood in American stories, peopled by Americans."[1] That is not unusual for any nation, but it became particularly poignant in Russo–American relations. These perceptions applied to the Soviet Union both before and after World War II. When Richard Pells said that it was difficult to get an accurate view of what Russia was about during the 1930s because "Americans generally saw what they wanted to see," and that different views of Russia "frequently depended on whatever issues and problems seemed uppermost in the United States," he could have been speaking of the entire history of the relationship between the two countries.[2]

During the nineteenth century, American perception of Russia was, despite its being ruled by a czarist dynasty, that of a nation friendly to the new democracy. Toward the century's end, when repressions by the czars were widely publicized in the American press, these views changed. New despotic images replaced old images of a benevolent aristocracy. Americans greeted the overthrow of the Romanov dynasty in 1917 as a triumph of democracy. But, before the year was over, Americans went to the other extreme of seeing the Bolshevik Revolution as a betrayal of the Russian people. In one sense the previous demonic characterization of czars was simply transferred to the new Soviet leaders. But a new dimension was added. Americans went through a short period of domestic hysteria known as the Red Scare. The nation became overwhelmed with fear of domestic radicals, especially Bolsheviki revolutionists. Anti-Soviet rhetoric subsided somewhat during the next two decades due to the end of the Red Scare and the beginning of financial exhilaration in the 1920s, and due to the recognition of the Soviet Union and the onslaught of financial deprivation in the 1930s. But when Stalin and Hitler signed a non-aggression pact in 1939, the old rhetoric boiled up again into angry denunciations and condemnations. Within two years all this would swing in the opposite direction once again when Germany invaded the USSR in 1941. War conditions dictated a new war rhetoric among the allies. The Soviet Union became a brave friend, Marshall Stalin "Uncle Joe," and old antagonisms were muted or forgotten. In other words, the rhetorical history of American views of Russia and the Soviet Union has witnessed wide swings from one extreme to another. But we need to inquire more extensively into this history because it provided a stockpile of images American officials and opinion leaders drew upon in the cold war rhetoric.

AMERICAN IMAGES OF CZARIST RUSSIA

Looking back from the perspective of post-World War II, it is tempting to read an impending cold war into the history of American–Russian relations from the very beginning. In her critique of history textbooks used in public schools, Frances Fitzgerald concluded that in the 1950s the "morbid fear of Communism becomes an overriding passion—to the point where in some books the whole of American history appears a mere prologue to the struggle with the 'Reds.' "[3] This stream of historical interpretation explains the relationship between the two nations by the sense of manifest destiny each felt.[4] This narrative stresses that the two nations did not truly become competing world powers until after World War II, but that a sense of destiny was present from the beginning albeit in latent form. When the two nations first became aware of each other at the end of the eighteenth century, the one was emerging from colonial tutelage, the other from feudalism. Each was torn between a desire for isolation and the need to take an active role in world affairs. As each nation came out of isolation to take an active role, each was forced to compete more and more with the other. This competition intensified, so this narrative goes, until "two missionaries with two mutually exclusive visions competed for the hearts and minds of their peoples. Little room for accommodation remained where two Manifest Destinies collided."[5] This reading is not inaccurate, but incomplete. It fails to explain the contradictory rhetorical images that competed in this history.

Another view of Russia, however much based on momentary political expediency, pictured American–Russian relations as guided more by friendship than enmity. A reading of this rhetorical history portrays Russia, for the most part, as a benefactor of U.S. interests. Encounters between the two were episodic, therefore becoming critical or representative moments that yielded moralistic political interpretations made public through a romantic rhetoric. Three episodes illustrate this rhetoric.

During the Revolutionary War Americans portrayed Russia as a friend in the struggle for independence. The major reason for this portrait lay in one incident. In 1775, British King George III asked Catherine the Great of Russia for 20,000 mercenaries to help battle the rebellious American colonies. Her refusal marked the first legend in American perception of Russia. Catherine became known in America as the "Mother of Independence." Her refusal to send cossacks to aid the British became a sign in the United States that the czarina did so out of approval for American democratic goals. The truth was a space apart from the legend. Strengthening the maritime British was not in landlocked Russia's national interest, so Catherine steered a neutral course in the American Revolution. In retrospect it hardly seems likely that a czarina would foster democracy, but the myth of Russian support for the Revolution remained. "The conclusion that must be drawn," Stoessinger observed, "is that the Russian empress dealt with the American question on grounds of pure realpolitik."[6] Nonetheless the myth of Russian support and friendship had begun and persisted for some time.

A second critical episode occurred during the American Civil War. In 1863 with the outcome of the war in doubt, the federal government feared the intervention of a European power to aid the Confederacy. When six Russian ships sailed into New York harbor and another six entered San Francisco Bay, a rumor swept the North that the Russians had sent their fleet to serve notice that European interference in America would not be tolerated. Again the myth belied the facts, but the myth combined with Russia's refusal to recognize the Confederacy served to strengthen the legend of Russian friendship toward the United States. Russia's actual purpose for the fleet's visit was not revealed until 1915 when czarist records were made available to an American historian.[7] Those records indicate Russian leaders feared expanding British power, what the Russian minister to Washington during the Civil War called the "ambitious projects and political egotism of the Anglo-Saxon race."[8] The British and French posed a threat to Russia in a potential war over Poland. Were war to come, the Russian fleet would have been trapped in the Baltic Sea. Hence the order to drop anchor in a neutral warm-water port. Since most ports were controlled by nations that Russia had reason to distrust, ports in a country beset by civil war seemed relatively safe. The myth that the Russian fleet had sailed to the aid of the Union strengthened Northern morale and, of course, intensified the notion of Russian friendship, born in the struggle for American independence.

When the Civil War was concluded, the perception of Russian friendship framed the debate over the purchase of Alaska, the third critical episode. Congressional approval of the purchase in 1867 was, in part at least, out of gratitude for Russia's assistance during the war. The rhetoric of the congressional debate about Alaska indicated a belief that the United States was doing Russia a favor in taking "Seward's Folly" off her hands. Secretary of State William Seward enlisted the aid of Charles Sumner, chairman of the Senate's Committee on Foreign Relations, in convincing the Senate to approve the purchase. In Sumner's major speech advocating the purchase he cited economic benefits that might accrue from Alaska, but reminded colleagues that they ought not to vote against the only real supporter of the Union during the Civil War. He cited the visit of the Russian fleet in 1863 "which was intended by the Emperor and accepted by the United States as a friendly demonstration."[9] The House of Representatives also approved because members were reluctant to vote against the only true friend of America during its recent troubles. Russia had expressed "unequivocal assurance" of support for the Union during the Civil War. But again the myth was larger than the facts would support when it came to Alaska. Alaska had become an economic liability to Russia and was difficult to defend. Russia acted out of national interest in unloading what was believed to be a worthless piece of frozen territory. Later, when the actual value of Alaska began to be realized, there was gratitude to the Russians for their generosity in selling Alaska. Stoessinger put it this way: "The legends of the generosity of Czar Alexander, myths though they were, still exercised a remarkable influence, especially on the American side, in delaying for some time the decline of Russo–American relations into suspicion and hostility."[10] But perceptions were soon to change radically.

The last two decades of the nineteenth century witnessed the rise of patriotic Americanism and a concomitant xenophobia. The "closing of the American frontier" saw an expansion of urban population with an increase in industrial problems and the growth of labor unions. The American farmer faced intensified competition in the world market even as agricultural prices declined. The birth of the Grange in rural areas paralleled the spread of unions in cities. A sharp increase in immigration exacerbated these problems. Between 1880 and 1900 the number of immigrants expanded to an average of nearly 400,000 a year. There was also a shift in the countries of origin, as a majority of immigrants came from southern and eastern Europe. The new arrivals had cultures and languages different from earlier immigrants who had come from northern and western Europe. By 1890 four of every five residents of New York City, the gateway for immigration, were foreign born. The perception in America that the new arrivals from Europe were especially alien was due to several influences: their languages were strange, their customs were different, they were largely Roman Catholic, and they were a cheap source of labor. The perceived threat resulted in a nativistic response. Anti-alien groups formed agitating to restrict immigration and to teach only the American language in schools, accompanied by general suspicion of all things alien.

Of the 1.5 million Jews who arrived in the United States between 1880 and 1910, more than 70 percent were from Russian areas, often fleeing to avoid persecution. Alexander III came to power in 1881 when Czar Alexander II was assassinated, and he instituted an excessively repressive regime, one marked by Jewish pogroms that resulted in large number of Jews emigrating. As they came to the United States, they brought tales of terror and oppression that began to alter the previous myths about "friendly" Russia.

The writings of George Kennan, an uncle of George F. Kennan who was to author the cold war policy of containment, are striking examples of the new rhetorical images of Russia that grew between the last two decades of the nineteenth century and World War I.[11] The elder Kennan was twenty years old when he journeyed to Siberia as a member of a survey team for the Western Union Telegraph Company. He lived in Siberia for two years, publishing his adventures in *Tent Life in Siberia* in 1870. In 1885, *Century Magazine* commissioned Kennan to return to write a series of articles on prison conditions there. Kennan, who spoke fluent Russian, found conditions appalling. His first-hand reports were published in a series of articles from 1888 to 1890. Thomas Bailey concluded that these articles had a significant impact on American perceptions:

They were not only widely circulated but, what was more important, they were read by editors, lawyers, preachers, and others who were in a position to give wide currency to the author's discoveries. The series stirred up a heated controversy in the press, and Kennan was tireless in defending himself and his methods against critics. He also supplemented the printed word by several hundred popular and somewhat sensational lectures.[12]

Americans were getting a new picture of Russia, one that showed, in Kennan's words, that "you cannot live, move, or have your being in the Russian Empire without permission."[13] Because he spoke as an American citizen, Kennan provided validation of the tales of terror that were told by Russian expatriates. The new images of a barbaric autocratic state gave rise to an alternate rhetoric about Russia that provided the basis for public debate among Americans about the appropriate relationship between the two nations.[14]

The year 1917 proved to be a crucial one. The rhetoric swung violently from antagonism to alliance to bitter antagonism. The prevailing anti-Russian rhetoric began to subside when on Good Friday, April 6, 1917, a joint resolution of Congress thrust the United States officially into World War I. Russia and the United States were allies against the hated Hun. But by the end of the year, with the war going badly for the allies, the Bolshevik Revolution erupted in Russia and the new government sued for peace. The inauguration of peace negotiations at Brest-Litovsk just before Christmas released hundreds of thousands of German soldiers for the western front. This event created an outpouring of hostile rhetoric that surpassed even the antagonistic images of the czar in its intensity.

AMERICAN IMAGES OF THE SOVIET REVOLUTION

Czarist Russia had been threatened with revolution for nearly a century before the October Revolution of 1917: the Decembrists in 1825; the "Bloody Sunday" revolt of 1905; and the February Revolution that ended the Romanov dynasty. For understanding part of American anti-Bolshevik rhetoric an understanding of the Provisional government is needed. When Czar Nicholas II abdicated, Prince George Lvov became premier of the Provisional Government. Many Americans hailed the overthrow of the Czar as, in George Kennan's words, the "complete triumph of democracy."[15] Such expectations were extravagant. The continuing problems of a losing war, acute food and material shortages, a paralyzed transportation system, and a war-weary citizenry contributed to continuing unrest rather than political stability. As crisis followed crisis, Prince Lvov resigned to be replaced by Alexander Kerensky in July. The political situation in Russia in the spring of 1917 was hardly conducive to democratic rule, but the Provisional Government talked about reforms that sounded compatible with U.S. democratic institutions. Americans held the "common-sense" notion that when a dictator is overthrown the succeeding government will be the opposite, that is a democratic government American-style. The common sense perception prevailed, even though there "was little in the Russian historical experience, in Russian social conditions, in the Russian cast of thought to suggest that a western conception of democracy, with safeguards for individual liberties, would spring up on Russian soil."[16] Nonetheless, a new myth arose, fed in subsequent years by Russian Whites who escaped during the civil war to the West, that said there was a fragile opportunity for democracy in Russia, represented by the Provisional Government, but brutally crushed by the Bolsheviks.

After the October Revolution, the Bolsheviks signed a separate peace treaty with Germany giving them relief from the exigencies of war. The Brest-Litovsk Treaty was costly. The Russians surrendered control of

Finland, Ukraine, Poland, Lithuania, Latvia, and Estonia and thereby were stripped of one-third of their population. Equally important the separate peace enraged the allied powers.[17]

There was an ironic reversal in Russia's leaving the war, with the rhetoric once again belying the facts. American isolationist resistance to entering the war had been lessened with the overthrow of the czar and the installation of a parliamentary government. Ronald Steel noted: "No longer did a tyrannical Russian dictatorship taint the Allied cause."[18] Although German submarine warfare provided an immediate cause for declaring war, President Wilson had, in a January speech to the Senate, advocated a negotiated settlement of the war, a "peace without victory." In his war message of April 2, 1917, he stressed that the United States was entering the war to make the world "safe for democracy." When the Bolsheviks overthrew Kerensky's government, they discovered a secret treaty that the czar had entered into with Britain, France, Italy, and Japan to carve up the territories of Germany, Austria-Hungary, and the Ottoman empire among the victors. The Bolshevik government published the details of the secret treaty in order to repudiate what they regarded as capitalist duplicity and to unmask the "war for democracy." Only one American newspaper, the New York *Evening Post*, published the complete Russian report, with just nine newspapers publishing short excerpts. Wilson's "Fourteen Points" doctrine was an effort to repudiate both the specifics and the nature of the secret treaty. But what emerged was an image of a duplicitous Soviet leadership that dared to betray the Western war effort, despite Russian attempts to explain their motives.[19]

The new Soviet government represented the very antithesis of American ideals, and the announced values and goals of the new regime provided new wine for the old wineskins of the anti-czarist myth. The Bolsheviks initiated extensive internal reforms, organized the army to fight a civil war against the Whites, separated church and state while nationalizing church property, and abolished all private ownership of land. But what was more shocking was to hear the Soviet leaders talking about a new world order. Even though Russia was leaving the war to confront her own internal struggles, the Soviet rhetoric spoke of world revolution. In a February 24, 1918 article in *Pravda*, Lenin said that the continuing war would unmask Western imperialism and "a socialist Soviet Republic in Russia will be a model for all other peoples." The thought struck horror in Western minds. The advocacy of social revolutions for other nations, in the words of Adam Ulam, was perceived in the West as "impudent baiting of the foreign governments, open declarations by the highest Bolshevik officials of their forthcoming doom at the hands of their aroused peoples."[20]

In the summer of 1918 an Allied Expeditionary Force invaded Russia, occupying Murmansk and Archangel. The official justification for intervention was to guard military stores lest they fall into the hands of the German army. A similar force moved into Siberia to rescue marooned Czech soldiers. Both forces supported the Whites against the Reds in Russia's civil war, and by the time U.S. troops were finally withdrawn in 1920, more than 500 American lives had been lost. The intervention intensified Bolshevik suspicions of the capitalist Western world, suspicions that would grow into paranoia under Stalin.

The notion that the new leaders were enslaving the Russian people just as the people had gained freedom from the czars became a rhetorical justification for U.S. intervention in Russia. Peter Filene stated "that by intervening to put Russia on her democratic feet, Kennan and other respected figures assured Americans, the United States would have the support of the vast majority of Russians."[21] Kennan drew upon the distinction he had made earlier between the czars and the people. Using the structure of that myth he simply replaced the czars with the new Soviet leaders. Thus were Americans led to believe that the Bolshevik leaders were as despicable to Russians as they were to Americans, which may or may not have been accurate.

One can see the contours and content of the rhetorical reaction to events in the USSR forming. In the aftermath of her withdrawal from the war, it bubbled over: "In newspapers, books, magazines, and meetings, the dispute over the Soviet phenomenon raged ceaselessly. Fundamental principles were at stake; the meaning and success of American values were involved. When talking about the USSR, Americans were really talking about their own nation and themselves."[22] This anti-Bolshevik rhetoric expressed itself in three different ways: (1) the general railings against the Bolsheviks; (2) newspaper reporting of events in the Soviet Union; and (3) the government-conducted Red Scare.

Just as the American rhetoric of the prerevolutionary period was characterized by various myths about the intentions of the czars, the rhetorical portrayal of the Soviet revolution focused on the perceived inimical character of the leaders of the new government. The moral dimensions of that rhetoric shaped perceptions of Soviet actions. When Soviet actions were inimical to U.S. interests, they provided verification of the stereotypes about the sinister nature of the Russian leaders. The rhetorical prism through which Americans viewed the Soviets was refracted by the American self-image, a blending of the political and the religious that portrayed America as a people with a special relationship to God, a people who valued morality and individual liberty above all else. The Bolsheviks' insistence on the doctrine of class conflict, their commitment to government ownership of property, and their espousal of atheism stood in sharp contradiction to the values that Americans cherished.

The Western hatred of "the Soviet phenomenon" was based on Soviet ideological rhetoric, rather than on fear of Russian might because, although "Soviet Russia lay prostrate, in the throes of war and economic chaos," as Ulam put it, she "was the locus of an infection sapping the strength of Europe."[23] Part of this hatred and fear came from the feeling that Russia has betrayed the West by leaving the war, part from a sense that the Russian people had been betrayed by the revolution. Americans responded with disbelief to the Bolshevik seizure of power. The myth that the Russian people had once again been betrayed received new life. Americans expressed their sympathy for the average Russian who was again being enslaved. Westerners were particularly shocked to hear the new Soviet leaders talking about establishing a new order in the world modeled after their new order. Even though Russia was leaving the war to attend to her internal struggles, the Soviet rhetoric spoke of world revolution, especially the words from Leon Trotsky. That rhetoric became the target for American responses: "Suddenly, Americans were hearing their own gospel, in Bolshevik translation, returning to them like an ironic and ominous echo. Two missionaries were now competing for the souls of the peoples of the world."[24] Two competing manifest destinies were in rhetorical competition. The leaders of the two nations reflected this competition, as John Lewis Gaddis observed, "both Wilson and Lenin believed in the universal applicability of their philosophies of government and in the inevitability of their eventual triumph; both sought to alter the traditional structure of international relations in such a way as to end imperialism and war; both, in their own way, looked to democracy as the ultimate objective."[25] Such an agreement in form accompanied by such a clash in content was bound to provide vitriolic responses. The anti-Bolshevik rhetoric went far beyond objecting to Russia's action in abandoning the war to mounting an attack on the moral character of Soviet leaders and their ideology. E. Malcolm Carroll said that during this period there was "virtual unanimity in condemning the Bolshevik methods: the dictatorship of the proletariat and the Red Terror. No one, whatever his politics might be, could speak, or write about Soviet Russia without a scathing moral denunciation."[26] Even the czars had not been subject to the bitter attacks that characterized the anti-Bolshevik rhetoric. If anything, the ideology and practices of the Soviets seemed more alien and threatening to American values than had that of the former czarist aristocracy.

Newspaper reports of the civil war fueled the anti-Soviet reaction in America. Russia had been devastated by world war, by revolution, by a bitter civil war, and by the allied intervention. The U.S. press covered the civil war from an anti-Soviet perspective and a geographical distance, both due to the new government barring foreign reporters from Russia. The press was forced to report events either by accompanying anti-Bolshevik armies or from a listening post in nearby Riga, Latvia. Journalists' news sources were often enemies of the Soviets, including refugees who had left homes and homeland to flee, bringing with them stories that were confusing and inaccurate.

Walter Lippmann and Charles Merz conducted a classic study for the *New Republic* of the coverage of Russia by the *New York Times* ("one of the really great newspapers in the world") between 1917 and 1920.[27] They concluded that the reporting was strongly anti-Soviet and sensational. "In large," they stated, "the news about Russia is a case of seeing not what was, but what men wanted to see."

During the period between the overthrow of the czars and the Bolshevik Revolution, they judged the reporting to be fair, if overly optimistic about the success of the Russian army against Germany. After the initial shock of the overthrow of the Kerensky government, there were numerous reports indicating that the Bolshevik regime would not last. In the two years from November 1917 to November 1919, the imminent collapse of the Soviets was predicted no fewer than ninety-one times. The newspaper based its early reports on the assumption that the new government would continue the war effort. When the Soviets withdrew from the war, the nature of reporting changed drastically.

In the five-month period following Brest-Litovsk in March 1918 and continuing until the allied intervention in August, Lippmann and Merz counted some 285 items relating to the issue of intervention. The main reason given for Allied military action was the German threat. With the Armistice in November 1919, the German "peril" was no longer an available justification for U.S. troops on Russian soil. But although that justification vanished, the troops stayed. Three days after the Armistice, this headline appeared in the *Times*: "Bolshevism is Spreading in Europe: All Neutral Countries Now Feel the Infection." The German peril was being replaced by the Red peril, and the metaphor of disease was central. An unidentified dispatch from London followed stating that the "most serious question of the hour, in the opinion of some newspapers here, is how far Europe is infected with Bolshevism." On December 18 a headline in the *Times* announced: "Red Peril Pictured As Alarming." The wartime enemy, Germany, was gone. In its place was a new diabolic enemy spreading an ideological disease.

At the Paris Peace Conference that produced the Treaty of Versailles the Big Four devoted more time to the Russian question than to any other single issue. Many decisions of the conference were made against the backdrop of the Bolshevik Revolution: territorial concessions and economic aid to nations that bordered Russia, military intervention inside Russia, an economic and military blockade of the Bolsheviks, support for anti-Bolshevik parties in Russia's civil war, and even the charters of the International Labor Organization (I.L.O.) and the League of Nations were intended to immunize against the ideological virus of the

Bolshevik Revolution. Each delegation used the specter of bolshevism to advance its government's foreign policy and to bolster political positions at home. When Woodrow Wilson faced difficulties getting approval for the plan for food relief to Europe, he used an appeal to the horrors of bolshevism to frighten Capitol Hill. On January 11, 1919 he sent a cable to chairmen of both the Senate and House Appropriation Committees. At first they were asked to keep the message confidential, but when it was deemed necessary to the passage of the legislation, the cable was read on the floor of both Houses. Stating that food relief was the key to peace in Europe, the cable said that "Bolshevism is steadily advancing."[28] When Herbert Hoover needed support for the American Relief Administration in Russia, he justified it rhetorically by saying that the entire operation was part of a plan "to effect the ultimate Americanization of the Russian economy."[29] Thus did the Soviet threat become in these early days a focal argument to convince representatives to pass legislation. Although the term "bolshevism" would later be replaced by "communism," this rhetorical pattern was portentous. And it would be repeated in arguing for aid to Greece and Turkey as well as for the Marshall Plan.

With no American reporters in Russia the only news was second-hand, replete with misinformation, confusion, and distortion of what the new Soviet government was doing. Sometimes facts were turned upside down. For example, the world was warned of an impending invasion of Poland by the Soviets, even though Poland had seized the opportunity created by the Russian civil war to attack the USSR in the spring of 1920 and had penetrated 180 miles inside Soviet borders. George F. Kennan wrote that "the editors of the daily press walked gingerly around the Russian problems in the 1917–1918 period, as bewildered as anyone else."[30] The images the American public received of Soviet leaders and their new government were stereotypical. "A disquieting amount of information that we received about Russia was one-sided, warped, or completely false," wrote Thomas Bailey.[31] The more exaggerated the distortions the more credence they seemed to receive, as the press wrote about the alleged "nationalization of women" and the "Bureau of Free Love." This vivid example comes from the *New York Times* in 1919. Headlined "Soviets Make Girls Property to State: Decrees Compel Them to Register at 'Free Love Bureau' on Attaining 18 Years," the article went on to report:

Russian maidens under the jurisdiction of certain provincial Bolshevist Soviets become the "Property of the state" when they reach the age of 18 years, and are compelled to register at a government "Bureau of Free Love," according to the official gazette of the Vladimir Soviet of Workers' and Soldiers' Deputies, which recently published that Soviet's decree on the subject.

Under the decree, a woman having registered, "has the right to choose among men between 19 and 50 a cohabitant husband." The consent of the man chosen is not necessary, the decree adds, the man chosen having no right to make any protest.

A similar privilege of choosing from among the registered women is given every man between 19 and 50, "without the consent of the women." This provision is described as "in the interest of the state."[32]

Such exaggerated stories only fed the fears of Americans about the Bolsheviks. Eventually, reporting from outside the Soviet Union ended in 1921 when a famine forced the Soviets to open their borders to the American press as a condition for U.S. aid, but the reporting of Soviet affairs was still being hampered by limitations from the government and limitations within the press. Whitman Bassow noted that "correspondents were handicapped because almost without exception, they did not know the language, the history, the politics, or very much about the men who shaped the visible events."[33] This handicap would not diminish noticeably in the ensuing years.

Finally, there was the domestic Red Scare. While Americans might become frightened by events in the Soviet Union, they became bitterly hysterical when it appeared that communism had invaded their homeland. In 1919 a subcommittee of the U.S. Senate investigated the extent to which American society, particularly labor unions, had been infiltrated by bolshevism. Such investigations served two purposes: they intensified the hatred of Soviet leaders, and they brought the Red Scare home to America. The investigations were in many ways similar to the HUAC investigations of the 1940s and the McCarthy hearings of the early 1950s, although not as long-lasting nor as pernicious. But a cycle was created: the distrust of the Soviets led to fear on the domestic scene, while fear of communism at home led to an intensified hatred for far-off Russia. As this cycle was repeated, distortions and exaggerations grew in a climate of fear resulting in a paranoia about everything remotely connected with communism or aliens. Subsequent events then filtered through the refracted lens of previous perceptions.

The Red Scare also had its roots in domestic politics. In 1919 when an epidemic of labor strikes swept the country, a natural result of postwar inflation, the anti-Bolshevik climate made it seem to many that the strikes were inspired by Moscow. These were not fantasies based solely on imagination, but they did require enormous leaps of logic. American radicals, who had been dispersed among a variety of left-wing organizations prior to the Russian Revolution, saw in the Bolshevik victory the first real sign of a proletariat revolution and, more important, the practical ideology and organization to achieve it. Radicals began deserting their old affiliations to join new organizations associated with or directed by communists. The Industrial Workers of the World, once the romantic ideal of radicals, lost an estimated 2,000 members to the communists. Big Bill Haywood, one of the most prominent of the Wobblies, switched to the communists declaring: "Here is what we have been dreaming about; here is the IWW all feathered out."[34] Radicals had been active in labor disputes and continued to be active during the postwar years. But it required a great leap in evidence and logic to see the postwar strikes as directed by Moscow through these radicals who already had a history of involvement before the Russian revolution was any more than a gleam in Lenin's eye. Nonetheless, the connection was made in the eyes of some officials and among many suspicious American citizens. Robert Murray concluded:

Employers . . . were brought to the realization that the issue of radicalism could be helpful in their fight against unionism. To certain politicians it became obvious that radicalism would make an excellent political issue by which free publicity as well as votes could be obtained. The general press . . . found in the issue of radicalism an immediate substitute for waning wartime sensationalism and eagerly busied itself with reporting exaggerations instead of facts.[35]

The foreign enemy, in other words, gave a convenient rationalization for understanding domestic strife.

In 1919 more than four million Americans struck, with the actual number of strikes recorded as 3,630. A walkout in Seattle, Washington that closed its port for a week was seen as evidence that bolshevism was infecting American life. Seattle Mayor Ole Hansen gave credence to that interpretation in the vitriolic speeches he gave denouncing the strikers.

The actual relationship between Bolshevik influence and American labor relations was tenuous at best. The vast majority of American workers were simply caught up in the economic conditions of the postwar, as they would be again after World War II. The main factors contributing to strikes were the transition from a war-time economy to peacetime, along with the generally deplorable working conditions of that period. In the steel industry, for example, the normal working day was twelve hours. Often workers were called on for twenty-four-hour shifts. There was more than sufficient reason for strikes within domestic industrial practices. There would have been labor unrest had Soviet Russia not existed, but the rhetoric of the day cast much of the blame on forces operating from outside the United States.

The verbal attacks upon Russian beliefs and actions created a rhetorical climate that made it simple for Americans to believe that the social unrest was created by an external enemy. Peter Filene noted that "the Bolsheviks were an evil which the Wilson Administration diplomatically boycotted and which the majority of American observers vehemently opposed."[36] The American fear and hatred of Russia's repressive regime resulted, as it would again in the future, in the U.S. government becoming more repressive. Democratic institutions in the United States weakened, ostensibly to protect them from an antidemocratic attack.

A Red Scare swept the country. There were, without doubt, revolutionary groups active in the United States. A scattering of terrorist acts served to validate the perception of a Bolshevik menace. Red-baiting Mayor Ole Hansen found a bomb in his mail. A maid of Georgia Senator Thomas Hardwick had her hand blown off as she opened a package addressed to the Senator. An investigation in the New York City Post Office revealed sixteen packages containing bombs, each addressed to a prominent public figure. Although such incidents were more an index of tense times than a sign of a pending revolution, the actuality of these incidents validated the rhetoric that saw the roots of America's domestic problems growing out of Soviet Russia.[37]

Anti-Bolshevik rhetoric led to antiradical action, especially against aliens regardless of whether they had any connections with political activities. U.S. Attorney General A. Mitchell Palmer led a crusade to eradicate Bolshevik influence from the United States. In well-publicized raids hundred of aliens were arrested and then deported to Russia, in some cases merely for having a foreign name. Moderate socialists who were elected to the New York legislature were not allowed to take their seats. Such high-profile government activities against radicals "further seared into the American public mind the familiar stereotype of a bloodthirsty, bewhiskered, bomb-throwing, free-loving Bolshevik."[38] Palmer hammered home the alien-radical connection: "My information showed that Communism in this country was an organization of thousands of aliens . . . direct allies of Trotsky, aliens of the same misshapen caste of mind and indecencies of character."[39] Radical automatically meant Red, with the accompanying image of a tattered but wild-eyed alien holding a bomb ready for revolution. Contrasted with this alien image was the image of Americanism, usually personified in Uncle Sam, standing resolute and ready to defend the homeland.[40]

With the election of Warren Harding to the presidency, the great first fear of communism subsided. Nonetheless, many of the rhetorical patterns for interacting with the Soviet Union were established. Frightening images had been created, arguments against bolshevism utilized, links between a foreign ideology and domestic political activities drawn, metaphors of disease employed, narratives of sinister Soviet actions and motives written, and a general rhetorical pattern of political universalism emerged that would be drawn from in the future. It was not complete, but it was fulsome.

AMERICAN IMAGES OF THE SOVIET GOVERNMENT
AFTER THE RED SCARE

In the period between the end of World War I and the Nazi–Soviet pact in 1939, the threat of a Soviet menace dissipated as domestic issues replaced foreign policy in the forefront of American consciousness, and the growing menace of fascism loomed more threatening. The election of Harding began twelve years of Republican control of the White House. During those years nonrecognition of the Soviet government remained the official policy of the United States. The rhetoric used to justify not recognizing the Soviet government during this period indicated that the images defining the moral and ideological character of the Soviets had been subdued, not forgotten. Three main reasons were given: Soviet leaders had repudiated their war debts; they had refused reparations for confiscated U.S. property inside the USSR; and they continued to talk about a worldwide communist revolution. President Coolidge's secretary of state, Charles Evans Hughes, repeated these charges about confiscating property and violating personal liberties, but emphasized "what is most serious is that . . . those in control at Moscow have not given up their original purpose of destroying existing governments wherever they can do so throughout the world."[41] These reasons supported continued Republican opposition to recognition of the Soviet Union.

The image of a diabolical enemy bent on world revolution, however, began mellowing somewhat during the 1920s. Lenin died in 1924, and Americans believed Stalin to be less fanatic. In his break with Trotsky in 1926, Stalin announced in a speech that the Russians "have had enough of that idiotic slogan, 'The World Revolution.' "[42] Part of his war with Trotsky had concentrated on the issue of spreading the revolution. The fiery Trotsky pressed for perpetual revolution whereas the cautious Stalin sought to consolidate "socialism in one country."[43] That is not to say that Stalin eschewed spreading socialist doctrine to other countries. He made that clear: "To win fully, to win definitely, we must see to it that the current capitalist encirclement be changed to a socialist one; we must strive for the proletariat's winning in at least a few other countries. Only then will our victory be full and final."[44] But Stalin was less cosmopolitan than Trotsky and certainly more guarded politically and personally. Make certain socialism is firmly in control in the Soviet Union, Stalin seemed to reason, before embarking wildly upon exporting it to other countries. Whether he ever felt secure enough at home for such Trotskyite ventures remains a matter of intense speculation. With the expulsion of Trotsky from the Soviet Union in 1928 (an expulsion that split both Soviet communists and American radicals with disastrous results for the Russian "Trotskyites"), Stalin emerged triumphant and curiously more palatable to Americans. Or at least palatable enough for President Roosevelt to recognize the Soviet government in 1933, although this is not to say it was the only reason for recognition.

The 1930s were a tumultuous time. Depending on one's point of view it was a "decade of destiny," or "the Red decade," or "the heyday of American communism." But whatever one's political view, it was the time of the Great Depression in Western nations and the rise of fascism in Europe. In terms of American images of the Soviet Union we may divide this time prior to the Nazi–Soviet pact into images coming from abroad and the rhetorics that developed at home.

First-hand reports by American correspondents in the Soviet Union were still limited by a lack of knowledge about Russian language and customs. Whitman Bassow noted that the selection of reporters to cover the USSR was not based on any special knowledge of the country but that "the key factor in the coverage" was who was available.[45] Eugene Lyons went to the USSR sympathetic to the Soviets, only to return six years later filled with hostility. His 1937 book, *Assignment in Utopia*, was a scathing appraisal of the Soviet regime, "a bitter, angry work" wrote Bassow, "that could only have been written by a true believer whose vision of communism was destroyed by the Communists themselves."[46] He followed this book with another, *The Red Decade*, in 1941 about domestic communists during the 1930s, which kept alive a distorted view of the depression and native radicals. Walter Duranty, whose fourteen years in the Soviet Union was the longest stay of anyone from the *New York Times* bureau, wrote sympathetically of Soviet conditions and government, "its utter difference from anything one has known before and its Alice-in-Wonderland topsy-turveyness as compared with the Western world."[47] For example, upon Hitler's assumption of power in 1933, Duranty wrote in the March 2 issue of the *New York Times* that Soviet leadership might not be as hostile toward the Nazis as their official rhetoric said: "It is beyond question that Moscow would welcome even a one hundred per cent Hitler regime on the grounds that it would conjure away the nightmare that has harassed the sleep of Soviet statesmen for the past five years: namely, an anti-Bolshevik European coalition or a 'holy war against the Red Peril.' "[48] Such reporting from sympathizers and antagonists was as divided as before and usually as uninformed, reinforcing established views and doing little to enlighten people at home.

Back in the United States, Americans—those in power and those out of jobs—were more concerned with the Depression than with foreign affairs. However, when attention did turn to the Soviet Union and communism, three different rhetorics dominated discussion of these subjects. The first proselytized for the Communist cause. With the United States in the depths of the Great Depression, the Soviet Union became an "experiment" in progressive government for some, the "wave of the future" for others.[49] Malcolm Cowley summarized the romantic faith embodied in this rhetoric:

All through the 1930s the Soviet Union was a second fatherland for millions of people in other countries, including our own. It was the land where men and women were sacrificing themselves to create a new civilization, not for Russia alone but for the world. It was not so much a nation, in the eyes of Western radicals, as it was an ideal, a faith and an international hope of salvation.[50]

This radical rhetoric progressed through two distinct periods. The first phase from 1929 to 1935 was one of "ultra-militance, sectarian politics, and revolutionary rhetoric."[51] Within the American communist rhetoric Roosevelt's New Deal was hardly distinguishable from Hoover's republicanism, both instruments of Wall Street and corporate capitalism. However, when the Soviet Union joined the League of Nations in 1934, and then advocated action against Mussolini's attack on Ethiopia and Hitler's occupation of the Rhineland in 1936, the party line changed. It was the time of the "popular front" coalition with progressives, and the topics of their rhetoric changed from sectarian condemnations of capitalism to collective security against the fascists and continued social progress at home. When the Soviet Union became the only nation, except for Mexico, to aid the antifascists in the Spanish civil war, radicals saw this action as proof that the Soviet Union was the progressive beacon in an increasing dark and reactionary world.

The revolutionary rhetoric of radicals and the chaotic conditions of the Depression ignited a new round of anticommunist condemnations in reaction, the second dominant rhetoric of the period. It was kept up through a steady drumbeat in the press. There was, for example, the Catholic press. Originally it had followed the Vatican in welcoming the Soviet revolution as an opportunity to spread the faith in Russia. Under the czars the Russian Orthodox Church had been a barrier to Catholic proselytizing and bolshevism was seen as an opportunity to convert Russians. But by the 1930s the Soviets had repressed the Catholics as they had other religious groups, and from that time on the Catholic Church regarded the atheistic Soviets as a supreme evil, a rhetorical tradition that would extend throughout the war and become a prime channel of condemnation in the cold war.[52] Condemnation of the Soviet Union on religious grounds, which predated the Catholic Church's attacks, became a major theme in the anticommunist rhetoric and was perpetuated from the 1930s on.

Among the secular press, Henry Luce and William Randolph Hearst loomed prominent in their persistent anticommunism. Luce, the publisher of *Time* and *Life*, had opposed recognition of the Soviet Union and advocated an economic boycott of the USSR. He exercised firm editorial control in a continuing condemnation of the Soviet government. Hearst attempted to launch another Red Scare by sending spies onto university campuses to expose communist teachers and teachings. He secured the "services of 'reformed' Communists who had written for *The Daily Worker* to help him sniff out Reds."[53] DeWitt Wallace, publisher of *Reader's Digest*, and Robert McCormick, publisher of the *Chicago Tribune*, contributed their share to the anticommunist "reporting" and editorials. This anticommunist rhetoric was primarily an update of the same rhetoric that had circulated during the time of the Bolshevik Revolution: strident hatred of the communists, fears of Russian power, linkages between alien doctrines and domestic radicals.

The third rhetoric of the period sought to link the Roosevelt administration and its policies to the communist menace. Only a few examples will be used here to demonstrate the flavor of this rhetoric. Generally, the favorite targets were Eleanor Roosevelt, Henry Wallace, and Harry Hopkins. In 1934 Elizabeth Dilling published a book entitled *The Red Network* in which she "named" some 1,300 Red conspirators including Eleanor Roosevelt, Mahatma Gandhi, and Chiang Kai-shek.[54] Although the people lumped together in her little book made her charges incredible, the linkage began, with a special place for Mrs. Roosevelt in most of the charges. In the 1936 campaign her husband, the president, also became a target. William Lemke of the Union party stated: "I do not charge that the President of this nation is a Communist but I do charge that Browder, Dubinsky and other Communist leaders have laid their cuckoo eggs in his Democratic nest and that he is hatching them."[55] But the most vigorous exponent of this linkage was Representative Martin Dies who chaired the Special Committee on UnAmerican Activities, the committee established in 1938. Although the committee's primary target was supposed to be American fascists, Dies was more interested in American communists and their infiltration of labor unions, schools, and the government. His book, *The Trojan Horse in America*, noted his hysterical concern for domestic communism's influence in the New Deal. He saw the Works Progress Administration, in general, and the Federal Theatre Project, in particular, as "the greatest financial boon which ever came to the Communists in the United States. Stalin could not have done better by his American friends and agents."[56] Partisan and ideological intentions motivated many of these attacks. The leaders in the attempts to link communism and the administration's policies came from southern reactionaries (such as Dies) and Republican conservatives, both of whom abhorred Roosevelt's programs for recovery. The distinctive feature of this rhetoric was guilt by idea or policy association, that is, linking the administration's policies to socialist or communist ideas, and thus calling administration figures "dupes" or "pawns" of radicals, or in some cases, of Stalin himself.

The designations "dupe," "pawn," or "apologist" took on additional meanings with the Moscow purge trials of 1936 to 1938.[57] When the Soviet Union put many prominent officials, including some of the great names of Bolshevik history (Bukharin and Rykov, for example) on trial for subversion or treason, the West was confused and shocked. They did not know what to make of these events. Some saw them as attempts to replace doctrinaire revolutionaries with nationalists in the Soviet Union.[58] Others saw them as convincing evidence of basic brutality of communism. The shock and confusion was even more anguishing in radical circles, and they led to angry divisions. Some publicly left the American Communist party in disgust; others deserted the party in less flamboyant fashion. Whittaker Chambers claimed he broke with the party at this time. Although his claims are still questionable, they symbolize one very real response to the purges. Others did not leave and instead adjusted to the new party line. Those true-believing radicals who sought to rationalize the purges or who believed the accused were actually traitors to the Soviet Union devised an incredible rhetoric of apology for Stalinism that would come back to haunt them in later years. Later when the "show trials" were exposed for the paranoid purges that they were, they would seem to prove how easily American radicals can be duped into becoming apologists for the Soviet Union and their words of *apologia* would be flung back in their faces with vehemence.

All of this was to change abruptly in 1939. New events caused the competing rhetorics to collapse and a new anti-Soviet rhetoric to dominate, at least for a brief period.

AMERICAN IMAGES OF RED FASCISM

The period between the Nazi–Soviet pact in August 1939 and the Japanese attack on Pearl Harbor on December 7, 1941 marked a resurgence of the vitriolic anti-Soviet rhetoric. When the Soviets signed a non-aggression agreement with Germany, the outburst of indignation in the United States was reminiscent of the response to the Soviet–German peace treaty at Brest-Litovsk in 1918. In each case Americans (and indeed much of the Western world) saw Soviet behavior as a betrayal of monumental proportions, but this time the betrayal went beyond abandoning a struggle with a demonic enemy to joining forces with that evil enemy itself.

Before proceeding to the intense condemnation heaped upon the Soviet Union, we might pause to consider Soviet reasons for this unholy alliance. The agreements at Munich are perhaps the key to Stalin's decision to seek the pact with Hitler. Great Britain and France struck a deal that for all practical purposes consigned Czechoslovakia to Germany in 1938. The very name "Munich" became synonymous in the war and postwar rhetoric with "appeasement" of aggressors. But for the Soviets it bore a more sinister connotation. In a 1958 interview with Walter Lippmann, Nikita Khrushchev explained the Soviet view of Munich. Czechoslovakia, Khrushchev said, was "an arrow aimed at the heart of Russia."[59] From his view, the Western powers had "appeased" Hitler in order to turn the Nazi threat away from the West eastward toward the Soviet Union. A year later von Ribbentrop and Molotov negotiated the non-aggression pact. The Pact contained a secret agreement that conceded Estonia, Latvia, and Finland to the Soviet sphere of influence and Lithuania to the Germans. Within a week Hitler invaded Poland and World War II was underway. A little more than two weeks later the Soviet Union moved into eastern Poland and soon invaded Finland. Whether Stalin's actions were motivated by an opportunity for expansionism or for the purpose of defending Soviet interests, they were brutally ruthless.

American public reaction to these events was swift. On the rhetorical level, fascism and communism became immediately linked as only two different faces on the same totalitarian coin. It should be noted that this convergence of different ideologies was underway even prior to the pact. In April 1939, Westbrook Pegler announced that communism and "Nazifascism" were one and the same, although "Hitler bolshevism" was the more immediate threat.[60] Just as important, a number of political thinkers in the late 1930s were popularizing the word "totalitarianism" and lumping fascism and communism under the same label. Walter Lippmann was one of these people. In his influential book *The Good Society* (1936), Lippmann devoted an entire chapter to "Totalitarian Regimes" and divided the space almost equally between fascism and communism.[61] Others followed suit. Just after the pact the *New York Times* proclaimed: "Hitlerism is brown communism, Stalinism is red fascism."[62] *Time* named Joseph Stalin as "Man of the Year" in 1939, dubbing him "Ivan the Terrible" and saying that he had "matched himself with Adolf Hitler as the world's most hated man."[63] With a multitude of similar statements springing forth, the two governments were merged so that the motives and acts of the one became indistinguishable from the motives and acts of the other.

Out of this period of upheaval and reversals came three rhetorical developments that later contributed to the rhetoric of the cold war or to its acceptance. First, the word "totalitarian" became the generic term to apply to dictatorial or ideological governments regardless of whether the actual ideas of those governments were in conflict with one another.

"Red fascism" captured perfectly this intellectual collapsing of different and divergent political ideas into one concept. From this convergence came conclusions that fascism and communism were different not in goals ("world domination") nor in ideas, but only in some strategies and tactics. What this meant rhetorically was that future speakers and writers had a rich motherlode of symbols, images, and analogies to mine when speaking or writing against the Soviet Union. Conversely, those who believed otherwise and sought more conciliatory policies to reach practical arrangements with the Soviet Union ran into a brick wall of preconceptions and linguistic obstacles that the heat of the cold war made almost impossible to surmount.

Second, the Hitler-Chamberlain agreements at Munich impressed an indelible historical analogy upon Western consciousness for the next several generations. "Munich" became synonymous with giving in or "appeasing" dictatorial aggression. It would become more than an analogy; it would become the central lesson to be learned about the nature of aggression, of diplomacy, and of any sign of weakness. Any kind of concession to an adversary, partisan critics cried, amounted to appeasement, and the specific consequences of Munich with all the attendant images of Nazi atrocities would be aroused.

The third and final development was a general and widespread distrust of diplomacy as an effective means for resolving international disputes. This predisposition would have far-reaching consequences in the postwar period as policymakers vacillated at first between diplomatic and military responses to situations that arose. In general Americans would view military preparedness with favor and diplomacy with suspicion. One can readily understand this predisposition. Americans had long been distrustful of European diplomacy. That was one contributing reason for isolationism. But the events in the last prewar years increased that distrust. At Munich Hitler cynically manipulated Western illusions and then just as cynically broke his agreements. The Nazi–Soviet non-aggression agreement shocked the world as two diametrically opposed ideologies made temporary common cause with one another. The secret agreements only intensified the shock. The last straw occurred with the Japanese attack on Pearl Harbor. Japanese diplomats were in Washington negotiating with Americans even as Japanese warlords planned and carried out the sneak attack on Pearl Harbor. The Alexandria *Gazette* voiced the outrage of millions of Americans when it denounced "the sly, cowardly attack executed at the very hour Japan's Machiavellian envoys were conducting 'peace' negotiations with our government. . . ."[64] The dastardly attack on Pearl Harbor remained a symbol of diplomatic duplicity for a generation of Americans, making them deeply suspicious of negotiations and staunch supporters of military preparedness.

CONFLICTING AMERICAN IMAGES OF THE SOVIET UNION IN WARTIME

The change from an anti-Soviet rhetoric to another began in Europe immediately after Hitler launched his invasion of the Soviet Union on June 22, 1941. It began with Winston Churchill. The British prime minister went on radio just hours after the invasion in a broadcast heard by millions of Americans over NBC and reprinted widely in American newspapers the next day. Churchill described Hitler in the theological terms historically used in war rhetoric: "the monster of wickedness, insatiable in his lust for blood and plunder."[65] Although few in the past had consistently opposed and condemned Soviet socialism as vigorously as he, Churchill now presented a different view of the Soviets: "I see Russian soldiers standing on the threshold of their native land guarding the fields where their fathers have tilled from time immemorial. I see them guarding their homes, where mothers and wives pray." Not only did Churchill portray "godless communists" in prayer, but he now remembered when they were allies with the West and had been cheated of the fruits of victory:

Behind this storm, I see the small group of venomous men [Hitler and the Nazis] who planned, organized and launched this cataract of horrors upon mankind. Then my mind goes back across the years to the days when Russian armies were our allies against the same deadly foe, when they fought with so much valor and constancy and helped gain a victory, from a share of which, alas, they were, from no fault of ours, utterly cut out.

Churchill ended with a warning that Hitler, if not stopped, would topple nations one by one until the whole Western Hemisphere was under his control.

Thus, Churchill drew upon an older rhetorical stockpile to recreate a wartime picture of an old antagonist, now a new ally. He drew from the commonplace stockpile of war rhetoric, that of brave and innocent people as defenders of native soil contrasted with evil enemies bloodthirsty for conquest and dominion. More specifically, he drew from the alliance of the British people and Russian people in World War I that fought the Germans decades before. The rhetorical division based its arguments on common human traits, innocent people, and defense of homeland. Omitted from the rhetoric was the communist government, its ideology and its history of rule under the Bolsheviks. The former were idealized; the latter ignored. This division eventually became fundamental in the rhetoric needed for victory, but it would be pursued with somewhat different twists in the United States.

Winston Churchill's reconstitution of the Soviet Union as a brave people opposing fascism spread in the United States through editorials favoring aid to the USSR. But the rhetorical rehabilitation was not completed until the Japanese attacked Pearl Harbor making the Soviets and Americans instant allies. In the interim between Hitler's attack on the Soviet Union and America's entry into the war, American responses moved slowly from the need to aid the Soviets as a necessity to the fact of embracing them as an ally. The analogical linking of the Soviet Union and Germany had been so powerful that it could not be dropped instantly. Thomas G. Patterson cited the statement by the *Wall Street Journal* shortly after the invasion that succinctly captured part of the mood of the time: "The American people know that the principal difference between Mr. Hitler and Mr. Stalin is the size of their respective mustaches."[66] In a statement made famous later, Harry Truman announced: "If we see Germany winning we ought to help Russia and if Russia is winning we ought to help Germany and that way let them kill as many as possible, although I don't want to see Hitler victorious under any circumstances. Neither of them think anything of their pledged word."[67] These sentiments were echoed by a number of Americans, including Charles Lindbergh, that seemed to resonate from the old isolationist tradition and suspicions of Europeans. They said in unmistakable terms, "a pox on both your houses."

When it became apparent that Nazi Germany might indeed dominate Europe and perhaps the world unless successfully resisted, it became politically easier to lend aid to the Soviets. In a short time a new rhetoric began to shape a new vision of the Soviets. Both radio and newspaper carried daily accounts of the Soviet–German war with more favorable images of the Soviets emerging. Following the rhetorical lead of Churchill, American opinion leaders portrayed brave Russians valiantly defending their homeland against sadistic hordes of Nazis.[68] This rhetoric stressed the traditional division made in wartime between the communist government and the innocent Russian people. With the attack on Pearl Harbor, public opinion changed radically. For the duration of the war the overriding emphasis was on the courageous Soviet allies fighting the demonic Nazi enemy.

During the war two different rhetorical portrayals of the Soviet Union coexisted: one dominant, the other subordinate. The first was the standard war rhetoric in which allies are gallant and stalwart and the enemy evil and bestial. *Time* magazine made Stalin "Man of the Year" again in 1942, but this time the caption read: "He took all that Hitler could give."[69] The siege of Stalingard provided a particularly poignant example of Soviet bravery and perseverence in the face of the German onslaught. Americans followed the siege of that Soviet city in the autumn and winter of 1942, and it must have reminded them that the courageous Soviets fighting on the streets were fighting an army that was dedicated to killing

Americans on their streets. The story was made into a movie, one of about 25 propaganda films that depicted the Soviets favorably.

Walter Duranty, *New York Times* correspondent, now found sound reasons for the Soviet Union's inexplicable policies in the past. The pact with Germany had enabled the Soviet Union to get much-needed industrial goods in order to prepare its defenses against an anticipated Nazi invasion. The Soviet attack on Finland now became a defensive maneuver, again in preparation for war with Germany. Even the purges had been beneficial, if excessive, in cleansing Soviet leadership of potential "Quislings." Duranty concluded: "What foreigners failed to realize . . . was the deep and bounding love of Russians for their country, their Rodina, their birthland."[70] In sum, the Bolshevik government had improved the lives of the Soviet people, giving them hope for the future and love of the Motherland.

In 1941 Joseph E. Davies, a wealthy businessman who had been ambassador to the Soviet Union from 1936 to 1938, published his impressions in a best-selling book, *Mission to Moscow*. He wrote of the "honest convictions and integrity of purposes" of the Soviet leaders and added that in his opinion the policies they pursued were "consistent with their own security . . . [and] are devoted to the cause of peace for both ideological and practical reasons."[71] Hollywood adapted the book into a successful movie in 1943, one used to flame the war effort. After the war it would be used to flame the cold war hysteria.

Wendell Wilkie, Republican presidential candidate in 1940, toured the world by air in 1942, spending some time in the Soviet Union. In his best-selling book, *One World*, he spoke warmly of his experiences in the USSR, comparing the country to the American midwest and stating baldly that "we do not have to fear Russia."[72]

Ralph Levering summed up the dramatic change in the public's view of the Soviet Union in reference to Davies's observations:

It seems unlikely that such remarks about the good faith of Russia's leaders would have made it to the printing presses of an established American publishing company six months before. After 22 June [1941] but before 7 December they were the words of a liberal; after Pearl Harbor they were words which almost any moderate could accept.[73]

The significance of these books lies not so much in the role they played in creating public opinion, for they had a relatively small circulation in comparison with images and ideas coming from radio, movies, newspapers, and mass circulation magazines. They are important, rather, as indicators of the prevailing beliefs of the time. Publishers printed these books because they believed there was a market for them. The topics they choose to publish are an indication of the ideas they believe the public is willing to entertain. And during the war the American public wanted to believe, needed to believe its allies in the East shared common values and aspirations with them.

Much of the extravagant war rhetoric about the Soviet Union infused and animated *Life*'s special issue on the USSR on March 29, 1943. The magazine, with a Margaret Bourke White photograph of a benign Stalin on its cover, described Lenin ("The Father of Modern Russia") as perhaps "the greatest man of modern times," "that rarest of men, an absolutely unselfconscious and unselfish man" who was dedicated "to rescuing 140,000,000 people from a brutal and incompetent tyranny. He did what he set out to do."[74] Soviet leaders were described as "tough, loyal, capable administrators." Writers at *Life* reported Kamenev had been executed in 1936 after a trial for "conspiring to kill government leaders." Trotsky was depicted as the Soviet Union's "traitorous Benedict Arnold."[75] In its biographical sketch of Beria *Life* stated that he was head of the N.K.V.D., "a national police similar to the FBI."[76] The issue included an interview with Davies, stories and the inevitable *Life* pictures about Soviet cultural activities and history, stories and scenes of cooperative efforts of Russians and Americans in facing the diabolical foe—Hitler and fascism. Rivaled only by patriotic speeches and newsreels, this issue of *Life* was the apotheosis of the dominant war rhetoric of the time, a rhetoric that stressed American–Soviet cooperation, embraced internationalism, portrayed the Soviets as Russian nationals rather than communist ideologues, and painted a picture of them as one-sided in its emphasis on the positive aspects of leaders and government in the Soviet Union as the later anticommunist rhetoric would be in painting a picture of Soviet depravity and evil.

Even as the patriotic rhetoric rallied Americans to the allied cause, a second subordinate rhetoric persisted throughout the war years. It continued the ideological rhetoric of anticommunism of previous years. Just as the ruling rhetoric ignored ideological differences between the two nations, the secondary rhetoric emphasized them; even as the former stressed trusting the Russians, the second sowed the seeds of distrust. George Sirgiovannia in his doctoral dissertation study concluded:

The resilience of such attitudes in what surely were the most auspicious years of U.S.–Soviet relations contributes to our understanding of why a far more virulent and widespread Cold War mentality of mistrust and hostility burst forth so soon after the Allied victory. Many of the issues that contributed to the Cold War, such as political and territorial makeup of Eastern Europe, had been raised during the alliance by those who assumed that the USSR could never be trusted to act in a spirit of justice and compassion. Such people also insisted that the domestic Communist movement—despite its "patriotic" wartime line—remained in the service of today's ally but tomorrow's possible adversary, Joseph Stalin's USSR.[77]

Sirgiovannia noted four groups that carried on this rhetoric: various labor unions, the right-wing press, Catholics and fundamentalists, and certain socialists. The variety of these groups only served to lay out a variety of vantage points from which to attack domestic communism or the alliance with the Soviet Union. Socialists continued in their bitter ideological struggle with communists for the heart and soul of the Left; religious groups denounced atheistic communism; the right-wing press kept alive the issue of communist influence in the Roosevelt adminis-tration; and unions, especially some in the American Federation of La-bor, repeated charges that the communists and fascists were struck from the same totalitarian mint, the only difference between the two being that fascism was our official enemy and more dangerous than com-munism at the time. Thus, the anticommunist rhetoric of the war years persisted. It was played more like the steady rhythmic section in the background of a concerto performance while the Roosevelt administra-tion and leading opinion-makers played the main themes of allied co-operation.

CONCLUSION

The relationship between the United States and the Soviet Union has historically veered from one extreme to another, a love-hate relationship which has swung from outlandish hopes to excessive despair, from trust to fear. As times have changed and particular events have brought the two in contact with one another, Americans have adjusted their attitudes toward the USSR to suit the times and events. Like the two countries themselves, these reactions have been larger than life, greater than sit-uations demanded. And they have been usually accompanied by an exaggerated rhetoric of salvation or condemnation as situations or cir-cumstances seemed to require.

From the Bolshevik Revolution through World War II, the various periods of agitation and fear about the Soviet Union and domestic com-munists created a rich tradition from which anticommunist advocates could draw in the postwar years, a tradition made even more believable merely by its long history. That tradition would not only serve as a fertile resource but also as an intellectual imprisonment to those who adopted it. What has not been noticed as often is that the excessive hopes attached to American relations with Russia and later the Soviet Union also created a tradition, though not as deeply embedded among primary policy-makers and opinion leaders, but a tradition nonetheless. The optimistic buoyancy that had greeted incidents or periods of American–Russian collaboration provided a very limited and eventually dangerous rhetor-ical grounds from which advocates of continued cooperation would be forced to draw. Its excessive hopes would mislead some as much as the excessive fears of communism would mislead others. In this sense, both traditions—being extravagant and idealized—created the conditions for the breakdown of collaboration and the development of confrontation between the two mighty nations.

NOTES

1. James Oliver Robertson, *American Myth, American Reality* (New York: Hill and Wang, 1980), p. 8.

2. Richard H. Pells, *Radical Visions and American Dreams: Culture and Social Thought in the Depression Years* (New York: Harper and Row, 1973), p. 63.

3. Frances Fitzgerald, *America Revised: History of Schoolbooks in the Twentieth Century* (Boston: Little, Brown, 1979), p. 56.

4. Vera Micheles Dean, *The United States and Russia* (Cambridge: Harvard University Press, 1948), p. 4.

5. John G. Stoessinger, *Nations in Darkness* (New York: Random House, 1971), p. 139.

6. Ibid., p. 104. Stoessinger goes on to note that the view of the czarina swung in the other direction when she divided Poland with Austria and Prussia. American sympathies went out to the Polish "underdog." However, this image faded after her death and the "Mother of Independence" legend resurfaced.

7. Frank A. Golder, "The Russian Fleet and the Civil War," *American Historical Review* (July 1915), p. 805. The legend and the actuality are summarized in Stoessinger, *Nations in Darkness*, pp. 106–9.

8. Dean, *The United States and Russia*, p. 7.

9. Charles Sumner, *Speech of Hon. Charles Sumner of Massachusetts on the Cession of Russian Alaska to the United States* (Washington, DC: Congressional Globe Office, 1867), p. 15.

10. Stoessinger, *Nations in Darkness*, pp. 112–13.

11. For a detailed examination of his life and writings, see Frederick F. Travis, *George Kennan and the American-Russian Relationship, 1865–1924* (Athens, OH: Ohio University Press, 1990).

12. Thomas A. Bailey, *America Faces Russia* (Ithaca, NY: Cornell University Press, 1950), p. 128.

13. George Kennan, "The Russian Police," *Century* 37 (April 1889), p. 891.

14. See the chapter, "Civilization Versus Barbarism," in Travis, *George Kennan*, pp. 249–315.

15. George Kennan, "The Victory of the Russian People," *Outlook* (March 28, 1917), p. 546.

16. William Henry Chamberlain, *Beyond Containment* (Chicago: Henry Regnery, 1953), p. 8.

17. On the full impact of the peace treaty, see George F. Kennan, *Russia Leaves the War* (Princeton: Princeton University Press, 1956).

18. Ronald Steel, *Walter Lippmann and the American Century* (Boston: Little, Brown, 1980), p. 112.

19. For a more extensive rendering of these events, see ibid., pp. 132–36.

20. Adam Ulam, *Expansion and Coexistence: Soviet Foreign Policy, 1917–1973*, 2d ed. (New York: Holt, Rinehart and Winston, 1974), p. 54.

21. Peter Filene, *Americans and the Soviet Experiment, 1917–1933* (Cambridge, MA: Harvard University Press, 1967), p. 43.

22. Peter G. Filene, ed., *American Views of Soviet Russia, 1917–1965* (Homewood, IL: Dorsey Press, 1968), p. ix.

23. Ulam, *Expansion and Coexistence*, p. 98.

24. Filene, *Americans and the Soviet Experiment, 1917–1933*, p. 37.

25. John Lewis Gaddis, *Russia, The Soviet Union, and The United States: An Interpretative History* (New York: Alfred A. Knopf, 1978), pp. 82–83. Gaddis continues by citing significant differences between the two. Lenin thought of democracy only in economic terms, endorsed violent revolution, and sought to overthrow the existing international order whereas Wilson conceived of democracy primarily in political terms, sought evolution within a liberal-capitalist framework, and sought to alter it from within.

26. E. Malcolm Carroll, *Soviet Communism and Western Opinion, 1919–1921*, ed. Frederic B. M. Hollyday (Chapel Hill, NC: University of North Carolina Press, 1965), p. 8.

27. Walter Lippmann and Charles Marx, *New Republic* (August 4, 1921), supplement.

28. Arno J. Mayer, *Politics of Peacemaking: Containment and Counterrevolution at Versailles, 1918–1919* (New York: Alfred A. Knopf, 1967), p. 270.

29. William Appleton Williams, *American–Russian Relations, 1781–1947* (New York: Rinehart, 1952), p. 201.

30. George F. Kennan, *Soviet–American Relations, 1917–1919: The Decision to Intervene*, vol. 2 (Princeton: Princeton University Press, 1958), p. 332.

31. Bailey, *America Faces Russia*, pp. v–vi.

32. *New York Times*, October 26, 1919, p. 5.

33. Whitman Bassow, *The Moscow Correspondents: Reporting on Russia From the Revolution to Glasnost* (New York: William Morrow, 1988), p. 49.

34. Quoted in Robert K. Murray, *Red Scare: A Study in National Hysteria, 1919–1920* (New York: McGraw-Hill, 1955), p. 52. The estimate of Wobblie defections is also from this source.

35. Ibid., pp. 67–68.

36. Filene, *Americans and the Soviet Experiment*, p. 41.

37. Ibid., pp. 67–81.

38. Bailey, *America Faces Russia*, p. 248.

39. Quoted in David H. Bennett, *The Party of Fear: From Nativist Movements to the New Right in American History* (New York: Vintage, 1990), p. 193.

40. See the various cartoons of the era reprinted in Murray, *Red Scare*.

41. Quoted in Gaddis, *Russia, The Soviet Union, and The United States*, p. 107.

42. *The Literary Digest* 91 (October 30, 1926), p. 8.

43. On this divisive issue, see Adam Ulam, *Stalin: The Man and His Era*, expanded ed. (Boston: Beacon Press, 1989), pp. 263–72.

44. Quoted in ibid., p. 269.

45. Bassow, *The Moscow Correspondents*, p. 64.

46. Ibid., p. 87.

47. Ibid., p. 88.

48. Quoted in Max Nomad, *Political Heretics: From Plato to Mao Tse-tung* (Ann Arbor, MI: University of Michigan Press, 1963), p. 347.

49. The studies of the American communist movements in the 1930s would fill a small library. As a sampling of some of these studies, see Harvey Klehr, *The Heyday of American Communism: The Depression Decade* (New York: Basic Books, 1984); John Gates, *The Story of an American Communist* (New York: Thomas Nelson, 1958); Irving Howe and Lewis Coser, *The American Communist Party: A Critical History, 1919–1957* (Boston: Beacon Press, 1957); Vivian Gornick, *The Romance of American Communism* (New York: Basic Books, 1977); Daniel Aaron, *Writers on the Left* (New York: Harcourt, Brace, and World, 1961). For an extensive background detailing the 1920s, see Theodore Draper's two volumes, *The Roots of American Communism* (New York: Viking, 1957) and *American Communism and Soviet Russia* (New York: Vintage, 1986).

50. Malcolm Cowley, "Russian Turnabout," *New Republic* (June 14, 1943), pp. 800–1.

51. Pells, *Radical Visions and American Dreams*, p. 84.

52. On the later period, see George Sirgiovanni, "An Undercurrent of Suspicion: Anti-Communist and Anti-Soviet Opinion in World War II America" (Ph.D. diss., Rutgers University, 1988), pp. 25–70, 241–88.

53. W. A. Swanberg, *Citizen Hearst* (New York: Charles Scribner and Sons, 1961), p. 469.

54. Robert McElvanine, *The Great Depression: America 1929–1941* (New York: Times Books, 1984), p. 203.

55. Quoted in Arthur Schlesinger, Jr., *The Politics of Upheaval* (Boston: Houghton Mifflin, 1960), pp. 619–20.

56. Quoted in Eric Bentley, *Thirty Years of Treason* (New York: Viking, 1971), p. 3. See also Bentley's reprinting of Hallie Flanagan's testimony before the committee, pp. 6–47.

57. See Robert C. Tucker, "Introduction: Stalin, Bukharin, and History as Conspiracy," in *The Great Purge Trial*, ed. Robert Tucker and Stephen C. Cohen (New York: Grosset and Dunlap, 1965), pp. ix–xlviii. See also Robert Conquest, *The Great Terror* (New York: Macmillan, 1968).

58. See Hugo Dewar, "How They Saw the Moscow Trials," *Survey* (April 1962), p. 94.

59. Walter Lippmann, *The Communist World and Ours* (Boston: Little, Brown, 1958), p. 17.

60. Westbrook Pegler, "What Strange Bedfellows," *American Legion Magazine* (April 1939), pp. 10–11.

61. Walter Lippmann, *The Good Society* (Boston: Little, Brown, 1936), pp. 54–90.

62. Quoted in Patterson, p. 7.

63. "Man of the Year," *Time* (January 1, 1940), p. 15.

64. From the Alexandria (Virginia) *Gazette* (December 8, 1941), quoted in Gordon W. Prange, in collaboration with Donald M. Goldstein and Katherine V. Dillon, *At Dawn We Slept: The Untold History of Pearl Harbor* (New York: Penguin, 1982), pp. 582–83.

65. This quotation and those following are from Winston S. Churchill, *Winston*

S. Churchill: His Complete Speeches, 1897–1963, ed. Robert Rhodes James, 6 (New York: Chelsea House, 1974), pp. 6,427–431.

66. Quoted in Thomas G. Patterson, "Red Fascism: The American Image of Aggressive Totalitarianism," Meeting the Communist Threat: Truman to Reagan (Oxford: Oxford University Press, 1988), p. 7.

67. New York Times (June 24, 1941), p. 7.

68. On changes in public opinion toward the Soviets during this period, see Ralph B. Levering, American Opinion and the Russian Alliance (Chapel Hill, NC: University of North Carolina Press, 1976).

69. Time (January 4, 1943).

70. Walter Duranty, The Kremlin and the People (New York: Reynal and Hitchcock, 1941).

71. Joseph P. Davies, Mission to Moscow (New York: Simon and Schuster, 1941), p. xviii.

72. Wendell L. Wilkie, One World (New York: Simon and Schuster, 1943).

73. Levering, American Opinion and the Russian Alliance, p. 203.

74. Life (March 29, 1943), p. 29.

75. Ibid., p. 32.

76. Ibid., p. 40.

77. Sirgiovanni, "An Undercurrent of Suspicion," pp. 11–12.

Chapter Three

Prologue to the Cold War

The year 1945 was a triumphant one. The Allies defeated both the Germans and the Japanese within a space of four months. The war was over. But 1945 was also a year of confusion and enigmas. Before the European war ended President Roosevelt died. Shortly thereafter Prime Minister Churchill was turned out of office. Of the Big Three only Joseph Stalin remained. The war had bound the three leaders and their nations together in common cause against a common enemy. Now the enemy had been vanquished, only one of the three leaders remained in power, and their common cause no longer had its central element to hold them to each other.

In the United States life had also changed. The older America had been secure in its isolation, dominated by Protestantism, a rural nation interrupted by industrial centers, but a rural nation nonetheless. The Depression had shocked Americans out of their self-complacency as it exposed the weaknesses within industrial capitalism. Americans experienced a psychic displacement that had not been felt since the Civil War. World War II had yanked them out of their isolationism and bound them together even more than World War I had. There were plenty of additional displacements as civilians moved into the cities and soldiers went to far-off lands. Now the war was over. Confusion came with it. Veterans returning home found a different world from the one they left. Women had left their homes to join the workforce and now were being asked to return home. Farmhands had left the fields to work in war plants. Various ethnic groups that once were outcasts in Protestant society now had prominent places in a new society. The war had been a great melting pot, but in its wake it had left ambiguities and disjunctions.

It was within the hope and fears of the first postwar year that the new president, Harry Truman, and other policymakers sought to secure the peace. As the year progressed the confusions became more baffling, the fears greater, the hopes dimmer. President Truman publicly reaffirmed his hope that the United States and its allies could work together, that the United Nations would prove to be effective, and that a world peace could be achieved based on the "four freedoms" and the Atlantic Charter. This rhetoric of accommodation through principle dominated 1945. However, on the private level the president and policymakers were concerned about the turn of events in relation to the Soviet Union. Two questions vexed them. What are the Soviets up to in eastern Europe? What appropriate U.S. response could they make? Both questions plagued the president and his advisers throughout the year and into the next. Slowly, they settled into an answer about the Soviet Union, prompted as much by George F. Kennan's "long telegram" as anything else. But they kept their answer within the administration as they sought different ways of testing the Soviets, sometimes with the carrot, sometimes with the stick. Before proceeding to the world Truman created, we need to note the legacy that Franklin Roosevelt left his successor.

THE ROOSEVELT LEGACY

As William Leuchtenburg noted, FDR cast a long shadow over subsequent presidents.[1] But it was not only presidents who fell under this shadow. Almost everyone who participated in government felt his presence. After his death each of the major Democratic figures who engaged in foreign policy decisions thought he or she was carrying out Roosevelt's plans for the postwar, and they were not deluding themselves. One can find in FDR's public or private statements justifications for just about any policy one wanted to advocate in regard to the Soviet Union or the postwar world. For example, he often bragged that he could "handle Stalin" and described him as "truly representative of the heart and soul of Russia." He told a national radio audience that "we are going to get along very well with him and the Russian people—very well indeed."[2] Those who advocated a conciliatory approach to the Soviet Union could quote these and other statements to demonstrate they were the heirs of FDR's hopes for peace. On the other hand, Averell Harriman quoted Roosevelt as saying in his last weeks: "we can't do business with Stalin. He has broken every one of the promises he made at Yalta."[3] Those who advocated a policy of firmness could likewise cite FDR and stake an equally legitimate claim to carrying on his policies.

The truth of the matter was that Roosevelt conducted relations with

Stalin in a highly individual fashion. He was his own secretary of state, foreign minister, primary adviser, and chief diplomat. For the most part he left the State Department's Soviet specialists out of policy-making. He trusted his genius for improvisation, his gift for personal relations, and his ability to postpone commitments (especially about the postwar world) until the last minute. The legacy he left was one of high hopes and ambiguous policy. It was classic FDR.

Nowhere was the ambiguity greater than in the attempts during the last six months of Roosevelt's life to forge a lasting peace. In October 1944, Churchill made his famous attempt to put percentages on respective spheres of influence for the Soviets and the West in eastern Europe after the war: Greece—90 percent British; 10 percent Soviet; Romania—10 percent British, 90 percent Soviet, and so on through Hungary—50/50, Bulgaria—25/75, and Yugoslavia—50/50.[4] What is important is not whether these were carried out or formed the basis for Soviet postwar policy in eastern Europe, but that Churchill appeared to base the approach to the postwar world in terms of spheres of influence. This would become a contentious point. The Yalta Conference seemed to contradict it. At Yalta in February 1945 the Big Three agreed on a United Nations, Soviet involvement in the war against Japan, and a "Declaration on Liberated Europe" that promised to "enable the liberated peoples to destroy the last vestiges of Nazism and Fascism and to create democratic institutions of their own choice."[5] In speaking on March 1, 1945 to a joint session of Congress, Roosevelt said that the recently concluded Yalta accords meant the end of the old ways of world politics, with spheres of influence and balances of power.[6] In their place would be a world organization for peace, the United Nations. Despite these lofty sentiments there is substantial evidence that Roosevelt understood some accommodation would have to be made for Soviet concerns about its security in the eastern European nations. If that understanding did not proceed from hard agreements, it had to take into account that Soviet armies already occupied many of those countries. Stalin himself had said: "This war is not as in the past; whoever occupies a territory imposes on it his own social system. Everyone imposes his own social system as far as his army can reach. It cannot be otherwise."[7] However these different events were perceived and interpreted by the major participants, the point remains that few agreements had been reached about the postwar world to which all concerned could be said to be unequivocally committed. The question of whether the Soviet Union should be treated in a conciliatory or firm manner remained up in the air. The question of whether international disputes should be settled in a United Nations or through unilateral action was put high on the shelf until the war was over.[8] The question of whether spheres of influence should be accepted as part of the new world order or should be banished from international relations remained a matter of dispute depending on which nation addressed the question in what circumstances. But these questions were disputes among leaders to be settled in the future. The ambiguity continued.

Quite simply the Big Three spoke with different voices. Although Stalin agreed with the principles of a liberated Europe, he persistently pressed for recognition of Soviet security interests in eastern Europe, especially in Poland. Churchill vacillated between private denunciations of Stalin and attempts to work out agreements with him. His doctor noted that he "seems torn between two lines of action. . . . At one moment he will plead with the President for a common front against Communism and the next he will make a bid of Stalin's friendship. Sometimes the two policies alternate with bewildering rapidity."[9] Roosevelt also was torn in several directions. With the Soviets he talked power politics, the language of the "four policemen" (the United States, Soviet Union, Great Britain, and China) securing the peace. But in the United States "he continued to obscure this basic program in the idealistic Wilsonian language, which by then had become the lingua franca of postwar thinking."[10] In other words, power politics vied with idealistic principles for direction of the postwar world. And the two created ambiguity and tension. Stalin was getting different messages from his western allies.

Suspicions about the Soviet Union had circulated among government officials during the war, but the imposing presence of Franklin Delano Roosevelt prevented them from being aired publicly. FDR dealt with foreign policy in a personal manner, both because the war crisis gave him the power to do so and because of his confidence he could deal successfully with Churchill and Stalin. His aim was to win the war, and he permitted little criticism of his Soviet ally to dilute that overarching goal.

In April 1945 Roosevelt was dead, the unifying rhetoric of the war was no longer relevant, and the ecumenical rhetoric for peace began to be challenged. Some said that the USSR was pursuing traditional national interest, protecting borders by establishing a sphere of influence in eastern Europe and working from a balance of power politics. That struck a fearful note among American policymakers. Most U.S. officials "were, with the exception of a few eccentrics like Henry L. Stimson and Henry A. Wallace, opposed to spheres of influence—at least in Europe, and particularly in Eastern Europe."[11] That belief would become a fundamental constraint on future American analysis and action. Others complained that the Soviet Union was breaking agreements and warned of Soviet intents to rule the world. Much of this was done in private, but a new period of competing rhetorics about the world and about Soviet–American relations was beginning to emerge.

TRUMAN ENTERS THE WHITE HOUSE

With the death of Roosevelt, Harry Truman inherited the Oval Office, or Oval Room as it was called at the time. Having been vice president for less than three months, Truman had little first-hand knowledge of foreign policy, in general, much less about the agreements that his predecessor had reached with Stalin and Churchill.[12] Still, Truman was determined to continue the general policy of cooperation among the allies and to honor agreements that had been made. Being in the dark about U.S. foreign policy, Truman began to rely heavily upon the State Department and his White House advisers to help him through the difficult early weeks and months of his administration. Thus, members of the Truman administration were free to voice individual opinions as they had not been before in the Roosevelt administration. They would eventually play significant roles in determining the course of American–Soviet relations.

Various people within the administration, such as Chief of Staff Admiral William Leahy, U.S. Ambassador to the USSR Averell Harriman, and Secretary of Navy James Forrestal, were skeptical of Soviet intentions and expressed their fears to the president. The effect of this new freedom was soon apparent. Harriman flew to Washington from Moscow five days after Roosevelt's burial to brief Truman. He advised the president that the Soviets were not living up to their agreements. Truman told Harriman at that first meeting on April 20, 1945 that he intended to stand firm. Nothing enraged the new president more than people breaking their word. Harriman recorded that he was relieved to hear that "there would be no departures from American principles or traditions to win favor from Stalin."[13] What Truman apparently meant by the impression that he gave Harriman was that he would stand by the international principles of the "four freedoms," the Atlantic Charter, and the Declaration on a Liberated Europe.

Much of the remainder of 1945 was dedicated to continuation of Roosevelt's principles as Harry Truman understood them. In April the San Francisco Conference opened to create the United Nations. For 63 days representatives labored to produce a workable result. When the Charter of the U.N. was completed and signed, President Truman who had flown out to San Francisco for the historic occasion walked to the podium and spoke to the assembled delegates:

The Charter of the United Nations which you have just signed is a solid structure upon which we can build a better world . . .

If we fail to use it, we shall betray all those who have died in order that we might meet here in freedom and safety to create it.

If we seek to use it selfishly—to the advantage of any one nation or any small group of nations—we shall be equally guilty of that betrayal. . . .

Let us not fail to grasp this supreme chance to establish a world-wide rule of reason—to create an enduring peace under the guidance of God.[14]

Truman rightly believed he was fulfilling Roosevelt's promise to the American people and the people of the world by his words. But in time his words would also become both prophetic and ironic. As the administration later believed the Soviets were using their veto power for selfish purposes, it would therefore by-pass the U.N. to take unilateral action to thwart those purposes. Such actions, however, lay in the future. For the time being the rhetoric of accommodation and principle prevailed.

In July 1945 President Truman sailed to Europe to meet with Stalin and Churchill at the Cecilianoff Palace in the Berlin suburb of Potsdam. Whether or not one agrees with Charles Mee's harsh assessment of Churchill as a Machiavellian leader interested in playing the United States and the Soviet Union off against each other, the prime minister did show every indication of pursuing British interests above all else.[15] Churchill tried in vain to get Truman to meet in advance of the conference in order to confront Stalin with an Anglo-American alliance. Truman's resistance to these overtures indicated his resolve to bargain with Stalin in good faith, in the belief that an accommodation was possible.

Churchill's defeat for reelection during the conference left Truman to play a lone hand with Stalin. There was, nonetheless, a compelling reason for Truman's confidence: the atomic bomb. Truman was informed of the successful explosion of the test bomb at Alamogordo just five days after the conference opened. The president regarded the possession of the atomic bomb as the final proof that the United States was the strongest nation in the world. It appeared that the United States would have the determinative role in future world events by virtue of its sole ownership of the most powerful weapon the world had ever known. Though ensuing events would support the validity of Henry Wallace's observation that the bomb gave "the erroneous hope of being safe behind a scientific Maginot Line," Truman was thrust into a position of *prima inter pares* with the knowledge that his country alone had the atomic bomb.[16]

The Potsdam Conference did not yield major results. A Council of Foreign Ministers was formed to begin the process of drawing peace treaties for the defeated nations. The question of Poland was not settled, but papered over with typical diplomatic language. Germany was divided into separate zones and a formula for reparations was worked out. After gaining certain geopolitical concessions, the Soviet Union agreed to come into the Japanese War. Some of the Americans concluded that it would be difficult to work with the Soviets in the future. President

Truman later noted: "Force is the only thing the Russians understand. . . . What Stalin wanted was control of the Black Sea straits and the Danube. The Russians were planning world conquest."[17] But that was a private conclusion. The public statements emphasized continued co-operation among the allies through Soviet entrance into the war against Japan and through the desire to negotiate those issues upon which they could not immediately agree.[18]

After the surrender of Japan, President Truman stated the principles upon which he believed a new world order should be established. On October 27, 1945 the president spoke at the Navy Day celebration in New York's Central Park. Truman listed twelve principles that would guide the United States in foreign policy in the postwar world. Central to these twelve was his belief that in the "sovereign rights" and "self-government" of all peoples. Countries prepared for self-government should choose their own form of government "by their own freely ex-pressed choice, without interference from any foreign source." To back up this principle, Truman declared that the United States would not recognize any government that was imposed upon people by a foreign power. The president acknowledged that the current period was a "dif-ficult phase of international relations," but he added that "the world cannot afford to let the cooperative spirit of the Allies in this war dis-integrate." He concluded with words that appeared to take Soviet con-cerns into account:

Differences of the kinds that exist today among nations that fought together so long and so valiantly for victory are not hopeless or irreconcilable. There are no conflicts of interest among the victorious powers so deeply rooted that they cannot be resolved. . . . For our own part, we must seek to understand the special problems of other nations. We must seek to understand their own legitimate urge toward security as they see it.[19]

Norman Graebner noted: "President Truman's principles, like those of Wilson and Hull, assumed that there were no conflicts of interest in the world which could not be settled by peaceful adjustment and thus largely on American terms."[20] In essence, Truman was establishing the terms for the postwar peace, but he also seemed to be saying that the Soviets' need for security, which they had made abundantly clear, could be resolved within the principles he articulated. Thus, Truman's rhetoric relied on U.S. standards for self-government, but left the door open for accommodation with the Soviet Union. Or so it seemed at the time. Eventually the Soviet's "legitimate urge" would be redefined as aggres-sion, and the principles Truman articulated would become the only standards by which disagreements could be resolved.

On November 14 Dean Acheson, undersecretary of state, repeated the themes of Truman's Navy Day speech. In an address about American–Soviet friendship in New York, Acheson traced a history of relations between the two nations from the time of Thomas Jefferson through joint membership in the United Nations, noting that never "has there been any place on the globe where the vital interests of the American and Russian people have clashed or even been antagonistic." He added that "there is no reason to suppose that there should, now or in the future, ever be such a place." Any current problems, said Acheson, were capable of rational examination and solution. The Soviet Union's devastation in the war made it easy to "understand and agree with them that to have friendly governments along her borders is essential both for the security of the Soviet Union and for the peace of the world," analogous to the need of the United States "to look for security through bases and methods which will keep danger far from us." Acheson concluded with a call to heed Stalin's request to judge the Soviets "upon facts and not rumors."[21] The speech was to the National Council of American–Soviet Friendship, an organization that would be on the attorney general's list of subversive groups in two years.[22]

But all was not as cordial as the public rhetoric during this period might lead one to believe. Truman had assured Harriman back in April that he intended to stand firm against the Soviets. When Soviet Foreign Minister Vayacheslav Molotov met the president on April 23, 1945, Truman gave Molotov a dressing down. " 'I have never been talked to like that in my life,' said Molotov. . . . 'Carry out your agreements and you won't get talked to like that,' " replied Truman.[23] Although the conversation was private, Truman's language was not the language the Soviets were accustomed to hearing from Roosevelt. Truman's words were, perhaps, the first syllables in the new language of the cold war.

The Soviets became exposed to the new language again several months later. The meeting of the Council of Foreign Ministers in London between September 11 and October 2 brought into the open the disagreements between the Soviet Union and the West over the shape of the postwar world. The meeting had been called to negotiate peace treaties with the defeated enemies. However, the Soviet Union "vehemently resisted Anglo-American demands for representatives regimes in Rumania and Bulgaria."[24] Unable to bridge these differences, the conference broke up without even issuing a joint communique. With these disagreements publicly aired came a round of criticism of the Soviet Union from Republicans and Conservatives. Part of it came from the failure of the Foreign Ministers conference, part from the perception of the administration's attempts to "paper over" the differences.

Dean Acheson sought to preserve the appearance of cooperation with his speech in November about Soviet–American friendship. But Senator Vandenberg rose in the Senate to answer him. Referring to Acheson's concern for international friendship, the senator from Michigan called for the lifting of constraints on the press in the USSR and bordering nations. The theme of his speech was a plea for "frank cooperation" between the two nations. "When the iron curtain of secrecy falls around an area suspicion is unavoidable, restless conjecture substitutes for knowledge, and dependable trust is out of the question," said Vandenberg.[25] But the senator did not limit his criticism to the Soviet Union. He alluded to "our own iron curtain" drawn around international conferences, notably Yalta. Yet, in all, the speech was not terribly harsh when contrasted with the anticommunist rhetoric of the next year. Vandenberg pointed out that the Soviets had allowed some press coverage in Rumania, Bulgaria, Hungary, and Finland. Quoting Acheson's admonition, given in the words of Stalin, to judge "upon the facts and not rumors," Vandenberg asked "how can we judge the Soviets objectively . . . if the Soviets themselves discourage us from doing so?" Vandenberg used the term "iron curtain" some eight times in the speech, but those words did not make the headlines they made after Churchill's speech several months later. Vandenberg's speech did not have the spotlight of the presidency giving prominence to his address, but equally important, Vandenberg concluded "not with a challenge but an appeal," pleading for openness on the part of the Soviet Union. (Privately, Vandenberg had been more disturbed. During the San Francisco Conference he worried that Stalin wanted to "pick us off piece-meal [just as Hitler used to do]." He asked himself: *"At what point is it wisest to stop appeasing Stalin? Otherwise a new 'Munich' will be followed by comparable tragedies."*[26] The analogies Vandenberg voiced privately would soon become the public ways of understanding Soviet behavior.)

Conservatives, both Republican and Democratic, were even more antagonistic. Senator Burton Wheeler of Montana told the Senate in late November that the country faced "the greatest crisis in history," an aggressor Soviet nation that wanted raw power. Wheeler attacked the notion of "appeasement" in terms that conjured the image of Munich.[27] In early December Senator James Eastland of Mississippi rose to inform the Senate that Stalin was following the same road of aggression that Hitler had used to set the world on fire. In the analogy, the USSR had designs on the world similar to Nazi Germany, and a Munich appeasement of Soviet ambitions, he warned, might lead to World War III.[28] These men saw a world in crisis. The enemy had a different name, but it was the same old enemy: totalitarianism.

As 1945 drew to a close, there was no rhetorical consensus. The Truman administration continued to speak a rhetoric of principles, but it also harbored hopes for negotiations with the Soviet Union within the framework of those principles. Conservatives in government and in the press began to attack Soviet leaders as aggressors bent on world conquest. Internationalists, such as Senator Vandenberg, held out hope for peace, but in terms that were increasingly critical of the Soviet Union.

THE PRIVATE QUEST FOR MEANING AND POLICY

On the public level the Truman administration continued to voice confidence that the United States, Great Britain, and the Soviet Union could work together productively to secure the peace in the postwar world. Much of this rhetoric was needed until the war with Japan was concluded. But even after that, the administration extended this rhetoric for the remainder of the year, usually including brief references to the Soviet Union's "special" need for security on its borders.

But privately the administration grew increasingly worried. It began seeking to determine Soviet motives and goals for the postwar world. In the State Department several papers were drawn up speculating about these motives and goals as a preface to preparing U.S. postwar policy. On this private level greater emphasis was given to Soviet concerns about a buffer zone between the USSR and eastern Europe than was given in public statements. During the second half of 1945 State Department officials drew up several papers theorizing about these matters. The differences among them point to the lack of consensus within the administration, especially the State Department, about what kind of postwar policy should be constructed.

Three of these documents deserve attention as they point to the struggle in the State Department to grapple with relations between the United States and the Soviet Union. All were written in the aftermath of the September Council of Foreign Ministers meeting. Robert L. Messer and Eduard Mark documented the alternatives to the eventual policy of containment that these proposals explored.[29]

On October 18, 1945 Charles E. Bohlen, special assistant to Secretary of State Byrnes, wrote a memorandum attempting to address the problem of Soviet influence in eastern Europe. Bohlen sought a middle ground between the principle of self-determination for eastern Europe and recognition of Soviet interests in that area. He attempted to make a distinction between a legitimate or "open" sphere of influence and an "exclusive" sphere of influence. Bohlen argued that the United States should make it clear to the Soviets that "complete domination" of the countries of central and eastern Europe would not be tolerated. On the other hand, he stated that the United States should not attempt to deny the Soviet Union its legitimate influence in the smaller countries on its borders. Bohlen summarized his position in this fashion: "It is important, therefore, to distinguish between a fair and reasonable definition of legitimate influence on the part of a great power in such areas and the illegitimate extension of such interest in the direction of domination and absolute control." The historical analogy he used to clarify what he meant was U.S. policy toward Latin America as stated in the Monroe Doctrine and practiced historically. Latin America lay within America's sphere of influence which meant that it was forbidden to conclude military or political alliances with a "European or Asiatic power." However, Bohlen continued, U.S. influence in Latin America did not mean that cultural exchanges or normal trade or other international relations were forbidden. The analogy was intended to clarify the kind of influence over eastern Europe that Bohlen thought might be acceptable to the United States. As Eduard Mark entitled his article analyzing this memorandum, Bohlen sought to describe the limits of Soviet hegemony.[30] The problem with the memorandum was the vague language of "legitimate" and "illegitimate" spheres of influence, the unspecified difference between "influence" and "domination," and above all, the embarrassing analogy that required Americans to admit they had a sphere of influence in Latin America that could be made comparable to a Soviet sphere in eastern Europe. Clearly Bohlen was attempting to walk a very fine line between the principles of self-determination and the power politics of spheres of influence. He appeared to be saying that the Soviets had a legitimate interest in exercising their influence over eastern European nations, but should not use that influence to close off the area from the West or to exercise complete political domination over it. Bohlen did not make clear how the United States should respond if the Soviet Union did not act in accordance with what Americans took to be normal international procedures, nor did he propose policies to achieve the goals he outlined.

Cloyce K. Huston, who also had served as a career foreign service officer for twenty years, wrote a second memorandum dealing with the same subject on October 24, 1945. Huston gave a very different view of Soviet intentions based on a different narrative of the prewar years. According to Robert Messer, he "turned Churchill's iron curtain inside out."[31] Huston argued that anti-Soviet eastern Europeans, aided by American and other foreign interests, had erected a barrier between the Soviet Union and Europe in the years before the war so as to bar the Soviets from European resources. Soviet policy in eastern Europe in the postwar world was aimed at preventing the resurrection of that barrier, that prewar "*cordon sanitaire* so that Russia would no longer be isolated from her neighbors nor have to suffer their being used as the springboard from which some future attack can be launched."[32] He advocated a policy of U.S. support for Soviet aims of establishing "friendly governments" in eastern Europe through a forthright and direct declaration of that support. Huston even went so far as to draft a public statement that explicitly outlined which actions the United States deemed acceptable and which unacceptable. Such a declaration, he argued, was consistent with the Atlantic Charter and the Yalta agreements and might cause the Soviet Union to relent from its repressive methods in establishing its influence in these disputed areas. Messer correctly noted that Huston proposed a *redefinition* of American foreign policy for the postwar world.

The final memorandum came from Bohlen and Geroid T. Robinson, a Columbia University professor on leave to serve in the State Department. This memorandum was probably an attempt to develop policies consistent with Bohlen's previous analysis. Completed in December 1945, the Bohlen-Robinson study set forth two policy options, Policy A and Policy B, as they called them. They based these options on the belief that the United States held a powerful advantage over the Soviet Union, militarily and economically. In their view Soviet ideology was pragmatic rather than doctrinaire and therefore was not a rigid formula for revolutionary expansion or world domination. The vacuum in Europe in the aftermath of the war provided the United States with an opportunity for leadership in shaping the postwar role of the Soviet Union. The key to peace could be found in avoiding any unnecessary friction between the two allies. To achieve positive results, Bohlen and Robinson proposed two policy options, A and B, of which B was most certainly a fallback policy. Policy A, which they preferred, was to share atomic knowledge with the USSR and to work to establish buffer states in eastern Europe acceptable to both nations. Policy B was to build a balance of power in Europe so that the Soviet Union could be held in check in case Policy A did not work.[33]

These three memoranda illustrate the diversity of opinion that resided in the State Department about Soviet intentions and U.S. policy in the immediate postwar period. Each sought to analyze Soviet motives in eastern Europe and to develop policies to accommodate Soviet interests while protecting U.S. interests. Equally important, each treated the Soviet Union as a great power intent on exercising its prerogatives of victory which included a legitimate influence in eastern Europe. The authors paid little attention to communist ideology either in their analysis of the Soviet Union or in their proposals for American responses. Messer noted that Huston's interpretation represented a "vestige in the department [of state] of Rooseveltian wartime priorities" and added that the striking thing about his memorandum was the reception it received. There was no substantive objection to it.[34] The Bohlen and Bohlen-Robinson studies apparently were accorded the same reception. However, it is clear from these forays into analysis that the State Department was concerned that the postwar world could not be created solely in accordance with the high principles of the Atlantic Charter or the Declaration on Liberated Nations and therefore was seeking alternative ways of dealing with the Soviet Union.

The public expressions of the two Bohlen memoranda came with President Truman's Navy Day speech on October 27, 1945 and with Secretary of State James Byrnes's speech before the New York *Herald-Tribune* forum four days later. The secretary reiterated U.S. commitments to human rights and democracy, to peace and understanding among nations, to a policy of nonintervention in the internal affairs of other nations. But he also denounced "local tyranny," and said that the United States had learned from the Nazis and Fascists that "external aggression" begins with tyrannies at home. Secretary Byrnes went on to hold out the hand of accommodation to the Soviet Union repeating and elaborating on Truman's hope that differences between the two nations could be resolved peaceably through mutual understanding:

Far from opposing, we have sympathized with . . . the effort of the Soviet Union to draw into closer and more friendly association with her Central and Eastern European neighbors. We are fully aware of her special security interests in those countries and we have recognized those interests in the arrangements made for the occupation and control of the former enemy States.

We can appreciate the determination of the people of the Soviet Union that never again will they tolerate the pursuit of policies in those countries deliberately directed against the Soviet Union's security and way of life. And America will never join any groups in those countries in hostile intrigue against the Soviet Union. We are also confident that the Soviet Union would not join in hostile intrigue against us in this hemisphere.[35]

The secretary drew, as Bohlen had in his first memorandum, on the analogy to America's Good Neighbor policy toward Latin America in describing and justifying a sphere of influence for the Soviet Union in eastern Europe.

The importance of this speech was twofold. It demonstrated the continuing attempt by the administration to balance the principles of democracy with the demands of power politics in walking the diplomatic tightrope between adhering to the Atlantic Charter but conceding Soviet strategic interests. The second matter of import were the analogies used to support this two-pronged approach. On the one hand, the secretary cited America's Western sphere of influence in Latin America as analogous to the Soviet Union's legitimate interests in eastern Europe. On the other hand, he cited the analogy to Hitler's Germany as a potential analogy to justify U.S. opposition to aggression. Within two years the first analogy would all but disappear from official rhetoric, except by a few dissidents, and the second analogy would not only dominate but became one of the primary explanations for Soviet behavior and appropriate U.S. actions.

During the last months of 1945, the public rhetoric reflected private ambiguities. Even as officials in the State Department privately voiced different interpretations of Soviet actions and diverse policies to respond

to these actions, higher officials, including the president and the secretary of state, proclaimed the hope for cooperation within the framework of democratic principles and the actualities of power politics. In
all probability, they were confused about what Stalin intended to do in
eastern Europe and they were equally confused about what kind of
unilateral policies the United States should adopt, should the United
Nations not function as effectively as some hoped. But a radical change
would soon occur in February 1946, when Stalin delivered his election
speech, and shortly thereafter the State Department received a long
telegram from its charge d'affaires in Moscow, George F. Kennan. U.S.
policymakers had been asking: What does the Soviet Union want? In
these two statements, they seemed to get their answer.

STALIN'S ELECTION SPEECH

On February 9, 1946 Joseph Stalin made a rare speech over Moscow
radio on the eve of a Soviet election. Had the speech come the previous
year, it is doubtful that it would have been noticed in the United States.
However, by early 1946 mounting tensions over the postwar world made
the speech more prominent and more ominous. *Time* called the speech
"the most warlike pronouncement uttered by any top-rank statesman
since V-J Day."[36] James Forrestal recorded in his diary that Supreme
Court Justice William O. Douglas remarked the speech was "the declaration of World War III," and his own opinion that it was "a major
pronouncement of the most ominous kind."[37] Looking back much later,
Charles Bohlen described the speech as one of the principal causes for
the origin of the cold war.[38] The primary reason for this interpretation
of Stalin's speech was that U.S. policymakers, especially in the State
Department, took it as a definitive policy statement about Stalin's foreign
policy goals, rather than as an election speech pointing to domestic plans
for the future. Considerable controversy still exists over which interpretation is correct. Let us begin with the interpretation that it was an
election speech.

Isaac Deutscher analyzed the speech as an attempt to reassert the
ideological foundations of the Soviet state and to prepare Soviet citizens
for rebuilding Soviet economic strength.[39] The Soviet Union was holding
its first election since 1937, and Stalin was a candidate for reelection to
the Supreme Soviet. In all probability the elections had been called to
achieve three purposes. First, holding an election would confirm Stalin's
pledge at Yalta for establishing a new world order based on free elections
freely held. Given his absolute control over the nation, Stalin had little
to fear in holding an election and could thereby demonstrate his good
faith in the electoral processes. If these elections were not free in the
Western sense (since only a single slate of Communist party candidates

were offered to the voters), they would be free in the Soviet sense and thus fulfill the technical strictures he had agreed to previously. Second, Stalin wished to replace certain political figures with others and used the election to reorganize the government for the postwar period. For example, Nicolai Bulganin was elevated to the Ministry of War and General Zhukov, the hero of World War II, was shuffled off to an obscure provincial garrison.[40] These changes pointed to the final reason for elections. After relying on a patriotic war-time rhetoric exhorting Soviets to defend the Motherland, Stalin was shifting from nationalistic appeals to the ideological foundations that gave the Soviet state its legitimacy.

Stalin began his 4,000-word address by signaling this change in rhetoric from wartime to peacetime. During the war ideology had taken an inconspicuous backseat to nationalistic pride as Stalin sought to rally Soviets to defense of the homeland. But now that was past, and the change was immediately emphasized. Instead of addressing his audience as "brothers and sisters, my friends, my countrymen" as he had during the war, he opened simply with the ideological form of greeting: "Comrades."[41] He proceeded with a brief text from standard communist ideology, a reference to Marxist-Leninism, another signal that the rhetoric had changed due to changing circumstances. Stalin made these references specific by charging that the "capitalist system of world economy conceals elements of crisis and war," because an uneven distribution of raw materials and exports methods existed. However, the "catastrophes of [a future] war could be avoided" if redistribution could be carried out with equity. But, he added, this redistribution "could not be achieved under present capitalist conditions." In tracing recent history, Stalin declared that World War I had been caused by an economic crisis. But World War II was different. It had been caused by the rise of fascist states that had destroyed all "the last remnants of bourgeois democratic liberties at home" and had expanded for the purpose of imposing a fascist domination throughout the world. The war, therefore, had been fought to defeat the fascists. "On this basis was established," Stalin stated, "the anti-Fascist coalition of the Soviet Union, the United States of America, Great Britain and other freedom-loving countries." Speaking with ideological pride, Stalin proclaimed that the Soviet system had triumphed and thus demonstrated that it was not a "risky experiment, doomed to failure" or a "house of cards without any roots in life." Victory had proved that the Soviet system was "perfectly viable," that it was "a form of organization superior to all others." The sections of the speech dealing with World War II and foreign policy comprised only about 10 percent of the entire speech, about 400 words.

The remainder of the speech centered on defenses of Stalin's administration throughout the war and his new five-year plans for the future. Stalin answered critics who had doubted the capabilities of the Red Army by asserting that victory had demonstrated that it and the Soviet system had "successfully stood the test in the fire of war and . . . proved its complete vitality." He also answered those who had criticized his lack of preparation for war by cataloguing impressive Soviet victories, such as those at Moscow and Stalingrad, and by arguing that these would not have been possible without the preparation of previous five-year plans. From this recital, Stalin launched into a lengthy comparison of capitalistic methods of production with Soviet methods. Capitalists started with light industries, which over a period of time developed into heavy industries. The Soviets did not have this luxury, he said, and therefore were forced to plunge directly into developing heavy industry. A similar case was made for agriculture. There was so little time, given the civil war and World War II, that the Soviet Union had gone from a small scale peasant economy to large scale agriculture through collectivization, without which "we would have not been able to eliminate the age-old backwardness of our agriculture in so short a period of time." The effectiveness of these methods, Stalin argued, showed that the Communist party was not "sleeping over the chestnuts."

This lengthy recital of past successes set the stage for Stalin's purpose in the speech: to announce a new Five-Year Plan, one he conceded might be only the first of several that would be necessary to restore industry and agriculture to prewar levels and eventually to exceed them. He went into lengthy detail about how the plan's goals would be achieved. He included a special reference to scientific needs: "I have no doubt that if we render the necessary assistance to our scientists they will be able not only to overtake but also in the very near future to surpass the achievements of science outside the boundaries of our country." The new Five-Year Plan laid down the directions for the future, directions that resurrected the call for immediate sacrifices and hard work to insure a more comfortable future. Stalin concluded his address by expressing his gratitude for being nominated to the Supreme Soviet and said, "I will try to justify this confidence."[42]

The critical question about this important speech was who was Stalin addressing, who was his audience? Deutscher and a variety of others have interpreted the speech as directed primarily, if not solely, to a domestic audience. Anders Stephanson concluded that it was a reaction to the Soviet Union's internal situation, a transition from concern with the outside world to concern with internal domestic matters. He stated: "The future, Stalin was probably intimating, now seemed a bit murky, and one had better be prepared [for any eventuality]."[43] B. Thomas Trout interpreted it in a similar manner stating that "war had necessitated adjustments in both political and ideological demands on Soviet citizens with a relative loosening of the entire social structure."[44] Stalin therefore was reasserting ideological control in the war's aftermath. War had devastated the Soviet Union. The western part of the nation was in ruins. A thousand cities and villages had been leveled. Industrial output had been cut nearly in half; the agricultural system was in chaos; some twenty million people had been killed. Ulam concluded that "against this background it becomes clear why the regime felt it could not afford relaxation or liberalization, why on the contrary the outside world had to be presented in a hostile light and the atmosphere of urgency and vigilance inculcated."[45] Even without the natural Soviet xenophobia or personal paranoia of Stalin, an appropriate political reaction to the weakened national condition in the face of uncertainty would no doubt have been to call for sacrifice and vigilance. Both Dean Acheson and Averell Harriman agreed with this conclusion at the time. Because the capitalist forces still controlled much of the world outside the Soviet Union, Acheson noted, the Soviet Union thought it had to be capable of guarding against any eventuality which might erupt.[46] Harriman believed Stalin was speaking to his own people so as to motivate them to further sacrifice, rather than speaking to the outside world to declare Soviet foreign policy aims in the postwar world.[47] Even Harry Truman dismissed the speech in an informal remark at the Women's Press Club dinner. He said it reminded him of a senator who said, "Hell, you know we all have to demagogue a little sometimes."[48]

Stalin's election speech was a Soviet-styled campaign speech. It was not intended to seek votes because the leader already had the election secured. Instead, the speech was intended to reassert the fundamental values upon which Soviet society was based, Marxist-Leninism. Just as an American candidate for national office places proposals within basic American values in a campaign and argues from them, so too Stalin reaffirmed communist values and argued that these made victory in the war possible. Just as an American candidate outlines what policies are needed for the future, so too Stalin outlined a new Five-Year Plan to recover from the devastation of the war. Just as an American candidate calls for vigilant solidarity against any potential foreign adversary, so too Stalin called for his people to sacrifice to build a strong Soviet society as the best defense against "any eventuality." To read the speech within the genre of campaign speeches is to interpret the speech as one directed primarily to Soviet citizens with little import for Soviet foreign policy.

The growing tensions and uncertainties in the United States, however, contributed to a different interpretation of the speech. A week after Stalin's address, headlines in the *New York Times* announced that Canada had seized twenty-two persons believed to be spies engaged in attempts to secure atomic secrets.[49] The following day in the Sunday edition the front page headlines proclaimed: "More Canadians Rounded up; Russians Implicated." The same edition reported speculation about the meaning of Stalin's statements about wars being economic and that the

USSR needed to increase economic production. Furthermore, Stalin's reference to lending assistance to Soviet scientists might mean, the newspaper ventured, that the Soviets were dedicating themselves to building their own atomic bomb. The *Times* put forth three theories: (1) there was unrest in the USSR, and Stalin was using the threat of a hostile world to regain unity after the war; (2) the speech was Stalin's blessing on a shift in party doctrine from nationalism back to Marxist-Leninism; and (3) the Five-Year Plan was what the Soviets needed to recover from the war.[50] It was the second theory that sparked fears in certain corridors of American power.

Herbert L. Matthews devoted his column in the *Times* a week later to the speech suggesting a sinister interpretation of it. He based this interpretation as much on what Stalin did not say as what he said. He noted that the Soviet leader did not mention the United Nations or give credit to the United States for helping to win the war. He speculated that the USSR was "interested" in the Middle East, that she was anti-British, and that Stalin had been "flirting" with the Arab world. Even though he ruminated about these possibilities, Matthews had to admit that "there have been no direct moves [by the Soviet Union] in the Middle East." Nonetheless he concluded that we do not know what "limits the U.S.S.R. places on her own conception of security."[51]

Gradually this second interpretation became dominant. The offending or precipitating statements that were extracted from the speech concerned the return to Marxist-Leninist ideology, assertions about the inevitability of crises and wars within the capitalist world, talk of preparing for any eventuality. Some within American leadership circles, such as Forrestal and Bohlen, took Stalin's speech as a definitive foreign policy statement, thus lifting it out of the genre of Soviet election speeches directed to a domestic audience to read it as a policy statement directed toward the rest of the world. Later scholars called the address Stalin's "declaration of Cold War" on the West, with Churchill's Fulton address complementing it as the Western counterpart.[52] They would see it as the resumption of Soviet ideological war with the West as well as a blueprint for future expansionism. That interpretation came from the way the State Department officials became alarmed at the time. One official called it "the most important and authoritative guide to post-war Soviet Policy."[53] This interpretation caused the State Department to request an analysis of Soviet intentions from the charge d'affaires in the U.S. embassy at Moscow, George F. Kennan.

KENNAN'S "LONG TELEGRAM"

Prior to Stalin's speech, several analyses of Soviet motives and intentions had circulated within the State Department. The memoranda by

Bohlen, by Huston, and by Bohlen and Robinson, as we have seen, had been drafted and read. They had neither been accepted uncritically nor rejected out of hand. But now with tensions growing an additional analysis was needed.

Winston Churchill once said, in a much quoted statement, that the USSR was a "riddle wrapped in a mystery inside an enigma." What is less remembered is that Churchill continued to say: "Perhaps there is a key [to the riddle-mystery-enigma]. That key is Russia's national interest."[54] But in 1946 the focus—partly as a result of Stalin's speech, partly due to an anticommunist mentality among some administration figures—concentrated not only on the Soviet Union's national interest but on communist ideology. The times were ripe for an ideological analysis, and George F. Kennan did much to provide it.

The particular reason for requesting Kennan to comment on Soviet motives was the Russian refusal to join the International Monetary Fund and the World Bank. But the real reason was Stalin's speech and the increasing confusion about how to understand Soviet actions. On February 22 Kennan sent an 8,000-word "long telegram," an impressive and persuasive document that later became one of the most controversial documents in the early cold war.[55] Kennan had been submitting ideas for some time, only to see them ignored. But this time he found, much to his surprise, that the effect of his telegram was "nothing less than sensational."[56]

Although the telegram is repeatedly referred to as a document, it should be remembered that it was, like other major statements on Soviet motives and goals during these early years, a specifically *rhetorical* document. Kennan's purpose was to persuade policymakers in Washington that his view was a "realistic" understanding of the Soviets in contrast to what he believed were the naive and dangerously optimistic understandings then dominating strategic thinking in Washington.[57] He set his task as one in which he would demolish such naivete and replace it with hardheaded "realism."

Kennan divided his analysis into five parts. In the first part he sought to locate the primary source of Soviet conduct for the postwar period. He located that source specifically in Marxist-Leninist-Stalinist ideology. He delineated seven premises that comprised that ideology and four "deductions" that resulted from them. Thus, at the very outset of his telegram Kennan emphasized the ideological motivations behind Soviet actions and cited statements from Lenin and Stalin to support these contentions. Part two dealt with a background in which Kennan attempted to qualify this ideological analysis by pointing out that most Soviet citizens did not share the ideological fervor of Soviet leadership, that the premises that made up the ideology were false, and that the Kremlin's "neurotic view of world affairs" stemmed as much from an instinctive "sense of insecurity" as from ideology. However, he concluded that

no one should underrate importance of dogma in Soviet affairs. Thus Soviet leaders are driven necessities of their own past and present position to put forward a dogma which [views the] outside world as evil, hostile and menacing; but as bearing within itself germs of creeping disease and destined to be wracked with growing international convulsions until it is given final coup de grace by rising power of socialism and yields to new and better world.[58]

Kennan stated that this drive to expand represented a "centuries old movement" within Russia. But he warned that no one should doubt that this "new guise" of worldwide Marxism now posed a more insidious and dangerous threat than ever before. Thus, despite the qualifications he had voiced, he returned to the ideological theme of his analysis.

Part three outlined the practical ways in which the Soviet Union sought to implement its universal ideology in world affairs on the "official" level. It is appropriate to call it "universal" since Kennan, for the most part, saw Soviet intentions as stretching far beyond such traditional areas of Soviet interest as eastern Europe and the Middle East to reach out to colonial and "backward" areas, South American countries, and other unspecified ("etc.") targets. He saw the Soviets acting to "penetrate" in each of these areas in order to extend Soviet domination.

Part four concentrated on the ways in which the USSR might seek to extend its influence on the "unofficial, or subterranean plane." Again, he enumerated the ways in which this insidious ideology would seek to penetrate and eventually weaken Western democracies including using the Russian Orthodox Church and its foreign branches, infiltrating "labor, youth and womens organizations," utilizing pan-Slavic groups, and above all maneuvering subversively through "underground lines" that are "tightly coordinated and directed by Moscow." The communists sought to infiltrate, influence, and finally dominate each of these, as well as other organizations in its quest to "tear down sources of strength" in the Western world. Implicit in this analysis of the subterranean efforts lay the disease metaphor, a spreading virus that if left unchecked might sap the strength of Western resolve.

In part five Kennan finally turned to what measures the United States should take to repulse this Soviet ideological challenge. His recommendations were curiously prosaic. He pleaded with Washington to inform the American people about the challenge they faced, advised policymakers that the Soviets were "highly sensitive to the logic of force" rather than reason (thus planting the seeds for his later theory of containment), and urged a dispassionate development of constructive policies that remained consistent with America's own "methods and conceptions of human society." Making the disease metaphor explicit, Kennan remarked that much depended on the "health and vigor of our own society" because "communism is like [a] malignant parasite which feeds only on diseased tissue." He closed his long telegram with the warning that the greatest danger the United States faced in coping with communism rested in allowing "ourselves to become like those with whom we are coping." In subsequent years the warning would fall by the wayside.

Kennan's analysis differed remarkably from other analyses at the time. Unlike Bohlen and the others who located Soviet motives primarily in national self-interest or fear of invasion, Kennan located them in communist ideology. Unlike the others who concentrated on Soviet moves in eastern Europe and the Balkans, Kennan saw a worldwide movement that functioned both on the official and the unofficial (or secret) levels to infiltrate governments and private organizations alike. Unlike the others who believed the Soviet Union sought hegemony, Kennan saw the Soviet Union as expansionist seeking domination. Unlike the others who sought to develop specific policies to counter Soviet moves either by supporting the Soviet's need for security or by devising different options, Kennan remained vaguely ambiguous by advocating public education, vigilance, traditional American values, and the "logic of force" rather than the "logic of reason." These differences, despite the weakness of not advocating a precise policy, set Kennan's analysis in sharp contrast with others.

As Robert Messer pointed out, it was not only the content but also the style and rhetorical stance of Kennan's analysis that made it persuasively appealing. Whereas Bohlen and the others saw complexity in Soviet intentions and proposed tentative solutions, Kennan "was direct, positive, and betrayed no doubts about the validity of his analysis."[59] It was his rhetorical stance of attempting to persuade directly that the other analyses lacked. Bohlen's own analysis as well as his study with Robinson were more analytic explorations of possibilities and problematic answers than persuasive briefs for a particular point of view. Kennan saw his opportunity and seized it with all the literary and rhetorical skill he could muster for the occasion. He was authoritative, direct, and nonequivocal. Kennan himself later noted ruefully that his telegram read like "one of those primers put out by alarmed congressional committees or by the Daughters of the American Revolution, designed to arouse the citizenry to the dangers of the communist conspiracy."[60] But that's exactly the effect the telegram provoked, and alarm was certainly the effect Kennan sought.

However, Kennan's rhetoric could not have had this power if it had not reached a receptive audience in Washington and if it had not touched some primordial fears among its readers. At the time the State Department, as already noted, and others in the Truman administration were searching for a conceptual framework for understanding Soviet behavior. Kennan's telegram came at just the right time. Furthermore, in James Forrestal, secretary of the Navy, Kennan found his most receptive audience. The secretary was known for his antipathy and suspicions about Soviet intentions, in particular, and communism, in general. Had someone else, say Secretary of Commerce Henry Wallace, been the primary reader of the telegram, it might have been filed away and forgotten, much as Bohlen's and Huston's were. But it was Forrestal not Wallace who read it and publicized it within the administration. Kennan's ideological analysis meshed with the secretary's preconceptions, gave intellectual validity to them, and stated in simple language what Forrestal had only groped to express. It was the right message at the right time read by the right audience that made it so effective. Forrestal read the telegram with excited enthusiasm. He ordered copies distributed to Truman's cabinet and circulated it as required reading among high-ranking officials at home and abroad. Letters commending Kennan poured in. Secretary of State Byrnes described his analysis as splendid.[61] The telegram made Kennan's career. Soon Forrestal recalled him to Washington and installed him in the National War College as the administration's resident expert on Soviet policies and as the State Department's senior adviser on Soviet affairs.[62] For many within the administration, including Bohlen, the private, behind-the-scenes search for a basic understanding of the Soviets was over. The "correct" interpretation had been discovered.

CONCLUSION

In the period between the death of Franklin Roosevelt and Churchill's "Iron Curtain" speech, President Truman maintained a public rhetoric of alliance and cooperation with the Soviet Union. The president and other officials continued to express a dedication to the principles of the Atlantic Charter and the Yalta agreements as the standards that would guide the Allies in constructing a postwar peace. Their understanding of these principles was an American understanding of them. Seldom did Truman evidence any sympathy or comprehension that the Soviets might interpret these principles differently. His "dressing down" of Foreign Minister Molotov in the early days after he assumed the presidency exhibit his lack of comprehension about any different interpretation. Nonetheless Truman and his secretary of state also mentioned that they understood the Soviet "special" need for secure borders. How exactly they meant these words is still problematic. If they really believed the Soviets needed a buffer zone in eastern Europe, they might not have become as alarmed as they did when Stalin began to consolidate it. And certainly that was what Stalin intended. He had previously preached the doctrine of socialism in one country. In the aftermath of the war, he seemed intent on establishing socialism in one zone of Europe.[63] However much Truman may or may not have understood Stalin's intent, he was caught up in the contradictions of the rhetorical legacy he had inherited from Roosevelt, one that created the dilemmas for a new U.S. foreign policy rhetoric. On the one hand, there was the universal rhetoric expressed in the principles of self-determination, free elections, and a secure peace based on the Atlantic Charter and the war-time alliance. This presumed a commonality of principles to which all adhered and to which each would submit when disputes arose. On the other hand, Roosevelt had assured Stalin that he understood the Soviets' fear of invasion and their need for security on their borders. Churchill had gone further and proposed to divide Europe into spheres of influence with Stalin. That private rhetoric appeared to approve different spheres of influence among the allies just as the veto power accorded each in the U.N. Security Council institutionalized this approach and appreciation for national self-interests. That was exactly what Stalin was attempting to create in eastern Europe, and more to the point, the Red Army was already stationed in those countries. When the rhetoric of Truman and Byrnes spoke of understanding the need for Soviet security on its borders, they undoubtedly were taking this private understanding into account.

Roosevelt had left another rhetorical legacy. He had publicly proclaimed an end to spheres of influence as a method of constructing a peaceful world, and Truman felt obliged to adhere to that principle. Thus, when specific matters had to be negotiated, the public rhetoric of universal principles of democracy and free elections clashed with the private rhetoric of spheres of influence. Cut off from a public rhetoric of spheres of influence, the administration had to search for new meanings of Soviet actions. Perhaps Roosevelt, who had repeatedly balanced these conflicting goals but had also postponed dealing with them until the war was over, could have juggled them long enough to come up with a new rhetoric that combined the conflicting rhetorics in ways that the American people could accept.

But Truman was no Roosevelt. In attempting to stand by universal principles but at the same time recognizing Soviet "special" interests in eastern Europe, he created a peace-time rhetoric that had little direction for practical policies in dealing with the Soviet Union or explaining Soviet maneuvers in eastern Europe to the American people. At some point he had to choose between the universal rhetoric and the "special" interests rhetoric. The emphasis he and Secretary Byrnes gave to each as well as Roosevelt's promise of an end to spheres of influence indicated which would eventually be chosen, but for the time being that choice did not have to be made. It would come later.

Republicans and conservative Democrats compounded Truman's problems by voicing suspicions of Soviet motives or condemnations of Soviet actions. Already in these early days an incipient anticommunist rhetoric was publicly reemerging. Even such an internationalist as Senator Vandenberg voiced his skepticism about the Soviet Union by saying that Soviet leaders had lowered an "iron curtain" over their activities. At the beginning of the 1946 election year Republicans made it clear that any further compromises with the Soviets would require them to attack the administration.[64] Lines were being drawn, and the rhetoric was narrowing.

In the late part of 1945 and in early 1946 the Truman administration became more worried about Soviet activities. The Soviets were not acting like Americans and this created confusion and fear. The London Foreign Ministers Conference had ended without any agreements. In January Albania proclaimed a People's (Communist) Republic. In Iran the Soviets were dragging their feet about withdrawing their troops. Within this milieu the administration began searching for a conceptual framework to understand and prepare for future moves by the Soviet Union. Several prominent members of the State Department tried their hands at such an analysis, but it was an obscure charge d'affaires in the American embassy in Moscow who provided the persuasive rationale for that understanding. However, the time was not ripe for presenting it publicly nor were members of the administration convinced that a modus vivendi was completely impossible. A fundamental reorientation was in the making, but it was only in its beginning stages. Neither the president nor leading members of his administration was willing to speak out, despite Kennan's urgings to do so, in direct antagonism to the Soviet Union at this time. Those first words of warning would have to come from elsewhere, from a voice friendly to Truman, not a partisan opponent. And in the oratory of Winston Churchill, the great war-time ally now a private citizen, the new conception of world affairs and world dangers that was taking hold privately would find its first eloquent Western voice.

NOTES

1. William Leuchtenburg, *In the Shadow of FDR* (Ithaca, NY: Cornell University Press, 1983).

2. Quoted in Hugh Thomas, *Armed Truce: The Beginnings of the Cold War 1945–1946* (New York: Atheneum, 1987), p. 171.

3. W. Averell Harriman and Elie Abel, *Special Envoy to Churchill and Stalin, 1941–1946* (New York: Random House, 1975), p. 444.

4. For the original Churchill proposals and subsequent percentages worked out by Eden and Molotov, see Thomas, *Armed Truce*, Appendix 3, p. 555.

5. "The Declaration on Liberated Europe," in Appendix 5, ibid., p. 558.

6. "The Crimea [Yalta] Conference . . . ought to spell the end of the system of unilateral action, the exclusive alliances, the spheres of influence, the balances of power, and all the other expedients that have been tried for centuries—and have always failed." Quoted in James MacGregor Burns, *Roosevelt: Soldier of Freedom 1940–1945* (New York: Harcourt Brace Jovanovich, 1970), p. 582.

7. Quoted in William Taubman, *Stalin's American Policy: From Entente to Detente to Cold War* (New York: W. W. Norton, 1982), p. 90.

8. See Roosevelt's concept of the "four policemen" in John Lewis Gaddis, *The United States and the Origins of the Cold War: 1941–1947* (New York: Columbia University Press, 1972), pp. 24–27. And one could point to the creation of a Security Council in the United Nations to which the great powers belonged as permanent members with veto power as an example of the recognition of the "policemen" concept institutionalized.

9. Quoted in Daniel Yergin, *Shattered Peace: The Origins of the Cold War and the National Security State* (Boston: Houghton Mifflin, 1977), p. 59.

10. Ibid., p. 57.

11. Eduard Mark, "Charles E. Bohlen and the Acceptable Limits of Soviet Hegemony in Eastern Europe: A Memorandum of 18 October 1945," *Diplomatic History* 3 (Spring 1979), p. 202.

12. In fact, it appears that he had no idea what the "Manhattan Project" was and was not informed until he had been president for several weeks. See Leuchtenburg, *In the Shadow of FDR*, p. 7.

13. Harriman and Abel, *Special Envoy to Churchill and Stalin*, p. 448.

14. Quoted in Cabell Phillips, *The Truman Presidency* (New York: Macmillan, 1966), p. 82.

15. Charles Mee, Jr., *Meeting at Potsdam* (New York: M. Evans, 1975), p. 29.

16. John Morton Blum, ed., *The Price of Vision: The Diary of Henry A. Wallace* (Boston: Houghton Mifflin, 1973), p. 485.

17. Harry Truman, *Memoirs: Year of Decisions*, vol. 1 (Garden City, NY: Doubleday, 1955), p. 412.

18. See "The Berlin (Potsdam) Conference, July 17-August 2, 1945," *A Decade of American Foreign Relations: Basic Documents 1941–1949* (Washington: Government Printing Office, 1950), pp. 34–50.

19. Harry Truman, "President Truman's Navy Day Speech, October 27, 1945," in *Ideas and Diplomacy*, ed. Norman A. Graebner (New York: Oxford University Press, 1964), p. 692.

20. Ibid., p. 690.

21. Dean Acheson, "American-Soviet Friendship," *Vital Speeches of the Day* 12 (December 1, 1945), pp. 110–12.

22. D. F. Fleming, *The Cold War and Its Origins, 1917–1960*, vol. 1 (Garden City, NY: Doubleday, 1961), p. 332.

23. Truman, *Memoirs: Year of Decisions*, vol. 1, p. 82.

24. Mark, "Charles E. Bohlen and the Acceptable Limits of Soviet Hegemony in Eastern Europe," p. 202.

25. Senator Arthur H. Vandenberg, "Raise the Iron Curtain," *Vital Speeches of the Day* 12 (December 1, 1945), pp. 115–19.

26. Arthur H. Vandenberg quoted in *The Private Papers of Senator Vandenberg,* ed. Arthur H. Vandenberg, Jr. (Boston: Houghton Mifflin, 1973), p. 177.

27. Quoted in Fleming, *The Cold War and Its Origins,* pp. 334–35.

28. Ibid., p. 335.

29. We are indebted for this discussion to the following two articles: Robert L. Messer, "Paths Not Taken: The United States Department of State and Alternatives to Containment, 1945–1946," *Diplomatic History* 1 (Fall 1977), pp. 297–319; Eduard Mark, "Charles E. Bohlen," pp. 201–13.

30. Mark, "Charles E. Bohlen." All quotations from the memorandum are taken from this article as published on pp. 207–9.

31. Messer, "Paths Not Taken," p. 303.

32. Quoted in Mark, "Charles E. Bohlen," p. 206.

33. For further details on the proposals, see Messer, "Paths Not Taken," pp. 297–319.

34. Ibid., p. 303.

35. Brynes's speech, "Neighboring Nations in One World," is printed in *Vital Speeches of the Day* 12 (November 15, 1945), pp. 68–70.

36. Quoted in Gaddis, *The United States and the Origins of the Cold War,* p. 300.

37. James V. Forrestal, *The Forrestal Diaries,* ed. Walter Millis (New York: Viking, 1951), p. 134.

38. Charles E. Bohlen, *The Transformation of American Foreign Policy* (New York: W. W. Norton, 1969), pp. 75–76.

39. For Deutscher's analysis, see his *Stalin: A Political Biography,* 2d ed. (New York: Oxford University Press, 1967), pp. 573–80. See also Adam Ulam, *Stalin: The Man and His Era* (Boston: Beacon Press, 1989), pp. 630–37.

40. See Adam Ulam, *The Rivals* (New York: Penguin, 1976), pp. 112–13.

41. Ulam, *Stalin,* p. 630.

42. "Stalin's Analysis of Victory," *A Documentary History of Communism,* vol. 2, ed. Robert V. Daniels (New York: Vintage Russian Library, 1962), pp. 142–47.

43. Andres Stephanson, *Kennan and the Art of Foreign Policy* (Cambridge, MA: Harvard University Press, 1989), p. 292.

44. B. Thomas Trout, "Rhetoric Revisited: Political Legitimation and the Cold War," *International Studies Quarterly* 19 (September 1979), p. 263.

45. Adam Ulam, *Expansion and Coexistence* (New York: Holt, Rinehart and Winston, 1974), p. 401.

46. Dean Acheson, *Present at the Creation,* (New York: W. W. Norton, 1969), p. 150.

47. Harriman and Abel, *Special Envoy to Churchill and Stalin,* p. 547.

48. Quoted in Hugh Thomas, *Armed Truce* (New York: Atheneum, 1988), p. 481.

49. *New York Times* (February 16, 1946), p. 1.

50. *New York Times* (February 17, 1946), p. 2E.

51. *New York Times* (February 17, 1946), p. 4E.

52. Walter LeFeber, *American, Russia, and the Cold War 1945–1975,* 3rd ed. (New York: John Wiley, 1976), p. 39.

53. Quoted in Yergin, *A Shattered Peace*, p. 167.

54. James C. Humes, *Churchill: Speaker of the Century* (New York: Stein and Day, 1980), p. 271.

55. The complete text is printed in Barton J. Bernstein and Allen J. Matusow, eds., *The Truman Administration: A Documentary History* (New York: Harper Colophon, 1966), pp. 198–212. All subsequent quotations are from this text.

56. Kennan, *Memoirs*, p. 294.

57. See Kennan's own recollections of his motives in his *Memoirs*, pp. 292–95.

58. Bernstein and Matusow, *The Truman Administration*, pp. 202–3.

59. Messer, "Paths Not Taken," p. 315.

60. Kennan, *Memoirs*, p. 294.

61. David Mayers, *George Kennan and the Dilemmas of U.S. Foreign Policy* (New York: Oxford University Press, 1988), p. 100.

62. For an interesting account of Kennan's lectures at the War College during the following year, see Thomas A. Bailey, *The Marshall Plan Summer* (Stanford, CA: Hoover Institution Press, 1977), pp. 8–9.

63. For an incisive account of Stalin's attempts to establish socialism in one zone, see Deutscher, *Stalin*, pp. 551–55.

64. Gaddis, *The United States and the Origins of the Cold War*, p. 283.

Chapter Four

Churchill's "Iron Curtain" and Beyond

Although it seems virtually impossible to speak about the origins of the cold war without discussing the significance of Winston Churchill's "Iron Curtain" speech at Fulton, Missouri in early 1946, there is anything but consensus about the role it played. Did it merely reflect the actual state of relations between the United States and the Soviet Union or was it instrumental in defining a new set of relations? John Spanier stated plainly that "Churchill, in short, said bluntly that the cold war had begun."[1] It is that perspective that we share. But the question remains, how did Churchill's great speech contribute to the cold war reality?

There has been widespread recognition that the speech came at a crucial time in the development of the strained relations among the war-time allies. There is a weight of evidence to support John Blum's con-clusion that "at least until the time of Fulton, the possibility existed of a practical accommodation between the United States and the Soviet Union."[2] But Churchill proclaimed an international crisis, ideological in character, global in scope. He declared that the one world the allies hoped to build after World War II had been divided by an "iron curtain" into two antagonistic camps. By giving popular currency to this vivid metaphor of division, Churchill set in motion the dynamic of a public rhetorical process that was to give Americans a new interpretation of the world and their place in it. Churchill supplied basic elements for a vocabulary that would be picked up and widely spread by opinion lead-ers, so that these linguistic elements eventually became *the* way to per-ceive and to talk about disputes between the Soviet Union and the West, to the exclusion of other interpretations. Louis Halle observed that "in a matter of months this term [iron curtain] would be an accepted part of everyone's vocabulary.... Those who responded with initial disapproval would shortly be using it themselves."[3] Churchill's call for an Anglo–American alliance was rejected, for the most part, by the general public; his "iron curtain" metaphor, however, was accepted as an accurate description of the world. This striking metaphor became more than a convenient designation for one interpretation of world tensions; it became the shorthand way of stating the political context within which issues were perceived and interpreted, the way they were discussed and debated, and the ideological context within which subsequent decisions were made.

THE CONTEXT OF THE SPEECH

The background of Churchill's invitation to speak at Westminster College in Fulton, Missouri is straightforward and hints of no political intrigue. Churchill had been voted out of office during the meeting of the Big Three at Potsdam in July 1945. His unexpected defeat struck him like "a physical blow" and he returned home to become a private citizen. Lord Moran, his personal physician, reported the former prime minister's view of what his defeat meant to negotiations with Stalin: "After I left Potsdam, Joe did what he liked. The Russian's western frontier was allowed to advance, displacing another eight million poor devils. I'd not have agreed and the Americans would have backed me."[4] When he was invited to speak at a college in Missouri in 1946, Churchill emerged from his "black dog" depression because he saw a new opportunity to persuade Americans to his view of international affairs.

The invitation to speak came about in this fashion. In August 1945, Dr. F. L. "Bullet" McCluer, president of Westminster College, a small Presbyterian school, needed a speaker of "international reputation" to fulfill the terms of an endowment. He sought the aid of a former classmate, General Harry Vaughan, who was military aide to the White House, in getting Churchill. Vaughan took the invitation to the president, who added a note saying: "Dear Winnie, This is a fine old school out in my state. If you come and make them a speech there, I'll take you out and introduce you."[5] The prospect of being introduced by the president of the United States promised extensive attention for what Churchill might say. He quickly accepted the invitation.

If there was political intrigue between Truman and Churchill, it occurred as the date for the speech approached. Any postwar ambiguities that Churchill had expressed regarding the Soviet Union were gone by the time he arrived in the United States in January 1946. He had reverted to his earlier antibolshevism with a vengeance. He was already using the term "iron curtain," a metaphor originally coined by Joseph Goebbels in the last days of the war, in both private letters and public speech.[6] Now, he would make it famous worldwide. By the time of Fulton, Churchill had excised ambiguity from his thinking in favor of an alliance between the United States and Great Britain that he believed was necessary for dealing with the Soviet expansionism in Europe.

Churchill arrived in Florida in January to vacation before his historic address. He wrote Truman telling him that he needed to talk with him before the speech. He said that under the president's auspices his speech would command attention and that "there is an opportunity for doing some good to this bewildered, baffled and breathless world."[7] Clearly, Churchill realized that disputes over the postwar world had confused both the American and the English public. He intended to give clarity by expressing a new meaning of recent events, and he chose to use his considerable oratorical skills to present that meaning. There is evidence that Truman and Secretary of State Byrnes knew what Churchill would say, although Truman apparently did not read the actual speech until aboard the train traveling to Missouri.[8] Later, Truman's refusal to endorse the ideas of the speech publicly indicated either his reluctance to abandon the possibility of accommodation with the Soviet Union, or his fear that an abrupt change from the rhetoric of cooperation to one of confrontation would shock and anger the American people. But already the administration was taking a harder line in negotiations, and an Anglo–American alliance was at least in de facto existence. On the day after the Fulton speech, Secretary Byrnes sent a stiff note to Moscow calling for the immediate withdrawal of Soviet troops from Iran. Such protests were sufficient for the time being. In an election year it would serve little purpose to endorse the Anglo–American alliance against the Soviet Union, especially since anti-British and isolationist feelings still ran deep. Above all, Truman did not want the public onus of being the one who split the war-time alliance.

The interpretation of Soviet intentions expressed in Kennan's "long telegram" was fast catching hold within the Truman administration. The coincidence of Churchill's speech provided the first public statement of this analysis. That is not to say that Churchill spoke from Kennan's work, but rather that he and Kennan had come to similar conclusions about the nature of the Soviet Union. In a real sense Churchill, an Englishman, gave the public its first inkling of what those inside U.S. government circles were now discussing. The most likely explanation for Truman's appearance with Churchill and his subsequent reluctance to embrace Churchill's ideas publicly is that the president was waiting to see what kind of political reception the speech received. Fulton provided a convenient trial balloon. A shift from one political reality to another is not easily or quickly accomplished. Without first preparing the groundwork for public receptivity, the announcement of a new policy based on a new reality is politically dangerous. Churchill happened along at a time that was propitious for the administration to test public and congressional reaction.

Churchill met Truman in Washington, and the two traveled by private train to Jefferson City, Missouri. When the subsequent motorcade arrived in Fulton on Tuesday, March 5, the community of some 7,000 swelled to nearly 40,000, including some 300 members of the press. About 2,500 people crowded into the Westminster College gymnasium to see Churchill receive an honorary degree and to hear him speak. Truman gave Churchill the promised introduction, saying that he understood that Mr. Churchill would have something useful to say. Of course the man who had rallied his countrymen to their finest hour needed no introduction as an orator. His reputation as the man who had "mobilized the English language and sent it into battle," as John F. Kennedy was to characterize him, was world-famous. Also, in the months before Fulton, the American conservative press had kept Churchill in the public eye. *Reader's Digest* lionized him as "a personality unsurpassed in history," who "will be quoted as long as Shakespeare."[9] In its January 7, 1946 issue, *Life* reproduced some of Churchill's paintings and described him as a "superb orator" and "talented historian."[10] Who better then than an orator-historian-statesman to survey the broad stretches of the postwar world, its confusions and fears, and to give clear meaning to it?

CONTENT OF THE SPEECH

In characteristic style, Churchill began by validating the unique occasion. Expressing his gratitude for the honorary degree, he said that he was glad to have come to Westminster: "The name Westminster is somehow familiar to me. I seem to have heard of it before. Indeed it was at Westminster that I received a very large part of my education in politics, rhetoric, and one or two other things."[11] Having thus established his connection with the Missouri college, while at the same time foreshadowing the Anglo–American alliance theme of the speech, Churchill then underscored the special significance of having the U.S. president travel a thousand miles to "dignify and magnify" the speech of a private citizen, giving him the opportunity to address "this kindred nation" as well as people in nations afar. By noting that he had full liberty to speak for himself, not only because the president had so stated, but because he had already satisfied his political ambitions beyond his "wildest dreams," Churchill emphasized the significance of his message while maintaining a distance between what he would say as a private citizen and what others might say as official policy. The message was clear. Churchill could speak about the "real" nature of the world without the restraints that an official governmental position placed on others, others such as the president of the United States who sat in rapt attention during his address.

Churchill defined a new political reality for the postwar world. He brought clarity to confusion. The new world was not one world, as the war-weary allies had hoped, but two worlds: "From Stettin in the Baltic to Trieste in the Adriatic, an iron curtain has descended across the continent. Behind that line lie all the capitals of the ancient states of Central and Eastern Europe." With a few short sentences the former prime minister captured a new vision of the world. "Warsaw, Berlin, Prague, Vienna, Budapest, Bucharest and Sofia," all, proclaimed Churchill, now lay behind the iron curtain. It was an ominous litany.

In the iron curtain world view, a bipolar view, there was no longer a multilateral political reality, consisting of Great Britain, the United States, the Soviet Union, and every other nation, each with its own national interests. Nor was there a group of victorious allies striving for peace. Now there were but two sides. On the one side lay the repository of "the joint inheritance of the English-speaking world and through which Magna Carta, the Bill of Rights, the Habeas Corpus, trial by jury, and the English common law find their most famous expression in the Declaration of Independence." On the other side lay a tyrannical communism controlled by the Soviet Union and desiring "the fruits of war," a growing challenge and peril to "Christian civilisation." In this ideological dichotomy there was no middle ground. The sharp division was a paradigm in which European nations were already either on one side of an iron curtain or the other, and the other nations of the world had become the battlegrounds to determine on which side they would eventually fall.

The speech was based on two pillars: the Soviet Union posed a massive threat to world peace, and only an alliance of Great Britain and the United States could respond effectively to this threat. Churchill planted the ideological seeds for what would later blossom into a tiresome rhetorical litany about the Soviet menace. In fact, his speech foreshadowed the primary themes of Truman's declaration of American policy a year later, even as it struck additional themes that Truman chose to omit because they received negative responses.

The sections of the speech describing the communist menace struck many of the major chords of anticommunism.[12] The Soviets were tyrannical and totalitarian. He drew upon comparisons to Nazi Germany to magnify the threat. Communism, Churchill asserted, was expansive seeking to extend its control over other nations in the Middle East and Far East. One method they used to achieve this goal was through subversive "fifth columns" in other nations, although he carefully noted that domestic communism was only "in its infancy" in England and America. In all, he painted, as befits an amateur painter, a dark and foreboding picture of the Soviet Union (where "control is enforced upon common people by various kinds of all-embracing police government, to a degree which is overwhelming and contrary to every principle of democracy") and her intentions in the world ("Nobody knows what the Soviet Union and its Communist international organization intends to do in the immediate future, or what are the limits, if any, to their expansive and proselytizing tendencies."). Although he denied knowing Soviet intentions, Churchill described the Soviet Union as expansionist and international. Thus, in a single sentence he had both denied knowing intentions and attributed intentions to the Soviet Union. It was the latter that left a lasting impression.

The second pillar of his speech concerned an Anglo–American alliance to meet the threat communism posed in the world. Harbutt pointed out that this alliance was not presented as an effect caused by the first. Rather Churchill used it as a theme running parallel to the theme of Soviet expansionism within the address so that no one could miss his meaning, but so that he also could deny that he actually stated it. Only the United States, Churchill said, could provide the leadership necessary to prevent catastrophe at this "breathless" moment in history. He assured Americans that Great Britain was ready to join in that great effort. The two nations were bound together through common language and law, and therefore fit to repulse the new "danger" to the world. He contended that the alliance should not seek a balance of power in Europe because the two nations could not "afford to work on narrow margins." Instead he said an alliance must be established that enforced the principles of the United Nations, even to the point of creating an international armed force for the U.N. Churchill avowed his loyalty to the nascent United Nations Organization, but declared that an association between Britain and America would be not only beneficial to the success of the world organization but indispensable, lest the U.N. become nothing more than a "Tower of Babel." Nonetheless he returned again and again to his primary theme: the need for the United States, now at the pinnacle of its power, to take the lead in recognizing the new threat to world peace and the forceful means needed to confront that threat.

Although Churchill divided the world into two camps on either side of an iron curtain, he hedged his bets. He paid lip service to establishing "lasting friendships" with the Soviets. He claimed to understand the Soviets "need to be secure on her western frontiers from renewal of German aggression," but this brief mention was overwhelmed by the hostile argument of the speech. Like other Western speakers before him, Churchill avoided saying what measures nations on his side of the iron curtain could take to reassure the Soviet Union that its frontiers were secure. That omission stood in stark contrast to the specific action he urged upon Americans to meet the growing danger directed from the other side of the iron curtain. In sum, Churchill's great speech exploded the belief that the world could be made whole after the devastation of World War II. Instead, the whole point of Churchill's address was that the world was already divided even more dangerously after the war than it had been before the war. His transcendental metaphor for that division dominated all other concerns he voiced, and it was on that metaphor that all his subsequent arguments rested.

THE BIOGRAPHICAL AND RHETORICAL RESOURCES FOR CHURCHILL'S THEMES

As we have seen, Churchill's speech was based on two pillars: the Soviet Union posed a massive threat to world peace, and only an alliance of English-speaking nations, led by the United States, could meet that threat. Neither idea was new in Churchill's thinking. Each had deep roots in his political past.

The advocacy of an Anglo–American partnership dated back to World War I. The linking of the two countries in a cultural-political bond had been one of his key themes in the period between the two world wars. During the early years of World War II Churchill had seen a union with the United States as Britain's salvation. After Pearl Harbor swept the U.S. into the war, Churchill, as he later wrote, "went to bed and slept the sleep of the saved and thankful."[13] His only fear was that the United States would concentrate its efforts in the Pacific to the temporary subordination of the war in Europe and, with the brief suspension of lend-lease after the Japanese attack, that seemed a possibility. So Churchill came to the United States to address a joint session of Congress the day after Christmas 1941. His choice of language indicated more than merely fleeting interest in a union promoted by the crisis of war.

Churchill began his speech to Congress by noting that if "my father had been American and my mother British, rather than the other way around, I might have got here on my own."[14] Getting to the subject of the Japanese attack, he referred to "the outrages they have committed upon *us* at Pearl Harbor," asking "[w]hat kind of people do they think *we* are?" (emphasis added). In closing Churchill again sounded the Anglo–American theme. "It is not given to us to peer into the mysteries of the future. Still I avow my hope and faith, sure and inviolate, that in the days to come the British and American people will for their own safety and for the good of all walk together in majesty, in justice, and in peace."

In the later days of the war Churchill magnified the same theme in a speech in Boston. During a visit to the United States in 1943 he received an honorary degree from Harvard University and, in a speech that pre-figured Fulton, he spoke of America's responsibility for leading the civ-ilized world on a course between world anarchy and world order. In the exercise of that leadership he urged the union of the British and American people. After tracing the common history, culture, and lan-guage of the two nations, Churchill went beyond merely suggesting close ties to advoacting a political unity: "This gift of common tongue is a priceless inheritance, and it may well someday become the foun-dation of a common citizenship."[15] This suggestion went further than he was prepared to go two years later at Fulton, but clearly the idea of a "fraternal association of the English-speaking peoples" was not a new idea for Churchill in March 1946.

Neither was the second pillar of the Fulton speech new. Harbutt wrote that the "Iron Curtain" speech "may be viewed as a highly compressed repetition . . . of his great anti-appeasement campaign."[16] But now it was turned to another long-time theme, anticommunism. In an editorial re-sponse to the speech the *Canadian Forum* wrote: "He is reverting to type . . . in his fervor against Russia. After the Russian revolution in 1917, it was Winston Churchill who was most determined of all British or French Statesmen in intervening to defeat it, and he was the most violent of all responsible leaders in his abusive language against Bolshevism."[17] The editorial did not overstate the case. As secretary of war, Churchill had indeed urged Allied intervention against the Soviets in the Russian civil war and had expressed his regret that the intervention was not inten-sified. He regarded Lenin as a plague, saying that the Bolshevik leader "was sent into Russia by the Germans in the same way you might send a phial containing a culture of typhoid or cholera to be poured into the water supply of a great city, and it worked with amazing accuracy."[18] The disease metaphor, later so prominent in American anticommunist rhetoric, described Churchill's early and enduring view of Bolsheviks.

In 1931 Churchill made another of his frequent visits to the United States, this time for a lecture tour in which he concentrated on what he regarded as the Soviet threat, expressing his belief that "the two great opposing forces of the future . . . would be the English speaking peoples and Communism."[19] Harbutt, in his extensive documentation of Churchill's antipathy for the Soviets, concluded that the hatred was essentially visceral, that "his identification of Bolshevism as the main political enemy came from emotional rather than philosophical sources."[20] That hatred was a recurring theme throughout Churchill's career, one that was suppressed only when the threat of war made it necessary. On being asked how, given his record of inflexible animosity toward the Soviet Union, he could ally himself with Stalin, Churchill replied that "if Hitler invaded Hell, I would at least make a favorable reference to the Devil in the House of Commons."[21] Churchill's abhorrence of Soviet communism was a well-worn tenet, like his call for an Anglo–American alliance.

THE FAILURE OF CHURCHILL'S SPEECH

Churchill painted a rhetorical picture of Soviet communism as an ominous threat to the Western way of life, with democratic tenets and traditions at stake. He advocated a realpolitik solution (even as he decried balances of power), a return to the development of force as a way of combatting that threat. The American public was ill-prepared to grant the suppositions for such a solution. The public assumed what David Rees ascribed to the prevailing "liberalism" of the time, namely

that force and "power politics" are always to be deprecated in international relations, and that the conflicting policies of countries and power groups can usually be harmonised by the same means that govern internal domestic differences— due process, reason, common sense, elementary morality and institutions such as the United Nations.[22]

The American people, after all, went to war only as a last resort. War was rarely admitted as a rational instrument of foreign policy. Realpolitik was a dirty word, not the central ingredient of foreign policy. More than a century of isolation, made possible by wide oceans and British sea power, had enabled Americans to think of a relationship between power and diplomacy as something European, a part of the Old World that ignited two world wars, both of which Americans had entered reluctantly to set the Old World right. When the United States had been forced to enter these wars, they fought them as crusades waged in the spirit of Wilson's Fourteen Points and Roosevelt's Atlantic Charter. Each war had ended in spectacular victories and the vindication of American principles. The long years of isolation had another effect. Americans had precious little in their political vocabulary to conceive of and therefore to express a power-oriented foreign policy. Indeed, Americans had only a primitive conceptual language to envision any kind of foreign policy beyond a crusade for victory over a diabolic enemy or withdrawal for purposes of maintaining their privileged moral status among nations of the world. Thus, they were not disposed to adopt Churchill's version of power politics because they had no sophisticated political vocabulary to understand it.

Some American political leaders were quick to reject the proposed alliance. The day after the speech the *New York Times* was replete with statements by members of Congress disassociating themselves from the notion.[23] Senator Brewster of Maine told reporters that "we cannot assume the heritage of British colonial policy," while Senator Pepper of

Florida said that it was, indeed, British colonial policy that was at issue. Senator Johnson of Colorado conceded that there was already an unwritten alliance but he was not sure that the United States was ready for "a military alliance that would impose upon us the duty of enforcing Britain's foreign policy." Representative Ellis of West Virginia said that the speech was just a "build-up" for the loan to Britain that was under consideration in Congress. Senator Ball of Minnesota saw global implications, believing that a collaboration between England and the United States would be justifiably interpreted by the Soviet Union as ganging up against her and would be almost certain to foster counter-alliances. The following Sunday the *New York Times* put American responses to the speech in the perspective of the Churchillian bent for asking Americans to pull British chestnuts out of the fire, noting "Britain's extremely limited home area, her perilously exposed position on the edge of the Continent in an atomic age; her dwindling resources; her exhausted savings; her fearfully difficult imperial problems; her domestic social problems, and so on."[24] The call for a partnership between the United States and Great Britain fell on skeptical or suspicious ears, except for the president of the United States and some members of his administration.

Despite the draconian description of their national plight, the British response was also something less than enthusiastic. The *London Evening News* looked upon the proposed alliance as merely "a call to strengthen Anglo-American comradeship within the framework of the United Nations."[25] The *London Times* was of the opinion that, while such an alliance might be an element in British policy, it should not be the "sole and all-sufficient one."[26] Lord Samuel argued that such an alliance might tend "to dominate the proceedings of the United Nations and the actions of the world."[27] The liberal *Manchester Guardian* and the conservative *London Daily Mail* welcomed the speech, but only in general terms, while the *News Chronicle* expressed the fear that the speech might confirm the Soviet Union's worst fears about the intentions of the capitalist world.[28] The general opinion in Great Britain reflected a continued hope for the United Nations in preference to a bilateral military alliance.

In the Soviet Union the official reaction was delayed, but vociferous when it came. On March 13 Stalin responded using his standard form of ostensibly replying to a request from *Pravda* to comment on Churchill's speech. Stalin accused Churchill of calling for a "war with the Soviet Union." He described the former prime minister as an English racist for advocating an alliance of English-speaking people against the Soviet Union. Stalin reminded readers that Hitler had made the same racial appeals to Germans, and he castigated Churchill as a "Hitler-like warmonger." Churchill, according to Stalin, was attempting to organize a new military opposition to the Soviet Union, much as he had tried after

World War I. He failed then, and the Soviet leader predicted he would fail again.[29] Stalin limited his blistering attack to Churchill, and he significantly did not include the United States in the plan he denounced.

The official American public reaction was cool. Secretary of State Byrnes disassociated the United States from Churchill's proposals. He stated that he had not been consulted about the speech in advance. But at the same time Byrnes acted upon the premise of firmer statements toward the Soviet Union by issuing a protest over Soviet troops in Iran. President Truman tried to keep his own counsel. But reporters hounded him trying to learn whether he agreed with Churchill's views. In his press conference on March 8 he too tried to dissociate himself from the speech although he left a door open for future consideration of the proposals. He denied that he knew in advance what Churchill intended to say and lamely added that Churchill had merely exercised his right to free speech. For this kind of talk, he was described by some as "bewildered" after the Churchill speech, most likely because he privately agreed with Churchill but did not want to endorse his views publicly.

The call for an Anglo–American alliance was not publicly embraced at the time, even though Churchill soon regarded the eventual results as a vindication of his purpose. In an article for the *New York Times* a year hence and just after the announcement of the Truman Doctrine, Churchill took satisfaction that, given a year to digest the principal ideas he presented at Fulton, the burden of guarding the civilization of the Western world had passed from Great Britain to the United States. Noting that "[i]t may be true that the British withdrawal from India and Burma, now in somber progress, marks the end of the mighty empire and mission in the East," he predicted that the British nation "will rise again, if not to its former pre-eminence, at least in solid and lasting strength." Meanwhile, he warned, the United States must assume the burden, having no choice "but to lead or fall."[30] But the immediate result of the alliance a year before was rejection.

There are several reasons that account for the public failure. An Anglo–American alliance would have split the war-time alliance. Americans were slow to disown the association with the Soviets that had defeated the Nazi powers and that, in the aspirations of many Americans, had to form the basis for postwar peace. Second, by naming an "iron curtain," Churchill seemed to be advocating spheres of influences and Americans were reluctant to adopt a policy that conflicted with the altruistic hopes and universal rhetoric that had been the basis for winning World War II. Third, Churchill's Anglo–American alliance sounded as if he wanted to bypass the United Nations, replacing it with power politics. Even though the United Nations was not functioning with demonstrated success in addressing world problems, it was still prized by Americans as a real hope for solving international disputes. Finally,

Churchill, by saying he understood the need for a buffer between the USSR and European powers, had appeared to condone the Soviet domination of eastern Europe. This reference also seemed to reinforce the elevation of spheres of influence over the United Nations. These reactions were common among Americans who still maintained, to a certain degree, their isolationist sentiments and their suspicions of British colonialism.[31] That is not to say that Americans rejected Churchill's blasts against the Soviets. There is considerable evidence to the contrary.[32] Rather Americans appeared initially to accept a major part of Churchill's statement of the problem, but not the solution he proposed. The old political reality, cultivated during the war, was still dominant in the general public. It was firmly embedded in the American view that rejected power politics. An intense effort over time would be needed to dislodge it and transform antipathy toward an alliance between the British and the Americans into a full-fledged crusade against communism.

THE SUCCESS OF CHURCHILL'S SPEECH

Although the Fulton speech met with mixed immediate reactions, in the following months, Churchill succeeded beyond his wildest dreams. His address sowed the seeds for a rhetorical process that was to blossom into a new world order, a new political reality. These effects lay not in his arguments, but in his language, especially his dominant metaphor, the iron curtain. As his terms for describing the meaning of international disputes were spread by the news media, they were adopted by opinion leaders in speeches and editorials so that Churchill's way of talking about the world became the prevailing coin for discourse. Lewis Broad correctly concluded, just five years after Fulton, that "today the terms of this address are the commonplace of the weekend speaker."[33] While the policies that Churchill advocated were discussed and debated, the language of Churchill's rhetoric became the dominant language for those discussions and debates. Gradually, over a period of time, the language of Fulton, expanded and reinforced by Truman and others, became accepted as the commonsense perception of the "real" meaning of the actual events and disputes that caused the original confusion. For example, Senator Maybank of North Carolina declined to endorse a military alliance because he doubted that it would curb what seemed to be the "indefinite expansion" of the Soviet Union's "power and doctrine."[34] Still, he accepted that Soviet expansionism and communist ideology posed the central problem, using almost the exact words the prime minister had used to state the problem. Senator Robertson of Wyoming went further. He said that he believed the cooperation with Britain and other nations of the United Nations was important until the USSR "rolls up the iron curtain."[35] In other words, the discussion proceeded within the division Churchill had drawn, especially by adopting the dominant metaphor, iron curtain, to symbolize that division.

Churchill's speech is best understood, not as argumentative, but as epideictic. In an argumentative speech the propositions, supported by facts and figures, interwoven by logical and emotional appeals, can be weighed and evaluated. The effects of such a speech can be measured by the changes in the attitudes and beliefs of the auditors, as reflected in public opinion polls or in the passage of policies. But Churchill's call for an Anglo–American alliance convinced few, and those who were convinced, primarily major figures within the Truman administration, kept quiet for a while about their conversion to his call.

The success of an epideictic speech, however, cannot be determined by judging the efficacy of its propositions. The key to judging an epi-deictic speech is the language used by the speaker. Its success rests more in the moral meaning assigned to the state of the world than in the specific policies advocated to meet a specific situation. The funeral or-ation is the most typical example of the epideictic speech. In such speeches the orator recites the life of the deceased in a calculated mixture of biographical history and moralistic myths. The purpose is to give consolation to the living. When—as in Pericles's "Funeral Oration" or Isocrates's "Evagoras"—the purpose is to eulogize those fallen in battle or the death of the father of a new ruler, a new dimension is added to the discourse. As Takis Poulakos pointed out in his analysis of Isocrates' eulogy, history and myth converge. The ceremonial speech is used to instruct the new leader on political policies and wise governance.[36] The great achievements of the past are related in mythological form so as to recount the heroic traditions to which the current generation must as-pire. To put it another way, as Christine Oravec did, the speaker "re-ceived common values and experiences from his audience and by reshaping them in artistic language returns these experiences heightened and renewed."[37] But the purpose of such a mixture of history and myth is to instruct toward moral ends. If the artistic language is compelling enough, the mixture becomes reality for those willing to believe. That is what happened with Churchill's speech. The will to believe is not based on specific pragmatics in such speeches as it is on the willingness to believe in heroic and demonic myths that combine fact with value. As people assimilated the terms of the speech as part of their everyday talk about Soviet–American relations, especially their use of the iron curtain metaphor, they also adopted the definitions and meanings sub-sumed in these terms. Once a definition of a situation is accepted as "the nature of things," that is, once it gives meaning to events, it creates the reality of those events. From that point on, particular policies and responses to events seem preordained, leading from a rhetorical meaning to specific policies consistent with those meanings as naturally as day follows night. The success of Churchill's speech lay in the future, in the day-by-day use of the division he had memorialized.

A single speech cannot accomplish a major change in political reality overnight. Such a change requires a rhetorical process of some sophistication. Churchill initiated that process at Fulton. As the process proceeded, was expanded, maintained, and legitimated by the rhetoric of the Truman Doctrine and other rhetorical efforts, it altered the prevailing reality. Ordinary Americans eventually responded, not in terms of realpolitik, but in terms of a moralistic crusade. Churchill drew a picture of the Soviet Union as a massive threat to Americans in order to argue for a political alliance. In this sense, he relieved the confusion of the present through the clarity of his interpretation of the current state of the world. To paraphrase Ricoeur, Churchill's epideictic speech was the result of a "productive imagination," and his purpose was not to refer to actual conditions in order to copy them, but "in order to prescribe a new reading" of them.[38] Within the new political clarity he gave to events, he called for his audience to live up to the heroic actions and venerated principles of the recent past. Americans, confused by the failure to secure a universal peace in the aftermath of war, rejected his alliance at first, but accepted his description of the division in the world and later embarked upon a universal crusade to keep the American body politic pure.

THE IRON CURTAIN RHETORIC AND POLITICAL REALITY

Political reality is changed by a rhetorical process, for that reality is, from beginning to end, a creation of persuasive language. Kenneth Burke explained this by distinguishing among three realms of word and reality.[39] The first is the realm of words that are used as signs for objects in the natural world, that actual world that "would be left if all word-using creatures and their verbalizings were suddenly obliterated."[40] The second realm is the verbal realm itself, "their terms of grammar, rhetoric, poetic, logic, philology, etymology, semantics, symbolism, etc."[41] The third is the order of what Burke called "sociopolitical reality," which depends on the verbal world for its existence and meaning, for this realm has no exact counterpart in nature: "Sociopolitical institutions, with the personal and social relations involved in them, and the vast terminology of attitudes, acts, and motives that goes with them, do not enjoy exactly the kind of extraverbal reality we find in the commonsense vocabulary of the natural realm."[42] Thus the words of the sociopolitical world, such as "family, democracy or dictatorship," are rhetorical constructs defining relationships. Political reality does not consist of objects that we might bump into in the natural world, but rather it comes into meaningful existence through vivaciously persuasive language.

Political reality is not easily changed because people tend to believe that the language they use to describe actual events really describes the way things naturally are. Language originally used in a creative way to give new meaning to the external world gradually loses its creativity and becomes static, becomes the unchanging and only meaning to be attached to the external world. Much of this fossilizing of meaning comes through community. People inherit meanings through their communities, for to be human is to live in community. A common political language is the glue that holds together the conglomerate elements that constitute a nation. People acquire the language of a political community as they learn to think about politics within that community. In another context Joseph Church illuminated this procedure:

Developmentally, it is clear that one comes to terms with reality only through a continuing dialectic in which language plays an intimate and indispensable role, and which orients us schematically to a multi-dimensional universe infinitely broader and more variegated than anything that can be known perceptually and at first hand.[43]

On a national and international level, language plays an even greater role since events and actions are far-removed from firsthand experience and involve greater complexities than can be understood individually by referring solely to personal experience. In the shared knowledge that animates a nation, public rhetoric serves the indispensable purpose of giving meaning to national affairs that cannot be known directly or validated personally. Events, as they are reported or described, give validity or legitimacy to the a priori meanings people have about the political world.

The old political reality Americans believed was one of cooperation among the war-time allies, hopes for the United Nations as the principal organization for resolving international disputes, longings for a universal peace now that the diabolical Nazi forces had been defeated, expectations for a return to normalcy after the temporary interruptions caused by the war, confidence in U.S. superiority throughout the world, and desires to return from war-time sacrifices to the day-to-day practical problems of living. They believed these things because the dominant rhetoric during the war had promised them. However, in the first months after the war ordinary Americans had had this prevailing view disturbed by the confusing events in Europe, but these had not destroyed their beliefs in this reality, only confounded them.

Churchill's speech at Fulton provided the rudimentary elements necessary to initiate a rhetorical process that would, over time, radically change this political reality, the meanings people attached to events, the expectations they had for the future. Churchill defined a new world situation as an impending crisis. There was no explicit external event that all could point to that made it a crisis. The situation in eastern Europe had existed since the Red Army had pushed the Nazi forces from the streets of Stalingrad to the suburbs of Berlin. The Soviets occupied and claimed power in the nations they had liberated from the Nazis, just as the United States occupied and claimed power in Japan and the formerly Japanese-dominated islands of the South Pacific. In so many words Churchill recognized this by citing a list of political moves by the Soviet Union in eastern Europe, the establishment or encouragement of Communist parties in those countries as well as western European countries "beyond their numbers and are seeking everywhere to obtain totalitarian control." As he acknowledged, the threat was not of marching armies, but the spread of a political ideology he detested. Thus, it was a dangerous condition rather than a dramatic event that occasioned his dire warnings.

Central to Churchill's clarion call was his division of the world into two competing antagonistic ideologies, symbolized by the iron curtain. The new conditions required new words to describe this schism, and the metaphor succinctly provided that new view. The crisis Churchill proclaimed was potentially more a threat than the old prewar crisis because of atomic weapons. What was at stake was nothing less than the survival of democracy itself. On the one side of the iron curtain was "Christian civilisation," representing all that was sacred to Americans and the British, who shared traditions from the past and aspirations for the future. On the other side was the profane, a tyrannical dictatorship with sinister designs on the world and determined to spread a doctrine that negated all that Americans cherished.

The Rhetorical Stockpile

Churchill drew upon the rhetorical stockpile of the past to refine the sense of crises. He reminded his audience that he had seen war coming in the past and had cried aloud, but to little avail. The analogical linking with Munich was unmistakable. The image of Munich, synonymous with appeasement, provided the linkage with a recent past that could not be easily dismissed. In the comparison, the old tyranny of Hitler's Germany was replaced by the new tyranny of Stalin's Russia. Churchill cast the new situation in terms of the old. "There never was a war [World War II] in all history easier to prevent by timely action," Churchill said, thereby implying that "timely action" now could prevent another war. Churchill clearly was assuming the role of political prophet, once again sounding the political alarm. It was a time of crisis that called for resolve and unity. The failure to see the crisis and to act would result in another Munich. The time was critical because "the Communist parties of fifth columns constitute a growing challenge and peril to Christian civilisation."

Churchill's prophetic rhetoric might be called a secular version of what theologian James Wharton called a rhetoric of the "occasion of the Word of God."[44] Wharton drew his example from the Old Testament Israel of Nehemiah's time. These Israelites were as far removed from the exodus from Egypt as postwar Americans were from Lexington and Concord. Yet that memory, through their rhetorical retelling of the exodus, was the basis for Israeli identities as a people and as a nation. Their religious reality was, in other words, constructed through the sacred myths they chose "to recall and preserve this many sided and endlessly variegated set of memories" that delineated Israel's "own identity, its present and its future."[45] Such memories can fade and people need to be recalled to or reminded of their greatness. Wharton described the characteristics of a rhetoric that recalls a people out of their current disinterest. First, such a rhetoric must draw upon the stockpile of previous images, selectively remembered, that are the essence of the nation's identity. These images constitute what the nation holds to be its sacred values. The concept of the sacred, as used here, need not be synonymous with the specifically religious: "It is rather the utilization of the religio-sacred as a perspective for the understanding of ostensibly non-religious phenomena such as authority, community, and personality."[46] The concept of the sacred is endemic to community, for no nation can exist continuously without such values, without what Emile Durkheim called "the collective sentiments and the collective ideas which make its personality."[47] Churchill clearly drew from the primary values of the dominant rhetoric of World War II, the protection of sacred rights and democratic procedures, to give a new sense of understanding and mission in the postwar world. The speech was prophetic. The sacred values of the American people were at stake, a crisis was at hand.

But just as he was reasserting the values of the dominant war rhetoric, he was also subverting other aspects of that rhetoric. That rhetoric had maintained that the Soviet Union was a major power allied with and friendly to the United States. It ignored the differences between the two nations and stressed instead their similarities. Inherent in this rhetoric was the belief that the Soviet Union could be trusted to act in alliance with Western nations not only to defeat the Nazis, but also to secure the peace after their defeat. The iron curtain metaphor subverted this part of the dominant rhetoric as it drew from the subordinate rhetoric of anticommunist that had lain latent during the war. This subordinate rhetoric emphasized the ideological differences between communism and Western democracy and warned against Soviet intentions.

The Power of Metaphor

The power of Churchill's stylistic figure drew from this tradition as well as the unique American experience. It was rich in associations and connotations. The iron curtain created a warlike image of two sides divided by a line. With the memory of the frontier firmly imbedded in the American experience, drawing a line was a familiar concept pregnant with meaning:

When Americans felt themselves or their beliefs threatened, they drew a line and dared their enemies to cross it. . . . They gathered their friends behind the line; by definition, those on the other side of the frontier were enemies. The expected response to the drawing of a line was a violent effort to cross it; a line was a "dare," a challenge which had to be accepted. The expected response to a violation of such a frontier line was violent defense; the American was not fighting merely for a boundary or for a piece of territory but for the primary distinction between Americans and others. What was at stake in the drawing of lines and the establishment of frontiers was *identity*, personal, communal, and national.[48]

This divisive image plucked powerful memory chords within Americans, catalogued in countless stories and songs, enacted by children who played "cowboys and Indians" and by film stars from William S. Hart to John Wayne. In his speech Churchill carefully said that the Soviet Union had drawn the line in eastern Europe. This served two important purposes. First, he placed blame for the split among the allies solely on the Soviet Union. Throughout the early period of the cold war blaming the Soviets for breaking the war-time alliance was of paramount importance. It was a recurring theme in both private decisionmaking and public rhetoric that the United States not appear as the one who destroyed this alliance. In the emerging ideological rhetoric the Soviet Union was malevolent and aggressive, the Western powers innocent and defensive. Responsibility for dividing the world had to be placed on the Soviets to justify Western actions in response so that they would seem defensive rather than offensive. The Western meaning, then, attached to Churchill's speech that divided the world was that the former prime minister only described a division already in place. Second, interpreting events in eastern Europe as a line drawn by the Soviets fit his purpose of urging Americans to summon up their moral resolve to confront this dangerous dare that had been flung in their faces. Recalling the heroic myths of American society and wedding British and American democratic principles, Churchill sought to unite the moral purposes of the two as a prelude to brave the perils that lay ahead.

The image of an iron curtain also connoted mystery. A curtain is a theatrical convention that divides the audience from the mysteries that accompany a live drama. A curtain conceals the various elements that go into preparing for a public presentation: actors being people rather than characters, stagehands rushing to move scenery or props to simulate an illusion of location, lights being tested to throw just the right brightness or shadow over the places that the director wants illuminated. The impenetrable "iron" (with its concomitant reference to the German Iron Cross) only served to make the curtain more mysterious and fearful. Thus, Churchill combined the conventional mysteries of the theater with the image of wilderness, that area beyond the frontier "line" that held unknown and potentially savage terrors. Once the curtain goes up, what the audience sees is a carefully contrived semblance of reality, as emotions are manipulated to evoke laughter or awesome terror. This conception subsequently pervaded interpretations of Soviet actions. Specific actions were never what they seemed, and one had to lift the masks from actors to interpret those actions for what they were. Expert interpreters functioned much as drama critics searching beneath the surface of the drama to find its real meaning. The ideological consciousness of those expert interpreters provided the categories for this interpretation, and much of that ideology began to be articulated by Churchill at Fulton.

The Dominant and Subordinate Rhetorics

Churchill drew both from the dominant and subordinate rhetoric of World War II. He used the dominant rhetoric of cooperation in the battle against a totalitarian enemy for the purpose of sustaining democratic principles, but stressed only British–American collaboration. He incorporated the content of the subordinate rhetoric of anticommunism to define the new diabolical enemy of these principles. This speech, therefore, relied on the form of the old reality (an all-out war to defend the arsenals of democracy), but created a new reality of content by substituting communism for fascism as the new enemy (a diabolic enemy bent on imposing tyranny and totalitarianism on the rest of the world). Churchill made the new reality frightfully vivid through the iron curtain metaphor. Max Lerner, writing a week after Fulton, accurately predicted that the term would have enormous currency because "it rolls up into a single image all the fears that the Soviet state has invoked since the Russian Revolution almost thirty years ago."[49]

CHURCHILL AS POLITICAL PROPHET

The classical role of the prophet is useful in understanding Churchill's rhetoric, although not in the sense of the prophet as a predictor of the future, as is usually meant when Churchill's speech is described as prophesy.[50] The classical role of the prophet in the ancient Eastern world was not as "foreteller" but rather as "forthteller."[51] Such prophets often did predict what future would arise out of the conditions of their time unless those conditions were changed, but the idea of prediction was a by-product of prophesy and not of its essence. The prophet's role was to describe the political situation of a people in a rhetoric that presented that situation in moral terms. The prophet was interested in the affairs of state, but not as an official leader because "the place for a prophet is not in office, but rather as a mentor of the state."[52] The prophet thus spoke, not for official purposes, but for moral purposes. The message had been given to the prophet; he had been raised up to do this work. In the case of the Hebrew prophets this calling was distinctly from God, but in proximate cultures, such as China, the calling was described in general terms of a moral imperative. One of the functions of prophets who lived during the establishment of Israel's monarchy was to define Israel as God's chosen nation, morally superior to foreign nations. The prophets "were ready to stir up king and people against foreign foes and to promise the help of the God of Israel."[53] While later prophets were concerned with social reform and social justice, the early prophets were concerned with national survival. The authority of the prophets came not only from God, but also from the message they preached, a message of survival in the face of heathen enemies.

Churchill's role at Fulton fit the model of the early prophets of Israel. His authority did not come from any office he held, for he was now a private citizen. While his reputation, bolstered by an introduction by the president, gave him a hearing, his ultimate authority came from his message itself. Churchill felt compelled to present a new picture of the world; one divided between good and evil, between "God's people" and malevolent foreigners. As mentor to the official leaders he warned that national survival was at stake. The principles that defined Christian civilization were in danger. It was a time for a recognition of the new state of the world. The world had been divided by an iron curtain, behind which an expansionist Soviet Union plotted to conquer eastern European nations and directed the subversion of others as well. Its virus threatened democratic principles and Western survival. The line Stalin had laid down was a challenge to Western nations to recall their recent heroic past and the moral values that sustained them, or else all was lost. The sonorous language and precisely timed delivery gave even greater impact to Churchill's role as mentor to officials, as prophet to people.

THE IRON CURTAIN AS COMMUNITY EVENT

Churchill's greatest influence was not so much on the general public as upon governmental officials and journalists. His prophetic proclamation with the connotations of crisis associated with it was immediately picked up by the press. The headline on the front page of the *New York Times* the day after Fulton announced: "U.S. Sends Two Protests to Russia; Churchill Assails Soviet Policy." A sub-headline stated: "Iron Curtain Dividing Europe Is Not What We Fought For, Churchill Says At Fulton, Mo."[54] The president, on his way back to Washington from Fulton, stopped in Columbus, Ohio to address a meeting of the Federal Council of Churches of Christ in America. Truman underscored that "mankind now stands in the doorway to destruction," with the knowledge of atomic energy. The Council of Churches had just issued a report by a special commission of twenty church leaders on atomic energy that spoke of the "possibility of a speedy end to man's life on earth."[55] The specter of atomic power, as Churchill had noted in his speech, provided a framework that made it easy to believe that crisis was indeed at hand. *Time* magazine commented on the president's trip to Columbus with Churchill's analogical linkage from the past on its editorial mind: "In a week that was oddly reminiscent of the weeks before Munich, a bewildered Harry Truman traveled from Missouri to Ohio."[56] This foreboding was announced even though the Soviet Union had done little to precipitate such an analogy. One must conclude that Churchill's words, rather than Stalin's actions, shaped this perception.

The heightening atmosphere of crisis continued in subsequent political discourse among officials in government. Secretary of State Byrnes, in a speech in New York on March 16, spoke of America's commitment to peace through the United Nations. "We do not propose," said Byrnes, "to seek an alliance with the Soviet Union against Great Britain or an alliance of Great Britain against the Soviet Union," and thus rejected the explicit proposal of Fulton. But those sentiments were expressed in the context of his speech devoted to keeping the United States militarily strong, based on an analogy between current conditions and the prewar years. "This tragic experience makes us realize that weakness invites aggression," said Byrnes. Churchill had said that the only thing the Soviets respect is military strength. Churchill's reference to military strength and weakness as well as his use of the Munich analogy made Byrnes's talk of military preparedness less a political risk than it had been just weeks before Fulton.

Representative Karl Mundt of South Dakota spoke in Detroit on April 8, saying that the most searching question in the "District of Confusion" was: "Can we get along with Russia?" After describing Soviet leaders as confident and realistic, he launched into a diatribe against the USSR as "a completely totalitarian state, much like Hitler's." Mundt reached back two years to recount his visit to the Soviet Union. His primary evidence was that the N.K.V.D. office building's lights were on at 3:00

A.M. and implied that they were busy arresting "the people who dare to try to oppose anything supported by the communist regime in Moscow."

The Soviet Union Mundt described was a country on the march, using three techniques: absorption, adoption, and assimilation. Not only were these techniques working in eastern Europe, but also in the United States where Americans were "not immune to the method which the USSR has so successfully developed," because "the processes of assimilation are directed here at home by American Communists through nice-sounding organizations attracting the support of well-meaning but completely gullible Americans." Mundt said that he was gratified that he had seen an about-face in foreign policy during the past thirty days. But he felt that if we had maintained a tough stance previously "we would have broken open this iron curtain."[57] As the iron curtain metaphor was repeated, it began to assume a reality that made it politically easier to see the growing specter of a Communist threat. Mundt added, however, that he was not worried about this military threat because the United States had the atomic bomb and was clearly superior to the Soviets in navy, army, air force, and industrial capability. The threat had not yet assumed the massive proportions it later would, but Churchill had begun to focus attention on this new political reality.

THE "CRISIS" IN IRAN AS LEGITIMIZING EVENT

The perception of a threat grew in subsequent weeks. The "event" that transpired immediately after Fulton that provided an early application of the new definition of political reality was not an action but an announcement. Two days after Churchill's speech the New York Times carried a front-page headline: "Soviets in East Iran Despite Promise."[58] The Soviet announcement was that, while they were removing some of their troops from Iran, others were staying in northern Iran until the situation stabilized. Iran, along with Greece and Turkey, comprised what was known as the "Northern Tier," an oil-rich area that was the nexus of important trade routes and traditional Anglo–Russian rivalry. The Soviet announcement was treated as a crisis, even though up till that time there had been little expressed American interest of significance at stake in Iran.

In late 1945 Herbert Matthews had written about the Soviet Union's need for oil and of the rivalry in the area. The Soviets, he said, were seeking security for their great and valuable oil region.[59] In two articles for the New York Times in December 1945, Clifton Daniels had reported his investigation in Iran, detailing the chaotic political and economic conditions there. Landlords owned more than 99 percent of the land, he wrote, with the rest of the population being a "nation in rags."[60] The press, in short, described the situation in Iran as unstable, but wrote about it in terms of geo-political interests, not ideological imperatives.

By the time of Churchill's speech at Fulton, however, journalists began to characterize Iran as being of such interest to U.S. goals that the continuing presence of Soviet troops constituted a crisis, reminiscent of Munich. The background, briefly, was this. There had been an agreement at Potsdam that British and Soviet forces would be removed from Iran six months after the war's end. Both had defended the oil fields from the Nazis since 1942. The date for removal of troops fell on March 2, 1946. Although the Soviets had said at the Moscow Conference in December that the date might be premature in light of the political turmoil in Iran, Western officials expected that the original date for withdrawal would be observed. The growing concern about Soviet intentions within the Truman administration created the perception of a crisis when the Soviets announced that they were withdrawing their forces on the agreed date, except for those in the northern province of Azerbaijan.[61] Not getting all the Soviet troops out of Iran by the scheduled date created the crisis and the belief that the U.S. government had to act swiftly to get them removed. The day after Churchill's speech Secretary Byrnes sent a harsh note to Moscow demanding Soviet withdrawal, and soon thereafter they did.

The Iranian crisis is instructive. Coming as it did shortly after Kennan's long telegram and immediately after Churchill's speech, the U.S. response may be taken as the first application of the doctrine of containment (though it had not yet been publicly announced) which both the American diplomat and the former prime minister had advocated. Undoubtedly speeches calling for firmness given by Senator Vandenberg on February 27, by Secretary Byrnes on February 28, and by John Foster Dulles on March 1 also contributed to the decision to send the harsh note. That Byrnes made it public without waiting for a Soviet response indicated that he intended to be tough with the Soviets. The administration's perception was that the Soviet refusal to withdraw symbolized both a broken promise (caused by the sinister motives Kennan had attributed to the Soviets) and its policy of expansionism (that both Kennan and Churchill believed to be their primary policy). They eventually came to believe that the stern note they had issued caused the Soviet withdrawal. Thus, a pattern was established. According to the administration, Soviet actions in Iran validated its belief that she was inherently expansionist, and the precipitate action by the United States was the most practical response to expansionism. Both legitimized the chilling rhetoric of Kennan and Churchill. The pattern would be repeated endlessly in the future, each time with escalating responses by the United States.

To understand how Iran functioned within the rhetorical process one must understand the nature of political knowledge. Jacques Ellul wrote: "A fact does not become political except to the extent that opinion forms around it and it commands public attention."[62] Such a fact finds its meaning in the rhetoric—both private and public—used to explain that fact, but with two conditions attached to it: that "the government or a powerful group decides to take it into account and, secondly, if public opinion considers it a fact, and at that, a fact of political nature."[63] In the case of the "crisis" in Iran, opinion had already formed about Soviet motives in the eastern Mediterranean due to a variety of rhetorical efforts, Kennan's private telegram and Churchill's public speech being only the most conspicuous examples for administration officials and journalists, respectively. Since Kennan and Churchill generally agreed on Soviet intentions to expand, the events in Iran became self-fulfilling prophecy of the anticommunist rhetoric that preceded these events. More important, the Iranian crisis legitimized the rhetoric by seeming to provide a specific set of events that confirmed these warnings about the Soviet Union, when it could just as easily be argued that the meaning the administration attached to Iran arose simultaneously with its growing anticommunism.

At the time, however, the Truman administration was unwilling to make a complete break with the Soviet Union. A note of protest sufficed to achieve a limited objective. During the remainder of the year, diplomatic relations continued to dominate, but the emerging new political reality of division and confrontation made compromise more and more difficult. The public rhetoric of the iron curtain thus received a rudimentary legitimization during the Iran crisis, falling as it did hard upon the heels of that speech.

BEYOND THE IRON CURTAIN

The initial rhetoric of Churchill carried an authority of its own, beginning with the reputation of the man himself and extending from his prophetic message. But to alter political reality the rhetorical process must be expanded by additional spokespeople and an additional vocabulary. That reality must be maintained and legitimated to become ultimately authoritative, driving out alternative interpretations. This process was to reach its apotheosis following the rhetoric of the Truman Doctrine, but it began in incipient form after Fulton.

After Churchill's speech the newspapers could not write enough about Soviet affairs.[64] Editorials soon changed their stance to focus on the Soviet Union with growing damnation. Liebovich remarked that "a speech by a single man, who no longer held public office, had far greater impact on the news organizations than did the movements of millions of soldiers or hundreds of edicts in occupied parts of the world."[65] He concluded that "Churchill had altered the states of mind of editors," and added that in the ensuing months while the Soviets reduced hostile actions, "the news organizations expressed increasing alarm over the perceived threat of world communism."[66]

What had happened in the aftermath of Churchill's speech and the Iranian "crisis" was that a terministic screen of anticommunism had developed in the consciousness of many reporters and editors. Kenneth Burke described the effects of this screen in this fashion: *"many of the 'observations'* [of actual events and people] *are but implications of the particular terminology in terms of which the observations are made.* In brief, much that we take as observations about 'reality' may be but the spinning out of possibilities implicit in our particular choice of terms [about that reality]."[67] Once Churchill announced a bipolar division, journalists adopted it and began "observing" events within that division and set about "spinning out" the possibilities implicit in it as they reported on succeeding events. Most prominent in this terministic screen was the threat the Soviet Union posed to Christian civilization. And the perception of threat prompted rhetoric of nihilation for enemies of the United States and therapy for heretics. Such subsidiary rhetorics served to maintain, legitimize, and extend the iron curtain rhetoric. This process would assume ritual proportions later, but it began in incipient form in the months after Fulton.

Nihilation of the Enemy and Therapy for Heretics

H. V. Kaltenborn exemplified the rhetoric of nihilation. In the 1940s Kaltenborn was the most listened to of all American radio commentators and, with his seeming encyclopedia knowledge of world affairs, probably the most credible. He had demonstrated repeatedly that he had no deep-seated ideological bias against the Soviets but his commentaries can serve as a reflection of changing opinion about the Soviets. Kaltenborn had visited the USSR some five times and, in 1937, had "explained that he felt the Soviet people sought only peace and goodwill."[68] When Hitler and Stalin signed their non-aggression pact in 1939 he refrained from criticizing the Soviets, but when both Germany and the Soviet Union invaded Poland, he attacked Stalin's action bitterly. That all changed when war broke out. In 1943 he told his listeners that the United States was in no position to tell the Soviet Union what to do in the postwar world, since she had done more to win the war than anyone among the Allies. In 1944 he advised his audience to ignore those who argued that the Soviets wished to spread bolshevism. But by early 1946 Kaltenborn was becoming more critical of Soviet behavior, and on the night of Churchill's Fulton speech he devoted his entire broadcast to the speech. He concluded his program by saying that Churchill "spoke as a great orator, a great leader, a great believer in democracy and peace. We will do well to heed his words."[69] Throughout the remainder of the year he grew more vociferous in his criticism of the Soviet Union, until by February of the following year he had concluded that "the communist has no respect for truth, for pity, for human life, for individual dignity. The leaders in the Kremlin are ruthless revolutionaries whose constant objective is the Communist revolution."[70] Thus were Soviets transformed in this rhetoric of nihilation into subhuman monsters devoid of human feelings, a rhetorical characterization necessary for war with a foreign enemy, necessary for suspension of basic liberties for domestic enemies.

While the rhetoric of nihilation began to validate the authority of the iron curtain interpretation of communists by consigning the enemy to the ranks of the subhuman, the rhetoric of therapy enabled repentant heretics within American society to confess their past sins and convert to political orthodoxy. Their testimony to their conversion also served to validate the emerging reality. The most prominent of the ex-communist witnesses of this early period was Louis Francis Budenz, who testified before the House Committee on UnAmerican activities in late 1946. Budenz was no ordinary ex-communist, but one who had worked his way up in the party to become managing editor of the *Daily Worker*. At the end of the war he had become disillusioned with the party and had reconverted (with the assistance of Monsignor Fulton Sheen) to catholicism. By agreeing to testify about his past associations and to name names, he demonstrated the authenticity of his rejection of communism and his conversion to emerging orthodoxy:

Once launched, he never looked back: from October 1946 until his "retirement" in 1957, he testified thirty-three times, wrote four books and numerous articles, and established a reputation not merely as an *informer* whose role might be confined to the perpetual reiteration of his own experiences, but also as an *expert* capable of generalizing about the nature of Communism, its aims and philosophy.[71]

In his first appearances before HUAC Budenz "named Gerhart Eisler as the Kremlin's top agent in the United States and told HCUA that all Communists were 'a part of the Russian fifth column.' "[72] On the basis of his testimony the Eisler family was hauled before the HUAC in early 1947. Gerhart Eisler refused to answer questions, but his sister testified against him including her interesting description of him as having "Bolshevik-trained eyes."[73] She accused him of being a communist agent and of having been responsible for various political murders. When Gerhart Eisler stowed away on a ship after jumping bail, his escape and reappearance in East Germany seemed to confirm the truth of his sister's testimony and Budenz's accusations.[74]

Budenz set the pattern for ex-communists. He recanted his previous political allegiances. To prove his sincerity—as if it were therapeutic—he proffered names of others he knew or believed to be communists. In return the committee praised his conversion as well as his honesty in testifying, mutually satisfactory congratulations. Richard Rovere concluded that no one "has had any greater influence on the public view of the Communist problem than Louis F. Budenz."[75] Joseph Alsop concurred: "Louis Budenz has played the decisive part in convincing numbers of our people that treachery teems in all departments of our national life." He observed that Budenz had gained such authority that "valid proofs" were no longer needed by the press or the public. An accusation by an ex-communist was enough to garner the next day's headline and "the accused is marked thereafter as a traitor to his country."[76] To achieve the status of loyal citizen, Americans called before the committee had to engage in this kind of therapeutic rhetoric of confessing past sins and proving the therapy had worked by proffering names of others. There were those, of course, who did not avail themselves of this rhetorical means for rehabilitation. They would be banished to live outside the moral order, consigned to the blacklist or unemployment line. Refusing the rhetoric of therapy, they would have the rhetoric of nihilation imposed upon them. Budenz set the pattern and a frightening pattern it was.

PERCEPTIONS NARROW

In retrospect, September 1946 was a momentous month within the Truman administration. Since Churchill's speech the president had been pursuing a two-track approach to the Soviet Union. On the one track he refused to embrace publicly the division among the allies Churchill had drawn at Fulton. Throughout the year, in fact, he continued to express his hope for cooperation among the allies to secure the peace.[77] In private he tolerated Secretary of Commerce Henry Wallace's criticism of a hardline approach to the Soviets. On the other track Truman was using tough words toward the Soviet actions in Iran and toward its proposals for sharing joint Russian–Turkish defense of the Black Sea Straits. In both cases the firm protests worked. Balancing peaceful cooperation with stern protests was a delicate rhetorical task that was bound eventually to cause Truman to tip one way or the other. There is considerable evidence to support the belief that Truman had already made up his mind about which of the two tracks was more effective in dealing with the Soviet Union, but it was in September that perceptions within the administration narrowed so significantly that the official anticommunism of the following years became almost inevitable. The two events that influenced this constriction were the firing of Henry Wallace and the Clifford-Elsey report. The former removed the rhetorical stream of cooperation and coexistence from the administration; the latter coalesced the emerging rhetoric of strident anticommunism within the executive branch.

The Firing of Henry Wallace

Henry Wallace had been the voice of conciliation toward the Soviet Union within the Truman administration from the beginning.[78] Although he was critical of the growing momentum toward a harder line in foreign policy, Wallace remained loyal to the Democratic party, often expressing his views to Truman in private, rather than airing them publicly. In a now-famous letter to the president on July 23, 1946, a letter later made public, Wallace expressed his views clearly. Asking how U.S. actions since the end of the war must look to other nations, Wallace answered his rhetorical question:

I mean by actions the concrete things like $13 billion for the War and Navy Departments, the Bikini tests of the atomic bomb and continued production of bombs, the plan to arm Latin America with our weapons, production of B–29s and planned production of B–36s, and the efforts to secure air bases spread over half the globe from which the other half of the globe can be bombed. I cannot but feel that these actions must make it look to the rest of the world as if we were only paying lip service to peace at the conference table.[79]

Wallace concluded that it must appear that we were either preparing for an inevitable war or that we were preparing to intimidate the rest of mankind. As the Truman administration grew more adamant about the Soviet Union, a confrontation was inevitable between the president and his secretary of commerce.

The political crisis that led to Truman's request for Wallace's resignation came as the result of the political uproar over a speech Wallace gave before the National Citizens Political Action Committee in New York City at Madison Square Garden on September 12, 1946. Wallace had been warned that the Department of State would never clear his speech on foreign policy, so he took it directly to the president. Wallace claimed that he had spent an hour with Truman, going over the speech page by page.[80] When the speech was released to the public in advance, Truman was asked about it at a press conference. He said he approved the whole speech and that what Wallace had to say was in line with the position his administration was taking. Richard Walton stated that it proved to be "one of the most explosive speeches in American political history."[81]

The audience of 20,000 that gathered in Madison Square Garden to hear Wallace was strongly opposed to a hard line toward the Soviet Union: "Before Wallace rose to speak, they passed a resolution assailing America's foreign policy and loudly cheered Claude Pepper's fervid denunciation of the diplomacy of the Truman administration."[82] The bias of the audience, which included some American communists, was reflected in the reception Wallace's remarks received. Boos, catcalls, and shouts interrupted the speaker whenever he voiced even mild criticism of Soviet actions.[83] When compared to Churchill's speech, Wallace's address was a moderate appeal for a nonideological foreign policy, "not an apologia for Soviet behavior or an extravagant condemnation of American diplomacy."[84]

If Churchill was a prophet in the manner of Israel's *early* prophets, rhetorically depicting a godly nation superior to foreign nations, Wallace was a prophet in the manner of Israel's *later* period, preaching the need for social reform within the nation itself and for justice in relations with other nations. Wallace said that an atomic age made war unthinkable, thus agreeing with Churchill that national survival could well be at stake in the choices world powers made at this critical point in history. But his prophetic answer to the crisis was not to take a stance of moral superiority in an effort to defeat foreign nations but to take a moral stance for social reform in the United States. Wallace began with a prophetic litany that decried injustice in America: "The price of peace—for us and for every nation in the world—is the price of giving up prejudice, hatred, fear, ignorance."[85] He followed with specifics, citing a recent lynching in Georgia, and a plea for the United States to contribute to economic justice in the world. Having established his moral position, Wallace moved to the central issue of his address, foreign policy.

Wallace's speech was a direct challenge to the iron curtain interpretation of Churchill's Fulton speech. He denied explicitly that he spoke from a pacifist position, stating that he had favored preparedness in the 1930s, thereby attempting to exempt himself from the Munich analogy. Since it was an election year Wallace used the occasion to attack Thomas Dewey for his support of an alliance with the British, while answering Churchill at the same time. Such an alliance, said Wallace, "may sound attractive because we both speak the same language and many of our customs and traditions have the same historical background." But he disavowed such an alliance. He said bluntly that "the British imperialistic policy in the Near East alone, combined with Russian retaliation, would lead straight to war unless we have a clearly defined and realistic policy of our own." He then outlined such a policy based on spheres of influence. By this he neither meant "getting tough" nor "appeasement" toward the Soviet Union. Instead, he stated in one of the most controversial sections of the speech: "On our part, we should recognize that we have no more business in the *political* affairs of Eastern Europe than

Russia has in the *political* affairs of Latin America, Western Europe, and the United States." This statement was a direct contradiction of the ideological policy Churchill had advocated.

Wallace concluded his address with prophetic predictions. He urged that competition between the United States and the Soviet Union be placed on a friendly basis. As the friendly competition continued, he predicted that the two countries would become more alike, the Soviets "forced to grant more and more of the personal freedoms" (at which point he was interrupted by hissing from the audience) and the United States "more and more absorbed with the problems of social-economic justice." Just as Israel rejected the later prophets of social reform, so too was the prophesy of Wallace rejected.

The storm erupted the next day. It seemed obvious to everyone, except Truman, that Wallace's speech was a sharp departure from the current policy toward the USSR. Many newspapers called for Wallace's dismissal. At first Truman tried to explain that he had only approved of Wallace's right to make the speech, not the speech itself. But his explanation only caused more questions to be raised. Senator Arthur Vandenberg wired the president from the Conference on Foreign Ministers in Paris, which he was attending at the invitation of the president, that he could only cooperate with one secretary of state at a time. Secretary Byrnes threatened to resign if Wallace was not silenced. The letter of July 23 was leaked to the press, and in a week's time Truman requested Wallace's resignation.

With his resignation Wallace was branded a heretic. A line had been drawn and one was on one side or the other. It is a measure of the degree to which the iron curtain interpretation of Soviet–American relations had entered the consciousness of opinion leaders both within and without governmental circles that an immediate uproar over Wallace's speech exploded. But advocates of the hard line had to account for Wallace in some way. If a responsible leader—and certainly a former vice president and secretary of commerce would seem to be such a person—could believe an alternate view, he represented a challenge to the authenticity of the new political reality that was inexorably emerging. Therefore a rhetoric of nihilation had to be applied to him.

Firing Wallace was the first step in subverting his beliefs. Truman seemed to have convinced himself that Wallace's views were caused by an unbalanced mind rather than a different interpretation of events. After meeting with him, Truman noted that he was not certain Wallace was "fundamentally sound intellectually."[86] In a letter home the president wrote: "Well, now he's out, and the crackpots are having conniption fits. I'm glad they are. It convinces me I'm right."[87] This private thought was echoed by the public press. *Time* magazine featured Wallace on its cover with the caption "America Must Choose." But in the lengthy cover article, it launched an attack on Wallace and his "counterfeit" view of reality. Speaking of a year of "bewildering confusions," *Time* stated that most citizens now believed the Soviet Union to be an antagonist with an "unnatural totalitarian scheme." As for Wallace, it described him as not merely mistaken about events, but as completely inauthentic: "a man who has read much but is not well read, thought much but is not a thinker, known too many people to have made many real friends. He is a scientist who is governed by his emotions, a believer who has rejected faith."[88] The *San Francisco Chronicle* succinctly summarized this nihilistic rhetorical characterization of Henry Wallace. It wrote that he did not recognize "reality."[89] Of course, the "reality" he did not recognize was the iron curtain reality that was beginning to permeate American consciousness.

The Clifford-Elsey Report on Soviet–American Relations

The political reality that Wallace was out of touch with was one that had been drawn together and presented to President Harry Truman in a sweeping report on September 24, only four days after firing his secretary of commerce. The report had been more than two months in preparation. Soon after the Iranian "crisis," Truman told Clark Clifford, his special counsel, that the Soviets were "chiseling" and that the time had come to take a stand. He directed Clifford to make a comprehensive study of relations between the two nations that he could use for policy-making purposes.[90] Clifford consulted with various members of the administration, including Kennan, and with George Elsey prepared the summary. Henry Wallace had spoken of national powers and conflicting interests. This report spoke of a worldwide ideological war between communism and capitalism.

In the words of Arthur Krock, "American Relations with the Soviet Union," as Clifford called his memorandum, supplied President Truman "with every detail of the wartime relationship with the U.S.S.R., it charted the postwar prospect with startling prescience in which the shape and thrust of Truman's subsequent great programs—the Greek-Turk aid legislation, the Marshall Plan, the North Atlantic Alliance (including NATO), and what later became known as the 'Truman Doctrine'—were outlined."[91] The report was divided into an introduction and six separate sections. It drew on the division Churchill had made at Fulton and especially from Kennan's "long telegram," which it quoted at length. However, Clifford and Elsey eliminated Kennan's references to Russia's historical desires to focus exclusively on ideological motives for Soviet actions. Section one stated with unmistakable clarity what would become the prevailing ideological interpretation of these motives:

The fundamental tenet of the communist philosophy embraced by Soviet leaders is that the peaceful coexistence of communist and capitalist nations is impossible. The defenders of the communist faith, as the present Soviet rulers regard themselves, assume that conflict between the Soviet Union and the leading capitalist powers of the western world is inevitable and the party leaders believe that it is their duty to prepare the Soviet Union for the inevitable conflict which their doctrine predicts. Their basic policies, domestic and foreign, are designed to strengthen the Soviet Union and to insure its victory in the predicted coming struggle between Communism and Capitalism.[92]

From this ideological perspective, Clifford went on to recount in the next two sections Soviet–American agreements from 1942 to 1946 and Soviet violations of those agreements. The account laid blame for conflicts solely on the Soviet Union. The melodramatic form pervaded these sections. (Interestingly, Clifford wrote that many of these conflicts were caused by the ways in which communists interpreted words of these agreements. He accused them of "exploiting . . . Soviet definitions of terms.") The fifth section stated that Soviet activities threatened the United States both in American foreign interests and American domestic life. Clifford contended that the American Communist party engaged in propaganda and espionage and therefore constituted a serious threat to U.S. national security. In the final section, the memorandum resonated with Churchill's division of the world and his plea for an Anglo–American alliance:

If we find it impossible to enlist Soviet cooperation in the solution of world problems, we should be prepared to join with the British and other Western countries in an attempt to build up a world of our own which will pursue its own objectives and will recognize the Soviet orbit as a distinct entity with which conflict is not predestined but with which we cannot pursue common aims.

But Clifford went further. He called for a global policy that would assist "all democratic countries" threatened by the USSR, that would maintain U.S. military forces sufficient to "restrain" Soviet expansionism, and that would expose and eliminate "communist penetration" within the United States. Although Clifford mentioned that economic aid to other countries would be needed and American economic might should form the basis of its policy of restraining the Soviet Union, he stressed military conceptualization of the problem. Indeed, the Clifford-Elsey memorandum was a militarization of Kennan's "long telegram" and Churchill's speech, and contained none of the subtleties of Kennan's analysis nor the recognition of Soviet security concerns given lip service by Churchill.[93]

Truman spent much of the evening reading the memorandum. The next morning he asked Clifford how many copies he had of it. When

Clifford answered ten, the president ordered all of them confiscated and put under lock and key. "This is so hot," Truman said, "if this should come out now it could have an exceedingly unfortunate impact on our efforts to try to develop some relationship with the Soviet Union."[94] At this time the president was unwilling to act directly on these recommendations. However, less than six months later he would not only act but use it to lay the foundation for a new foreign policy. Margaret Truman linked his Truman Doctrine speech directly with the memorandum, what she described and the administration seemed to accept as a *"realistic* assessment of the present and recent past."[95] In other words, the memorandum spelled out the reality to which Wallace had objected and for which he had been banished from the corridors of power, a comprehensive political reality that would guide future U.S. policy in both domestic and foreign spheres.

CONCLUSION

There is widespread agreement among historians that an unmistakable change in American–Soviet relations occurred during February and March of 1946. D. F. Fleming called it "a turning point," one that came, in Fraser Harbutt's words, with "remarkable suddenness."[96] In John Lewis Gaddis's view, the period "produced a fundamental reorientation of United States policy toward the Soviet Union," a reorientation that Robert Messer stated reversed "the premises upon which American Soviet policy had been based."[97] Daniel Yergin said that during this time "American officialdom for the most part had resolved the contradictory interpretations about Soviet behavior and intentions into a coherent view."[98] This reorientation can be ascribed to a number of factors including Stalin's speech and Kennan's interpretation of Soviet motives, the Iranian crisis, the hard line taken by the Truman administration, as well as Churchill's speech.

To attribute this sudden change to one speech would be hyperbolic. But Churchill supplied a prophetic view of a divided world, one that posed a threat to the civilized world's survival. His metaphor, "iron curtain," provided a shorthand means to spread that view so that his more elaborate interpretation of a new political reality eventually became an integral part of public discourse. More important, his speech provided a generic rhetorical moment for the public reorientation. Churchill argued for a specific policy, an alliance between Great Britain and the United States, but as public debate ensued, the American public heard that part of his message that fit its view of themselves and the world. What resonated in most Americans was not a realpolitik, but the utopian interpretation that had long defined America and was captured in the global division Churchill enunciated, a division between light and darkness, between a godly nation and the forces of evil. For the time that effect would suffice. In time it became profound.

But Churchill's address had a greater impact on two other audiences, audiences certainly more influential than the American public. To these listeners—the press and the president—he played both prophet and mentor about world affairs. Journalists who subscribed to Churchill's bipolar terministic screen began writing about Soviet–American affairs within the terms that Churchill had laid down. It should be remembered that for all the behind-the-scenes discussions, memoranda, and reports, the Fulton speech remained the dominant public effort of the year, a rhetorical focal point for subsequent public discussions both in support of his views and in opposition. When Henry Wallace sought to attack these terms and to substitute different terms for understanding Soviet–American disputes and prospects, he was fired from government and attacked for being mentally unbalanced. He was not merely urging a different interpretation; he was out of touch with "reality."

Churchill had even greater influence on President Truman, his final audience. In the aftermath of the speech and the events in Iran, Truman ordered the full review of relations between the United States and the Soviet Union. The Clifford-Elsey memorandum echoed the political perspective of Churchill by emphasizing the ideological conflict between the two countries but Americanized the need for an all-encompassing policy to combat communism. The year that began with the president still considering various approaches to deal with the Soviet Union ended with a much narrower perspective, as Ernest May pointed out: "The available evidence indicates that the perceptions of Truman and his advisers became less discriminating as time passed. . . . By the end of 1946 they no longer saw anything in Eastern Europe, the Mediterranean, or the Middle East except a baleful Soviet Union."[99] These perceptions and the ideological reasons for them remained confined to the White House for the most part, but they formed the perspective upon which the president was prepared to act. A new anticommunist consensus had begun to be formed and only awaited a propitious moment for its full public revelation. At the time, as Truman said, it was "too hot" to make public, but it was accepted within the ruling circles nonetheless.

Winston Churchill attested to the creation and growth of the new reality a year later. Feigning surprise that "such mild, mellifluous, carefully shaped and guarded sentiments should have caused so much commotion," he took satisfaction that in little more than a year "statements of this character are not seriously challenged in any part of the world today, outside the vast Communist or Communist-controlled regions."[100] His views, he observed, were now endorsed by American public opinion and formed official U.S. policy. "This is to me," Churchill wrote, "a very intense satisfaction."[101] The prophetic vision of a world divided that Churchill proclaimed at Westminster College in March initiated a public rhetorical process that would be expanded, maintained, and legitimated for years to come. It was the first public step. It would be elevated to the status of U.S. "doctrine" a year later and bear the eponym of the president who announced it: the Truman Doctrine.

NOTES

1. John W. Spanier, *American Foreign Policy Since World War II*, 9th ed. (New York: Holt, Rinehart and Winston, 1980), p. 24.

2. John Morton Blum, "Portrait of a Diarist," in *The Price of Vision: The Diary of Henry A. Wallace, 1942–1946*, ed. John Morton Blum (Boston: Houghton Mifflin, 1973), p. 47.

3. Louis Halle, *The Cold War as History* (New York: Harper and Row, 1967), p. 104.

4. Lord Moran, *Churchill, Taken from the Diaries of Lord Moran: The Struggle for Survival, 1940–1965* (Boston: Houghton Mifflin, 1966), p. 310. Churchill seemed to ignore the fact that the Soviets already occupied most of these territories by the time of the Potsdam meetings.

5. Quoted in Margaret Truman, *Harry S. Truman* (New York: Pocket Books, 1974), p. 339.

6. Hugh Thomas, *Armed Truce* (New York: Atheneum, 1988), pp. 504–5.

7. Quoted in Robert Donovan, *Conflict and Crisis: The Presidency of Harry S. Truman, 1945–1948* (New York: W. W. Norton, 1977), pp. 190–91.

8. On Truman's understanding of what Churchill would say at Fulton and the significance for U.S. policy, see Fraser J. Harbutt, *The Iron Curtain: Churchill, America, and the Origins of the Cold War* (New York: Oxford University Press, 1986), pp. 161–82.

9. Mark Sullivan, "Churchill—Greatness in Our Time," *Reader's Digest* (July 1945), pp. 1–2.

10. *Life* (January 7, 1946), p. 44.

11. All quotations from Churchill's speech, "The Sinews of Peace," are from *Winston S. Churchill: His Complete Speeches, 1887–1963*, vol. 7, ed. Robert Rhodes James (New York: Chelsea House, 1974), pp. 7,285–293.

12. For a fuller analysis of the speech, see Harbutt, *The Iron Curtain*, pp. 185–97.

13. Cited in James C. Humes, *Churchill: Speaker of the Century* (New York: Stein and Day, 1980), p. 207.

14. All quotations from Churchill's speech, "A Long and Hard War," are from *Winston S. Churchill: His Complete Speeches*, vol. 6, pp. 6,536–541.

15. All quotations from Churchill's speech, "Anglo–American Unity," are from *Winston Churchill: His Complete Speeches*, vol. 7, pp. 6,823–827.

16. Harbutt, *The Iron Curtain*, p. 184.

17. "Churchill and Russia," *Canadian Forum* 26 (April 1946), p. 3.

18. Humes, *Churchill*, p. 266.

19. Quoted in Harbutt, *The Iron Curtain*, p. 17.

20. Ibid., p. 28.

21. Humes, *Churchill*, p. 201.

22. David Rees, *Korea: The Limited War* (New York: St. Martin's Press, 1964), p. xi.

23. *New York Times* (March 7, 1946), pp. 5–6.

24. "Topics of the Times," *New York Times* (March 10, 1946), p. 8E.

25. "Europe's Capitals Stirred by Speech," *New York Times* (March 7, 1946), p. 5.

26. "Churchill Speech Hailed in London," *New York Times* (March 6, 1946), p. 6.

27. Quoted in *New York Times* (March 6, 1946), p. 5.

28. Jeremy K. Ward, "Winston Churchill and the Iron Curtain Speech," *The History Teacher* 1 (January 1968), p. 59.

29. All quotations are from the translation of the interview published in *New York Times* (March 14, 1946), p. 4.

30. *New York Times* (April 12, 1947), p. 19.

31. See D. F. Fleming's summary of Arthur Krock's five reasons for the failure of the address in *The Cold War and Its Origins*, vol. 1 (Garden City, NY. Doubleday, 1961), p. 352.

32. See Harbutt, *The Iron Curtain*, pp. 197–208. The first public opinion poll after Fulton said that of those who had heard about Churchill's speech, 40 percent opposed his ideas and only 18 percent approved. A month later, however, 85 percent approved.

33. Lewis Broad, *Winston Churchill* (New York: Hutchinson and Company, 1951), p. 572.

34. *New York Times* (March 7, 1946), p. 6.

35. *New York Times* (March 6, 1946), p. 6.

36. Takis Poulakos, "Isocrates's Use of Narrative in the Evagoras: Epideictic Rhetoric and Moral Action," *Quarterly Journal of Speech* 73 (August 1987), pp. 317–28.

37. Christine Oravec, " 'Observation' in Aristotle's Theory of Epideictic," *Philosophy and Rhetoric* 9 (Summer 1976), p. 171.

38. Paul Ricoeur, *Hermeneutics and the Human Sciences*, trans. John B. Thompson (Cambridge, UK: Cambridge University Press, 1981), p. 141.

39. Kenneth Burke, *Language as Symbolic Action: Essays on Life, Literature, and Method* (Los Angeles, CA: University of California Press, 1966), pp. 373–79.

40. Ibid., p. 375.

41. Ibid., p. 374.

42. Ibid., p. 375.

43. Joseph Church, *Language and the Discovery of Reality* (New York: Random House, 1961), p. 136.

44. James A. Wharton, "The Occasion of the Word of God," *Austin Seminary Bulletin* (September 1968), pp. 22–34.

45. Ibid., pp. 23–24.

46. Robert Nisbet, *The Sociological Tradition* (New York: Basic Books, 1966), p. 47.

47. Emile Durkheim, *The Elemental Forms of Religious Life*, trans. Joseph Swain (London: George Allen S. Unwin, 1915), p. 427.

48. James Oliver Robertson, *American Myth, American Reality* (New York: Hill and Wang, 1980), p. 92.

49. Quoted in Harbutt, *The Iron Curtain*, p. 208.

50. See, for example, Harbutt, *The Iron Curtain*, p. 208.

51. An excellent summary of the classical role of the prophet can be found in H. H. Rowley, *Prophecy and Religion in Ancient China and Israel* (New York: Harper and Brothers, 1956), pp. 1–17. See also Joseph Blenkinsopp, *A History of Prophecy in Israel* (Philadelphia: Westminster Press, 1983); and J. Lindblom, *Prophecy in Ancient Israel* (Philadelphia: Fortress Press, 1962).

52. Rowley, *Prophecy and Religion*, p. 37.

53. Ibid., p. 28.

54. *New York Times* (March 6, 1946), p. 1.

55. *New York Times* (March 7, 1946), p. 15.

56. *Time* (March 11, 1946), p. 17.

57. All quotations are taken from Karl E. Mundt, "Can We Get Along with Russia," *Vital Speeches of the Day* 12 (June 15, 1946), pp. 514–22.

58. *New York Times* (March 7, 1946), p. 1.

59. Quoted in Fleming, *The Cold War and Its Origins*, vol. 1, p. 341.

60. *New York Times* (December 7, 1945), p. 6.

61. For an analysis of the events leading to the crisis from one scholar who admittedly believes the Soviets were attempting to take over Iran and the Balkans, see Bruce R. Kuniholm, *The Origins of the Cold War in the Near East* (Princeton, NJ: Princeton University Press, 1980), pp. 304–42. For a different interpretation, one that stresses that the Iranian "crisis" was a "complication" arising out of the previous failure among the Big Three to reach concrete agreements and from the "political and economic fragility" of former colonial nations now freed from colonialism, see Adam Ulam, *Expansion and Coexistence: The History of Soviet Foreign Policy, 1917–1967* (New York: Praeger, 1968), pp. 425–29.

62. Jacques Ellul, *The Political Illusion* (New York: Alfred A. Knopf, 1967), p. 98.

63. Ibid., p. 100.

64. Louis Liebovich, *The Press and the Origins of the Cold War, 1944–1947* (New York: Praeger, 1988), p. 126.

65. Ibid., 128.

66. Ibid., pp. 129–30.

67. Burke, *Language as Symbolic Action*, p. 46.

68. Louis Liebovich, "H. V. Kaltenborn and the Origins of the Cold War: A Study of Personal Expression in Radio," *Journalism History* 14 (Summer-Autumn 1987), p. 48.

69. Ibid., p. 51.

70. Ibid.

71. David Chaute, *The Great Fear* (New York: Simon and Schuster, 1978), p. 123.

72. Ibid.

73. Testimony of Ruth Eisler, reprinted in *Thirty Years of Treason*, ed. Eric Bentley (New York: Viking, 1971), p. 65.

74. Hanns Eisler, his brother and a world-renowned composer, also testified.

He admitted that he had once made application to the Communist party in Germany, but never followed through on it. Nonetheless, Representative John Rankin of Mississippi treated him as a card-carrying communist anyway. Hanns also took off for Europe and lived in East Germany for the rest of his life.

75. Richard Rovere, "The Kept Witnesses," *Harper's* (May 1955), p. 34.

76. Joseph Alsop, "The Strange Case of Louis Budenz," *Atlantic* (April 1952), p. 29.

77. See his speech to the U.N. General Assembly in October 1946.

78. For a detailed discussion of Wallace's attempts to influence Truman to take a conciliatory line toward the Soviet Union, see Richard J. Walton, *Henry Wallace, Harry Truman, and the Cold War* (New York: Viking, 1976), pp. 33–117.

79. Quoted in ibid., pp. 89–90. This letter is analyzed in more detail in a subsequent chapter on critics of the new reality.

80. See *The Price of Vision*, pp. 617–26. Truman maintained that he only gave the speech a cursory glance. See his *Memoirs*, vol. 1 (Garden City, NY: Doubleday, 1955), p. 557.

81. Walton, *Henry Wallace*, p. 100.

82. J. Samuel Walker, *Henry A. Wallace and American Foreign Policy* (Westport, CT: Greenwood Press, 1976), p. 150.

83. Edward L. Schapsmeier and Frederick H. Schapsmeier, *Prophet in Politics: Henry A. Wallace and the War Years, 1940–1965* (Ames, IA: The Iowa State University Press, 1970), p. 155.

84. Walker, *Henry A. Wallace*, p. 153.

85. All quotations are from Henry A. Wallace, "The Way to Peace," *New Republic* (September 30, 1946), pp. 401–6.

86. Herbert Druks, *Harry S. Truman and the Russians, 1945–1953* (New York: Robert Speller and Sons, 1966), p. 107.

87. Harry Truman, *Off the Record: The Private Papers of Harry S. Truman*, ed. Robert H. Ferrell (New York: Harper and Row, 1980), p. 97.

88. *Time* (September 30, 1946), pp. 21–24.

89. Quoted in Liebovich, *The Press and the Origins of the Cold War*, p. 132.

90. Kuniholm, *The Origins of the Cold War in the Near East*, p. 369.

91. Arthur Krock, *Memoirs* (New York: Funk and Wagnalls, 1968), p. 224.

92. The memorandum was first published by Krock as an Appendix in his *Memoirs*, pp. 421–82. All quotations are taken from publication.

93. Despite his later protestations about having his telegram misunderstood by the administration, Kennan read the Clifford-Elsey memorandum, made some substantive changes, and wrote: "I think the general tone is excellent and I have no fault to find with it." Quoted in Deborah Welch Larson, *Origins of Containment: A Psychological Explanation* (Princeton, NJ: Princeton University Press, 1985), p. 295.

94. Quoted in Margaret Truman, *Harry S. Truman*, p. 379.

95. Ibid., emphasis added.

96. Fleming, *The Origins of the Cold War*, vol. 1, p. 347; Harbutt, *The Iron Curtain*, p. 153.

97. John Lewis Gaddis, *The United States and the Origins of the Cold War, 1941–1947* (New York: Columbia University Press, 1972), p. 284; Robert L. Messer,

The End of an Alliance: James F. Byrnes, Roosevelt, Truman and the Origins of the Cold War (Chapel Hill, NC: University of North Carolina Press, 1982), p. 181.

98. Daniel Yergin, *Shattered Peace: The Origins of the Cold War and the National Security State* (Boston: Houghton, Mifflin, 1977), p. 163.

99. Ernest R. May, *"Lessons" of the Past: The Use and Misuse of History in American Foreign Policy* (New York: Oxford University Press, 1973), p. 46.

100. *New York Times* (April 11, 1947), p. 27.

101. *New York Times* (April 12, 1947), p. 19.

Chapter Five

The Truman Doctrine

In his address to a joint session of Congress on March 12, 1947 President Truman officially committed the United States to an ideological cold war. *Newsweek* magazine called it "America's Date With Destiny."[1] With unmistakable clarity Truman stated the principle that would guide U.S. global strategy for the next four decades: "I believe it must be the policy of the United States to support free people who are resisting attempted subjugation by armed minorities or by outside pressures."[2] As many recognized at the time, it represented a new foreign policy for the United States. The day after the speech, James Reston of the *New York Times* compared its significance to that of the Monroe Doctrine, and it quickly became known as the "Truman Doctrine."[3]

The speech led to a transformation of Harry Truman and a transformation of U.S. foreign policy. Those transformations had been more than a year in the making. From the end of 1945 when concern over Soviet maneuvers turned to alarm, the administration had begun narrowing its perceptions and its options. Now, in March 1947 it was time to announce publicly this policy transformation. Truman's address built on the division Churchill had drawn at Fulton, placed ideological themes and arguments drawn from Churchill and from the Clifford–Elsey report in an American policy context, and transformed that policy (that, for all practical purposes, had been in effect for a year) into a doctrine, a doctrine that would form the basis for the anticommunist reality of subsequent decades. Truman described it as "this terrible decision" and Margaret Truman concluded that it was "the real beginning of the cold

war."[4] The president's speech defined a new ideological reality that
would dominate the American political arena in which foreign policy
commitments (and many domestic policies, as well) would be debated
and either implemented or rejected.

Truman's historic proclamation, taken with the other rhetorical events
of this period, resulted in a transformation of American society. The
questions we pose now are: why did the Truman Doctrine become an
ideological statement of universal policy and messianic mission for the
United States? In other words, why did Truman define the conflict with
the Soviet Union in ideological terms instead of diplomatic or other
political terms? And what role did Truman's speech play in the creation
of the cold war consensus?

BACKGROUND

The precipitating event that led to the Truman Doctrine was not an
act by an adversary but an announcement by an ally. On the afternoon
of February 21, 1947, the private secretary of Lord Inverchapel, the
British ambassador to the United States, called the State Department to
request an immediate meeting for the ambassador with the new secretary
of state, George C. Marshall. The purpose was to deliver a "blue piece
of paper," a code name for an important message from the British government. Since Marshall was away for a speaking engagement at Princeton University, Dean Acheson, undersecretary of state, suggested that
a copy of the message be delivered to him and the formal message be
delivered when Marshall returned. The British agreed, but delivered
two notes rather than one.

The British notes declared that the Greek government was on the
verge of collapse, that the British (due to their own economic problems)
could no longer provide economic and military support to Greece and
Turkey, and that the British government hoped the United States would
assume this burden thereafter. The British set March 31 as the deadline
for terminating their support for the two countries.

Acheson described the message as a "shocker."[5] It is unclear what he
was shocked about. It could hardly have been the news that the Greek
situation was becoming more unstable. The civil war in Greece had been
going on for several years and was now in its "third round."[6] It entered
this new phase in the aftermath of the March 1946 elections which had
given the right-wing royalists control of the government in Athens. Soon
thereafter, insurgents renewed their guerilla war, this time against the
new government. The strain of Nazi occupation during World War II
and the continuing civil strife within the country had left both the Greek
economy and its political structure in disarray. But the U.S. government,
far from ignoring Greece, had been monitoring these events carefully.

Turkey hardly qualified as a "shocker." The previous October the Soviets had withdrawn their proposal for joint control of the Black Sea straits. The administration perceived no immediate threat to the territory of Turkey, although maintaining a large military force was causing the Turks some financial strain.[7]

Finally, the withdrawal of British financial and military support had been anticipated. The British treasury had been depleted by the war. Like other European countries, the British economy was in a shambles in the early postwar years, and the hard winter of 1946–47 had exacerbated this financial crisis.

Neither the Greek civil war nor the British economic situation could have been shocking to Acheson. A number of memoranda about both situations had been circulating in the State Department for some time prior to the February notes.[8] The possibility that U.S. aid would be needed, as the British recommended, was already in the works. As early as September 1946 the government had quietly begun preparing for military aid to Greece. That month, the United States had granted Greek requests for economic credits to the government. More recently, Loy Henderson, who was in charge of Near Eastern Affairs, had discussed this continuing problem in a memorandum that Acheson retitled "Crisis and Imminent Possibility of Collapse." It called for substantial aid to Greece. Acheson had edited the memorandum and sent it on to Secretary Marshall. On the day before reception of the British notes, according to Acheson, Marshall instructed him to "prepare the necessary steps for sending economic and military aid" to Greece.[9]

In all probability it was the March 31 deadline that was the source of Acheson's "shock." In reaction, he immediately treated the situation as a crisis. That urgent mood pervaded both the private deliberations and public announcements from that day forward. The "crisis" was rhetorically manufactured by Acheson's preconceptions and his immediate reaction. "Crisis" is only a word, a description of a situation, but it is a description pregnant with urgency. In the medical world a crisis is a turning point for a sick patient, a crucial moment when a life or death decision must be made. That's the way members of the administration saw the British announcement and their opportunity. It should be stressed that what Acheson responded to, like Churchill before him, was not an act by the Soviet Union, but new conditions now that the British were withdrawing financial aid from Greece.

Working within the critical atmosphere he himself originated, Acheson took the lead in developing the official U.S. response. Secretary Marshall was preoccupied with preparing for the all-important Moscow Conference of Foreign Ministers on attempting to find common ground among the allies for a settlement over Germany and Austria. Marshall stayed intimately informed about the situation, and before leaving on

March 10, he participated as fully as his other duties allowed in discussions and with the decision President Truman made. But it was Acheson who was the driving force. Immediately after receiving the British notes he called President Truman and Secretary Marshall to inform them of the crisis. He immediately set the appropriate groups working on position papers for the U.S. response. He worked ceaselessly to coordinate this response. By the end of the first evening an initial draft of a position paper had been written. Throughout the weekend Acheson received updated progress reports by various groups within the administration that were developing American policy.

TRUMAN AS AUDIENCE AND AS DECISIONMAKER

By February 26, a more complete position paper had been worked out and approved by Secretary Marshall. On that day he and Acheson met with the president, and the undersecretary made an oral presentation. The memorandum, which President Truman described as a "result of studies by our experts," recommended that the United States step in to fill the void that would be left by the British withdrawal of financial and military aid to Greece and Turkey.[10]

In Harry Truman, the two State Department officials had a receptive audience. As early as January, 1946 he had focused on the East Mediterranean region as a Soviet target. In a "dressing down" letter to Secretary James Byrnes, which the president later said he personally read to him, Truman said:

There isn't a doubt in my mind that Russia intends an invasion of Turkey and the seizure of the Black Sea Straits to the Mediterranean. Unless Russia is faced with an iron fist and strong language another war is in the making. Only one language do they understand—"how many divisions have you?"

I do not think we should play compromise any longer. . . . I'm tired of babying the Soviets.[11]

But he did not act directly on his private feelings at that time. Perhaps his reluctance was due to the less than enthusiastic reception Churchill's speech at Fulton soon received. Perhaps it was due to the fact that 1946 was an election year and he did not want to split the Democratic party between those who sought conciliation with the Soviet Union and those who sought greater firmness. Perhaps it was because he did not yet feel secure enough in the presidency to make such a change in policy. Perhaps it was because he retained lingering hopes that some accommodation with the Soviets could be realized. There is enough historical and biographical evidence to support any of these suppositions and even more.

Moreover, he had already taken firm action against the Soviet Union. He had gotten the Soviets out of Iran. He had dispatched a naval force to the east Mediterranean when the Turkish dispute arose. He had approved the merger of the British and American zones in Germany. He had fired Secretary of Agriculture Henry Wallace for proposing a more accommodating stance toward the USSR. In sum, until February 1947 the president had kept his public option open even though his perception of the kinds of policies necessary to confront the Soviet Union had narrowed.

He was inclined to view Soviet–American relations ideologically. Kennan's "long telegram" had stressed these as the primary motives of the Soviets. Winston Churchill had proclaimed at Fulton that the new division of the world was between "Christian civilisation" and the communists. The Clifford-Elsey memorandum of September 1946 contended that the "key to an understanding of current Soviet foreign policy . . . is the realization that Soviet leaders adhere to the Marxian theory of ultimate destruction of capitalist states by communist states."[12] Drawing extensively from Kennan's telegram, Clifford had made the ideological challenge even more rigid to the virtual exclusion of any other motivation for Soviet intentions and actions. He had concluded: "The language of military power is the only language which disciples of power politics understand. The United States must use that language in order that the Soviet leaders will realize that our government is determined to uphold the interests of its citizens and the rights of small nations." This conclusion foreshadowed the language of the Truman Doctrine.

Unlike his predecessor, Truman did not like to postpone decisions. Instead, he loved to make decisions. He had more of the temperament of a judge than a diplomat, preferring clear rulings to the equivocations of power politics.[13] During the previous year he had grown increasingly impatient and angry with what he believed were blatant Soviet violations of their agreements with the allied powers. (He wrote his daughter the day after his speech that he "knew at Potsdam that there is no difference in totalitarian or police states, call them what you will, Nazi, Fascist, Communist or Argentine Republics.")[14] The president quickly approved the memorandum, and thus the decision was made. He would replace British aid to the two countries with U.S. financial and military aid.

The memorandum that Truman approved contained nine recommendations in all. For our purposes, the sixth and ninth recommendations of the memorandum are significant:

6. The problem [should] be discussed privately and frankly by the leaders of the administration with appropriate members of the Congress.

9. Measures [should] be adopted to acquaint the American public with the
   situation and with the need for action along the proposed lines.[15]

These were recommendations about the rhetorical handling of the president's decision. Truman quickly scheduled a meeting the next day with
leaders from Congress. Since Secretary Marshall would soon be off to
the Moscow Conference, Acheson continued his assumption of leadership in putting these recommendations into action, especially the rhetorical dimension.

Acheson later wrote: "This was my crisis. For a week I had nurtured
it."[16] In like manner, Halle summarized the reaction of those associated
with Acheson in the government: "This was once more the eleventh
hour—as in 1917, as in 1941. If the United States did not intervene now,
all would be lost."[17] Reading these reactions today is disconcerting.
There had been no dramatic event as in 1917, no attack on the United
States as in 1941. The Soviet Union had made no overt move in either
Greece or Turkey. There had been no spectacular turn in the Greek civil
war. Turkey was relatively stable.

In fact, neither Greece nor Turkey had asked for U.S. aid. In the furious
activity of the days following the British announcement, this omission
had been overlooked. When it was realized on February 28, Secretary
Marshall sent a cable to the American embassy in Athens asking the
Greeks to ask for U.S. assistance. Marshall even sent the text of exactly
what the Greek government should request.[18] In other words, the U.S.
government told the Greek government to request what the Americans
thought it should request.

What had occurred, then, was that a U.S. ally had announced it would
discontinue aid to Greece and Turkey in a little over a month and urged
the United States to take over that responsibility, a policy already under
consideration in the State Department. And the British deadline may
have been a deliberate bluff, as Wittner pointed out, because they continued aid to the two countries far beyond the cut-off date they themselves had set.[19] But the Americans, led by Acheson, saw the proposed
British withdrawal from the Near East as creating the possibility of a
Soviet takeover of the area and that possibility, they believed, required
an immediate response and firm action in anticipation of any Soviet
action.

The crisis rested not in the events themselves, but in the perception
of what they meant. More specifically, it was Dean Acheson's (along
with that of Loy Henderson and John Hickerson) immediate perception
of crisis. This attitude, shared by most others, spread among those who
participated in the historic events of the following days.[20] The mood of
critical urgency permeated the discussions and decisions that led to the

address by the president and much of its reception by the press and public.

PREPARING FOR A POSITIVE RECEPTION

After deciding to extend aid to Greece and Turkey, the primary issue became how to persuade Congress and the American public to support such aid. In simple terms, the rhetoric became the principal problem. The decision to act had been made with dispatch. During the past year the administration had been persuaded or had persuaded itself that the communist Soviet Union was driven by an ideological fanaticism to expand aggressively to conquer Europe and perhaps eventually the world. Of these ominous Soviet objectives they were convinced. The primary audience for the new foreign policy—elites in the administration—had by this time already been persuaded about the insidious Soviet motives and goals. Now other elites in Congress who shared this view had to be convinced that Greece and Turkey were sufficiently important to American national interests to cause the United States to abandon its traditional policy of isolationism in favor of a policy of international intervention. It was necessary to line up influential members of Congress on the president's side as an advance force to getting the full Congress to approve aid. At the same time, the second major audience—influential journalists—would have to be persuaded to accept the policy. Their support was critical to giving credibility to congressional support and in convincing the final audience—the American people. Constructing persuasive arguments to convince these others of the rightness of this policy, they feared, would be much more difficult than reaching the decision in the first place.

The administration launched a campaign targeted at these three specific audiences: congressional leaders, especially leaders from the majority Republican party; influential members of the press; and finally the American people. Members of the administration, led by President Truman and Acting Secretary of State Acheson, approached these audiences successively, beginning with influential senators and representatives. They magnified the situation they faced into a crisis confronting the entire Western world of which the United States, they said, was the only bulwark against a Soviet offensive intended to conquer western Europe. The existing apprehensions and fears among people in each of these audiences made them receptive prey for the messianic rhetoric of the administration. But it should be remembered that no dramatic act on the part of the Soviet Union precipitated this "crisis" atmosphere. The "crisis" was rhetorically constructed from the arguments and style in which the administration's case was presented to these various audiences. Indeed, later on, there would be much criticism of the crisis atmosphere that the administration had created so as to stampede others into accepting its policy of aid to Greece and Turkey. However, the crisis atmosphere became commonplace. This environment bred its own brand of fanaticism. Any small act by the Soviet Union would become as "critical" to "Western survival" as any other. It was in this urgent atmosphere that the administration first sought to convince congressional leaders of the need to act, then briefed reporters on the background of the "crisis" and the policy to meet it, and finally went before the public with an all-out speech that declared a universal ideological policy for the United States. It set a rhetorical pattern of perpetual crisis that was repeated by the administration and later adopted by its opponents to culminate in the great fear of the Fifties.

The administration embarked upon three simultaneous activities: convincing influential senators and representatives to support economic aid to Greece and Turkey, drafting a speech for the president, and preparing for positive reception by the press. Let us consider each of these in turn.

A Dress Rehearsal for Congress

On February 27, the day after the decision was made, the president, Marshall, and Acheson met with a small group of Republicans and Democrats from Congress. This meeting was crucial. "[W]e are met at Armageddon," is the way Acheson described it, and he was speaking not about the Soviets but about the representatives from Congress, especially the Republicans.[21] In the 1946 election Republicans had wrested control of both Houses of Congress from the Democrats, winning fifty-six seats in the House and thirteen in the Senate. They had campaigned on promises to cut the budget, to reduce taxes, and to bring the boys home. It was an all-out attack on Roosevelt's New Deal and, to a lesser degree, on internationalism. Republicans had emerged from the campaign triumphant and now they chaired and held the majorities on the committees that Truman's aid program would have to go through.[22] However, Republicans had left an opening in the campaign. Some had made communism, or the "communist threat" as they called it, a major issue in the campaign.[23] Since the president and his officials at this meeting shared this fear to one degree or another, it was an opening that could and would be exploited.

The congressional delegation included Senators Arthur Vandenberg (chair of the Senate Foreign Relations Committee), Styles Bridges (chair of the Senate Appropriations Committee), and Tom Connally (senior Democrat on the Foreign Relations Committee); Representatives Joseph Martin (Speaker of the House), Sam Rayburn (Democratic minority leader), Charles Eaton (chair of the House Committee on Foreign Affairs), and Sol Bloom (senior Democrat on the House Foreign Affairs

Committee).[24] Conspicuously absent was Senator Robert Taft, "Mr. Republican" and the leader of the isolationist forces in Congress. The official explanation for his absence, as voiced by Acheson later, was that it was an "accidental omission" that was rectified at a later meeting.[25] But that strains credulity. How could such politically sophisticated men "accidentally" omit one of the most prominent men in Congress and perhaps the Republican nominee for president the next year? A more plausible explanation for his absence is that he was deliberately not invited. Three reasons can be advanced for this belief. First, the administration did not want to alert the isolationist forces about the momentous change in policy upon which it was embarking. Second, the administration saw this meeting as critical in getting Republican support, it did not want the most prestigious Republican to voice his opposition, as Taft later did, and thus influence the other Republicans. Or at least not until the president had secured a commitment of support from these influential Republicans. Finally, ignoring Taft presented the administration with the opportunity to split the Republican party between its isolationist faction and its internationalists, a split that could increase the chances for Truman's election in his own right.[26] Later, at Senator Vandenberg's suggestion, Taft was invited to a meeting, but that was only after other Republicans had fairly well committed themselves to supporting the president.

These were the men who composed the audience for the first presentation of the president's new policy. If the administration were to be successful, that success was dependent on overcoming congressional skepticism and opposition. Thus, in rhetorical terms, this meeting was a dress rehearsal for the arguments that would be used to persuade Congress and the public to support the president's decision to extend aid to Greece and Turkey.

The president spoke first outlining the problem and what he intended to do about it. He then turned to Secretary Marshall for elaboration. There is a mythology that has grown up that Marshall spoke only in humanitarian and economic terms thereby "flubbing" his lines, as Acheson haughtily described it.[27] Reading Marshall's statement today hardly supports that conclusion.

The secretary began by saying that a "crisis of utmost importance and urgency" had arisen in Greece and Turkey that had a "direct and immediate relation to the security of the United States." He briefly described the political and financial problems of the Greek government and Great Britain's notice that it could not continue aid to the government. Then, he stated in succinct terms the threat that the potential collapse of the Greek government posed to the United States:

Our interest in Greece is by no means restricted to humanitarian or friendly impulses. If Greece should dissolve into civil war it is altogether probable that it would emerge as a communist state under Soviet control. Turkey would be surrounded and the Turkish situation, to which I shall refer in a moment, would in turn become still more critical. Soviet domination might thus extend over the entire Middle East to the borders of India. The effect of this upon Hungary, Austria, Italy and France cannot be overestimated. It is not alarmist to say that we are faced with the first crisis of a series which might extend Soviet domination to Europe, the Middle East and Asia.

Marshall went on to say that only the United States could help Greece. He mentioned the Turkish situation in less critical, but still serious, terms. The secretary concluded with the list of executive actions the president proposed and for which they sought congressional support.[28]

Whether it was Marshall's dry manner of speaking or the brevity of his remarks or the tentative way he talked about threat of Soviet domination, Marshall's presentation did not have the dramatic effect needed to persuade the representatives. The congressional delegation immediately began asking disconcerting questions rather than voicing their approval: "How much would the aid cost?" "Isn't this just pulling British chestnuts out of the fire?" Acheson was aghast. He asked to speak and did so with Truman's and Marshall's permission. The effect of his impromptu remarks was electric.

Marshall's statement had been brief, precise, and without stylistic flourishes. Acheson spoke for ten to fifteen minutes. He amplified the threat. He made the central issue an issue of confrontation between the Soviet Union and the United States, between an aggressive power from the East and the last defender of freedom in the West. He was not tentative, but authoritative. In addition, he emphasized the ideological conflict and cited a historical analogy to give it greater force. According to Jones, Acheson said:

We had arrived at a situation unparalleled since ancient times. Not since Rome and Carthage had there been such a polarization of power on this earth. Moreover the two great powers were divided by an unbridgeable ideological chasm. For us, democracy and individual liberty were basic; for them, dictatorship and absolute conformity.[29]

To stress the horrendous consequence of not acting, Acheson drew upon a well-worn metaphor:

Like apples in a barrel infected by one rotten one, the corruption of Greece would infect Iran and all to the east. It would also carry infection to Africa through Asia Minor and Egypt, and to Europe through Italy and France, already threatened by the strongest domestic Communist parties in Western Europe.[30]

He concluded by saying: "It is a question of whether two-thirds of the area of the world . . . is to be controlled by Communists."[31] In the later anticommunist rhetoric, the historical analogy would be changed from Rome and Carthage to Munich, but the disease metaphor would continue and be made more deadly. But for the moment, these sufficed. At the conclusion of Acheson's remarks, there was silence.

Finally, Vandenberg spoke. He said he had been impressed and even shaken. Others report that Vandenberg's language was more colorful and to the point. Cochran, for example, wrote that Vandenberg's words to Truman are: "If that's what you want, there's only one way to get it. That is to make a personal appearance before Congress and scare hell out of the country."[32] The others seemed to agree. None of them voiced opposition this time to the president's intention to extend aid to Greece and Turkey. Although no promises of support were given, Vandenberg and the others said they were inclined to support the president "*on the condition* . . . that the President should, in a message to Congress and in a radio address to the American people, explain the issue in the same frank terms and broad context in which it had been laid before them."[33] Thus, the style and theme for the president's address had been struck. Marshall's dry precise style would not do. The president would have to speak in the "frankest, boldest, widest terms" possible.[34] And the emphasis would have to shift from the problems Greece and Turkey were currently experiencing to an ideological confrontation between the United States and communism.

Drafting the Speech

After the meeting, feverish work began on the president's address. The eventual 2,200-word address went through nine drafts.[35] Joseph Jones was the principal writer, but he was aided by a variety of other people who suggested, edited, or wrote sections of the address. Among these were Clark Clifford (Special Counsel to the president and his principal adviser on speeches), Clifford's aide, George Elsey, Acheson, and even the president himself.

The first version presented to the president was unsatisfactory. Truman recalled that it was "filled . . . with all sorts of background data and statistical figures about Greece" that made it sound like an "investment prospectus." He returned the draft with the directive that it should have "more emphasis on a general declaration of policy." He also told Acheson that he wanted it toughened up and simplified. When the next draft came back to the president, it contained the famous policy statement. The writers' version read: "I believe it should be the policy." To achieve even greater emphasis the president struck out the word "should" and substituted "must," thus changing the meaning from the conditional to the compulsory.[36] As Jones noted, phrasing the decision in this way meant that Truman's decision had to be accepted in full or rejected. There was no middle ground.[37]

Between the initial version and the final version, those working on the speech grappled with greater problems than changing verbs. President Truman had told Acheson he wanted no hedging in the speech. But as the writers began putting it together they found that they had to do considerable hedging with the facts when dealing with certain problems. Three of these problems concern us here.

First, they had to decide on the exact way in which the confrontation between the adversaries would be described. The administration saw Turkey and Greece as important to strategic goals of the United States. Jones wrote that one reason why they did not emphasize this in the speech was because the American people were not accustomed to strategic thinking. Another reason could have been that if the speech emphasized that American aid was to be given these countries for strategic purposes, then the Soviet Union could use the same argument for consolidating its control over eastern Europe. Above all though, the president wanted a statement of broad principle, not a narrow strategic justification.

But how to describe the situation in Greece as symbolic of a confrontation between two great powers? There were practical and rhetorical reasons for not describing it as a struggle between the United States and the Soviet Union. Secretary Marshall was meeting with the Soviets at the very time the speech was to be delivered. Therefore, they were reluctant to name the Soviet Union as the enemy. In fact, the Soviet Union would not even be mentioned in the speech. It was a silly subterfuge since everyone who read or heard the speech immediately knew the president was talking about the Soviets. Nonetheless by omitting an explicit reference to the Soviet Union, Secretary Marshall would not have to defend such a belligerent anti-Soviet statement in Moscow.[38]

Furthermore, for rhetorical purposes they wanted something more elevated than a "spheres of influence" or "power struggle" definition of the issue. A foreign policy based on spheres of influence had long ago been ruled out. If there was one consistent theme running throughout U.S. foreign policy in the twentieth century, it was opposition to spheres of influence. President Wilson, President Roosevelt, and President Truman had all denounced divisions in the world dominated by specific powers, although they upheld the Monroe Doctrine with its explicit claim to American hegemony in the Western Hemisphere. Even though these presidents paid obedience to the Monroe Doctrine, they had developed no rhetorical tradition for recognizing spheres of influence by other nations, nor had they any inclinations for developing such a public language. American and British leaders often referred to the Soviet Union's concern about a buffer zone in eastern Europe, but their references were remarkably vague. They described this Soviet concern as a desire for "friendly associations," or remaining "secure on her western frontier" or having "special security interests." Such vague descriptions were intended to avoid using the hated words, "spheres of influence." Being so vague and usually buried in speeches devoted to enunciating universalist principles, they did little to establish a rhetorical ground for developing a public rhetoric based on appreciation for Soviet concerns over security. On the other hand, American and British officials pursued policies designed to strengthen Western influence over areas they deemed important to their security. Quite simply, American officials had no rhetorical heritage for devising a rationale or justification for recognizing spheres of influence in foreign policy, nor were they inclined to invent one.

How then were speechwriters to describe the political substance of the confrontation? The rhetorical forms they called upon were the universal rhetoric of Wilson (of making the world safe for democracy) and the war rhetoric that had rallied the American people against the fascists. The universal rhetoric had found expression in the Atlantic Charter, the Yalta agreement on a Liberated Europe, and the various speeches by President Truman, especially his Navy Day addresss. The rhetoric of World War II, like all war rhetorics, stressed an absolute division between "good allies" and "evil enemies." The forms of both the universal rhetoric and the war rhetoric had rich and evocative histories, especially in the immediate past. They were the dominate rhetorical forms available to speechwriters and decisionmakers. And they were used to justify the new policy.

But how to adapt these forms to the current problem? It was on March 3 that the advisers hit upon the "defending democracy" as the defining feature of Sovet–American disputes.[39] Yet, even this ideological description caused problems. They did not want to use a theme of "capitalism versus communism" because it would be repugnant to domestic liberals. They also rejected a "free enterprise versus communism" because they might have to extend aid in the future to governments that did not have a free enterprise system, especially since the Labor party still controlled the British government. Finally, they struck on the theme of the "free world" versus "totalitarianism" and described this division as a choice between "alternative ways of life," the most ideological section of the address.[40] That description avoided most of the pitfalls the writers had encountered; it was tough; and it laid down what seemed to be an idealistic line. Thus, the way around their original problems was to describe the challenge as ideological, the aggressive challenge posed by totalitarian communism to free nations around the world.

The resolution of the original problem created the second major problem in its wake. The writers had to find a way to reconcile aid to the undemocratic, corrupt, and reactionary Greek government (as well as the dictatorial Turkey) with the principle of defending "free" nations. "Hedging" would have to give way to "stretching" on this point. Again, Jones described with some detail how the writers grappled with this inconvenience. He remarked that "faith" and "realism" replaced "facts" in resolving the problem. The aid would be given so that Greece and Turkey could "develop" as democratic nations. In the final version considerable space was given to "explaining" this reconciliation:

No government is perfect. One of the chief virtues of a democracy, however, is that its defects are always visible and under democratic processes can be pointed out and corrected. The government of Greece is not perfect. Nevertheless it represents 85 percent of the members of the Greek Parliament who were chosen in an election last year. Foreign observers, including 692 Americans, considered this election to be a fair expression of the view of the Greek people.

The Greek Government has been operating in an atmosphere of chaos and extremism. It has made mistakes. The extension of aid by this country does not mean that the United States condones everything that the Greek Government has done or will do. We have condemned in the past, and we condemn now, extremist measures of the right or the left. We have in the past advised tolerance, and we advise tolerance now.

This verbal footwork provided a linguistic swirl for arguing that the administration recognized the true character of the Greek government even as it justified sending aid to the country through different appeals. These paragraphs were defensive parts of the speech laid down for defensive purposes in the future. No one could accuse the president of not recognizing the kind of government for whom he was proposing aid, even if it did not fit the principle the president was pledging the United States to defend around the world.

Finally, they had to find a way around the United Nations. Since the end of the war, Truman had been trumpeting the U.N. as the best way to resolve international differences and to insure peace among nations.[41] Jones pointed out that during the drafting of the speech the "United Nations . . . was never a major issue."[42] But others were concerned. Dean Rusk, who had just taken over the U.N. office in the administration, recommended a greater role for the United Nations and wrote paragraphs he thought appropriate for the speech. Only one of these was used. Inserted at almost the last minute, it read: "We have considered how the United Nations might assist in this crisis. But the situation is an urgent one requiring immediate action, and the United Nations and its related organizations are not in a position to extend help of the kind that is required." Such statements were merely lip service to an organization for which the president had raised such high expectations. Bypassing the United Nations to take unilateral action created serious problems later. There was no question that Truman was undermining the authority and prestige of the United Nations. Critics at home and the Soviets abroad immediately seized upon this point.[43] Even Senator Vandenberg recognized this rhetorical mistake and sought to rectify it by adding an amendment to the legislation that stated that aid could be withdrawn if the purpose of the aid could be better achieved under the direction of the United Nations.[44] This amendment, however, was meaningless in terms of what the United States actually intended to do. In other people's eyes it only compounded the original end run around the United Nations. Treating the U.N. in this fashion probably sent a clear message to the Soviet Union about how the United States intended to use that international organization in the future.

The final version of the speech did not have unanimous approval within the administration. George F. Kennan objected violently to the ideological thrust and universal commitment of the speech. He especially objected to the "alternative ways of life" language. So much did he object that he wrote a different version for the speech, but it was rejected.[45] The decision had already been made. And Kennan agreed with much of the policy toward Greece and Turkey, if not with the reasons that would be given for it. George Elsey presented a simpler objection. He wrote to Clark Clifford: "There has been no overt action in the immediate past by the U.S.S.R. which serves as an adequate pretext for 'All-out' speech. This situation in Greece is relatively 'abstract'; there have been other instances . . . where the occasion more adequately justified such a speech."[46] But Elsey was merely objecting to this occasion for the speech, not the ideological content. Thus, despite these and other objections, was the speech fashioned that would mark America's public entrance into an ideological war with the Soviet Union.

Preparing the Press

As work on the president's speech progressed, so too did work on the nation's journalists. The administration embarked upon an intensive campaign—and there is no other word for it—to persuade the press to support the new foreign policy of the United States. This campaign, euphemistically called a "Public Information Program," had three purposes:

1. To make possible the formulation of intelligent opinions by the American people on the problems created by the present situation in Greece through the furnishing of full and frank information.

2. To portray world conflict between free and totalitarian or imposed forms of government.

3. To bring about an understanding by the American people of the world strategic situation.[47]

On the evening of the congressional briefing, Acheson met with members of the press to give a detailed briefing. Simultaneously, those
congressional leaders who had been present at the White House meeting
began to exert their influence on their colleagues and their connections
among journalists and other influential elites. This persuasive campaign
was heightened when Secretary Marshall released the text of the appeal
from the Greek government for aid on March 3. He made no mention
of the British note, thereby implying that the sole cause for the current
crisis was the Greek government's call for help at a particularly critical
moment in history. Marshall stated that the "problems involved [in the
Greek "crisis"] are so far-reaching and of such transcendent importance
that any announcement relating to them could only come from the President himself."

This campaign continued right up until the time of the president's
speech. Put in rhetorical terms, the purposes of the campaign were to:
(1) create an atmosphere of crisis over Greece in anticipation of the
president's speech; (2) to emphasize the ideological struggle between
the United States and the Soviet Union; and (3) to gain full support from
the press for the president's new foreign policy so as to convince the
American people to support it. From the beginning Acheson wanted
the briefings of the press "pitched" in the broadest context. The role of
the press, as the administration saw it and as Jones plainly stated it,
was to act as an "advance agent to Congress and the public for the
President's message of March 12."[48]

Much of the press complied. This audience was arguably the easiest
audience to persuade. Much of the press had already accepted the division Churchill had proclaimed at Fulton. They had spent much of the
previous year "spinning out" the meaning of that division when new
events happened. They were ready to join in the administration in sum-
moning the American people to meet the new totalitarian challenge. On
March 1, James Reston posed three questions in the *New York Times* that
echoed administration thinking: Was the United States prepared to take
action in Greece to stop Soviet expansion in the eastern Mediterranean?
Was the United States prepared to replace Great Britain as the stabilizing
force in world affairs? Was it possible for the Democrats and Republicans
to reach agreement on unified policy supported by the English and
opposed by the Soviets?[49] Hanson Baldwin followed up the next day by
writing that the United States stood at the crossroads of history, a time
for decision that could determine whether Western Civilization was to
prevail or be swept away into a new Dark Ages.[50] (It should be remembered that the articles were written before Marshall announced that the

Greeks had officially asked for aid.) By March 8 the *New York Times* could report "growing excitement" for the president's address and the hope that it would outline the extent of America's new international role.[51] The stage had been carefully set not only for an historic announcement but for positive reactions as well.

ARGUMENTS OF THE TRUMAN DOCTRINE

On March 12, 1947 President Truman addressed a special joint session of Congress. His speech was a rambling address reflecting the many people who had a hand in its construction. The speech has been so thoroughly analyzed by so many scholars that a detailed analysis of it would be redundant.[52] Our purpose here will be to summarize the speech and point to the parts that played the major role in developing the anticommunism consensus. Despite the brevity of his remarks and the plain style he employed, Truman had the electrifying effect he sought.

In the preamble of his address, President Truman stressed the gravity of the recent events. He stated that these events involved the foreign policy and national security of the United States, a world situation he subsequently called a "crisis" and one that required "immediate action." The most pressing problem, "one aspect of the present situation," involved Greece and Turkey. Thus, right off the bat, Truman implied that Greece and Turkey were only symbolic of a far more fundamental problem confronting the United States, but also that each were inextricably part of U.S. national security.

Truman announced that Greece had issued an urgent appeal for aid from the United States and briefly described the economic problems that government faced. But the problem was even greater than these financial difficulties: "The very existence of the Greek state is today threatened by the terrorist activities of several thousand armed men, led by Communists, who defy the government's authority at a number of points, particularly along the northern boundaries." The Greek government, Truman stated, could not cope with these problems and only the United States was in a position to render aid. After further describing the plight of the Greeks and adding disclaimers about the character of its government, Truman briefly said that Turkey too needed additional aid from both the United States and Great Britain to maintain "its national integrity."

Neither Greece nor Turkey was the main issue in this crisis. Their problems were real, according to Truman, but they were primarily symbolic of larger issues. He reminded his listeners of the "real" meaning of World War II, that the United States had fought that war to keep some nations from imposing their way of life on others. This analogy linked the recent war to the present situation and set the stage for fundamental meaning to be placed on the current crisis. Declaring that he was "fully aware of the broad implications" of the policy he was to announce, Truman launched into the meat of his speech:

At the present moment in world history nearly every nation must choose between alternative ways of life. The choice is too often not a free one.

One way of life is based upon the will of the majority, and is distinguished by free institutions, representative government, free elections, guarantees of individual liberty, freedom of speech and religion, and freedom from political oppression.

The second way of life is based upon the will of a minority forcibly imposed upon the majority. It relies upon terror and oppression, a controlled press and radio, fixed elections, and the suppression of personal freedoms.

I believe it must be the policy of the United States to support free peoples who are resisting attempted subjugation by armed minorities or by outside pressures.

I believe that we must assist free peoples to work out their own destinies in their own way.

I believe that our help should be primarily through economic and financial aid which is essential to economic stability and orderly political processes.

Here was the new foreign policy for the United States and the justification for it pristinely and plainly stated. Truman declared in no uncertain terms the broad policy that would guide the country for decades. He had created the linguistic lens through which every American could see the central meaning of complex and difficult problems confronting the country in international affairs.

It should be noted that President Truman stated with equally unmistakable language that American help should "primarily" be offered through economic and financial assistance. However, by focusing almost exclusively on Greece, the country involved in a real civil war, and by describing the universal problem as one of "armed minorities" attempting to "forcibly" subjugate "freedom-loving peoples," the military images and implications overshadowed the precise call for economic aid to threatened countries.[53] Later, when Secretary Marshall recommended aid to European countries in his speech at Harvard, some interpreted Marshall's economic plan as an alternative to Truman's belligerence.[54] Even more to the point, Truman did not (and probably could not at the time) say what additional measures the United States would take if economic aid did not achieve the effect he desired. It became simple for the president and others then to advocate military aid as the next step in confronting communism.

As Truman viewed the world situation, there were only two choices and the question was: Which side are you on? His vision was that of an ideological dialectic with no synthesis in sight. The president had made his choice. He contended that failure to act at this critical moment in world history would have tragic consquences. Echoing Archeson's private presentation thirteen days earlier and presenting what would eventually be known as the "domino" theory, President Truman stated:

If Greece should fall under the control of an armed minority, the effect upon its neighbor, Turkey, would be immediate and serious. Confusion and disorder might well spread throughout the entire Middle East.

Moreover, the disappearance of Greece as an independent state would have a profound effect upon those countries in Europe whose peoples are struggling against great difficulties to maintain their freedoms and their independence while they repair the damages of war.

It would be an unspeakable tragedy if these countries, which have struggled so long against overwhelming odds, should lose that victory for which they sacrificed so much. Collapse of free institutions and loss of independence would be disastrous not only for them but for the world. Discouragement and possibly failure would quickly be the lot of neighboring peoples striving to maintain their freedom and independence.

Should we fail to aid Greece and Turkey in this fateful hour, the effect will be far reaching to the West as well as to the East.

Thus did President Truman describe the stakes in the problem and the policy he was presenting to Congress and the American people. He spent the remainder of his address detailing the legislation he sought and the amount of money needed. Though the principle Truman had stated was global in scope, the money he asked for ($400 million) was minimal in aid.

In eighteen minutes President Truman had announced a significant departure in America's traditional foreign policy and had created a new way of seeing its place in the postwar world. He had created a simple good-evil perceptual lens through which the American people could view, understand, interpret, and act upon events that the administration said symbolized confrontations between two mutually exclusive "ways of life." Differences within the so-called free world and within the so-called communist world were minimized or ignored, as the moral and mortal conflict between the two was accentuated. About such language as this, Alexis de Tocqueville had observed: "Democratic writers are perpetually coining abstract words . . . in which they sublimate into further abstraction the abstract terms of the language. Moreover, to render their mode of speech more succinct, they personify the object of these abstract terms and make it act like a real person."[55] The personifications would come later. For the moment, the abstract definition of the enemy and the abstract principle would suffice. As one Briton said: "We went to sleep in one world and woke up . . . in another."[56]

INITIAL RESPONSES TO THE SPEECH

If the responses to Churchill's Fulton speech were cool, the responses to Truman's speech were red hot. Probably the most accurate summary of reaction to the speech was that both the press and Congress recognized the speech as a landmark in U.S. history. The *New York Times's* headline stated: "TRUMAN ACTS TO SAVE NATIONS FROM RED RULE." The first paragraph of its news story succinctly captured the meaning of the speech: "President Truman outlined a new foreign policy for the United States today. In a historic message to Congress, he proposed that this country intervene wherever necessary throughout the world to prevent the subjection of free peoples to Communist-inspired totalitarian regimes at the expense of their national integrity and importance."[57] James Reston compared Truman's policy to that of the Monroe Doctrine and Roosevelt's announcement of the lend-lease program.[58] The lead editorial in the *Times* went further: "This was a speech comparable with President Roosevelt's famous 'quarantine' speech against aggressors, a speech made under analogous circumstances in 1937."[59] The Omaha *World Herald* rightly called the speech "the most breath-taking statement ever made in time of peace by any American President or statesman."[60]

The weekly magazines also joined the chorus of praise. *Life* editorialized that "the immediate task of America is to hold the door of history open for the kind of world government which lovers of freedom can approve."[61] *Time*, *Newsweek*, and the *New Leader* carried a number of stories on the speech that ranged from approving to enthusiastic. David Lawrence, editor of *U.S. News*, gave the strongest endorsement: "If American Presidents from 1920 to 1939 had made it plain beforehand that the United States meant to use her industrial, financial, and military power to checkmate aggression, the Second World War would never have been fought."[62]

Domestic criticism of Truman's speech came primarily from isolationist forces on the right and the old FDR forces on the left (left of Truman, that is). The reasons for their criticism or opposition were just as diverse. On the conservative side, Senator Taft remarked that if the United States assumed a "special position in Greece and Turkey . . . we can hardly . . . object to Russians continuing their domination in Poland, Yugoslavia, Rumania, and Bulgaria."[63] Representative Harold Knutson of Minnesota objected to the economic commitment: "I guess the do-gooders won't feel right until they have us all broke."[64] On the liberal side, both *Nation* magazine and *The New Republic* inveighed against the Truman Doctrine. The former stated: "Blindly, without general public understanding or consent, without even a clear picture of what lies at the end, the United States takes its first steps along the road of big-power politics."[65] Henry Wallace was even more vehement. He wrote that the speech had "scarcely a paragraph of fact or evidence. All was a mixture of unsupported assertions, sermonizing and exhortation. It was evident that in the name of crisis facts had been withheld, time had been denied and a feeling of panic had been engendered."[66] But the range of criticism as well as the range of political beliefs by the critics, as we shall later discuss, worked against them, especially in contrast to the single consistent message presented by the administration and echoed by the influential press.

The response from the target of the president's warning, the Soviet Union, was curious. On the one hand, *Izvestia* and *Pravda* denounced the speech as "adventurist." *Pravda* charged that Truman's arguments were borrowed from Hitler who "also referred to the Bolshevik danger when he prepared for the seizure of one state or another."[67] It charged that the United States had disregarded its obligations to the United Nations. Instead, according to *Pravda*, the Americans were extending the Monroe Doctrine to Europe. It was on this point that the Soviets would repeatedly dwell. On the other hand, the Soviets, according to at least one American scholar writing later, did not seem "unduly disturbed."[68] Soviet actions at the time appear to support that conclusion. Even as the party press was denouncing Truman, the Soviets were continuing the meetings in Moscow. When Secretary Marshall had an interview with Stalin on April 19, the eve of his departure, Stalin was in a relaxed mood, according to Bohlen. The Soviet leader suggested that if differences could not be resolved immediately, then six months later they could try again.[69] It appears that the Soviets did not originally take Truman's speech that seriously or as a direct threat to them. In October 1944, Stalin had agreed with Churchill that Greece lay within the British sphere of influence.[70] They were not directly involved in the Greek civil war.[71] And after the initial propaganda blasts at the United States, the statements from *Pravda* and *Izvestia* moderated. In sum, the Soviets seemed to understand the ideological statement Truman had made better than some others since they depended on an ideological rhetoric themselves. As Henri Lefebvre observed: "Only another ideology of true theory [that is, a theory taken by its advocates to be true] can struggle against an ideology."[72] Truman had constructed an anti-communist ideology to combat the spread of the communist ideology.

Conversely, Truman received support from presumed political opponents. Governor Dewey of New York, titular head of the Republican party, came out strongly for Truman. Alf Landon, FDR's presidential opponent in 1936, implied his approval by declaring that "the military dictatorship of Russia has reverted to original Marxism and is seeking to impose it on the whole world by force."[73] These statements lent bipartisan support not only to Truman's policy, but also to his view of the new meaning of the postwar world.

Overall, the reaction to Truman's speech was positive. Editorial writers around the country applauded it, Democrats rejoiced that he was acting like a president, and polls showed increasing support for both the president and his policy. Clearly, Truman had struck a responsive chord and could now play it for all it was worth.

THE TRUMAN DOCTRINE AND THE NEW REALITY: NEW DEFINITIONS AND OLD LANGUAGE

The three basic elements of creating a new political reality, as noted earlier, are actual events, the language used to interpret those events, and the widespread acceptance of that interpretation. All three are plainly visible in this situation.

The actual event that precipitated the speech was the British declaration that they could no longer provide aid to Greece and Turkey. But that would be mentioned only in passing. Instead, other events would be cited for Truman's speech, his policy, and his action.

Truman's address did not merely interpret events that were present without Truman's words. By defining certain events as he did and constructing arguments to support those definitions, the president called a new reality into being and gave it meaning. In essence, he set a new political reality in motion. But he did not do so by words alone. He drew upon a rhetorical stockpile that preexisted the speech, most notably Churchill's speech at Fulton, and had the new reality (i.e., the new language and arguments) extended by the reporting that followed it.

The first aspect of this reality called into existence by Truman was a crisis of world proportions. The core of the speech was based on three definitions, each intimately related to the others. These three laid the foundation for the assertion of the principle that would guide the United States in world affairs and for the immediate policy toward Greece and Turkey that would exemplify that principle.

The first definition was of crisis itself. The president spoke of "this fateful hour" and "gravity of the situation" that confronted not only the United States, but the world at large. Although the press and officials from the administration had prepared the way, the crisis came into full political existence by being spoken into existence.

But unlike Churchill who a year before had warned of an impending crisis but who could only speak in general and metaphoric terms about it, Truman could point specifically, as he did, to the war in Greece. Thus, he had a tangible situation to exemplify the "crisis" and also a tangible situation to lead into the greater issue that he wished to address: "The very existence of the Greek state is today threatened by the terrorist activities of several thousand armed men, led by Communists, who defy the government's authority at a number of points, particularly along the northern boundaries." The "crisis" was heightened, according to Truman, by the Greek government's "urgent" appeal for help. From that point on and in subsequent news reports, the situation in Greece was called a "crisis," a rhetorical description of a complex political situation.[74] The mood of the administration was thereby set and the environment in which Truman's decision would be considered was created. It would be difficult to point to an event of the preceding days that, like the attack on Pearl Harbor, could be construed as critical. It would be more accurate to say that the "crisis" lay in the perception of what the British notes meant to officials of the administration and in the language used to describe that meaning.

The second definition concerned the future of this world "crisis." Churchill had dramatically divided Europe into those countries on either side of an iron curtain, a divison that Truman drew upon in his address. But Churchill stressed the political nature as much as the ideological shape of the impending conflict—the rise of Communist parties on the western side, and the consolidation of the Soviet "sphere" on the eastern side. Churchill even went so far as to assert that the British understood the USSR's "need to be secure on her western frontiers from all renewal of German aggression." That admission weakened the argument he had made by giving some legitimacy to Soviet concerns for security against the West.

Truman would have none of this. Even as he drew upon Churchill's fundamental division, the president both contracted and expanded the meaning. He defined the world conflict as ideological, a Manichean choice between freedom and totalitarianism, or as he phrased it between "alternative ways of life." (By simple word count, Truman used the word "free" or one of its derivatives twenty-four times in the eighteen-minute speech, "totalitarian" four times, "democracy" three times. "Communist" is only used once, and the Soviet Union was never mentioned.) Truman made no reference to understanding the USSR's needs for security or for any other interpretation of the increasing disagreements between the United States and the Soviet Union. Instead, he gave Americans a linguistically created political reality in which the confusions of the present were clarified in the simple terms of a contest between the defense of freedom and the threat of totalitarianism, between two mutually exclusive ways of life, between political good and political evil. In this way Truman's language sought to transcend the actual conditions in Greece and Turkey and to transform their meaning so as to create a different public consciousness (and public reality) about the challenge the United States faced.

But even as he was constricting the meaning of the conflict, he was expanding its application to the entire world: "At the present moment in world history nearly every nation must choose between alternative ways of life." In addition, he was further expanding America's role.

Churchill had called for an Anglo–American alliance. That had caused some to claim that Churchill was asking Americans to rescue the crumbling British empire. Truman avoided this rhetorical trap. The president emphasized unilateral U.S. action in saving Greece from totalitarianism. "No other nation is willing and able to provide the necessary support." Truman asserted, nor was the United Nations "in a position to extend help of the kind that is required." Thus, Truman defined the new role of the United States in world affairs. If it is too harsh to call this speech a declaration of war (since Truman stated that U.S. assistance should "primarily" be financial and economic), the speech was at least the call to a holy ideological crusade in defense of freedom against the aggressive forces of totalitarianism.

From this second definition Truman proceeded to the final, more troublesome one: how to describe the situation in the Near East to conform to the general declaration of policy. Already we have seen the difficulty that writers and advisers had in describing the governments of either Greece or Turkey as democratic. Therefore, the definition of *free* ("free institutions, representative government, etc.") used in the policy section was expanded in those parts of the speech that dealt with Greece and Turkey to mean "independent." Indeed, in the case of Turkey, that was the only justification for aid: "The future of Turkey as an independent and economically sound state is clearly no less important to the freedom-loving peoples of the world than the future of Greece." Economic aid was needed, Truman said, to help Turkey maintain its "national integrity." In the case of Greece, an additional quality was present: the desire (only obliquely evident at the time) "to become a self-supporting and self-respecting democracy." Thus, the conditions for being recognized as a "free" nation were reinterpreted in these two instances, as they would be in many cases to come, to include "independent" nations or even nations that only "desired" to become democratic. The justification was thereby established for later alliances with nations that made no pretense to meeting the conditions of "free nations." The ways in which Greece and Turkey were treated in this original request for aid under the Truman Doctrine set the precedent for those alliances.

This definitional coin had more than these two sides to it. There was also the problem of describing the threat to Greece and Turkey. Neither the Soviet army nor communist troops from another country had invaded either Greece or Turkey. The administration clearly believed the Soviets were involved and acted upon that belief. But they had no proof. Therefore, they defined the meance in more abstract terms borrowed from the language of democracy (a "militant minority" or "armed minority") or from the language of community ("outside pressures"). The rhetorical problem was that the administration was attempting to define a strategic policy in universalist terms and attempting to justify it in ideological terms. The two constantly clashed even within the speech so what was intended as very clear (if abstract) language had to be constantly redefined and reinterpreted to fit specific situations. The linguistic result was a shifting contraction and expansion of commitment that the doctrine was supposed to allay. The practical result was that the United States was transforming the political reality through these definitions, but also leaving enough elasticity in the language to be able to apply the doctrine to a variety of situations that did not meet the exact conditions inherent in the doctrine.

These finer points were ignored, except by a few critics, at the time. The messianic language of Truman's speech transcended and transformed the mundane complexities of the existential world into a transcendental political reality in which ideological angels do moral and mortal combat with ideological devils.

THE TRUMAN DOCTRINE AS COMMUNITY EVENT: THE LANGUAGE OF SHARING AND THE SHARING OF LANGUAGE

Truman's speech was a community event in several ways. The most obvious way in which it was such an event was that it was broadcast and distributed not only nationally but internationally. But we mean something much more than that.

Truman built upon Churchill's speech. The former prime minister had described a world divided by an "iron curtain" into two opposing communities, one the familiar democratic community, the other the alien tyrannical community. Churchill advocated an Anglo–American alliance because the two countries were bound together by a common heritage and common language, quintessential prerequisites for community. A community requires sharing, a common language, common experiences, common aspirations.

Truman built upon Churchill's division but also expanded and redirected it. If Churchill spoke of a world divided into two opposing forces, Truman told how people lived on either side of this division. In the familiar community, which Truman asserted was America's responsibility to lead, people lived in freedom with freedom of speech, free elections, rule by the majority and above all, freedom of religion. Cowering behind the iron curtain, people in the alien community have no free choice, no free elections, are ruled by a minority forcibly imposed by terror and coercion upon them. Thus, Truman shifted the idea of commonality that bound the familiar community together from a literal common language, English, to a common political language of freedom and from a common heritage of democratic governments to common aspirations for independence. In practical terms this shift allowed Truman to include Greece and Turkey in the civilized Western community. This larger definition also held out future membership to other nations who sought to reject the alien community and to adopt the ways of democratic living. In political terms, the emphasis on a unilateral U.S. policy combined with this shift in definition of the free world avoided Churchill's mistake in calling for an Anglo–American alliance, a policy that had ignited anti-British suspicions in the United States.

Whereas Churchill had at least given lip service to the alien community's needs, Truman emphasized their illegitimate activities that he said posed a threat to the familiar community: "The Government of the United States has made frequent protests against coercion and intimidation in violation of the Yalta agreement, in Poland, Rumania, and Bulgaria. I must also state that in a number of other countries there have been similar developments." In speaking of "the other way of life" as Truman euphemistically termed it, he repeatedly described it in language usually associated with aliens: defying existing authority, exploiting human misery and want, creating chaos, and most pertinently, as a sinister minority. Such stereotypical descriptions evoke the fears of self-contained communities to intruders in their midst. In the past Americans had feared aliens from foreign countries. Now they were being called upon to fear a new kind of alien, one who had foreign ideas. In this sense, Truman's speech was intended to create communal fears of an alien community even as it was intended to evoke pride and determination in protecting the stereotypcial values of the existing community. All of this required a new common language that went beyond the narrow common language of English advocated by Churchill.

Again, Truman expanded Churchill's notion of a common heritage from that of the English-speaking world to another common heritage of more recent vintage. The community of free nations shared the common experience of World War II, and Truman likened it to the common danger that now existed:

One of the primary objectives of the foreign policy of the United States is the creation of conditions in which we and other nations will be able to work out a way of life free from coercion. This was a fundamental issue in the war with Germany and Japan. Our victory was won over countries which sought to impose their will, and their way of life, upon other nations.

In other words, what had bound free nations together before must now bind them together again to face the challenge of new representation of an old enemy. The repeated use of the word "totalitarian" rather than communist made this conceptual linkage. Communism and fascism, in the current political geneology, were only two different progenies of a common political parent, totalitarianism. Truman made his conceptual association explicit through the historical analogy he cited.

The narrative or dramatic form he used to present the conflict in Greece and America's response to it was the melodramatic form. In this script Truman presented a helpless heroine ("the Greek Government is unable to cope with the situation. The Greek army is small and poorly equipped") menaced by a sinister villain ("The very existence of the Greek state is today threatened by the terrorist activities by several thousand armed men, led by Communists"). Truman demanded that the stalwart hero, the United States, rush to the rescue of the beleagued heroine: "The United States must supply this assistance [to Greece]. There is no other country to which democratic Greece can turn." All that is missing from this scenario are pictures of the heroine tied to the railroad tracks, the villain twirling his moustache, and the fair-haired hero racing against odds and obstacles to the rescue. Although Truman termed the failure to act a potential tragedy, he really was using melodrama to demand support for his proposals.

The president's language was straightforward with few literary flourishes. However, in attempting to magnify the problem, he drew explicitly on the growth metaphor. If Greece fell, he contended, totalitarian regimes (by which he meant communist regimes) would "spread and grow." The result would be "confusion and disorder" throughout the Near East, increasing problems in Europe, and eventually a disaster for the world. The president linked the metaphor of growth with life itself, asserting that when totalitarian regimes reach full growth, "the hope of a people for a better life has died." The great Western hero, the United States, "must keep that hope alive." Implicit in these descriptions were the policy of containment and the disease metaphor, though Truman stated neither directly. But it was only a small step from the "evil soil" in which totalitarianism is nurtured to the "evil system" that spreads deadly infections. Likewise it was only another small step from how such regimes "spread and grow" to a policy to "contain" that spread and growth.

But language alone does not possess any magical qualities to change consciousness. That brings us to a second aspect of the Truman speech as a community event: the acceptance and sharing of the president's view of reality. We have already seen how the American press responded positively. The influential press had been carefully cultivated about what kind of policy was needed for the world and had printed stories in advance of the speech pointing to such needs so that Truman's address became self-fulfilling prophecy. Part of this was due to the extensive briefings of reporters by administration officials prior to and after the speech. Part was also due to journalistic responsibilities to add to the story with additional accounts of how the decision was made, what it meant, and so on. A primary reason for responding as they did was that most journalists agreed with the president on the nature of the "crisis" the country faced. Influential newspapers and magazines immediately filled in the blanks left by the president by naming the Soviets as the chief perpetrators of unrest in the world. They printed maps, some of them with menacing personifications of the USSR, that showed how large the Soviet Union was in comparison with the two small nations Truman proposed to aid. *Time* went so far as to give a prominent place in its "International" section to an interview with the ex-Trotskyite, James Burnham, upon the publication of his book, *The Struggle for the World*, five days after Truman's speech. Much of Burnham's ideological analysis of the world situation coincided with Truman's, with an even more pessimistic forecast.[75] But the press went beyond such reinforcements of the president's message, and in two distinctive ways.

It was at this time that the word "containment" first began to circulate as a description of U.S. strategy. The popularly held belief that it came later after George Kennan's "X" article was published is erroneous. In the March 17 issue of *Newsweek* which was published in advance of the speech and certainly as a preparation for it, the lead story in the "National Affairs" section read: "Policy: 'Containment' of Communism." The story gives the administration's version of the events requiring the speech, but attributed the policy to the secretary of state: "There could be no doubt what this [Truman's meeting with congressional leaders] meant. The word for Marshall's policy was 'containment'—containment of communism."[76]

Time magazine picked up on the word, but in a different context. Administration officials had feared that aid to Greece, especially military aid, might be interpreted as intervention or imperialism. It is this problem that *Time* confronted:

Was the program [aid to Greece and Turkey] a kind of U.S. imperialism? Those Americans made uncomfortable by this word might have to find another word which did not distress them so much. For the U.S. was in a world divided between two great antagonists. Communist imperialism must be contained. U.S. influence must expand to contain it.[77]

This brief excerpt succinctly summarizes so much of what we have been describing. The most influential national magazine of the time had repeated almost verbatim Truman's basic premises. Henry Luce and his writers might disagree on how the president's policy should be implemented, as they certainly did when it came to applying the doctrine to

China, but they shared the president's view of the new division of the world, the antagonists, and the ideological content of the worldwide struggle. Equally important, the magazine blithely noted that if people did not like the way some described the policy (imperialism), then a more congenial description (containment) should be adopted. It was as simple as that. Change the language and one changes the way people view the policy.

Second, some in the press began a line of argument against dissenters from Truman's policy that would become more widespread and lethal in the future. *Newsweek* ran a story about Senator Claude Pepper's criticism of the president's policy. The title of the story was simply "Red Pepper." Although it printed excerpts from Pepper, it described his reactions as "predictable" and "predictably vociferous." The writer of the story seemed to take delight in writing that Pepper's criticism appeared in *In Fact*, a weekly newsletter that "for years has followed the Communist party line with unflinching loyalty." The story was accompanied by a 1942 picture of Senator Pepper captioned "Pepper and comrades: When Russia called, he rallied—and rallies again." Two people in the five-year-old picture were identified in a footnote: Rep. Vito Marcantonio and Joseph Curran, president of the National Maritime Union (CIO).[78] With such "reporting," *Newsweek* was consigning Pepper to the alien community. Unfortunately, with the president's proclamation of a domestic Truman Doctrine—the Loyalty Program and its attendant Loyalty Review Board and attorney general's list of subversive organizations—only nine days after the foreign Truman Doctrine, such irresponsible charges would not only become commonplace, but would increase in fury.

THE TRUMAN DOCTRINE AND AUTHORITY: A NEW HARRY TRUMAN

The authority with which one speaks directly influences belief. Part of Churchill's authority came from his person. His reputation as spokesman for freedom during World War II required that others weigh his words seriously, even if they rejected them at the time. Harry Truman's authority came from his office. He was president of the United States and he was proposing a sharp departure from traditional U.S. foreign policy. Unlike Churchill, he was in a position to implement that policy. But in this particular case, the speech lent authority to Truman.

Ever since he had been propelled into the presidency, he had been hounded by questions, mainly privately spoken but sometimes voiced in public, about whether he was up to the job. He pondered the same questions himself. With the decisive language and bold policy of this speech, he began to be transformed. Again, this was no overnight or magical transformation. His appointment of General Marshall, probably the most esteemed American citizen of the time, as secretary of state in January 1947 enhanced his authority. The other appointments early that year conveyed the image that government by crony was being replaced with government by capability. Secretary Marshall's pointed deference to the president, especially noted in his announcement about the Greek request for aid, added further to recognition of Truman's ultimate responsibility for foreign policy. Yet, these only prepared the way.

Truman had made an historic decision. He had presented it to Congress in an historic speech. He had used little evidence in the speech, and the logic of relating Greece and Turkey to his doctrine was tortured. Yet, the sweep of his proposal and the fears he aroused created a new Harry Truman.

The transformation was immediately noted. Reporters noticed a new briskness to his step. *Newsweek* reported there was no question now whether he would run for election in his own right or not.[79] His personal approval rating that had stood at 32 percent just after the 1946 congressional elections, now had soared to more than 60 percent.[80] Long stories in major magazines now treated him with greater respect. Before the speech at least one writer had called America's upcoming new global strategy, Marshall's policy. Now and forever more, it would be known as the Truman Doctrine. The increasing prestige accorded to the president gave greater authority to his version of reality and the appropriate ways for Americans to deal with it.

CONCLUSION

On May 22 Truman signed the bill authorizing aid to Greece and Turkey into law. But in the days between February 21 and May 22 much more had happened than a partisan campaign for a political policy. A new reality about the world and America's place in it was announced and began to take hold. The process had begun with Churchill's speech but now it had been Americanized and given an enormous boost by Truman's address. Both Churchill and Truman described a world divided into two irreconcilable ideologies. Whereas Churchill called for an alliance, Truman insisted that only the United States was strong enough to engage in this ideological war. The American way of life was at stake. A world hung in the balance. When Secretary Marshall objected to the extravagance of the speech, the reply was that it was the "only way" the president could get Congress to pass the legislation for aid to Greece.[81] That reply suggests that Truman believed the rhetoric pertained only to this situation and that he had Congress in mind as his principal audience. He may have believed that such universal language and commitments were needed on this specific occasion to pass the enabling legislation and that later he could apply these principles selectively. There is considerable evidence that Truman and his advisers did not believe these principles should be applied to Asia, especially China. But Truman underestimated the powerful impact his speech had and the authority he possessed. The drama of the crisis, the melodramatic presentation of arguments, the sinister enemy who was linked to the just defeated but universally hated Nazis—all came together to produce a growing unity among Americans in opposition to communism. Indeed, the rhetorical threat of a diabolical enemy threatening the world all but obscured the policy of sending aid to Greece and Turkey. Bipartisan support from Democrats and Republicans, reinforced by leading journalistic opinion-makers, made it a common reality beyond partisan differences, beyond the president's power to control or recall it. The extensive publicity generated in the press overwhelmed criticism of this new reality. Those who had the fortitude to question or criticize found themselves consigned to the alien community in which questions about their patriotism were raised. In his brief speech President Harry Truman constructed only the bare bones of an American anticommunist ideology. Others would give flesh and muscle to it.

NOTES

1. *Newsweek* (March 24, 1947), p. 23. This description was a paraphrase of Senator Vandenberg's request to suspend senatorial discussion of the constitutional amendment to limit a president to two terms in office so that Congress could prepare for Truman's speech an hour later.

2. "Special Message to the Congress on Greece and Turkey: The Truman Doctrine," *Public Papers of the Presidents of the United States: Harry S. Truman, 1947* (Washington: U.S. Government Printing Office, 1963), pp. 178–79. All subsequent quotations from this speech are taken from this printed version, pp. 176–80.

3. *New York Times* (March 13, 1947), p. 3.

4. Margaret Truman, *Harry S. Truman* (New York: Pocket Books, 1974), p. 375.

5. Dean Acheson, *Present at the Creation* (New York: W. W. Norton, 1969), p. 247.

6. The "first round" in the civil war occurred in 1943–44; the "second" extended from 1944 to 1945. The election in March 1946 precipitated the "third round." For varying interpretations of the significance of the evolving events in Greece during this critical period and U.S. responses to them, see Howard Jones, *"A New Kind of War": America's Global Strategy and The Truman Doctrine in Greece* (New York: Oxford University Press, 1989); Lawrence S. Wittner, *American Intervention in Greece, 1943–1949* (New York: Columbia University Press, 1982); John O. Iatrides, ed., *Greece in the 1940s: A Nation in Crisis* (Hanover, NH: University Press of New England, 1981); Bruce Robellet Kuniholm, *The Origins*

of the Cold War in the Near East (Princeton, NJ: Princeton University Press, 1980). Although these writers differ on interpretations and the relative strength and influence of communists within the insurgent movement, they generally agree that it was indeed a civil war that was being fought in Greece.

7. For background see Kuniholm, *The Origins of the Cold War*, pp. 6–72, 303–82; George S. Harris, *Troubled Alliance: Turkish-American Problems in Historical Perspective, 1945–1971* (Washington, DC: American Enterprise Institute for Public Policy Research, 1972), pp. 23–25.

8. See Wittner, *American Intervention in Greece*, pp. 1–102.

9. Acheson, *Present at the Creation*, p. 217.

10. Harry S. Truman, *Memoirs: Years of Trial and Hope*, vol. 2 (Garden City, NY: Doubleday, 1956), p. 100. For Truman's memory of his thoughts at this time, see these *Memoirs*, pp. 93–102.

11. Harry S. Truman, *Memoirs: Year of Decisions*, vol. 1 (Garden City, NY: Doubleday, 1955), p. 552.

12. "American Relations with the Soviet Union: A Report to the President by the Special Council [*sic*] to the President September—, 1946, Top Secret," printed as Appendix A in Arthur Krock, *Memoirs* (New York: Funk and Wagnalls, 1968), p. 431. The complete document runs from pp. 421–82. All subsequent quotations are from this publication.

13. Henry Wallace noted in his diary: "It almost seemed as though he was eager to decide in advance of thinking." Quoted in Robert J. Donovan, *Conflict and Crisis: The Presidency of Harry S. Truman, 1945–1948* (New York: W. W. Norton, 1977), p. 24. On his love of making decisions and his temperament as a judge, see Donovan, pp. 23–24, and Richard Neustadt, *Presidential Power: The Politics of Leadership* (New York: John Wiley, 1980), pp. 125–31.

14. Margaret Truman, *Truman*, p. 375.

15. "Measures To Meet the British Request for Immediate Aid to Greece and Turkey," *Foreign Relations* (1947), pp. 59–60.

16. Acheson, *Present at the Creation*, p. 219.

17. Louis J. Halle, *The Cold War as History* (New York: Harper and Row, 1968), p. 113.

18. "The Secretary of State to the Embassy in Greece" (February 28, 1947), *Foreign Relations* (1947), 5, pp. 69–71. The actual text was written early in the day. Henderson received Paul Economou-Gouras, the Greek charge d'affaires, at the State Department on March 28 and wrote the request that Marshall sent to the Greek government.

19. See Wittner, *American Intervention in Greece*, pp. 64–67.

20. Among those who dissented was General James K. Crain, deputy chairman of the Policy Committee on Arms and Armaments. He thought the United States would only be repeating Great Britain's mistake by continuing its policy of economic and military aid. He preferred a military warning to the Soviets to stay out of Greece and Turkey and to save up U.S. military might to back up that warning if necessary.

21. Acheson, *Present at the Creation*, p. 219.

22. For background on Truman's difficulties with the Eightieth Congress, see Susan M. Hartmann, *Truman and the 80th Congress* (New York: Columbia University Press, 1973).

23. Most prominent, as later events would reveal, was Richard Nixon's 1946 campaign against Jerry Voorhis. But Nixon's was only the most publicized of these campaigns. See Roger Morris, *Richard Milhous Nixon: The Rise of an American Politician* (New York: Henry Holt, 1990), pp. 257–337; and Stephen E. Ambrose, *Nixon: The Education of a Politician 1913–1962* (New York: Simon and Schuster, 1987), pp. 117–40.

24. Representative John Taber, chief of the House Appropriations Committee, was invited but unable to attend. Senator Robert Taft, who later would lead congressional criticism of the Truman Doctrine, was not invited. At Vandenberg's recommendation, the president included Taft in the next meeting on March 10.

25. Acheson, *Present at the Creation*, p. 219.

26. See Charles L. Mee, Jr., *The Marshall Plan: The Launching of Pax Americana* (New York: Simon and Schuster, 1984), pp. 35–37.

27. Acheson, *Present at the Creation*, p. 219.

28. "Statement by the Secretary of State," *Foreign Relations* (1947), 5, pp. 60–63.

29. Jones, *Fifteen Weeks*, p. 141.

30. Acheson, *Present at the Creation*, p. 219.

31. Quoted in Wittner, *American Intervention in Greece*, p. 71.

32. Bert Cochran, *Harry Truman and the Crisis Presidency* (New York: Funk and Wagnalls, 1973), p. 187. Cochran was following Eric Goldman who first reported this remark in *The Crucial Decade*. No contemporary account, either by Vandenberg or other participants in the meeting, attributes this remark to Vandenberg.

33. Jones, *Fifteen Weeks*, p. 142. The idea of a national radio address was later dropped since the speech itself was broadcast nationally.

34. Ibid., p. 143.

35. Jones's account of writing the speech is still the basic and most important description of that process. However it should be augmented by two more recent studies. See John J. Iselin, "The Truman Doctrine: A Study in the Relationship Between Crisis and Foreign Policy-Making" Ph.D. diss., Harvard University, 1964; and Bernard Weiner, "The Truman Doctrine: Background and Presentation" Ph.D. diss., Claremont Graduate School, 1967.

36. Truman, *Memoirs*, p. 105.

37. Jones, *Fifteen Weeks*, p. 171.

38. Instead, as *Time* pointed out, Marshall had to attempt a definition of democracy that the world would understand, so as to make clear the extent of the new commitments Truman was making. See "New Definition Wanted," *Time* (March 24, 1947), p. 27. As difficult as this task was, it was a far easier rhetorical problem than defending anti-Soviet statements in Moscow.

39. See Wittner, *American Intervention in Greece*, n. 26, p. 344.

40. This part of the speech came not from the speechwriters but from the "Basic United States Policy" statement drafted by Francis Russell and the State-War-Navy Coordinating Committee that had been working on the president's new policy. Jones, *Fifteen Weeks*, pp. 152–53.

41. See Carl Wayne Hensley, "Harry S. Truman: Fundamental Americanism in Foreign Policy Speechmaking, 1945–1946," *Southern Speech Communication Journal* 40 (Winter 1975), pp. 180–90.

42. Jones, *Fifteen Weeks*, p. 160.

43. See *Time* (March 24, 1947), p. 21.

44. Thomas J. Schoenbaum, *Waging Peace and War: Dean Rusk in the Truman, Kennedy and Johnson Years* (New York: Simon and Schuster, 1988), p. 149.

45. See George F. Kennan, *Memoirs: 1925–1950* (Boston: Atlantic-Little, Brown, 1967), pp. 313–24.

46. Quoted in Mee, *The Marshall Plan*, p. 48.

47. Jones, *Fifteen Weeks*, p. 152.

48. Ibid., p. 145.

49. Summarized in ibid., p. 144–45.

50. *New York Times* (March 2, 1947), p. 4.

51. Jones, *Fifteen Weeks*, p. 163.

52. For a paragraph-by-paragraph analysis, see Wayne Brockriede and Robert L. Scott, "The Rhetoric of Containment: America Develops a Policy and an Ideology," *Moments in the Rhetoric of the Cold War* (New York: Random House, 1970), pp. 10–43.

53. Later Joseph Jones complained about this military emphasis rather than the economic emphasis in the speech.

54. For only one example of this interpretation, see the editorial "Phony Peace," *Life* (June 16, 1947), p. 43.

55. Alexis de Tocqueville, *Democracy in America*, the Henry Reeve text, rev. Francis Bowen, ed. Phillips Bradley, vol. 2 (New York: Vintage, 1945), p. 73.

56. *Time* (March 24, 1947), p. 25.

57. *New York Times* (March 13, 1947), p. 1.

58. Ibid., p. 3.

59. Ibid., p. 26.

60. Quoted in the *New York Times* (March 13, 1947), p. 4. See the other excerpts from a broad range of newspapers that the *Times* printed.

61. "Struggle for the World," *Life* (April 21, 1947), p. 38.

62. "Preventing a Third World War," *U.S. News* (March 21, 1947), p. 21.

63. Quoted in Henry W. Berger, "Senator Robert A. Taft Dissents from Military Escalation," in *Cold War Critics*, ed. Thomas G. Patterson (Chicago: Quadrangle Books, 1947), p. 177.

64. *Newsweek* (March 24, 1947), p. 23.

65. *Nation* (March 15, 1947), p. 290.

66. Henry Wallace, "The State Department's Case," *New Republic* (April 7, 1947), p. 12.

67. *New York Times* (March 16, 1947), p. 5. See the excerpts from Soviet Ambassador Gromyko's speech at Lake Success in *Time* (April 21, 1947), p. 25.

68. Adam B. Ulam, *Stalin: The Man and His Era*, expanded ed. (Boston: Beacon Press, 1989), pp. 657–59.

69. Charles E. Bohlen, *Witness to History, 1929–1969* (New York: W. W. Norton, 1973), p. 262–64. See these pages also for Marshall's reaction to this interview and the significance of that reaction.

70. See diagram of percentages of these spheres in Hugh Thomas, *Armed Truce: The Beginnings of the Cold War, 1945–1946* (New York: Atheneum, 1986), p. 555.

71. Most serious scholars, even some who support Truman's decision, now

doubt that the Soviets were directly involved in the events in Greece. See, for example, Kunniholm, *Origins of the Cold War in the Near East*, p. 426. Milovan Djilas went so far as to quote Stalin as saying at about this time: "The uprising in Greece must be stopped, and as quickly as possible." *Conversations with Stalin*, trans. Michael B. Petrovich (New York: Harcourt, Brace, and World, 1962), p. 182.

72. Henri Lefebvre, *The Sociology of Marx*, trans. Norbert Guterman (New York: Pantheon, 1968), p. 77.

73. *Newsweek* (March 31, 1947), p. 22.

74. On the rhetorical nature of "crisis" in political speeches, see Theodore Otto Windt, Jr., *Presidents and Protesters: Political Rhetoric in the Nineteen Sixties* (Tuscaloosa, AL: University of Alabama Press, 1990), pp. 3–6.

75. *Time* (March 24, 1947), pp. 26–27.

76. *Newsweek* (March 17, 1947), p. 27.

77. *Time* (March 24, 1947), p. 20.

78. *Newsweek* (March 31, 1947), p. 25.

79. *Newsweek* (March 31, 1947), p. 23.

80. *Time* (April 7, 1947), p. 23.

81. According to Bohlen, Marshall thought the speech "overstated the case a bit." See Bohlen, *The Transformation of American Foreign Policy*, p. 87.

Chapter Six

The Truman Doctrine Extended: The Loyalty Program

It was only a small step from the declaration of an American policy to defend against enemies abroad to the announcement of a program to defend the United States from enemies within. How could it be otherwise? In fact, the Loyalty Program announced by the president only nine days after his dramatic speech to Congress was a logical extension of the Truman Doctrine, on the one hand, and the next necessary act in rhetorically legitimizing the new cold war reality, on the other. A universal policy would not be universal were it not applied at home as well as abroad.

BACKGROUND

Investigations into communist influence in the United States had begun with the Red Scare during the Wilson administration. But it was congressional action in late prewar years that prefigured the witch hunts that occurred after the war. In 1938 Congress established a new committee, the House Committee on UnAmerican Activities, under the chairmanship of Martin Dies of Texas. Congressman Dies with the vocal support of J. Parnell Thomas, Republican from New Jersey, appeared more interested in investigations of the relationship between the New Deal and communism and of leftist subversives in government than in examining the Fascist threat of those anxious days.[1] But that was understandable. Dies was a conservative Democrat who detested the New Deal, and Thomas was a reactionary Republican whose passion was his opposition to communism. After some sensational charges in the prewar years, the committee faded into the public background during the war even as it continued its hearings into general matters about communist infiltration in the Roosevelt administration.

Measures to keep disloyal people from government employment had its roots in World War II. When war came, the Civil Service Commission issued a regulation disqualifying any applicant for employment in the federal government if the commission ascertained "a reasonable doubt as to his loyalty." In April 1942 the attorney general created an Inter-departmental Committee on Investigations to inform governmental agencies about procedures for determining employee loyalty and to prepare reports on "front groups." A year later President Roosevelt issued Executive Order 9300 through which he replaced the committee with an interdepartmental advisory board whose purpose was to "study the problem of subversion, to advise the Department of Justice on handling it, to receive FBI reports on accused employees and follow up on actions taken in the various departments and agencies as a result of these reports."[2] This committee survived the war, but by then it was more a paper committee than an investigative committee. Nonetheless, the contemporary precedent for barring suspected disloyal persons from federal employment had been established.

After Truman's ascension to the presidency, two streams came together that would merge into a raging river of hysteria, fear, and retribution. The first stream had as its source the great spy scare of the immediate postwar years. In 1945 the Office of Strategic Services raided the offices of *Amerasia*, an obscure scholarly journal devoted to Far Eastern studies, and discovered a cache of classified State Department documents which apparently had been passed by government officials to the editor. Although there was less to the incident than most histories record, it garnered sensational headlines at the time, especially in the Hearst and Scripps-Howard newspapers.[3] A year later the Canadian government announced that it had uncovered a Soviet spy ring operating within the government. The arrests were based on information given by a Soviet defector, Igor Gouzenko, who also confided he had been told that an aide to Secretary of State Edward Stettinius was a Soviet agent. This latter piece of information would put the FBI on the trail of Alger Hiss. But for the time being the Canadian announcement was sensational in and of itself. These highly publicized incidents of spying, the public's years of concern over Nazi spying as well as its growing fear of domestic communists—these combined to stir a strong current of suspicion within American life.[4]

The second stream was political, pure and simple. After fourteen years of being beaten over the head with responsibility for the Great Depression, Republicans found an issue to do some head-bashing themselves.

The issue was communism. In the election of 1946 some Republicans made it a major issue. The National Republican Committee sent out materials about communism that candidates could use. When they seized control of both houses of Congress from the Democrats, they sensed that they had a potent weapon to counterbalance the political potency of the Depression. If Republicans could be charged with not caring about the economic well-being of American citizens, Democrats could be charged with not caring about the political security of American citizens. If Republicans could be accused of leading the country into the Great Depression, Democrats could be accused of leading the country down the road to socialism, or worse, allowing America to be infiltrated with communists.

The new Republican Congress's zeal for an anticommunist crusade was not lost on Truman. To make certain he got the message, House Majority Leader Joseph Martin announced that the new Congress would put an end to the disloyal practice of "boring from within by subversionists high up in the administration."[5] He promised a housecleaning in Washington. The president reacted to protect both the administration and Democrats. On November 25, 1946, shortly after the election, the president established a Temporary Commission on Loyalty charged with determining whether existing procedures for screening government employees were adequate. On February 20, 1947 the commission delivered its report to the president. Although it was unable to agree on the extent of the threat disloyal government employees posed, the commission said that the threat was more than theoretical.[6] A month later President Truman issued Executive Order 9835, "Prescribing Procedures for the Administration of an Employee Loyalty Program in the Executive Branch of the Government."[7] Although Truman's Loyalty Program did not receive the extensive publicity his doctrine did, it was equally important, especially to the development of the cold war rhetoric. Richard Fried succinctly described its significance: "This act helped fix the assumptions, language, and methods that fueled the assault on American liberalism mounted by McCarthy and other anti-Communist politicians."[8]

TRUMAN'S LOYALTY PROGRAM

Unlike other rhetorical artifacts, an executive order states its justificatory arguments explicitly at the beginning, and therefore these are worth citing in full:

WHEREAS each employee of the Government of the United States is endowed with a measure of trusteeship over the democratic processes which are the heart and sinew of the United States; and

WHEREAS it is of vital importance that persons employed in the Federal service be of complete and unswerving loyalty to the United States; and

WHEREAS, although the loyalty of by far the overwhelming majority of all Government employees is beyond question, the presence within the Government service of any disloyal or subversive person constitutes a threat to our democratic processes; and

WHEREAS maximum protection must be afforded the United States against infiltration of disloyal persons into the ranks of its employees, and equal protection from unfounded accusations of disloyalty must be afforded the loyal employees of the Government.

As high-sounding as these sentiments seem, there were several problems with this raison d'etre, or to be more precise, *raison d'etat*. First was the problem of defining subversion and disloyalty, and second was the problem of procedures for protecting the rights of people accused of being disloyal. The remainder of the Executive Order addressed these problems as well as establishing the bureaucracy to deal with them.

The definition of disloyalty was not difficult. Disloyalty or subversion usually involves an overt act that can be determined as a clear violation of one's allegiance to the country, such acts as sabotage, espionage, treason, or sedition, all of which were included as definitions within the Executive Order. But Truman's Order expanded the definition from *activities* to *associations*, and these *associations* were defined as:

Membership in, affiliation with or *sympathetic association* with any foreign or domestic organization, association, movement, group or combination of persons, designated by the Attorney General as totalitarian, fascist, communist, or subversive, or as having adopted a policy of advocating or approving the commission of acts of force or violence to deny other persons their rights under the Constitution of the United States, or as seeking to alter the form of government of the United States by unconstitutional means.[9]

Such loose language opened the proverbial Pandora's Box for investigation. This section lifted people out of time, out of history. When would such "affiliations" or "associations" be considered subversive? In the far more innocent past or only in the immediate present? How could one determine whether an "association" was political or personal, treasonous or innocent? On what basis would the attorney general decide an "organization, association, movement, group or combination of persons" were totalitarian or fascist or whatever? By making a universal statement that transcended time and circumstance, the Order opened the way for any and all kinds of investigations into applicants' beliefs and friendships. It was only a small step to investigating any American for the same reason.

The procedures outlined within the Order did not protect individual rights as the preamble promised. The departments within the executive branch charged with responsibility for the loyalty of their employees were administrative, not judicial departments. Contrasting the high-sounding principles with actual practices, Francis Biddle, former attorney general under Roosevelt and a vigorous critic of the program, wrote:

Charges under the loyalty procedure must be specific—but only as specific as "security considerations will permit." The employee . . . is permitted to introduce evidence—but only "such evidence as the board may deem proper in the particular case." He may appear by counsel and cross-examine—but not cross-examine the informants. He may call witnesses—but cannot subpoena them. Nonconfidential informants may be called at the hearings and cross-examined, but their names are not in the notice of charges or interrogatories. Testimony is under oath—but not the testimony of informants.[10]

Beyond these considerations, there were others that in future years would become even more damaging. The Loyalty Program reversed usual judicial practice by requiring the defendant to prove a negative—that is, that one is not disloyal—one of the most difficult propositions to prove. If the program did not fully establish the principle of guilt by association, it did institutionalize the principle of suspicion by association.

Truman's program also required the attorney general to keep a list of

each foreign or domestic organization, association, movement, group or combination of persons which the Attorney General . . . designates as totalitarian, fascist, communist, or subversive, or as having adopted a policy of advocating or approving the commission of acts of force or violence to deny others their rights under the Constitution of the United States.[11]

Unlike the lists that previous administrations had kept, this one was made public, the first in late 1947. It included as designated "subversive" organizations the Ohio School of Social Sciences, the Walt Whitman School of Social Sciences in Newark, and the National Negro Congress.[12] There would be additional lists in the future, some expansions of the attorney general's list, some kept by private organizations, some pulled out of briefcases.

The principle upon which Truman's Loyalty Program was based was simple: the world crisis of defending the American way of life, summarized so succinctly in the Truman Doctrine, required that the security of the nation be placed before the rights of citizens, even in peacetime. After all, a war, even one that did not immediately involve direct military hostilities, still required a united public behind the government. Wars, be they hot or cold, cannot be fought with a divided public.[13]

In all fairness to President Truman it should be noted that Truman's primary motive for creating the Loyalty Program was political.[14] Republicans had made being "soft on domestic communism" an issue in the

1946 campaign. By creating his own mechanism for investigating the possibility of subversion in government, the president believed he could short-circuit partisan attacks on the administration on this issue. He could show that he was as tough on domestic subversives as the Republicans, and maybe more so. In addition, he apparently wanted to take the investigative lead away from the Republicans, who would control Congress and thus the House Committee on UnAmerican Activities, by creating his own investigative unit. As he said to one aide, he signed the Order "to take the ball away from Parnell Thomas," who became the new chair of the House Committee.[15] In addition, he could use the communist issue to attack the critics of his foreign policy on his Left. And so it was used, occasionally by the president, as in his 1948 St. Patrick's Day speech, and by his political surrogates in the presidential campaign that year.[16]

But more was involved than politics. Truman, who thought the domestic communist bugaboo had been "blown up out of proportion," also believed that "one disloyal person is too many."[17] Apparently, he believed that by creating the Loyalty Board he could control the currents that were rushing forth in America by dismissing disloyal people, whoever they might be, but at the same time protecting individual rights.[18] But it did not work out that way. *Time* magazine correctly predicted at the time: "In the last analysis, if the U.S. was to have real security and no witch hunts, everything would depend upon the men running the machinery, and how they interpreted their instructions."[19] Others would interpret the threat quite differently from Truman, and they would use the "machinery" available to them for quite different and more intimidating purposes.

THE HOUSE COMMITTEE ON UNAMERICAN ACTIVITIES: 1947

When the Executive Order was issued, members of the House Committee on UnAmerican Activities warmly embraced it. Some members of the committee congratulated the president for creating a commission to deal with subversion. Representative Karl Mundt went so far as to give credit to the committee for prompting the executive branch to act.[20] During the spring and summer of 1947 the committee issued reports and held hearings to draft additional legislation to augment the president's program. These efforts came to naught, but the committee hit pay dirt with its hearings into communist infiltration into the film industry in Hollywood. As Walter Goodman observed: "To [John] Rankin [the anti-Semitic representative from Mississippi and member of the House UnAmerican Activities Committee], Hollywood was Semitic territory. To [J. Parnell] Thomas [chair of the committee], it was New Deal territory. To the entire committee, it was a veritable sun around which the press worshipfully rotated."[21] Above all, it was in Hollywood that the committee could find a few communists to give some validity to its extreme fears of subversion in the United States.

The rhetoric of these hearings set a pattern for chasing domestic communists for years to come. Part of that pattern had already been established in previous investigations, but now it expanded beyond even the loose boundaries of prior hearings. In the spring of 1947 the committee held closed hearings in Los Angeles in preparation for the public appearances scheduled for the fall. Although these meetings were closed, Representative Thomas and his chief investigator, Robert Stripling, briefed the press each afternoon about the charges it had heard of communist infiltration and propaganda from "friendly" witnesses (that is, witnesses who were considered friendly to the committee through their approval of its activities and their willingness to name people as communists or subversives). Thomas claimed that one witness had said that "Hollywood is one of the main centers of Communist activity in America." The chairman concluded that the Screen Writers Guild was "lousy with Communists" and that "the government had wielded the iron fist in order to get the companies to put on certain Communist propaganda."[22] There is little question but that Representative Thomas intended these briefings to serve the twin rhetorical purposes of exalting the importance of the public hearings that were to come and of establishing the authority of witnesses who would "name names" of those engaged in subversive activities in the film industry.

The Hollywood hearings began calling witnesses on October 20, 1947. The committee devoted the first week to listening to "friendly" witnesses, among them the author, Ayn Rand; actors, Robert Taylor, Adolphe Menjou, George Murphy, Ronald Reagan, Gary Cooper; producers, Jack Warner, Louis B. Mayer, and Walter Disney; and others. The following week eleven of the nineteen "unfriendly" witnesses (that is, people accused of being communists or subversives) were called, all of whom were either writers or directors: Alvah Bessie, Herbert Biberman, Edward Dmytryk, Lester Cole, Ring Lardner, Jr., John Howard Lawson, Albert Maltz, Samuel Ornitz, Adrian Scott, Dalton Trumbo, and Bertolt Brecht. Brecht eventually fled the United States, and therefore the remaining "unfriendlies" were known as the Hollywood Ten. The pattern of testimony followed the melodramatic form of anticommunism: dauntless heroes standing against communism and mentally unbalanced or sinister villains. To make the theatrical atmosphere complete, the hearings were broadcast nationally over radio.

The rhetorical stance taken by the committee toward "friendly" witnesses allowed them to read opening statements praising the committee for its work, stressing the importance of weeding out communists from films, trumpeting their own "Americanism," and suggesting what they would do or what should be done to communists who attempted to get work in Hollywood. The committee then questioned the witnesses about subversion in Hollywood and its effects. Ayn Rand, who left the USSR in 1926, presented herself as an expert and rendered a long analysis of the motion picture, *Song of Russia*, produced during World War II. She found it filled with communist propaganda:

[The movie] starts with an American conductor, played by Robert Taylor, giving a concert in America for Russian war relief. He starts playing the American national anthem and the national anthem dissolves into a Russian mob, with the sickle and hammer on a red flag very prominent above their heads. I am sorry, but that made me sick. That is something which I do not see how native Americans permit, and I am only a naturalized American. That was a terrible touch of propaganda. As a writer, I can tell you just exactly what it suggests to the people. It suggests literally and technically that it is quite all right for the American national anthem to dissolve into the Soviet.[23]

This scene from the film, along with others she selected, led Rand to conclude that the "mere presentation of . . . [a] happy existence in a country of slavery and horror is terrible because it is propaganda."[24] Rand saw only two "ways of life"—one of slavery and horror contrasted with the American way.

Other witnesses denounced communism as an ideology and communists as dangerous to American society. Adolphe Menjou described himself as a student of "Marxism, Fabian Socialism, Communism, Stalinism and its probable effects on the American people if they ever gain power here."[25] Relying on these impressive credentials, Menjou stated that the film, *Mission to Moscow* should never have been made and declared that he did not know if John Cromwell was a communist, but "he acts an awful lot like one."[26] Guilt by association did not bother Mr. Menjou; rather he thought that anyone who belonged to a communist-front organization and took no action against the communists or attended "any meetings at which Mr. Paul Robeson appeared" or applauded or listened to Robeson's "Communist songs in America" was probably "acting" like a communist, "a very, very dangerous thing."[27] Indeed, in a very different sense, it would soon become dangerous to performers' careers to be associated with Paul Robeson or listen to suspected "subversive" songs. The arguments witnesses used parroted arguments previously used in the official rhetoric. Witnesses described communists in the film industry as dangerous subversives or mentally unbalanced, the two appellations consistently applied to those outside the growing anticommunist consensus. Menjou described them as "the lunatic fringe, the political idiots, the morons, the dangerous Communists."[28] Others saw them as sinister, persistently attempting to sneak communist propaganda into films so as to take over the industry, to "control it, or disrupt it."[29] Robert Montgomery, the actor, opined that he had given up his job in 1940 "to fight against a totalitarianism which was called fascism" and was willing to do it again "to fight against a totalitarianism called communism."[30] Menjou applied the disease metaphor with a twist by claiming that many people in California were being "cured" of communism by healthy doses of education in Americanism and exposure of the fallacies of communist propaganda by the committee. The committee itself praised several of the witnesses for being outstanding "experts" on communism, among them the mother of Ginger Rogers, Lela Rogers, who was a script reader for RKO and an original member of the Motion Picture Alliance for the Preservation of American Ideals. Her primary contributions to the hearings were to say she had "heard" that the playwright Clifford Odets was a communist, and that her daughter had refused to speak the line, "Share and share alike—that's democracy" in the film, *Tender Comrade*, because it sounded like communist propaganda.[31] Witnesses were allowed to roam over a wide variety of subjects including accusing unions of being communist influenced (to the delight of anti-New Dealers and Republicans) to urging legislation to outlaw the Communist party in the United States. They were able to charge that the menace of communism existed in Hollywood with little or no substantiation of their charges. Above all, the "friendly" witnesses—to a person—described communism as an alien political reality that had to be exposed and stamped out. Robert Taylor spoke fairly well for these witnesses when he said, "if I were given the responsibility of getting rid of them I would love nothing better than to fire every last one of them and never let them work in a studio or in Hollywood again."[32] In other words, the alien (usually described as "foreign") community had to be banished so that films could help the committee achieve what Chairman Thomas called making "America just as pure as we can possibly make it."[33]

The following week "unfriendly" witnesses or the Hollywood Ten were called. They had been subpoenaed, and when they appeared, they were not treated kindly. In preparation for their appearances they decided on a single rhetorical strategy: refusing to answer questions about political beliefs or associations basing their refusal on their First Amendment rights of freedom of speech. According to Ring Lardner, Jr., they sought to say that "the whole investigation was unconstitutional—that where Congress was forbidden to legislate, Congress was forbidden to investigate."[34] To put this strategy into effect, each drew up an opening statement justifying this rhetorical stance. But when the first "unfriendly," John Howard Lawson, was called before the committee, he was not allowed to read his statement.[35] Representative Thomas said that he had "read the first line" and decided that it was "not pertinent to the inquiry."[36] As the committee began to inquire into his political affiliations, Lawson grew belligerent accusing the committee of using Hitlerite tactics to create a new Red Scare. He charged that perjury had been committed and more was planned. But his protestations were to no avail. The committee was interested in only one question: "Are you a member of the Communist Party, or have you ever been a member of the Communist Party?" Lawson refused to answer the question and was physically removed from the hearings by guards. His exit was followed by testimony from Robert Stripling, chief investigator for the committee, testifying to the communist affiliations of Lawson. Lawson, of course, was given no opportunity to reply. Such was the procedural pattern established against the "unfriendly" witnesses. They were called to testify, refused the right to read their prepared statements, questioned briefly about their origins and careers, and then asked the sixty-four dollar question about whether they were or had been communists. (Ring Lardner replied to the question by stating: "I could answer it, but if I did I would hate myself in the morning.")[37] When they declined to answer, they were dismissed and Stripling came forward to testify to their subversive dossiers.

However, the committee reversed its ruling about opening remarks and allowed Albert Maltz to read his statement. Maltz, like the others, stood on his First Amendment rights and argued that he had been deprived of his rights of cross-examination as well as his right to sue for libel (due to congressional immunity granted to these witnesses). He accused Chairman Thomas of using the hearings to attack supporters of the New Deal quoting from a previous hearing in which Thomas had said that he believed the "New Deal is either for the Communist Party or it is playing into the hands of the Communist Party."[38] He concluded by asserting that the committee was the true subverter of the Constitution and stated: "The American people are going to have to choose between the Bill of Rights and the Thomas committee. They cannot have both. One or the other must be abolished in the immediate future."[39] When Maltz refused to answer the big question, he was dismissed with Thomas adding that his testimony had been the "typical Communist line." (Dalton Trumbo had been similarly dismissed with the accusation, again by Thomas, that his testimony exhibited "typical Communist tactics.")

Thus, the treatment of "unfriendly" witnesses demonstrated the rhetoric of nihilation used against those who were perceived as or consigned to the alien community residing outside the new reality of anticommunism. But this nihilation did not end with merely cutting off testimony. Congress cited the Hollywood Ten for contempt on November 24, 1947. That same day film executives began meeting at the Waldorf-Astoria Hotel in New York to consider their position toward the ten. Two days later they announced that the ten were being suspended without pay and that from thenceforth no subversives or communists would "knowingly" be hired in Hollywood. The blacklist had begun. Eventually, all ten of the "unfriendly" witnesses were found guilty of contempt and sentenced to varying terms in prison. Walter Goodman concluded:

The philosophy that flowered under the klieg lights of 1947 would be an inspiration for much of the Committee's later work; a philosophy that held not only that Communism was a subversive doctrine; not only that Communism in sensitive positions were threats to the nation, but that the presence in this land of every individual Communist and fellow traveler and former Communist who would not purge himself was intolerable; that the just fate of every such creature was to be exposed in his community, routed from his job, and driven into exile.[40]

Thus was the rhetoric of nihilation extended from cutting off the right to reply to cutting off livelihoods through the blacklist and cutting off freedom through prison terms.

CONCLUSION

The Loyalty Program was the logical extension of the Truman Doctrine. If communism was the enemy, it had to be "contained" at home as well as abroad. If "several thousand armed men" in Greece could threaten the national security and military might of the United States, so too could a small band of "subversives" much nearer to home—in fact, at home—threaten the constitutional form of American government. Just as it might not be the fall of Greece itself that would topple the United States, it would be what might happen to other countries if Greece did fall. So too, it might not be just one person or organization that actually threatened American institutions, but how that person or that organization might infect other people and organizations that demanded they be stopped now. In other words, the Loyalty Program was intended to protect American constitutional government (even as it and other attacks on subversives would suspend constitutional rights) and to prevent the dominoes from falling at home. The administration acted upon these premises.[41] Though the president apparently believed that his program would undercut Republican witch-hunts against Democrats, the effect was just the opposite. It fueled the flames.

However, it would be irresponsible to place the blame for the great fear that was to follow, the fear we now call McCarthyism, solely or even primarily on Truman. The causes of McCarthyism are more complex than that. Republicans and anti-New Deal Democrats had already raised the issue of domestic communism. In the future, others—most notably Pat McCarran, Joe McCarthy, and Richard Nixon—would give a new dimension to demagoguery on this issue. Each would bear personal responsibility for the particular way in which each used the issue. Truman himself would have second thoughts about the Loyalty Program in light of the new Red Scare as it developed in the last part of the decade.

Nonetheless there was a direct tie between the Loyalty Program and the UnAmerican Activities Committee's 1947 hearings in Hollywood. The committee followed the directives of the Loyalty Program by ferreting out suspected communists, compiling lists of "subversives," and so on. It expanded the directives by cutting off testimony and declaring refusals to answer as communist tactics. To reach these conclusions is not to say such hearings would not have occurred without the Loyalty Program. But one would be remiss in the rhetorical record if one did not conclude that Truman gave (whether wittingly or not) sanction to such investigations with his program. Much of the rhetoric used by "friendly" witnesses echoed the rhetoric used by the administration in justifying its foreign policy. The committee could and did say that it was merely carrying on in a more vigorous fashion the administration's tepid search for communists.

What then was the rhetorical significance of these events? Within the new political reality that was being rhetorically constructed, the Truman program gave legitimacy to the search for Americans believed to be disloyal to their government or (and more importantly in terms of what was to follow) for other Americans who had associations and/or affiliations that might be interpreted as making them risks for public positions, be they in government, in schools and colleges, in labor unions, in motion pictures, radio or television. The important words here, of course, are "perceived" and "interpreted." These were often defined as loosely as partisans wanted or their imaginations allowed or their hatreds could reach. Previously, the investigations of political beliefs of Americans had been confined to Congress, for the most part to the House Committee on UnAmerican Activities, and partisan (Republican) or regional (southern Democrats) politics. With the signing of the Executive Order, Truman *officially* stated that "subversives" were a threat to American national security and he established *official* mechanisms and procedures for investigating suspected "subversives." In this way, Truman gave bipartisan sanction to the search for subversives in government which Republicans extended to a search for subversives in other areas of American life. Truman made the search for domestic communists bipartisan just as Republicans had made the anticommunist issue in foreign policy bipartisan. With such apparent bipartisanship on both domestic and foreign fronts, Americans who would dissent from the vitriolic anticommunist consensus could be banished from the prevailing political reality to the fringes of either psychological or political unreality. The universal rhetoric was now truly universal.

NOTES

1. Richard M. Freeland, *The Truman Doctrine and the Origins of McCarthyism* (New York: Alfred A. Knopf, 1972), pp. 118–21. See also Walter Goodman, *The Committee* (New York: Farrar, Straus and Giroux, 1968), pp. 24–166.

2. Robert J. Donovan, *Conflict and Crisis. The Presidency of Harry S. Truman, 1945–1948* (New York: W. W. Norton, 1977), p. 292.

3. The best summary of the incident can be found in Earl Latham, *The Communist Controversy in Washington* (New York: Antheneum, 1969), pp. 203–16.

4. On the public's concern about domestic communists, see Richard M. Fried, *Nightmare in Red* (New York: Oxford University Press, 1990), p. 50.

5. Quoted in Donovan, *Conflict and Crisis*, p. 293.

6. See Freeland for additional information about the commission, pp. 124–30.

7. Excerpts reprinted in Barton J. Bernstein and Allen J. Matusow, eds., *The Truman Administration: A Documentary History* (New York: Harper Colophon Books, 1968), pp. 357–63. Complete text reprinted in Eleanor Bontecou, *The Federal Loyalty-Security Program* (Ithaca NY: Cornell University Press, 1953), pp. 275–85.

8. Fried, *Nightmare in Red*, p. 66.

9. Bernstein and Matusow, *The Truman Administration*, p. 363. (Emphasis added.)

10. Francis Biddle, *Fear of Freedom* (New York: Doubleday, 1951), p. 210.

11. Bernstein and Matusow, *The Truman Administration*, p. 361.

12. Donovan, *Conflict and Crisis*, p. 295.

13. Woodrow Wilson knew this long ago. On the evening before delivering his war message in 1917 he told a friend: "Once lead this people into war, and they'll forget there ever was such a thing as tolerance. To fight you must be brutal and ruthless, and the spirit of ruthlessness will enter into the very fibre of our national life. There won't be any peace standards left to work with. There will only be war standards." Quoted in Bert Cochran, *Harry Truman and the Crisis Presidency* (New York: Funk and Wagnalls, 1973), p. 353.

14. For the most vigorous argument that much of Truman's program was motivated almost exclusively by politics, see Freeland, *Truman Doctrine*. For a variation of this theme, see Athan Theoharis, *Seeds of Repression: Harry S. Truman and the Origins of McCarthyism* (Chicago, IL: Quadrangle, 1971).

15. Ibid., p. 356.

16. See David Chaute, *The Great Fear* (New York: Simon and Schuster, 1978), pp. 31–36; Richard J. Walton, *Henry Wallace, Harry Truman, and the Cold War* (New York: Viking, 1976), pp. 249–73.

17. Quoted in Donovan, *Conflict and Crisis*, pp. 292–93.

18. See "Statement by the President on the Government's Employee Loyalty

Program," November 14, 1947 in *Public Papers of the President: Harry S. Truman, 1947* (Washington, DC: U.S. Government Printing Office, 1963), pp. 489–91.

19. *Time* (March 31, 1947), p. 20.

20. Walter Goodman, *The Committee* (New York: Farrar, Straus and Giroux, 1968), p. 195.

21. Goodman, *The Committee*, p. 202.

22. Quoted in ibid., p. 203.

23. Eric Bentley, *Thirty Years of Treason: Excerpts from Hearings before the House Committee on Un-American Activities, 1938–1968* (New York: Viking, 1971), p. 112.

24. Ibid., p. 116.

25. Ibid., p. 120.

26. Ibid., p. 123.

27. Ibid., p. 131.

28. Ibid., p. 128.

29. U.S. Congress, House Committee on UnAmerican Activities, *Hearings Regarding the Communist Infiltration of the Motion Picture Industry*, 80th Congress, First Session, 1947, p. 285. (Hereafter cited as *Hearings*.)

30. Ibid., 205.

31. Goodman, *The Committee*, p. 203.

32. *Hearings*, p. 168. Taylor continued by saying that getting rid of them was "not his position," but then said that were he producing he would not let any of them within "100 miles of me or the studio or the script."

33. Bentley, *Thirty Years of Treason*, p. 147.

34. Ring Lardner, Jr., *The Lardners: My Family Remembered* (New York: Harper Colophon, 1977), p. 321.

35. Lawson's statement, along with those of all the others, was later printed in full in Gordon Kahn, *Hollywood on Trial* (New York: Boni and Gaer, 1948).

36. Bentley, *Thirty Years of Treason*, p. 153.

37. *Hearings*, p. 482.

38. Quoted in Robert Vaughan, *Only Victims* (New York: G. P. Putnam's Sons, 1972), p. 98.

39. Quoted in ibid., p. 99.

40. Goodman, *The Committee*, p. 225.

41. See Freeland, *The Truman Doctrine*, pp. 207–45; 293–360.

Chapter Seven

Maintenance and the Moral Imperative of the New Political Universe: The Marshall Plan and "X"

The Truman Doctrine officially created a new interpretation of international politics. It redefined America's mission in the world. It redefined the nature of aggression. It created a new reality out of the myriad events that had preceded the speech. The role of the United States would thenceforth be to defend the free world from communism. The Truman Loyalty Program extended the doctrine to government employees, and the House Committee on UnAmerican Activities extended it even further to reach out to other parts of American life. The growing bipartisan view of a universal and worldwide struggle between freedom and communism was accepted with little discussion and a minimum of opposition.

But one speech and one Executive Order are not sufficient to create the kind of all-pervasive reality that eventually developed in the United States. The new rhetorical universe that Truman had announced had to be made legitimate. Given the American penchant for crusades, it also had to be given a moral imperative. Old beliefs do not die easily, and new beliefs which replace them must be shown to be morally efficacious. Doubts about the new reality had to be banished, and the new rhetorical universe had to be maintained in a clear self-righteous manner.

In the events that quickly followed the announcement of the Truman Doctrine, the tools of language-event that had created the new political reality in the first place were now enlisted to maintain that universe. The president's Loyalty Program had been one step in that direction. The Marshall Plan and Kennan's "Sources of Soviet Conduct" were the next. Each played significant roles in developing, expanding, and maintaining that new universe. Previous writers on these events have interpreted them politically. We now turn to a rhetorical interpretation.

In his address to Congress President Truman had asserted that the United States must embark on an ideological war with totalitarianism which everyone knew meant with Soviet communism. But he relied primarily upon assertions in his brief speech. He presented only a bare skeleton of the reasons for the ideological battles. Furthermore, he used a melodramatic form of good versus evil in his two ways of life section of the address. Following the historic announcement of the administration's official policy, it fell to others—primarily Secretary of State George Marshall and the new head of the Policy Planning Staff, George F. Kennan—to provide the rhetorical sinew and muscle as well as the moral substance of the skeletal melodrama the president had only sketched.

THE MARSHALL PLAN: THE GOOD AMERICANS

Winston Churchill called it the "most unsordid act in history."[1] That was the moral imprint placed on the European Recovery Program (ERP), better known as the Marshall Plan, and the description stuck. In announcing America's willingness to assist in European economic recovery, Secretary Marshall did not resort to the anticommunist rhetoric that had characterized and animated the Truman Doctrine and the Loyalty Program. His speech did not exhibit the anti-Soviet animus of Churchill's "Iron Curtain" address. In fact, the speech stressed a humanitarian theme. Since that time various scholars have attempted to emphasize the economic or political motives for the plan, issues that were debated at the time of the announcement.[2] Actually, the Marshall Plan encompassed all these motives. It rested fully on the assumption that the financial recovery of Europe was essential to U.S. strategic interests in Europe, essential to American financial interests, essential as an alternative to war in containing communism. But in the public mind, the moral motive dominated and remained dominate. It is in that motive, rather than the others, that Secretary Marshall's speech at Harvard contributed significantly to the growing anticommunist reality in the United States.

From the end of the war, the rehabilitation of Europe's economy was a central topic not only in Europe but in the United States as well. When the hard winter of 1946–47 hit Europe, the American concern escalated. During the writing of the Truman Doctrine speech, Joseph Jones asked whether other countries were to be included in the request for economic aid to Greece and Turkey. Acheson replied: "If F.D.R. were alive, I think I know what he'd do. He would make a statement of global policy but confine his request for money *right now* to Greece and Turkey."[3] It was in this way that the Greek–Turkish bill provided the precedent for the comprehensive request for aid to European nations.

The impetus for the Marshall Plan came at the conclusion of the Moscow Conference on Germany in April 1947. Due to the French intransigence on the German question and Stalin's seeming indifference to finding a solution to the deadlock, the conference achieved very little. On the way back to the United States Marshall was quite agitated about the lack of progress and the deterioration of the economies of Europe. According to Bohlen, the secretary saw the two situations as creating the kind of turmoil the communists could exploit for their own purposes. He was determined to prevent that.[4]

Upon his return, Marshall put the new Policy Planning Staff, which he had created and had appointed George F. Kennan as director, to work developing an "initiative" that would address the European economic problems and the role the United States could play in implementing it. The work Kennan and his staff did, combined with a memorandum from William Clayton, undersecretary for economic affairs, produced the basis for the eventual recovery program.[5] They proposed to extend some 13 billion dollars over the next several years to rebuild the European economy. Such an enormous sum and such a serious commitment would require a major announcement by the administration and a persuasive campaign for its acceptance.

There were rhetorical precedents for Marshall's historic address. Four deserve mention. In his first major speech as secretary of state at Princeton on February 21, 1947—the reason why he was away from the State Department when the British notes arrived—Marshall stated:

You should fully understand the special position that the United States occupies in the world geographically, financially, militarily, and scientifically, and the implications involved. The development of a sense of responsibility for world order and security, the development of a sense of overwhelming importance of the country's acts, and failures to act in relation to world order and security— these, in my opinion, are great "musts" for your generation.[6]

This brief remark foreshadowed the commitment Truman was to make three weeks later to insure a world order, and it was that latter speech that established the second precedent.

For all the emphasis on the anticommunist thrust of the Truman Doctrine speech, the president had stated unequivocally that American help to other countries should come primarily "through economic and financial aid." The aid he sought at that time was a piddling sum and limited to Greece and Turkey, but these created a precedent in policy. Equally important, the president had argued that economic instability thwarted development of democratic processes and continued instability would encourage internal subversion. Both of these could be used—and they were—as justifications for the ERP.

The third effort came not from a government official but from the most prominent journalist of the era, Walter Lippmann. From February through May 1947, Lippman wrote columns describing the enormous economic problems in Europe, eventually suggesting that the United States launch an economic aid program ("on a scale which no responsible statesman has yet ventured to hint at") for the continent.[7] According to administration officials, Lippmann's columns were invaluable in alerting the public to the problem and pointing to the solution.

The fourth rhetorical effort preparing the way for the Marshall Plan was Dean Acheson's speech to the Delta Council at Delta State Teachers College in Cleveland, Mississippi on May 8. Acheson was substituting for the president who previously had been scheduled to speak.[8] The council was promised a major foreign policy speech, and Acheson was to deliver it. The address that Acheson presented was a "problem" speech, intended to impress upon his influential audience and the rest of the country (through newspaper reports) how completely devastated the European economies were, why they needed to be revived, and that the United States had to act to meet this crisis.[9] Acheson did not propose a policy to meet these needs. Secretary Marshall directed that no one was to propose a solution, only emphasize the problem. Consistent with this directive, Acheson's purpose was to convince audiences that something had to be done. It was in this sense that the speech was important. As the president said, the Delta speech was "prologue to the Marshall Plan." Acheson himself described it as a rhetorical "reveille," in preparation to Marshall's clarion call a month later.[10]

It was in proposing a solution that the officials faced two rhetorical problems: who would make the announcement and how would possible Soviet involvement in the program be handled. Let's examine these in reverse order.

The problem of Soviet inclusion in the proposal was a tricky one. After all the anticommunist rhetoric that had welled up in the wake of the Truman speech, Congress certainly would be reluctant to approve any program that appeared to improve the economic fortunes of the USSR. If by some stretch of the political imagination Congress did approve a program with Soviet participation, policymakers believed the Soviets would find a way to use the economic aid for their own subversive advantage or would torpedo economic recovery in Europe so they could expand even further in the economic chaos that would result from its failure.

On the other hand, Marshall, Kennan, and the other major policymakers knew they could not exclude the Soviet Union and eastern European countries without putting themselves on the record as deliberately splitting the war-time alliance. Avoiding public responsibility for that split had caused what little delicate language there was in Truman's speech about the Soviet Union. Beyond that, any plan for economic recovery that excluded the Soviet Union would be seen as economic imperialism on the part of the United States.

To put the matter directly, they wanted to exclude the Soviet Union from economic recovery but did not want to take responsibility for that exclusion. They wanted the blame placed on the Soviets. They saw Europe already divided into two spheres of influence, the world divided into two antagonistic ideologies, but they did not want the United States to be the one held publicly responsible for the division. That responsibility again would have to be placed on the Soviet Union.[11] (There is a great irony in their concern about this matter. A year before Churchill had publicly divided the world between those on either side of the Iron Curtain. Truman had publicly divided the world into two ways of life. Yet, even after these divisions had been announced, policymakers were concerned about being responsible for declaring an irrevocable split between the war-time allies. The most reasonable explanation for this concern is that policymakers and the American public believed their own rhetoric only described a division that the Soviets had already made.) Therefore, instead of an ideological speech, this announcement would follow the advice of Kennan to "play it straight." It would be in the specific conditions of the program that they would deviate from "playing it straight."

The question of who would present the proposal was resolved quickly. It would be Marshall. This decision appears to have been one taken without consultation with the president. On May 28 Marshall decided to propose large economic aid to Europe through a public speech. He chose Harvard University as the site for this announcement. For some time President Conant of Harvard had been after Marshall to name a date when the university could honor him. Marshall had been too busy on previous occasions, and even that year, had put Conant off about the June commencement. However, now at almost the last minute, he accepted the invitation and promised to make a few remarks and perhaps "a little more."[12]

A word must be said at this time about George Catlett Marshall. No American rivaled General Marshall in esteem and prestige at that time. Not even the president. Harry Truman had authority as president and the respect that goes with it. Marshall's authority came from his person, not his office, a strength of character that inspired not only respect, but awe. At his last press conference Secretary of State Henry Stimson said of Marshall:

I have never known a man who seemed so surely to breathe the democratic American spirit. He is a soldier and yet he has a profound distaste for anything that smacks of militarism. . . . His devotion to the nation he serves is a vital quality which infuses everything he does. During the course of a long lifetime, much of it spent in a position of public trust, General Marshall has given me a new gauge of what such service should be. The destiny of America at the most critical time of its national existence has been in the hands of a great and good citizen.[13]

Such sentiments were not isolated but widely held. People, such as President Conant of Harvard, drew one comparison repeatedly in describing him: George Marshall was the George Washington of his era, the citizen-soldier whose devotion to country transcended any personal ambitions. It may be difficult for the current generation to realize the great regard people throughout the world had for George Marshall, a career military man, and especially after the calumnies cast upon him by Senator McCarthy during the hysteria of the 1950s. But at the time Harry Truman understood it. When Marshall was nominated as secretary of state, the Republican Congress unanimously approved the appointment on the very day it was submitted. He honored Marshall by naming the European Recovery Plan after him.

There were practical motives as well for the latter honor. As the president later told Clark Clifford, a Republican Congress would have difficulties voting against a program sponsored by the secretary and would be more drawn to a plan named for Marshall than one named for Truman.[14] In sum, a humanitarian program proposed by a statesman would have greater chance of acceptance and passage than a program advocated by a partisan president.

Marshall's Speech and Its Effects

George Marshall's speech at the Harvard commencement on June 5, 1947 took only fifteen minutes to deliver.[15] He argued that much of the world, especially Europe, was in serious economic trouble, so serious that it was difficult for Americans to comprehend how desperate the situation was. This economic breakdown could have disastrous consequences for the economy of the United States and the cause of world peace. Within this world context, Marshall made his proposal:

It is logical that the United States should do whatever it is able to do to assist in the return of normal economic health in the world, without which there can be no political stability and no assured peace. Our policy is directed not against any country or doctrine but against hunger, poverty, desperation, and chaos. Its purpose should be the revival of a working economy in the world so as to permit the emergence of political and social conditions in which free institutions can exist. Such assistance, I am convinced, must not be on a piecemeal basis as various crises develop. Any assistance that this Government may render in the future should provide a cure rather than a mere palliative. Any government that is willing to assist in the task of recovery will find full cooperation . . . on the part of the United States Government. Any government which maneuvers to block the recovery of other countries cannot expect help from us. Furthermore, governments, political parties or groups which seek to perpetuate human misery in order to profit therefrom politically or otherwise will encounter the opposition of the United States.[16]

Marshall concluded his speech by saying that any program of assistance must be drawn up by the Europeans themselves, acting in concert, not individually. The U.S. Government would lend "friendly aid" in drawing up a plan that, Marshall added, should include all European nations.

The American press had not been alerted to the importance of Marshall's address. Although it was given page one treatment in some newspapers, it aroused little immediate commentary among columnists until the ramifications of the program became clear. However, the reaction in Europe was quite different. Acheson took it upon himself to brief British journalists and to make certain that a copy of the speech was sent to England as quickly as possible.[17] Western European countries responded immediately and positively.[18] The USSR, although initially critical and then wavering for a time, eventually agreed to join Great Britain and France in discussions about the recovery program.

On June 27 a tripartite conference opened in Paris. Foreign Minister Molotov represented the Soviet Union; Foreign Minister Georges Bidault, the French; and Foreign Minister Bevin, the British. It is not our purpose to detail the maneuverings and discussions that occurred at that series of meetings.[19] A brief summary instead should suffice. The proposal Bevin and Bidault agreed upon required participating nations to act in concert with one another rather than individually, required them to present a detailed list of their needs to the United States, and included Germany among the participating nations. Molotov objected to each of these. He argued that these proposals violated the sovereignties of European nations. He did not want the inclusion of Germany until a peace treaty had been signed that settled the issue of reparations. Molotov presented an alternative proposal, but it was rejected by Bevin and Bidault. Upon receiving a telegram from Stalin, Molotov walked out of the conference declaring that U.S. policy would divide Europe, not unify it.[20] As numerous commentators have pointed out, none of the Western officials was disappointed by Molotov's departure. In fact, it was exactly what they wanted. The preliminary proposals had been created to assure that result, and Bevin and Bidault did all in their power to place the blame for the failure of the Paris meetings on the Soviet Union[21] The conventional wisdom that grew out of Molotov's departure from Paris was that the Soviets refused to join in a humanitarian effort to relieve hunger and human misery and that later in prohibiting eastern European nations from participating in the Marshall Plan they demonstrated their real immoral colors. As late as 1986 Clark Clifford restated this mythology when he said:

It was one of our aims to continue working with the Soviets so that they might ultimately find that they could develop some kind of understanding with us. We continued our effort. It's generally forgotten . . . that we offered to include the Soviet Union in the Marshall Plan and attempted to use some influence to get them to accept the offer. They rejected it arbitrarily, out of hand.[22]

But the Soviet side of the story should be included in this summary. From the Soviet view, to obtain aid from the United States required the Soviet Union to turn over a detailed checklist of its economic resources, its strengths and weaknesses. Furthermore, according to Soviet experts, the U.S. program would eventually hamper them in instituting the Five-Year Plan that Stalin had announced in his February 1946 speech. The ERP would also interfere with Soviet plans for the eastern European countries to nationalize their economies. Finally, the Western powers, it appeared to the Soviets, were intent on reviving the German economy (or at least, the West German economy) while refusing Soviet claims to German reparations. These were terms that Stalin rejected.[23] Issac Deutscher observed: "[Stalin] could not agree to submit to the West a balance sheet of Soviet economic resources, in which he would have had to reveal Russia's appalling exhaustion and the frightful gap in her manpower that he was concealing even from his own people."[24] From the Soviet view, the Marshall Plan, even at this early stage, was critical. Here was action in central Europe, not in Greece or Turkey, and it was action in the form of economic aid, not merely a speech declaring a policy. Ulam concluded: "Everything during the next fifteen years—the Communist triumph in China, the successive confrontations over Berlin, the Stalin-Tito dispute, the Cuban Missile Crisis—were [sic] at least to some degree traceable to Stalin's reaction to the Marshall Plan."[25] This assessment may be overstated, but the rapid Soviet reaction to what they perceived as capitalist encirclement cannot be overstated. The ERP represented another turning point in the development of the cold war. For the Soviets, it meant that they would have to consolidate their eastern bloc. Whether this consolidation was already underway so that the Marshall Plan only provided a pretext or was taken in direct reaction to the ERP probably depends on one's political orientation. Whatever it meant to the Soviets, it meant something quite different to Americans.

The Marshall Plan and Anticommunist Rhetoric

Secretary Marshall deliberately avoided the strident anticommunist language of the Truman Doctrine. The language and arguments he utilized were humanitarian and generous, not ideological. In certain ways the speech was a far cry from the Truman Doctrine calling for cooperation rather than containment. In fact, many believed that Marshall's speech signaled an abandonment of the hostile language of the Truman Doctrine.[26] At least that seemed to be the direction of administration policy on the public level. On the private level Washington policymakers did not want Soviet participation because they believed that a program that included the Soviets could not pass Congress, or if it did, the USSR would eventually wreck the plan and ruin European recovery.

However, Marshall's proposals carried another message as well, one that fit neatly within the growing anticommunist reality that was being created. The new reality pictured two camps on either side of the Iron Curtain. Truman and others had portrayed the enemy as tyrannical and expansionist. The American (and British, according to Churchill) side was portrayed as democratic and peaceful. The Marshall Plan served to fill in the details of the portrait of the United States as a generous, peaceful nation ready to play the role of Good Samaritan, one that would give of its resources freely to aid sickly nations devastated by war and unable to recover on their own. The language habit of a "good" America grew stronger as Marshall reinforced it. It fortified a vision of the world divided. Although the USSR was not specifically named, there was little doubt of whom Marshall spoke when he warned that the United States would oppose any government that maneuvered to block recovery or sought to exploit the weakened condition of Europe for political purposes. Thus, the division of the world was reinforced and the sense of community now extended to economic and humanitarian relations.

In this way the Marshall Plan added an ethical or moral dimension to the new reality. *Time* magazine caught the significance almost immediately: "The [American] nation's moral position was clear."[27] By making this humanitarian proposal Marshall emphasized the generosity of the U.S. government and attributed ignoble motives to any who would maneuver to block European recovery. When Molotov walked out of the Paris meetings and Stalin later prohibited Czechoslovakia and other eastern European countries from participating, the Soviets played right into the hands of the new reality. Their refusal served to prove their sinister intentions. Marshall had already suggested the motive for refusal: the desire to perpetuate and profit from human misery. Of course, the ultimate aim of the Soviets, according to the new reality that was being created, was to conquer the world. But at this juncture the Marshall Plan perpetuated the growing polarization of the world, placed the conflict in an ethical context, and attributed noble and ignoble motives to those who participated and those who did not. That the Soviets may have had very practical reasons for not participating was hardly ever mentioned in the American press or in the official rhetoric. The lasting impression was that the Soviets acted from evil motives to achieve ideological goals. *Life* magazine summarized this interpretation shortly after Molotov walked out of the Paris Conference:

The purpose of the Marshall offer was to restore economic hope to Europe; but it was not George Marshall's idea that half of Europe should have this hope and half not. His offer was open to all; indeed it still is. It was Molotov who reacted to the offer by leaving the first Paris Conference after five days and forbidding the Eastern satellites to share its benefits. The Iron Curtain then began to sink remorselessly through the channels of East-West trade.

Thus it was really Molotov who decided to split Europe.[28]

As *Life* also noted, the Marshall Plan was one part of the overall "war" against communism. The Marshall Plan fit easily within the emerging moral war. From thenceforth, this ethical framework would be used to view Western and Soviet actions, actions that now transcended power struggles to involve combat between two mutually exclusive moral systems. In the melodramatic form of anticommunism, the United States wore a white hat and was rushing to the aid of the helpless and endangered heroine Europe. The image of an altruistic and stalwart hero embodied in the Marshall Plan remains even today.

"X": THE VILLAINOUS SOVIETS

Following hard upon the heels of Marshall's dramatic proposal for European recovery came the publication of the most controversial and widely publicized article on foreign policy to appear in an American magazine in the postwar period. In subsequent years it also became the most praised and criticized article of the early postwar years. Even now more than thirty years after its publication, George F. Kennan's "The Sources of Soviet Conduct" remains an essay of intense historical and political dispute.[29] Our purpose is not to rehash the arguments about what Kennan really meant. The variety of interpretations, including Kennan's own later "revisions," attest to how different people could read different meanings into Kennan's article. Rather our purpose is to see how this article contributed to the anticommunist consensus.

Quite simply, Kennan's article acted in counterpoint to the Marshall Plan in the moral melodrama of anticommunism. President Truman once said that his doctrine and the Marshall Plan were "two halves of the same walnut."[30] That was a bit mistaken. The Truman Doctrine established the general moral shell of the new world order in which ideological angels do mortal combat with ideological demons. Within that outer shell the Marshall Plan and Kennan's analysis of Soviet motives were the two halves of the same walnut. The ERP demonstrated the good intentions of U.S. policy; Kennan's essay argued the villainous motives of Soviet communism. To understand Kennan's contribution to the anticommunist consensus, we will focus on its rhetorical origins and intent, the ways in which his analysis was understood at the time, and the ways in which Kennan was elevated from an obscure State Department official to the status of supreme authority (or "the expert") on Soviet aims, methods, and motives as well as the proper U.S. policy response to the Soviet Union. Kennan's professional advancement, his promotions, and increasing responsibilities coincided with a critical time in U.S. postwar history, and because of the importance he assumed in the administration, he emerged as the foremost authority on the Soviet Union.

The Origins and Central Arguments of "The Sources of Soviet Conduct"

Kennan's published article, of course, had its origins in his famous "long telegram" of the year before. It was in that private document that he pulled together his thinking on Soviet–American relations. The impact that it had within the administration caused him to be recalled to Washington to teach at the National War College and to embark on a speaking tour during the summer of July and August 1946 on behalf of the State Department. His purpose, according to Mayers, was to explain Soviet behavior and to "generate support among businessmen, civic leaders, academics, and other prominent citizens for the emergent tougher line against Moscow."[31] In late April 1947, Marshall appointed Kennan director of the Policy Planning Staff, a new group created by the secretary to do long-range strategic thinking about foreign policy.

In late 1946 while Kennan was still at the War College, Navy Secretary James Forrestal, soon to be first secretary of defense, asked a number of people, Kennan included, to comment on a paper by Edward Willett. Willett, an academic from Smith College but temporarily working for Forrestal, entitled his paper, "Dialectic Materialism and Soviet Objectives." He argued that Marxism–Leninism motivated Soviet leaders and called for rearming America's military to assure the country's safety in light of the dangerous threat the Soviet Union posed. Kennan responded with a critique of Willett's paper and was asked by Forrestal to produce a paper of his own analyzing Soviet behavior, one that would be more "academically sound" than his original critique.[32] That paper turned out to be "The Sources of Soviet Conduct."

Kennan's analysis went through two drafts. The first was unacceptable to Forrestal so Kennan had to rewrite sections which made them "tougher sounding."[33] In light of the ways in which the article was later interpreted, probably the most significant change Kennan made from the first to the final draft concerned the central policy issue of containment. The first version stated that *diplomatic* "counter-pressure" and the United States' own "dignified" example in international relations were the best means to confront Soviet mischief.[34] The final version stated that U.S. policy should be "designed to confront the Russians with unalterable counter-force at every point where they show signs of encroaching upon the interests of a peaceful and stable world."[35] Indeed throughout the finished version the word "force" was used; "pressure" rarely.

The dominant argument of Kennan's essay was that communist ideology drove Soviet policies, even if the ideology was used merely as a convenient rationalization for maintaining the dictatorial regime of Stalin. In this sense his interpretation was more subtle than Willett's. He devoted the whole first section of the essay to explaining the nature and centrality of ideology in the Soviet system using selective quotations from Lenin and Stalin to support this persistent contention. There was precious little mention of Russia's historic fear of the outside world. Kennan stated that Russia's history and tradition gave sustenance and muscle to this ideological urge. The emphasis and narrative instead focused almost entirely on the ideological consistency of Soviet (as opposed to historic Russian) motives. In developing what little narrative there was, Kennan substituted persistent adherence to an ideology for the ambiguities of historical development. Indeed, his narrative became a series of ideological propositions announced by Soviet leaders rather than a retelling of significant events. In approaching the historical development in this fashion, Kennan validated the notion that communist ideas were more important than concrete actions in determining Soviet history, motives, and goals. Indeed, one no longer had to look to events, except to unmask the traps they contained, as a guide to understanding the Soviet Union.

As part of the developing anticommunist mentality, Kennan stated bluntly that the Soviets saw a world divided in which there can be no "sincere assumption of a community of aims between the Soviet Union and powers which are regarded as capitalist."[36] This statement clearly reinforced Churchill's and Truman's division of the world into two antagonistic camps. Kennan also contended that the Soviet Union was inherently expansionist. The primary analogy he used was that of a "persistent toy automobile wound up and headed in a given direction, stopping only when it meets with some unanswerable force."[37] Implicit within this mechanical analogy lay the conclusion that others drew, that

Soviet expansion was inexorable. Also implicit in this particular analogy of expansion was the call for a policy of containment to stop it.[38] Since Kennan described this policy on occasion as using a "counter-force," one can understand why others interpreted him as meaning a military force, rather than using political or diplomatic pressure. Because Kennan left the impression that ideology drove the Soviet Union to expand in a variety of areas in the world, one can further understand why others interpreted him as saying that the United States faced a worldwide challenge from communism. Although Kennan stressed that the United States should respond to areas of vital interest, his analysis of a worldwide challenge from communism overshadowed this restricted application of containment. If the challenge was worldwide, then the policy to meet it had to be worldwide. Read within the context of the Truman Doctrine, despite Kennan's restrictions, that was the logical conclusion to reach.

It should be noted that Kennan stressed the neurotic and fundamentally defensive sources of Soviet conduct, even as his metaphoric toy automobile suggested aggressive expansionism. He also emphasized that the Soviet Union did not seem to have a long-range plan for its political objectives. It should be further noted that Kennan did not compare Stalin's Russia to Hitler's Germany. In other statements he consistently denied that the two were analogous. Kennan saw or thought he saw the Soviet threat as unique unto itself, but he said later that he believed it to be a greater threat ("more sinister, more cruel, more devious, more cynically contemptuous of us") than the Nazi threat.[39] This sense of impending crisis permeates Kennan's essay.

Before rushing to judgment, one should also remember that Kennan's paper was meant for private circulation within the administration, not for publication; that he was writing in response to Willett's paper which he considered too limited in analysis of Soviet behavior and too harsh in recommendations for U.S. military action; and that his "audience" was his patron, James Forrestal, who was noted for his beliefs in rearming America, his hatred of communist ideology, and his equal penchant for grand theorizing. Thus, one reason for *some* of the internal "confusions," as Stephanson calls them, of Kennan's analysis may be attributable to his attempts to reconcile his various rhetorical tasks in writing it; that is, reconciling his own beliefs with Forrestal's hatred of communism and attempting to persuade the Navy secretary from Willett's singular emphasis on ideology to a more complex interpretation, all the while protecting his chances for advancement.[40]

This private paper became public because Kennan did not want to write another article on the same subject. He had delivered an address in January 1947 to the Council of Foreign Relations on the same general subject. Hamilton Fish Armstrong, editor of *Foreign Affairs*, invited Kennan, who had spoken from notes, to submit an article along the lines of the speech he had given. Instead of developing a new article, Kennan sought and received permission from the State Department's Committee on Unofficial Publication to publish the paper he had written for Forrestal. After telling the committee he intended to publish the article anonymously by replacing his name with an "X" he received clearance. In late June, the July 1947 issue of *Foreign Affairs* appeared and within weeks created first a sensation and then, in the words of Kennan himself, an "indestructible myth."[41]

Interpretations of Kennan's Article

The contemporary meaning of "The Sources of Soviet Conduct" may best be inferred not from an intensive analysis of the text, but from the reception it received upon publication. The contemporaneous supporters and critics of Kennan selected what they believed its most important message and arguments, and these became in large measure the meaning of his article.

In his column in the *New York Times* of July 8, Arthur Krock drew national attention to "The Sources of Soviet Conduct." He had seen the original paper in Forrestal's office. When the article was published without authorship, Krock put two and two together. He titled his article: "A Guide to Official Thinking About Russia."[42] Krock went so far as to claim that the thesis of the article had become U.S. policy ("after appeasement with the Kremlin failed") and that its central argument allowed the State Department to predict "precisely what [Molotov] would do and the reasons he would give for doing it" *before* the Soviet foreign minister went to Paris for the Marshall Plan talks. With this title and Krock's assignment of omniscience to its author, Kennan's article and Kennan himself began their rise to prominence.

In his summary of the article, Krock chose as the central thesis: Soviet leaders are captives of their own ideology. This central idea is then expanded to include the following:

1. The "nefarious" capitalist system cannot adjust to economic change and therefore a revolutionary transfer of power is "inescapable."
2. Capitalism will perish through a proletarian revolution which will begin in a capitalist country and spread to the rest of the world.
3. Current rulers of the Soviet Union therefore will not cooperate with the West because there can be no "sincere assumption of a community of aims" between the Soviets and powers "regarded as capitalists."
4. The Soviet Union cannot change from these aims until the internal power structure changes. Any deviation from its dogma should be considered only a subterfuge.

Krock, of course, quoted what would become the most famous passages from the article, the passages about a "vigilant containment" of Soviet expansionism and the application of an adroit "counter-force at a series of constantly shifting geographical and political points." The columnist seemed relieved that a policy had been developed to meet the Kremlin's challenge "not *necessarily* by war" (emphasis added), but by a variety of acts that would contain the Soviet Union.

The importance of Krock's column went beyond drawing national attention to Kennan's article. In a few hundred words he could not be expected to give a complete analysis of Kennan's argument. Therefore, what he chose to emphasize and what he omitted became even more important. Krock excerpted and stressed the ideological motivations and aims of the Soviet Union, and he concluded that the current Soviet leaders were incapable of changing their dogma or cooperating with the West. Such a summary gave greater credibility to the "two world" division that had emerged with Churchill's and Truman's speeches and to the policy of containment since the only alternative policy mentioned by Krock was war.

The second interpretation came from Walter Lippmann who gave added stature to Kennan's analysis by devoting fourteen successive columns of "Today and Tomorrow" in the *New York Herald Tribune* to it. Shortly after the completion of this series, these were collected and published in a slim volume, *The Cold War: A Study in U.S. Foreign Policy*.[43] Although Lippmann agreed with Kennan on various points, he dissented on three major issues.[44] He scored Kennan for placing too much emphasis on ideology to the neglect of Russia's history; he attacked the policy of containment because he believed it meant confronting them around the globe; and he criticized Kennan for ignoring diplomacy as a means for settling problems between the United States and the Soviet Union in preference for a forceful or military solution.

For this study it is not important whether Lippmann or Kennan was the more astute analyst of U.S. foreign policy. What is significant are the ways in which Walter Lippmann, the most insightful and influential journalist of the time, understood Kennan's arguments. He believed Kennan was offering a strictly ideological analysis of Soviet motivations and aims, that the policy of containment meant a global commitment of U.S. resources, and that Kennan believed differences between the two powers could not be settled by diplomacy. By isolating these premises as central to the doctrine of containment, Lippmann lent credence to this interpretation, even as he attacked it.

The final interpretation was printed in *Reader's Digest*. Most writers refer to it as an "excerpt" but "digest" is more appropriate since the digestive process usually involves changing something from one thing into another. The *Reader's Digest* version published in October 1947 was

entitled "The Only Way to Deal with Russia," and that gave some indication of how far along the original article was toward acceptance as
the definitive policy for the United States.[45] Several examples may demonstrate this acceptance.

Those who authored the digest of "The Sources of Soviet Conduct"
took liberties in summarizing it. Kennan had begun his article by stating
that the Soviets were motivated by ideology and circumstance and then
proceeded to an explication of four principles that originated the ideology. The version appearing in *Reader's Digest* began with a condensed
sentence clipped from the nineteenth paragraph and spliced it to its
version of part of paragraph ten:

We are going to continue for a long time to find the Russians difficult to deal
with. The outstanding circumstance concerning the Soviet regime is that down
to the present day the men in the Kremlin have continued to be predominantly
absorbed with the struggle to secure and make absolute the power they seized
in 1917. They have endeavored to secure it permanently at home but they have
also endeavored to secure it against the outside world. For their ideology taught
them that the outside world was hostile and that their duty was eventually to
overthrow the political forces beyond their borders.

The rearrangement of these sentences into the "lead" of the article re-
directs the reader to the threat posed to the United States by the ideologically motivated Soviets. What was a subordinate idea in the original
becomes the thesis of the digest. It is within this new opening context
that the remainder of the digest must be read. Thus, the thrust was to
explain why the Soviets acted as they did in the context of their attempts
"to overthrow political forces beyond their borders."

Another emblematic change was more subtle. Kennan wrote that the
antagonism between capitalism and socialism "means that there can
never be on Moscow's side any sincere assumption of a community of
aims between the Soviet Union and powers which are regarded as capitalism."[46] The *Reader's Digest* version read that the antagonism "means
that there can never be on Moscow's side any sincere community of
aims with capitalist powers." Kennan had left the door slightly open by
writing about an "assumption of a community of aims," but the *Digest*
article closes that door by saying there can "never be . . . any sincere
community of aims." Kennan put the responsibility on the Soviet Union
for "assuming" or not "assuming." *Reader's Digest* forecloses that choice
and responsibility. Kennan also placed responsibility upon the Soviet
Union for determining which countries constitute enemies ("are regarded as capitalists"). The *Digest* again forecloses that choice and responsibility by making "capitalist powers" a fixed entity.

The *Reader's Digest*'s version of Kennan's article stressed the ideological conflict between two implacable powers. Deemphasizing the circumstances that Kennan said motivated Soviet expansionism, *Reader's Digest's* version stressed only the ideological motivations, thus imputing to the Soviets only a doctrinaire determinism based on ideology instead of strategic choices based on circumstances as motives for their actions. Ideology, according to the "digest," does not change whereas circumstances might.

These remarkable interpretations of Kennan's article caused him great distress. Kennan believed he had written about a "political containment of a political threat" but saw it transformed by association with the Truman Doctrine into a "military containment of a military threat." It is hard to understand his distress in light of what he actually wrote. After he left government service Kennan repeatedly expressed his exasperation over this transformation, but that transformation (despite Kennan's disclaimer) contributed mightily to the anticommunist consensus.

"The Sources of Soviet Conduct" as Language-Event

George F. Kennan's explanation of Soviet ideology and his advocacy of a policy of "containment" to challenge it became a language-event parallel with the "Iron Curtain" and the "Truman Doctrine." As the analysis and policy he presented became transformed, ideology became the only motivating force behind Soviet actions, and circumstances became strategic or tactical opportunities for expansion. Writing about Kennan's article, *Newsweek* summarized this interpretation succinctly: "Russia may shift her line from time to time. She may give way here, appear to co-operate there. But *always* Russian rulers will work on the theory that communism and capitalism are in conflict and that Russia is the leader of an expanding communism."[47] It should be said that Kennan encouraged this interpretation of his comparison of Soviet actions and the proper reaction to the "toy automobile." This mechanistic analogy was buttressed by other mechanistic metaphors: "the whole Soviet governmental machine;" "the mechanism of diplomacy;" "individuals who are components of this machine." This imagery was consistent with Kennan's emphasis on ideology as moving "inexorably along a prescribed path."

The second image fitted Kennan's emphasis on circumstance: "Its political action is a fluid stream which moves constantly, wherever it is permitted to move, toward a given goal. Its main concern is to make sure that it has filled every nook and cranny available to it in the basin of world power." This image would seem both to confirm and contradict the other image. On the one hand, it confirms the sense of movement or expansion as inherent in Soviet behavior and the need to stop it ("contain" it). On the other, the "path" is described in the first image as "inexorable" but in the second as "fluid." However, the interpretation placed on Kennan's article resolved this contradiction by seeing the ideological motive as inexorable and only their strategy and tactics as fluid.

The U.S. response, however, is described in spatial images: containment, "unassailable barriers," "unanswerable force." By October U.S. News was describing Kennan as author of the policy of "walling Russia in."[48] Such images encouraged American policymakers to erect barriers to the movement of the Soviet Union and thus encouraged a static response, containment, even as Kennan called for flexibility in application of that response. But with the transformation of his ideas into its simplified military form it came to mean military barriers both in the uses of military forces and military alliances often to the neglect of economic and diplomatic responses.

Kennan's "X" article exhibited each of the five characteristics we have attributed to language-events that create political reality. First, Kennan gave an interpretation of raw events that made the changing and often contradictory actions by the Soviet Union comprehensible. But the article went beyond that to clarify the confusion created by the contrast between Truman's belligerent doctrine and Marshall's humanitarian plan. Again, Newsweek caught this function of his essay: "For the average American, bewildered by the ideological conflict that is turning one world into two, there was news out of Washington last week that did more to explain current United States policy toward Russia than anything released since the war."[49] They were referring to "The Sources of Soviet Conduct." Kennan had illuminated the reasons behind the skeletal ideological rhetoric of Churchill and Truman and reconciled the Marshall Plan with the Truman Doctrine. He had elaborated upon these efforts by giving an ideological basis for understanding Soviet motives for expansion and the appropriate U.S. response, containment.

But there was another language-event associated with widespread circulation of Kennan's analysis. That was the label placed upon his thinking: "realistic." Brooks Atkinson described Kennan as having a "realistic grasp on current affairs."[50] Soon that label caught on to characterize not only Kennan but his policy as well. It even persists down to the present as scholars refer to Kennan's policy and those who followed it as the "realist school" of international thinkers. Such a description reinforced the growing anticommunist reality: containment was a "realistic" policy. Those who supported Kennan with whatever disagreements they might have over interpretation of his analysis and those who supported containing communism regardless of how they might disagree over the implementation of that policy had appropriated the word "realistic." Since "The Sources of Soviet Conduct" was seen as the "guide to official thinking" in the administration, it meant that the administration was in touch with fundamental aspects of reality in ways that others could not be in touch with it. Moreover, describing the policy of containment as a "realistic" policy meant that any other global policy that had different assumptions must by definition be unrealistic. In the battle for establishing meaning (i.e., basis for any political reality) of the postwar world the administration had won a major linguistic and conceptual victory.[51] Anyone who would argue with Kennan's analysis and the policy of containment would be restricted to arguing strategy and tactics, if they wanted to be considered "realistic." To attack fundamental premises would place such critics outside the realm of reality. Since these critics seldom agreed upon a single analysis or consistent policy when they dissented from basic principles, they had to be described in a variety of ways from naive idealists to fellow-travelers to communist dupes. To name something and have the name stick is to own it, especially when influential figures had conferred the name rather than one naming oneself. As Kenneth Burke remarked, "the mere act of naming an object or situation decrees that it is to be singled out as such-and-such rather than as something other."[52] By naming the new policy as realistic, it also meant that the new policy was not unrealistic, not idealistic, not wooly-headed or thoughtless. Thus anyone who disagreed fundamentally with their analysis or with the policy of containment was by definition "not realistic," not in touch with reality.

Second, Kennan's article met the next criterion of a language-event. It was widely publicized and understood as an intellectual conception of political reality. *Life* magazine reprinted the full text of Kennan's essay, and others printed excerpts. The article functioned for the American public as his "long telegram" had functioned for government officials. Since 1946 the administration, in general, and the State Department, in particular, had been searching for "new intellectual moorings."[53] The "long telegram" fulfilled this need. With the introduction of two confusing policies (the Truman Doctrine and the Marshall Plan) to meet a confusing situation, the public also needed "new intellectual moorings." Kennan's article fulfilled this public need. And by the end of a very rapid transformation period, containment became the "only way to deal with Russia."

Third, Kennan's language was a community-event as well. He described the two ideological camps into which the world was divided. In this sense, Kennan reinforced the language habit that had rapidly been formed, reinforced and gave greater intellectual sustenance to it. Both Churchill's and Truman's speeches were not merely interpretations of reality but were also acts that created reality, so too Kennan's rhetoric was more than an objective analysis of Soviet motives and policies. Kennan added to the growing anticommunist vocabulary the word "containment." He broadened the population of language users by making it intellectually respectable to talk in this way. People in the street now had a proper lexicon to discuss what those in the centers of power and in the centers of learning were already talking about.

But equally important, Kennan supplied the theoretical blueprint to interpret future Soviet acts. F. L. Polak called this rhetorical movement "imaging":

[Our] conscious striving to fore-know the future plus [our] partly unconscious dreams, yearnings, . . . hopes and aspirations for that future, periodically and successively, are condensed, crystallized and clarified into different sets of more or less specific, outlined and projective expectations or ideational goals. Such a set, at its end-state of collective and positive, prospective and constructive development may be called . . . an image of the future.[54]

Kennan had "condensed, crystallized and clarified" Soviet behavior into a theoretical whole that explained in intelligent language ways to interpret future Soviet acts. By concentrating on the motives of Soviet actions Kennan oriented American responses for the future. When people believe they know why others act as they do, they then believe they know what to expect of adversaries and of themselves in terms of proper conduct and thereby shape decisions and policies to take such expectations into account, as if the expectations are the actual motives and goals.[55]

It is in the area of motives that we come to the fourth and fifth characteristics of language-event creating political reality: authority and the sacred. Kennan stated that Soviet motives were deceptive, using tactics of accommodation when it suited their purposes all the while aiming toward expansion and not true cooperation.[56] The Kremlin's policies were secretive, duplistic. Actions were seldom what they seemed. But who was to determine when Soviet actions were to be taken at face value and when hidden motives had to be exposed? Obviously, expert knowledge was needed.

George F. Kennan was one of the few experts on the Soviet Union in the year immediately following World War II. Russian studies in universities were still in their infancy. (The Columbia University's Russian Institute graduated its first class of advanced students in 1948). Experts in Russian language, history, and political thought were few. Kennan possessed these three prerequisites. In the 1920s the State Department had anticipated the recognition of the Soviet Union by training certain foreign service officers in Russian subjects, including the Russian language. To do so, however, these officers had to be sent abroad to undertake such studies. Kennan himself went to the University of Berlin. Thus, by the postwar period only a few such experts existed. Kennan and Charles Bohlen were two of them. (Interestingly, a letter to the editor of the *New York Times* by one Waldo Ruess commented that Bohlen was most assuredly an expert but that Kennan "tops" him because he "knows Russia, Russian affairs, philosophy, politics, and language better." Ruess did not give any reasons for his admiration of Kennan's intellectual skills other than his letter in response to an article Brooks Atkinson had written about Kennan.)[57] Such was the intellectual prominence accorded Kennan.

When "The Sources of Soviet Conduct" appeared, its scholarly language and elegant historical scope carried its own authority with it. Krock noted (without naming the author) that the article was "obviously written by someone who studied the masters of the Soviets for years and at the closest range possible to foreigners."[58] When the mysterious "X" was identified as Kennan, a plethora of articles appeared about him.[59] Brooks Atkinson did a long profile for the *New York Times Magazine* and described him as "America's Global Planner," one who does the "considered thinking" for the Secretary of State about the "infinitely complex" and "interrelated" world affairs.[60] Other articles in *Newsweek*, *U.S. News*, and other popular magazines followed suit; *Life* portrayed him as knowing the "Russians like the back of his hand."[61] Thus, his authority to analyze Soviet actions and to recommend policy rested on his expert knowledge, both exemplified by his training, his writing, and, most important, the authority attributed to him.

But Kennan's expertise functioned as universe maintenance on another level as well: the appeal to the sacred. Kennan closed his article with appeals to use the most important influence available to Americans, the example of their own national character. Only "exhibitions of indecision, disunity and internal disintegration" in the United States could encourage the Soviet Union. More blatantly, Kennan concluded his study by announcing that Americans should be thankful for the challenge:

[Americans] will . . . experience a certain gratitude to a Providence which, by providing the American people with this implacable challenge, has made their entire security as a nation dependent on their pulling themselves together and accepting the responsibilities of moral and political leadership that history plainly intended them to bear.[62]

Such appeals to American national character graced by God's imprimatur placed the policy of containment within the context of traditional American values and historical missions, thus conferring moral legitimacy upon such a policy.

Yet, Kennan's expertise provided another form of allegiance to the sacred in a more subtle manner. The sacred involves piety, and piety is, as Burke succinctly said, "a system-builder, a desire to round things out, to fit experiences together into a unified whole . . . *the sense of what properly goes with what.*"[63] There are three kinds of architectonic designs used to such systems that "round things out" into a "unified whole." The first is mythology. George Kennan, the relative of George F. Kennan, spun a mythology about Russia prior to his death in 1924. The elder Kennan had visited Russia and wrote in popular magazines of the slave labor camps, tales of free love, the pogroms against Jews, and the despotic tyranny of the czars. The mythology grew large. The revulsion it inspired reinforced American values which were (at least in mythological terms) antithetical. Such all-encompassing mythology requires first-hand knowledge and articulate story-telling skills, both of which the elder Kennan possessed to qualify as an expert.

The younger Kennan's expertise operated within the second type of universe maintenance, the theological or philosophical. Within this architectonic structure experts are more removed from people because they operate on a theoretical level with a more esoteric language—the language of ideology or theory. "The Sources of Soviet Conduct" operated on both the philosophic and theoretical levels. In analyzing Soviet behavior he stressed both circumstance and ideology, but soon, as we have said, circumstance was relegated to strategy and tactics while ideology became the motivating force behind Soviet actions. In pressing his policy of containment, Kennan operated on the theological level "prophesying" how the Soviets would respond to the policy in ultimate terms of their eventual disintegration and self-destruction. Communist ideology, Kennan asserted, had no conception of a truth that flowed from an "objective reality," but they believed it was "infallible." This ideology was disciplined, impervious to "normal logic." Counter-force along a "series of constantly shifting geographical and political points" alone could eventually exploit the exhaustion of a "physically and spiritually tired" people to the point that the system itself disintegrates. (Granted here we are ignoring Kennan's second possibility for the disintegration of the ideological system: the death of Stalin.) In this sense, Kennan was offering a rhetoric of nihilation based on his analysis and prophesy.

Even as he was presenting this nihilation of the alien political culture, Kennan was obliquely engaging in a rhetoric of therapy for members of the American political culture. Kennan's language and presentation were so clearly the intellectual formulation of an international reality that those who deviated from fundamental premises of this new reality could only be considered ignorant and in need of enlightenment or so misguided that they were in need of therapy. Even Kennan noted this:

There will always be some Americans who will leap forward with gleeful announcements that "the Russians have changed," and some who will even try to take credit for having brought about such "changes." But we should not be misled by tactical maneuvers. These characteristics of Soviet policy [belief in the innate antagonism of capitalism and communism, Soviet duplicity, secretiveness, and basic hostility toward the United States], like the postulates from which they flow, are basic to the internal nature of Soviet power, and will be with us, whether in the foreground or the background, until the internal nature of Soviet power is changed.[64]

Any who challenged the ideological motives attributed by Kennan to Soviet leaders or who might believe the Soviets could act with any degree of sincerity were in need of therapy to see the "reality" of "real" Soviet motives, tactics, and strategy. The new orientation presented by the architectonic ideological theory of Soviet motives and actions was in Burke's terms, pious. Those who disagreed were guilty of impiety in challenging it, an impiety intensified by the fact that they might mislead others and thereby encourage greater adventurism on the part of the Soviet Union.

In his article, "The Sources of Soviet Conduct," George F. Kennan supplied the intellectual undergirding that supported and extended the new reality of Soviet–American relations. Churchill and Truman had baldly stated the new reality. Kennan produced a supple and subtle theoretical rationale for it. Equally important, Kennan had provided a chilling portrait of Soviet behavior that stressed fanaticism, dictatorial powers unrelieved by any Western civilities, expansionist designs against capitalist countries, and a general corruption of political and moral thinking. This portrait of a sinister Soviet Union contrasted with the portrait of an altruistic United States as sharply as the traditional melodramatic villain contrasts with the traditional melodramatic hero. "The Sources of Soviet Conduct," despite Kennan's later disclaimers, served as the other half of the moral walnut called anticommunism.

CONCLUSION

The two major rhetorical acts considered in this chapter were extensions and elaborations on the new anticommunist reality that was emerging in the postwar years. Former Prime Minister Winston Churchill had divided the world into those on either side of an Iron Curtain the Soviet Union had dropped across Europe. President Truman had reinforced that division of one world into two and declared that the issue facing the world was an ideological struggle between two mutually exclusive "ways of life." He further extended it into domestic areas through the establishment of his Loyalty Program. Secretary of State Marshall provided the ethical proof for the innate righteousness of the American way of life through an altruistic offer to rebuild European economies. George

F. Kennan provided not only a theoretical validation of the ideological struggle but also the proof that the Soviets were unethical through his descriptions of their fanaticism, their desires for expansionism, and their internal corruption. He reinforced the moral imperative of the United States in meeting the challenge by calling for a *defensive* policy of containment rather than an *offensive* policy of rolling back or attacking communism. That would come later from others.

The universal policy of international relations that involved a deadly struggle between two ways of life now extended to domestic life as well. George F. Kennan inadvertently supplied the theoretical reasons for searching out subversives in domestic America as well as containing communism abroad. The new political reality had at its core an ideological struggle that matched the American way of life against the communist way of life. Kennan asserted that Soviet communists were at the time guided by a belief in an infallible ideology that demanded obedience to its discipline and created a fanatical adherence to the party line that moved inexorably along a prescribed path. Since Kennan emphasized ideology and not national interest as the motive force, it was a small step for others to extend these motives to domestic communists as well as Soviet communists. Conversely, Kennan had called for "containment" of Soviet moves and need for a unified citizenry in the United States. That unity would be enforced in ways Kennan could never have imagined when applied to domestic communists and other "subversives;" indeed, in ways that would horrify Kennan himself.

The rhetorical acts that we have analyzed here were "generic moments," moments when images and rhetoric come together to produce policy. At this point, the anticommunist ideology had been completely established. The universal rhetoric was complete. The policies were in place. These currents had been running for sometime flowing from both partisan and bipartisan sources, from both domestic and international fountainheads. The currents let loose by these rhetorical efforts quickly merged into a mighty ideological river that was to flood and rampage across the United States.

NOTES

1. Quoted in William Manchester, *The Glory and the Dream* (New York: Bantam, 1975), p. 440.

2. On the economic interpretation of the cold war, in general, and the Marshall Plan, in particular, see Joyce and Gabriel Kolko, *The Limits of Power: The World and United States Foreign Policy, 1945–1954* (New York: Harper and Row, 1972); on the predominately political interpretation, see Richard M. Freeland, *The Truman Doctrine and the Origins of McCarthyism* (New York: Alfred A. Knopf, 1972), pp. 167–200.

3. Joseph Jones, *The Fifteen Weeks* (New York: Viking, 1955), p. 159. Emphasis

added. At the very moment of Jones's inquiry, Acheson was initiating a survey of European economic needs as preplanning contingency for the request that was to come several months later.

4. See Charles E. Bohlen, *Witness to History: 1929–1969* (New York: W. W. Norton, 1973), pp. 262–64.

5. See George F. Kennan, *Memoirs: 1925–1950* (Boston: Atlantic-Little, Brown, 1967), pp. 325–45. For the most comprehensive recent study of the Marshall Plan, see Michael J. Hogan, *The Marshall Plan: America, Britain, and the Reconstruction of Western Europe, 1947–1952* (Cambridge: Cambridge University Press, 1987).

6. Quoted in Forrest C. Pogue, *George C. Marshall: Statesman, 1945–1959* (New York: Penguin, 1989), p. 162.

7. Quoted in Ronald Steel, *Walter Lippmann and the American Century* (Boston: Atlantic-Little, Brown, 1980), p. 441. Steel argues that Lippmann did more than write columns. He assisted in developing the actual program. See pp. 440–42.

8. The death of Senator Bilbo of Mississippi had thrown the Democratic party into a bitter feud over his successor. Neither Truman nor Mississippi Democrats wanted to put the president in the middle of that political blood-letting. Therefore, the president asked Acheson to stand in for him. See Dean Acheson, *Present at the Creation* (New York: W. W. Norton, 1969), p. 227.

9. For his own summary of the speech, see Acheson, *Present at the Creation*, p. 229.

10. Ibid., p. 230.

11. See Louis J. Halle, *The Cold War as History* (New York: Harper and Row, 1967), pp. 124–25. Of course, this was their view at the time and central to traditional analysis of the cold war. It ignores that Churchill had already publicly divided the world into two hostile camps and that Truman had joined in an ideological war with the Soviets.

12. Pogue, *Marshall*, p. 209. For additional background on the speaking occasion and Marshall appearance, see Larry G. Ehrlich, "Ambassador in the Yard," *Southern Speech Communication Journal* 38 (Fall 1972), pp. 1–12.

13. Quoted in Pogue, *Marshall*, p. 28. On other similar descriptions of Marshall's character, see Bohlen, *Witness to History*, pp. 268–71; Harry S. Truman, *Years of Trial and Hope* vol. 2 (Garden City: Doubleday, 1956), pp. 112–15; Kennan, *Memoirs*, pp. 345–47.

14. Robert J. Donovan, *Conflict and Crisis: The Presidency of Harry S. Truman, 1945–1948* (New York: W. W. Norton, 1977), p. 287.

15. The speech was written by Charles Bohlen working from the Policy Planning Staff's report, the report from Clayton, and his own knowledge of what Marshall had in mind. See Bohlen, *Witness to History*, pp. 263–64.

16. "George C. Marshall's Speech at Harvard University, June 5, 1947," *Ideas and Diplomacy*, ed. Norman A. Graebner (New York: Oxford University Press, 1964), p. 733.

17. See Acheson, *Present at the Creation*, p. 234; Charles L. Mee, Jr., *The Marshall Plan* (New York: Simon and Schuster, 1984), pp. 99–103.

18. Foreign Secretary Bevin went so far as to say of it: "The speech may rank as one of the greatest in the world's history." Quoted in *New York Times* (June 14, 1947), p. 1.

19. See Mee, *Marshall Plan*, pp. 107–37; Hogan, *Marshall Plan*, pp. 51–69.

20. Hogan, *Marshall Plan*, p. 52.

21. Ibid.

22. Clark Clifford, answer to a question from the floor in *Containment: Concept and Policy*, ed Terry L. Deibel and John Lewis Gaddis, vol. 1 (Washington, DC: National Defense University Press, 1986), p. 61.

23. Issac Deutscher, *Stalin* (New York: Oxford University Press, 1967), p. 583. Cf. Adam Ulam, *Expansion and Coexistence* (New York: Holt, Rinehart and Winston, 1974), pp. 432–50. For the official Soviet version in a pre-Gorbachev history, see B. Pnomaryov, A. Gromyko, and V. Khvostov, eds., *History of Soviet Foreign Policy, 1945–1970*, trans. David Skvirsky (Moscow: Progress Publishers, 1974), pp. 160–67.

24. Deutscher, *Stalin*, p. 583.

25. Ulam, *Expansion and Coexistence*, p. 657.

26. See Jones, *Fifteen Weeks*, pp. 232–34; see also the editorial, "Phony Peace" in *Life* (June 16, 1947), p. 34.

27. *Time* (July 14, 1947), p. 15.

28. "The Molotov Plan," editorial, *Life* (November 17, 1947), p. 40.

29. An annotated bibliography of analytical and critical works about Kennan's article is a book-length project in and of itself. As a sampling of this vast amount of writing, one should first reread the article, "The Sources of Soviet Conduct," *Foreign Affairs* 25 (July 1947), pp. 566–82. Kennan's discussion and repudiation of the meaning attached to his article was first published in his *Memoirs: 1925–1950*, pp. 354–76. For better elaborations on Kennan's thought by Kennan himself, see his *Realities of American Foreign Policy* (Princeton: Princeton University Press, 1954); *Russia and the West under Lenin and Stalin* (Boston: Little, Brown, 1960); *On Dealing with the Communist World* (New York: Harper and Row, 1964). Two recent biographies are important not only in the light they cast on Kennan but for the bibliographies they contain as well: David Mayers, *George Kennan and the Dilemmas of U.S. Foreign Policy* (New York: Oxford University Press, 1988); and Anders Stephanson, *Kennan and the Art of Foreign Policy* (Cambridge, MA: Harvard University Press, 1989). As an additional sampling of interpretations of Kennan's beliefs, see the following: John Gaddis, "Containment: A Reassessment," *Foreign Affairs* 55 (July 1977), pp. 430–41; Eduard Mark, "The Question of Containment: A Reply to John Lewis Gaddis," *Foreign Affairs* 56 (January 1978), pp. 430–40; Barton Gellman, *Contending with Kennan* (New York: Praeger, 1984); Terry L. Deibel and John Lewis Gaddis, eds., *Containment: Concept and Policy*, 2 vols. (Washington, DC: National Defense University Press, 1986).

30. Quoted in Jones, *The Fifteen Weeks*, p. 233.

31. Mayers, *George Kennan*, p. 106. The chronology of Kennan's activities given here is taken from Mayers's account. See pp. 105–12.

32. Ibid., p. 110.

33. Ibid., p. 111. See also Lloyd Gardner, *Architects of Illusion* (Chicago: Quadrangle, 1970), pp. 270–300.

34. Mayers, *George Kennan*, p. 111.

35. Kennan, "The Sources of Soviet Conduct," p. 578.

36. George F. Kennan, "The Sources of Soviet Conduct," in *American Diplomacy, 1900–1950* (New York: Mentor, 1952), p. 91.

37. Ibid., p. 97.

38. For a more detailed examination of the metaphors of expansion and containment as applied to the Vietnam War, see Robert L. Ivie, "Metaphor and Motive in the Johnson Administration's Vietnam War Rhetoric," *Texts in Context: Critical Dialogues on Significant Episodes in American Political Rhetoric*, ed. Michael C. Leff and Fred J. Kauffeld (Davis, CA: Hermagoras Press, 1989), pp. 121–41.

39. George F. Kennan, "The Origins of Containment," *Containment: Concept and Policy*, vol. 1, ed. Terry L. Deibel and John Lewis Gaddis (Washington, DC: National Defense University Press, 1986), p. 7.

40. On these confusions, see Stephanson *Kennan and the Art of Foreign Policy*, pp. 73–85.

41. Kennan, *Memoirs*, p. 356. Why Kennan wanted it published anonymously has never been satisfactorily explained. Certainly, his position within the government required discretion. But he must also have known that having his paper published without the author's name would be unusual, not the customary practice of *Foreign Affairs*, and substituting "X" for a name would most certainly draw considerable attention to his article. Kennan's explanation, as honest as it may be, remains unsatisfactory or else enormously naive—something Kennan has rarely been accused of.

42. *New York Times* (July 8, 1947), p. 22.

43. Walter Lippmann, *The Cold War: A Study in American Foreign Policy* (New York: Harper and Brothers, 1947). All quotations from Lippmann are from this source rather than the *Herald Tribune*.

44. These three are specified and developed by Lippmann's biographer, Ronald Steel, in *Walter Lippmann and the American Century*, pp. 443–46.

45. *Reader's Digest* (October, 1947), pp. 25–31. The article was described as "an authoritative analysis." We are indebted to Marilyn Young for pointing out some of these changes in the *Digest* from Kennan's original in her unpublished paper, "The Rhetorical Origins of American Anti-Communism," written as a special project for Theodore Windt in 1970.

46. Kennan, "Sources of Soviet Conduct," p. 95.

47. "Stop-Russia Policy for U.S.," *U.S. News* (July 25, 1947), p. 17. (Emphasis added.)

48. *U.S. News* (October 10, 1947), p. 52.

49. "The Story Behind Our Russian Policy," *Newsweek* (July 23, 1947), p. 15.

50. Brooks Atkinson, "America's Global Planner," *New York Times Magazine* (July 31, 1947), p. 32.

51. Professor Kenneth Thompson, certainly a sophisticated analyst of international relations, described Kennan, Hans Morganthau, Walter Lippmann, and Reinhold Niebuhr as the "Four Horsemen of Realism in Foreign Policy." *Interpreters and Critics of the Cold War* (Washington, DC: University Press of America, 1978), pp. 35–64.

52. Kenneth Burke, *Philosophy of Literary Form* (Baton Rouge, LA: Louisiana State University Press, 1941), p. 4.

53. Halle, *The Cold War as History*, p. 105.

54. From *The Images of the Future*, quoted in Jane Blankenship and Janette Kenner Muir, "On Imagining the Future: The Secular Search for 'Piety,' " *Communication Quarterly* 35 (Winter 1987), p. 2.

55. Kenneth Burke, *Permanence and Change* (Indianapolis, IN: Bobbs-Merrill, 1977), p. 18.

56. Kennan, "Sources of Soviet Conduct," p. 95.

57. Letter to the editor of the *New York Times* (August 5, 1947), p. 22.

58. Krock, *New York Times* (July 8, 1947), p. 22.

59. Krock pointed to the State Department as the origin of the article but apparently it was R. H. Shackford of United Press who named George F. Kennan as the author. See the accompanying "sidebar" to the reprint of the article in *Life* (July 28, 1947), p. 53.

60. Brooks Atkinson, "America's Global Planner," *New York Times Magazine* (July 13, 1947), p. 9.

61. *Life* (July 28, 1947), p. 53; see also *U.S. News* (July 25, 1947), pp. 17–19 and (October 10, 1947), pp. 52–55; *Newsweek* (July 21, 1947), pp. 15–17.

62. Kennan, "Sources of Soviet Conduct," p. 106.

63. Burke, *Permanence and Change*, p. 74. Emphasis in the original.

64. Kennan, "Sources of Soviet Conduct," p. 96.

Chapter Eight

Critics and Advocates of the New Reality

The cold war reality did not capture American thought and imagination without critics who wanted to restrict it or advocates who wanted to expand it. The criticism came from a variety of political directions. In all probability that was one reason for its relative impotence. The Truman administration spoke with one consistent voice and was supported by prominent Republicans in the spirit of bipartisanship. Even if Republicans and dissident members of the administration did not accept every detail of the new political world order or every policy advocated by Truman or every argument used to support both the new reality and its attendant policies (for example, Kennan dissented from the "red fascism" connection and from the Truman Doctrine), they generally agreed with the overall scope and content of the cold war reality. The administration had powerful platforms from which to speak and its representatives spoke from within the official language and rhetoric of anticommunism. In so doing they presented a united front against critics and reinforced the broad contours and basic language of the cold war.

Critics and advocates, on the other hand, seemed like a Tower of Babel speaking from a variety of vantage points often as much in conflict with one another as with the administration. They ranged from those who prepared a frontal assault on the new reality to those who criticized specific policies that emanated from it to those who wanted to extend the reality to other areas of international and domestic life. The least successful were the critics who offered a different analysis of Soviet–American relations and therefore advocated different policies. The most successful were the advocates who sought to extend the Loyalty Program to other aspects of American life and the Truman Doctrine to Asia. The former found themselves consigned to the category of "idealists" or "dupes" in conventional history. The latter greased the way for Mc-Carthyism and extended U.S. commitments in the Far East. Interestingly, most of the critics and advocates shared a fundamental view with the architects of the cold war. They saw themselves as standing in the middle between two extremes. President Truman believed his policies represented a realistic path between marching into all-out war with the Soviet Union and retreat into isolation. Henry Wallace believed his ideas presented an alternative to that same isolationism, on the one hand, and Truman's brand of anticommunism, on the other. Walter Lippmann saw himself as standing between the extremes of universal containment and mindless withdrawal from the world. Robert A. Taft sought a middle ground between bipartisan support for the militarization of American life and the isolationist demobilization of the past. Richard Nixon believed his approach represented a responsible search for domestic communists in a way that avoided the protection of them by Democrats and the indiscriminate attacks on them from the rabid Right. At this point, we may do well to consider representative critics and their criticisms, and how they were dealt with at the time.

CRITICS

Henry Wallace: Idealistic Critique

When Franklin Roosevelt died, Mrs. Roosevelt wrote to Henry Wallace: "I feel that you are peculiarly fitted to carry on the ideals which were close to my husband's heart."[1] At the time that sentiment was shared by many. Wallace was an internationalist and social democrat. He had served as secretary of agriculture for eight years under Roosevelt during the most difficult period farmers ever faced in the United States. In 1940 FDR chose him as his running mate. When he was replaced by Harry Truman on the 1944 ticket, he returned to the cabinet as secretary of commerce. Truman fired him in 1946. He served as editor of the *New Republic* for a time and then became the presidential candidate of the Progressive party in 1948. Throughout the early period of the cold war, he was the most conspicuous and consistent critic of the assumptions and language of the new worldview, first within the government and then from without.[2]

Henry Wallace came to be labeled as an idealist, but his idealism was not in the analysis of world events nor in the policies he proposed. His idealism rested in his belief that he could argue with the new anticommunist reality of the Truman administration by marshalling facts and presenting pragmatic arguments based on spheres of influence. He was naive. Universal principles of good and evil animated the crusade against communism. Facts and policies were judged by how well or how poorly they fitted within the rhetorical construction of this universal ideology. Those facts and policies that supported the crusade were readily seized upon and trumpeted; those that did not were dismissed as irrelevant or, in some cases, products of pro-Soviet thinking. It was an either/or world, and no middle ground, no matter how reasonable, could be admitted. Wallace had a further rhetorical problem. He had limited rhetorical traditions to draw from in constructing his criticism of Truman's policies. At times, he advocated an arrangement between the Soviet Union and the United States based on spheres of influence and balance of power. But that approach, as much as it was one of the animating bases for actual policies by the administration, had been publicly renounced by Roosevelt, Truman, and the general public (insofar as the public had any real conception of spheres of influence). Spheres of influence also smacked of imperialism. The name "imperialism" had been reserved for other countries, especially in the cold war to Soviet imperialism, and therefore made spheres of influence even more unpalatable. The only other rhetorical tradition available to Wallace was the allied cooperation during World War II. That rhetoric of brave friends and democratic Russians had long since grown obsolete. To speak of the Russians as friends gave additional ammunition to those who accused Wallace of being pro-Soviet or pro-communist. Nonetheless, Wallace ventured forward to attack the new reality of anticommunism despite the constrained rhetorical traditions he had to draw from.

To understand Wallace's clash with the prevailing anticommunism one needs to understand that he had constructed a very different narrative of Soviet history and motives from the cold warriors. That narrative was shared in varying degrees by some others on both the liberal and conservative sides, but few drew the conclusions Wallace did or were as vocal as he in urging a different course of action.

In his famous July 23, 1946 letter to President Truman Wallace presented a very different story of Russian history and Soviet motives from the one Truman heard from others. Wallace wrote that for over a thousand years Russian history "has been a succession of attempts, often unsuccessful, to resist invasion and conquest—by the Mongols, the Turks, the Swedes, the Germans, and the Poles." During the thirty years the Soviets had been in power, they had experienced a "continuation of their historical struggle for national existence" including the years spent in resisting attempts at overthrowing them by the Japanese, British, and French, "with some American assistance," and in the civil war by the White armies "encouraged and financed by Western powers." The struggle became more frightening when the Soviet Union was almost conquered by the Germans "after a period during which the Western European powers had apparently acquiesced in the rearming of Germany in the belief that the Nazis would seek to expand eastward rather than westward." He concluded this narrative by saying: "The Russians, therefore, obviously see themselves as fighting for their existence in a hostile world."

From this brief recitation the secretary of commerce drew lessons quite different from those that had been drawn by Kennan in his "long telegram." Wallace pleaded with Truman to see recent U.S. actions through Soviet eyes:

Our actions to expand our military security system—such steps as extending the Monroe Doctrine to include the arming of the Western Hemisphere nations, our present monopoly of the atomic bomb, our interest in outlying bases and our general support of the British Empire—appear to them as going beyond the requirement of defense.

He noted that Americans might feel as fearful as the Soviets if they were the only capitalist nation in the world and found themselves surrounded by socialist nations armed as they never had been before. Citing the loans to Great Britain, U.S. resistance to the USSR's attempts to secure warm water ports and, more important, resistance to the Soviet Union's attempts to form a security system of "friendly" neighboring states in eastern Europe—all these, Wallace wrote, contributed to Soviet fears of encirclement by an anti-Soviet bloc that might serve as a "springboard of still another effort to destroy her." This analysis, based on a contrary telling of Russian history and stressing Soviet fears, led to another set of recommendations about how to conduct U.S. foreign relations with the Soviet Union. Wallace advocated what would later be called detenté, a recognition of genuine security concerns on the part of the Soviet Union, the establishment of an atmosphere of mutual trust using concrete agreements to achieve that end, and the development of mutually beneficial economic relations.

But Wallace recognized the formidable rhetorical task his position would require as well as the political courage it would need:

We should be prepared, even at the expense of risking epithets of appeasement, to agree to reasonable Russian guarantees of security. . . .

We should make an effort to counteract the irrational fear of Russia which is being systematically built up in the American people by certain individuals and publications. The slogan that communism and capitalism, regimentation and democracy, cannot continue to exist in the same world is, from a historical point of view, pure propaganda. Several religious doctrines, all claiming to be the only true gospel and salvation, have existed side by side with a reasonable degree of tolerance for centuries. This country was for the first half of its national life a democratic island in a world dominated by absolutist governments.

We should not act as if we too felt that we were threatened in today's world. We are by far the most powerful nation in the world.[3]

In these comments, Wallace was remarkably prescient about the emerging ideological rhetoric Truman would soon embrace, the slogans that rhetoric would use and the absolute division it would create. However, as an insider and still a member of the cabinet, he did not know the insurmountable linguistic edifice that it would erect. But he quickly learned.

Henry Wallace's speech at Madison Square Garden on September 12, 1946 was political dynamite. In it he ran head-on into the emerging ideological rhetoric of anticommunism, although he had not anticipated its force. "Russian ideals of social-economic justice," Wallace declared, "are going to govern nearly a third of the world. Our ideas of free enterprise democracy will govern much of the rest." Reciting the story of Russia's fears of encirclement and invasion, he stated that the emerging "get tough" policy toward the Soviet Union would produce the opposite result from what Americans anticipated: "The tougher we get, the tougher the Russians will get." He contended that the two nations should mutually agree to put this competition on a "friendly basis" instead of conniving and scheming against one another. In the most controversial section of the speech Wallace stated:

The real peace treaty we now need is between the United States and Russia. On our part, we should recognize that we have no more business in the *political* affairs of Eastern Europe than Russia has in the *political* affairs of Latin America, Western Europe and the United States. We may not like what Russia does in Eastern Europe. Her type of land reform, industrial expropriation, and suppression of basic liberties offends the great majority of the people of the United States. But whether we like it or not the Russians will try to socialize their sphere of influence just as we try to democratize our sphere of influence. This applies also to Germany and Japan. We are striving to democratize Japan and our area of control in Germany, while Russia strives to socialize eastern Germany.

His call for spheres of influence directly contradicted the administration's policy. Recognizing that his words were provocative in their moderation, Wallace declared that he was "neither anti-Russian nor pro-Russian." But he compounded the problem by announcing that President Truman had read these words and that "he said that they represented the policy of his administration."[4] That statement created controversy both at home and abroad, especially because Secretary of State James F. Byrnes was at that very moment at the Paris Peace Conference reiterating his government's opposition to spheres of influence. On September 20 Truman asked for Wallace's resignation from the cabinet and got it.[5]

Once outside the administration Wallace stepped up his criticism of President Truman's foreign policy. He opposed the Truman Doctrine saying: *"No loan to undemocratic and well-fed Turkey: No loan to Greece until a representative Greek government is formed and can assure America that our funds will be used for the welfare of the Greek people."*[6] He later opposed the Marshall Plan, NATO and, of course, ran against Truman in the 1948 presidential campaign. He predicted that Truman's Loyalty Program would "turn Americans against each other. It will threaten everything in America that is worth fighting for. Intolerance is aroused. Suspicion is engendered. Men of highest integrity in public life are besmirched."[7]

Henry Wallace spoke from outside the developing rhetorical reality of the cold war. In practically every respect, his view of the world and the policies he advocated clashed directly with those of the Truman administration and the growing consensus among Americans. The narrative of Soviet history he told was not one of a world divided between two competing ideologies, not one of Soviet expansion and U.S. determination to support free people everywhere, not one of melodramatic heroes and villains. He saw a divided world, no doubt about it, but it was divided by competing spheres of influence. He described the United States as powerful and generous and the Soviet Union as fearful of encirclement. He believed that relations with the Soviet Union should be based on mutual respect for each other's spheres of influence. Wallace argued that the Soviets had vital national interests and, though these might clash with the vital interests of the United States, there was nothing sinister involved. Moreover, his view of the Soviet Union, unlike that of the administration, was of a severely weakened nation ravished by war.

The primary metaphor he used in his speeches and writings to describe Soviet–American relations was the "game" metaphor, a peaceful and friendly competition. A second metaphoric cluster used by Wallace was the "sick" cluster, usually applied to American leaders who supported the Truman Doctrine. Robert Ivie concluded that,

Wallace's critique of the Cold War was driven by an ideal image . . . of a spiritually awakened America engaging the Soviet Union in peaceful competition to heal an economically sick world and eventually to win the allegiance of humankind. . . .

Wallace's ideal image [was] rhetorically flawed by its preponderant criticism of the United States, blaming the American government and reactionary capitalists almost exclusively for the Cold War, . . . [and] it also lacked a characterization of the Russians that was well suited to [Wallace's description of] their designated role as responsible players in the friendly game of power politics.[8]

Thus, not only did Wallace urge policies different from cold warriors, he had a very different vision of international reality and a different rhetoric in narrative, premises, and metaphors.

Wallace could not find an effective language to describe the Soviet Union and the kind of accommodations that the United States should seek with that nation. Here he too was a captive of history. The extremes of American–Soviet historical relations had veered from excessive hostility to excessive friendliness. The language of hostility had been used by the cold warriors to describe their positions. Wallace had only the tradition of the language of friendship to draw upon to describe his position. When he sought to go outside that traditional way of talking about the Soviet Union, he was accused of not talking about the Soviet Union at all, at least not the Soviet Union that was emerging in American consciousness. When he reverted to the language of friendship and its attendant arguments, drawn primarily from the war-time alliance, he played into the hands of his enemies who labeled him idealistic or a dupe of the communists. In either case, he was attempting to address the same problem as cold warriors, but by the time he went public with his reservations and alternative views, he found that he was already outside the evolving political reality of the times.

Because he argued from outside the new reality of the cold war, Wallace had to be discredited, his ideas banished. Just before he fired Wallace, Truman wrote a memorandum in which he said:

[Wallace] is a pacifist one hundred percent. He wants us to disband our armed forces, give Russia our atomic secrets and trust a bunch of adventurers in the Kremlin Politburo. I do not understand a "dreamer" like that. The German-American Bund under Fritz Kuhn was not half so dangerous. The Reds, phonies and the "parlor pinks" seem to be banded together and are becoming a national danger. I am afraid that they are a sabotage front for Uncle Joe Stalin.[9]

For presenting a competing reality about world affairs, Wallace had to be banished from government. That is understandable since he was urging a different foreign policy from that of the president and his secretary of state. But it does not explain the vitriolic attacks on him after his resignation. To understand that we need to know that the new cold war reality was an ideological reality, one that can accept no challenges to its fundamental premises, let alone a wholesale attack upon it.

Wallace's disagreement was basic, for he refused to acquiesce to the central assumptions and language inherent in the new political reality created by Churchill, Truman, and the others. One critical problem he encountered was that he accepted a world divided between the two major powers and even occasionally acceded to the official description of that division, an "iron curtain." By accepting these terms, he weakened his argumentative stance, even as he sought to argue a different nature of the conflict within that division. However, from the cold warrior's point of view, he was not to be engaged in debate, for one does not debate a universal reality that one has already "discovered" and designed policies aligned to it. Instead, all that is left to argue are the reasons a person would have for presenting such alien ideas, especially when they accept the basic division and its basic metaphor.

The attacks on Wallace took two lines of invective. One line was to portray him as a dreamer, a crackpot, an idealist. In the world of practical politics such epithets are derogatory. Each of these suggests that the person to whom they are attached does not live in the same universe as others, and does not have practical or realistic policies to confront the problems within that universe. On the first point, such criticism was undoubtedly correct. Wallace was offering an alternative vision of reality. Whether his policies would have been appropriate and practical at the time is another matter entirely since they found little favor and were not attempted.

The second line of invective attacked Wallace's patriotism. When Wallace went to England after the announcement of the Truman Doctrine and gave a series of speeches there, Senator Vandenberg rose in the Senate to denounce him as an "itinerant saboteur."[10] Dean Acheson later wrote: "Public distrust [opposition to aid to Greece and Turkey] was accentuated when Wallace established a foreign base in England from which to attack the Administration, and Gromyko joined in from Moscow. We were fortunate in our enemies."[11] Suddenly, England was a foreign base and Wallace was in camp with Gromyko. Acheson's recollection apparently captured distinctly the subversive image officials had of him, and the fanaticism that led an intelligent man to link Wallace with Gromyko. In his famous campaign memo for Truman in November 1947, Clark Clifford warned of the political danger of a Wallace third-party campaign and advised: "Every effort must be made *now* jointly and at one and the same time—although, of course, by different groups—to dissuade him and also to identify him and isolate him in the public mind with the Communists."[12] When Wallace announced his candidacy in December 1947, Stewart Alsop wrote: "The Wallace third-party has been indecently exposed for what it is: an instrument of Soviet foreign policy. Since the PCA invited him to head a third party, the whole movement has been stripped bare. The bones revealed are communistic bones."[13] The campaign against Wallace received its primary boost from the fact that communists did support him. In that era of growing fear, the communists in Wallace's presidential campaign were enough for many people to believe that Wallace was a "front," at best, and communist controlled, at worst. *Time* magazine stated: "But by all evidence, Moscow, more prescient, sensed the prize within its grasp and ordered the U.S. Communists to seize [Wallace]. Quickly the peace front corrected its faulty line and hails its new-found hero."[14] This drumbeat of vilification reached hysterical proportions. Coming from a variety of sources, including labor unions and the Americans for Democratic Action, the guilt-by-association not only indicted Wallace but supporters as well:

It was demanded that everyone stand up and declare himself. Support for Wallace was taken as ipso facto proof that the culprit was a fellow traveler or Communist dupe. . . . In at least six colleges and universities, professors declaring for Wallace found themselves out of jobs or otherwise penalized. In West Frankfort, Illinois, the Wallace senatorial candidate was refused police protection when stoned by a mob.[15]

It should be noted that President Truman's main argument against voting for Wallace was that it was a wasted vote, a vote for a third party that had no chance of winning.[16] And for that reason, as much as any other, Wallace lost in the 1948 presidential campaign badly which contributed even more to his being discredited. Nonetheless, Truman declared in his St. Patrick's Day speech that he would "not accept the political support of Henry Wallace and his Communists."[17]

During the formative years of the cold war Henry Wallace was the most outspoken critic of the major assumptions and policies that created the American side of the cold war. He clashed directly with the new reality as it was being formed, and ran into an ideological brick wall. He seemed to think that foreign policy like domestic policy should be open to discussion and debate. Instead, he found that the basic premises were closed to debate. By continuing to question these premises he had to be banished from the realm of effective discourse, from the arena of "realistic" thinking. When he presented his ideas as a member of the administration, he was fired. When he presented them from outside the administration, he was vilified. With the development of the closed ideological system of anticommunism, there was no room for debate on fundamental issues, only disagreements about the application of these principles to events and policies—the strategy and tactics of policies. Wallace was amazed and frustrated by this closed rhetorical universe, and he expressed his exasperation in the *New Republic* by writing that Truman's speech on aid to Greece and Turkey had "scarcely a paragraph of fact or evidence. All was a mixture of unsupported assertions, sermonizing and exhortation. It was evident that in the name of crisis facts had been withheld, time had been denied and a feeling of panic had been engendered."[18] The world had been divided into two warring ideological camps, and there was no room for someone like Wallace who

denied basic assumptions in the ideological rhetoric of anticommunism
or sought to find a different way of describing the conflicts between the
United States and the Soviet Union. The division was so complete and
its premises so melodramatically universal that when he voiced a different interpretation of events and people, he found himself castigated
for being a dupe of domestic communists or an apologist for Soviet
actions. The futility of his efforts eventually led Wallace to recant his
heresy, and heresy is the exact word to describe Wallace's early ideas.[19]
It was not until the Vietnam War that questioning basic assumptions of
U.S. foreign policy received any widespread discussion, the kind of
discussion Henry A. Wallace attempted to encourage in the early days
and for which he paid the price.

Walter Lippmann: "Realistic" Critique

Walter Lippmann belonged to another group of critics of the cold war,
a group that included Hans J. Morganthau, Reinhold Niebuhr, and eventually George F. Kennan. They were called the "realists" because they
sought to define the limits of U.S. power in devising policies to confront
the postwar world, but they did so within the ideological framework of
the new reality.[20] Among them, Lippmann commanded the broadest
audience.

In his lifetime Walter Lippmann rose from a precocious student of
philosophy and politics to the most influential journalist of his generation, an independent journalist but also an intimate of the powerful.
He had been a member of the committee that helped prepare President
Wilson's delegation to the Versailles peace conference, but soon thereafter he soured on active participation in politics and devoted himself
to a career as a political journalist and writer. In a long series of books
and from a variety of distinguished journalistic posts, Lippmann poured
forth his analysis and criticism of American policies in an eloquence
rarely achieved by other writers on politics. In his writing he sought to
merge reason with practicalities and usually took as his guide the principle that policies should not exceed the resources available to carry
them out.[21]

Given his previous disillusionment with the post–World War I peace,
it was understandable that he took an early and intense interest in the
kind of peace that would be established after World War II. During the
war he wrote two important books, *U.S. Foreign Policy: Shield of the
Republic* (1943) and *U.S. War Aims* (1944), which looked to the kind of
world order that would be realistic not idealistic, the tragic flaw as he
saw it, of Wilsonian diplomacy. Lippmann and some of the other realists
stood between the Truman camp and the Wallace camp. Lippmann
accepted that the postwar world was divided into two conflicting sys-

tems, that Soviet communism was as totalitarian as fascist Germany, that the United States should ally itself with Great Britain in the struggle for collective security, that power politics and military preparedness were essential to being able to react to world events, and that a "durable understanding" between East and West had to be reached through the Soviet Union accepting the elemental principles of human rights and political freedom.[22] In this sense, Lippmann kept one foot firmly planted in the Truman camp. He criticized U.S. foreign policy from *within* the rhetorical framework of the new reality and confined his criticism to specific matters of policy, for the most part, thereby not moving "outside the orbit of 'responsible' criticism or [jeopardizing] his prestige."[23]

What then did Lippmann criticize and from what bases? Lippmann's other foot was outside Truman and Acheson's conception of the cold war. From that vantage point, he criticized the national self-righteousness that motivated the anticommunist crusade as expressed in the Truman Doctrine, stressed the need to recognize the limitations of American power and resources in implementing the policy of containment, preferred diplomatic negotiations to military confrontations, and emphasized that national self-interest, not ideology, motivated the Soviet Union. He conducted his critique of the issues and policies that eventually formed the American version of the cold war in the dispassionate fashion that marked his entire career. Although he had already endorsed an Anglo–American alliance, he dissented from Churchill's "Iron Curtain" address because he thought it was an anti-Soviet alliance that would undermine any possibility of fruitful negotiations with the Russians. He deplored the messianic language of the Truman Doctrine, even as he supported the economic aid bill Truman presented.

As a minor example of how fervently members of the administration held to the beliefs of the Truman Doctrine, we may cite the exchange of Dean Acheson with Lippmann at a private dinner party while the aid bill was before Congress. Acheson had launched into a vigorous defense of Truman's assessment of the world and accused Lippmann, who had questioned the reasons the president had given for aid, of "sabotaging" U.S. foreign policy. That slander brought on a spirited confrontation between the two. As Steel described it: "Words flew, fingers were jabbed into chests, faces grew red . . . [and eventually] the two distinguished gentlemen stalked off in opposite directions."[24] The tenacity of belief in the new reality was so intense it could arouse vehement passions to the point that even Acheson, a man who prided himself on being devoted to reason and gentlemanly disagreements, could accuse a respected friend of sabotage.

Although Truman's claims for a universal policy of anticommunism sparked Lippmann's specific responses, it was George Kennan's "The Sources of Soviet Conduct" that drew his most sustained critique of the emerging new world reality. He devoted fourteen successive columns of "Today and Tomorrow" in the New York *Herald Tribune* to it and thus gave added stature to Kennan's analysis. Shortly after the completion of this series, these columns were collected, revised, and published in a slim volume, *The Cold War: A Study in U.S. Foreign Policy.*[25] Although Lippmann agreed with Kennan on various points, he dissented on three major issues.[26]

First, Lippmann scored Kennan for placing too much emphasis on ideology to the neglect of Russia's history. He argued that the Russians were not so much motivated by a messianic urge but by legitimate concerns for their security. It was not Soviet expansionism that had placed Soviet armies in eastern and central Europe, but were a result of Hitler's aggression against the Soviet Union. This narrative was closer to Wallace's than anything else, even if Lippmann disavowed Wallace's conclusions and policies. Thus, Lippmann argued that the charges of Soviet expansionism driven by communist ideology were misleading, at best, a serious misreading of history, at worst.

Second, Lippmann attacked the policy of containment because he believed it meant confronting them around the globe. He called this policy a "strategic monstrosity" doomed to fail, because it meant we would end up supporting any regime that was anticommunist regardless of whether it was democratic or not. It was based on "hoping for the best" instead of devising strategies to deal with the hardest and worst possible cases the United States might face.[27] Such an approach encouraged wishful rather than hard thinking. It undermined America's claim to moral leadership and at the same time might extend U.S. commitments beyond our capacity to fulfill them.

Finally, Lippmann criticized Kennan for ignoring diplomacy as a means for settling problems between the United States and the Soviet Union in preference for a forceful or military solution. He reminded Kennan that rival powers without common goals had been part of all history, but that previously diplomats had reached settlements. In a column for the *Herald Tribune*, he wrote:

A settlement with Russia does not depend on a change in heart in Moscow, upon an abandonment of Russian imperialism and a renunciation of the communist ideology. . . . It depends upon the restoration of a balance of power. . . . What will matter in the end is not what the Politburo would like to do, but what in fact it knows it cannot do.[28]

This balance of power had to recognize not only the limitations of Soviet power, but the limitations of U.S. power and prospects as well.

By isolating these premises as central to the doctrine of containment, Lippmann lent authority to this interpretation of Soviet–American relations, even as he attacked it. That was the paradox of the realists' critique. Lippmann accepted the primary language and view of the cold war originated by anticommunists. He accepted that the Soviet Union was totalitarian. He accepted a world divided between the two great powers. He presented a careful set of distinctions: distinctions between Soviet power and communism, between protecting U.S. national security rather than defending democracy and freedom everywhere, between restraining Soviet influence instead of containing Soviet expansion. In his political thinking such distinctions were crucial, but in the public arena they were much too finely drawn because in the long run it was the picture of the world that proved determinative, not the dissenting particulars that Lippmann articulated.

But Lippmann did more than reinforce the worldview of policymakers, he added to it in a way that severely undercut his criticism. He popularized the description, "cold war," as *the* interpretation of the state of Soviet–American relations. As William Safire pointed out, it was one of the two "great coinages [the other being "iron curtain"] of the post-World War II period."[29] And so it was, so much so that people often forget that the phrase is metaphoric, not literal.

The cold war generally refers to any activities short of a shooting war or formal declaration of war in describing Soviet–American relations. But it had and has a greater meaning than that, conjuring up images and attitudes that extend far beyond a simple description. The word "cold" implies a freezing atmosphere which was taken at the time to mean that the two mutually exclusive political systems were frozen in ideological place. To those who understood the *cold* part of the cold war in this way, it reinforced Truman's distinction between two ways of life that were mutually exclusive.

Using the war metaphor in 1947 went beyond Truman's policies at the time, even as it foreshadowed the policies to come. Lippmann's choice to name the conflicts between the Soviet Union and the United States as a *war*, be it cold or not, had far-reaching consequences. To talk about a situation in terms of *war* is to see adversaries as enemies, differences as conflicts, setbacks as defeats, concessions as appeasement, and to envision victory over the enemy as the only means for resolution. The language of war is much different from the language of diplomacy. Diplomats take publicly stated positions as posturing for negotiating advantage, differences between groups as always open for discussion, antagonists as adversaries, concessions as a normal part of diplomacy, and mutually acceptable agreements which respect the interests of both sides as reasonable resolutions of conflict. The war metaphor suggests military solutions to conflicts; diplomatic metaphors suggest discursive agreements. Equally important, defining a relationship as *war* sets in motion not only attitudes toward a foreign nation, but toward one's own citizens as well. A nation cannot conduct a war without a unified public. Citizens are called upon to enlist in the domestic war effort; unity and perseverance are the continuing rallying cries; and loyalty to the government's cause becomes primary. In fact, in wartime new laws are often needed to enforce unity and punish disloyalty. War rhetoric is an either/or rhetoric of brave friends and sinister enemies, and none is so sinister as those citizens who do not support the war effort fully. Within the either/or rhetoric, those who dissent are considered subversive to unity, sabotaging the war policy, or forming a fifth column by spreading confusion or undermining the resolve of both the government and the people. Those who dare to agree even on small points with the enemy are perceived to be pro-enemy.[30] Once the metaphor becomes acceptable as the actual description of the world, such psychological structures of thought and the attendent language of war become embedded in consciousness to the point that few even recognize they are using them and what the political consequences are.

The coining of the description, cold war, by Lippmann undercut his advice to see differences between the Soviet Union and the United States as differences to be handled diplomatically as well as through the establishment of a balance of power between the two nations. Instead, once the cold war became accepted as the definitive description, it encouraged the militarization of U.S. foreign response and the hunt for subversives on the domestic side. Lippmann should not be charged with these excessive consequences. He continued to criticize both Democrats and Republicans who stridently embraced his own metaphor and who eschewed any negotiations in preference for militant confrontations. In fact, years later, he recommended that President Kennedy change the word "enemy" in his inaugural address to "adversary" so as to signal a shift from confrontation to negotiation in Soviet–American relations.[31] He had no love for the McCarthyites either, nor did he ever give them encouragement. Nonetheless, it was those very McCarthyites who used the metaphor so effectively to wage their domestic war against subversives and fellow travelers so as to impose their form of Americanism upon everyone else. Indeed, their principal argument came directly from the war metaphor as they contended that the United States was in a deadly struggle with an implacable enemy that required the suspension of civil liberties and the banishment or punishment of domestic enemies. Such was the ironic paradox of Lippmann and of the other realists, who by their very criticism of the new world reality within the prevailing language and arguments that created it, both reinforced and extended that new reality. For that reason Lippmann and the other realists were seldom subjected to vilification, except by extreme McCarthyites. They served too valuable a purpose—wittingly or not—in legitimizing the rhetoric of the cold war.

Robert A. Taft: Conservative Critic and Asian Advocate

Senator Robert A. Taft is not that well known as a critic of the cold war. There are two primary reasons for this neglect. First, after the 1946 elections when the Republicans gained control of Congress, Taft and Vandenberg divided their responsibilities within the party. Taft concentrated on domestic issues and Vandenberg on foreign affairs. Among the domestic issues closest to Taft's heart was his belief that the Democrats were pursuing policies that eventually would lead to socialism. His consistent criticism of "creeping socialism" gradually evolved into supporting attacks on domestic liberals as subversives. As this occurred, his opponents lumped him with other strident anticommunists. Second, Taft did have impeccable anticommunist credentials, and for the most part, he agreed that communism posed a threat both domestically and internationally. Like members of the Truman administration, he considered communism only a different form of totalitarianism. Prior to the war he said that communism was more dangerous to the United States than fascism, but in amplifying this statement later he noted privately that the danger was ideological, not military.[32] It was a position he was to maintain throughout the early days of the cold war. Even though he appeared to many at the time as an anticommunist conservative, Taft contributed his own critique of the growing cold war from a conservative perspective.

Although often labeled an isolationist, Taft recognized in the postwar world that isolationism had run its course and that a different approach was necessary.[33] It was in that context of trying to balance some assumptions from the old noninterventionism with new international responsibilities that led to the complexities of Taft's criticism. Add to these concerns, Taft's personal ambitions for the presidency, his concerted goal of dismantling the New Deal, his attempt to balance partisanship with leadership, and his critique becomes even more intricate. Two of Taft's basic ideas concern us here: his fear of war with the Soviet Union, and his belief that U.S. efforts in Europe ought to be restrained both militarily and financially.

Senator Taft was skeptical about the messianic spirit of U.S. foreign policy. As early as 1943 he warned Americans that if they truly believed "that the United States can properly go to war to impose our ideas of freedom on the rest of the world, then it seems we must admit that the Soviets have a right to crusade to impose Communism on the rest of the world because they believe Communism to be the final solution to the world's problems."[34] In the postwar period, he combined this concern with his fear of war. When Truman announced his doctrine, Taft accused the president of dividing the world into two antagonistic zones and warned that such a division might make war more probable. He stated flatly, "I don't want war."[35] Reluctantly, he supported aid to Greece and Turkey, but did so believing that the aid would be limited to a time in the near future when a popular government could be elected or the United Nations could take over the responsibility of providing this assistance. Taft recognized the reactionary Greek government for what it was and did not intend his support to mean he approved of a military anticommunist crusade against the Soviet Union.[36] On the same grounds, he reluctantly supported the Marshall Plan, but he did so not because he thought the Soviet Union posed a military threat to Europe, but because it posed an ideological threat. On the floor of the Senate he announced that he knew of no indication "of Russian intention to undertake military aggression beyond the sphere of influence which was originally assigned to them."[37]

Furthermore, Taft believed the United States did not have the resources to respond quickly to any actual Soviet threat in Europe. These beliefs came together in his opposition to the North Atlantic Treaty Organization. Opposing that treaty he warned that it was easy "to skip into an attitude of imperialism where war becomes an instrument of public policy rather than its last resort."[38] In other words, Taft originally advocated a restrained response to the ideological conflict with the Soviet Union, denied that the Soviet Union posed a military threat, and eventually opposed NATO because he believed, as he did with other policies of the administration, that it might provoke the USSR to a military response.

Finally, Taft opposed the growing concentration of power in the executive branch of government. As a conservative, he believed in limited government, and he had a history of criticizing what he thought to be unconstitutional usurpation of power by presidents. He had fought the New Deal on this basis, opposed many of Roosevelt's policies of preparation in the prewar years, including the draft, and lend lease.[39] In the postwar period he worried that the president was abandoning principles of law and liberty to embrace "force as the controlling factor in international action."[40] This approach to foreign affairs had, in Taft's view, the corollary consequence of expanding presidential power to the point that it meant "a benevolent executive must be given power to describe policy and administer policy according to his own prejudices in each individual case. Such a policy in the world, as at home, can lead only to tyranny or to anarchy."[41] His concerns came together when President Truman took the United States into the Korean War. Taft believed the president had overstepped his bounds by entering the war without a congressional declaration of war or even congressional approval.[42] However, like other Americans, Taft was reluctant to pull away from Korea once the president had fully committed the United States to that war.

Senator Robert Taft's conservative critique brought down upon him the charge that he was an old-fashioned isolationist cut off from the concerns and responsibilities of the new world that was in the making. Newspaper reporters repeatedly referred to him as leader of the isolationist wing of the Republican party. Marquis Childs described him as a man with his "head in the sand" and charged that his brand of isolationism was no different in the post war years than in the years before World War II when he refused to admit that Japan had aggressive intentions against the United States.[43] These were rhetorical attempts to banish Taft's criticism of the cold war policies of the Truman administration to the dustbin of history along with the senator himself, representing him as a relic of the past. Taft recognized these attempts for what they were: "anyone who varies from the pattern established by our State Department is to be cast into outer darkness."[44] Indeed, casting dissenters into "outer darkness" was exactly the rhetorical banishment that those who believed in the new universal reality of communist aggression sought. In this sense, both Henry Wallace and Robert Taft, two prominent figures so different in beliefs, shared a common fate.

But even as Senator Taft dissented from some of the beliefs and policies of the Truman administration and was unsuccessful for the most part in restraining those policies, he reinforced the conceptual framework that animated those beliefs and produced those policies. His criticism rested on a different understanding of Soviet motives, a belief that the Soviets had a legitimate claim to their sphere of influence in eastern Europe, and his concern that military aid and alliances would overextend the United States and possibly cause war with the Soviet Union. He argued his principles in attempts to restrain rather than overturn President Truman's policies. More often than not he saw the commitments being made as ones that would bankrupt U.S. economy. Nothing was closer to Taft's heart than achieving an annual balanced budget. But attempting to restrain the universal rhetoric for financial reasons seemed like nit-picking or timidity in the crisis atmosphere that the administration created. Beyond that, some of the language he chose proved ineffective. He labeled certain actions or policies as "imperialistic." In his address to the American Bar Association in 1943, he attacked Walter Lippmann's call for a postwar American–British–Russian alliance by saying such a confederation would lead to national armaments "in all parts of the world," create a "profession of militarists," and possibly lead to war. Such a policy, he declared was "imperialism."[45] After the war he quickly discovered the public would brook no such description of U.S. actions. It had embraced containment instead of imperialism as the legitimate description of foreign policy just as it had accepted the change of the name of the Department of War to the Department of Defense in

July 1947. But Taft's efforts were unsuccessful primarily because his own deep-seated anticommunism prevented him from attacking the fundamental language and rhetorical framework of the cold war.

If Taft was unsuccessful in restraining the Truman administration, he had greater success than he imagined in helping to extend the Truman Doctrine in different directions. In opposing the nomination of David Lilienthal to head the Atomic Energy Commission, Taft charged among other things that Lilienthal was "soft on the subject of communism."[46] Taft's fear of domestic communism had a long history. Forged from his conservative principles and his experiences with the radical unrest of the 1930s, his anticommunism flamed in the aftermath of the 1948 Republican presidential defeat. Although he continued to concentrate on domestic economic issues, he encouraged the anticommunist campaign in the United States, even to the point of accepting Joseph McCarthy's tactics because they got results.[47]

The other direction in which he sought to extend the Truman Doctrine was toward Asia. While Democrats concentrated their attention almost exclusively on Europe, a significant number of Republicans viewed Asia as foremost. In the midst of the debate over the Marshall Plan, Taft advocated extending aid to Nationalist China in its civil war with the Chinese communists.[48] The pleas for aid to Jiang Jieshi (Chiang Kai-shek) began to fill the air in Republican circles. Although Taft agreed with these, it was the China Lobby that carried the rhetorical ball.

Senator Robert Taft's criticism of Truman's conception of the cold war was paradoxical. He warned about the United States committing itself too extensively around the world, but also called for including Asia within the circle of anticommunist crusade. He was skeptical about the Democrats' assertion of Soviet intentions to conquer the world, but at the same time feared a communist conquest of China. He criticized the concentration of power in the presidency even as he was reluctant to tie the president's hands when he was conducting foreign policy. He opposed many of the policies that made up the cold war but added a vigorous voice to the condemnation of communism at home and abroad. In so doing Senator Taft reinforced the conceptual framework of the new reality of the anticommunist crusade in such a way that others "who shared Taft's general outlook became more frustrated, doctrinaire, and extreme in their view of the decade that followed the senator's death in 1953 . . . [and thus produced] some of the very policies of which Robert A. Taft had been so critical."[49]

ADVOCATES

Richard Nixon, Alger Hiss, and Domestic Communism

Allen Weinstein noted in his exhaustive study of the Hiss case that "Hiss became the linchpin in a 'Communist conspiracy' to take over the

American government under Roosevelt and Truman."[50] He called Hiss an icon for the age of chasing down domestic subversives. Richard M. Fried went even further to say that the Hiss case "offered a fulcrum on which tilted the political balance of the McCarthy era."[51] The Chambers-Hiss case was central to the development of McCarthyism and to the great fear that engulfed the United States in the decade to follow. And it launched the national political career of a little-known congressman from California, Richard M. Nixon. Hiss and Nixon would be forever linked in U.S. history.

The Hiss case is so well known that only the barest of essentials will be summarized here.[52] On August 3, 1948 Whittaker Chambers, one-time communist underground courier and now an editor at *Time* magazine, appeared before the House Committee on UnAmerican Activities to accuse eight people of being communists, among them Alger Hiss. Hiss immediately demanded an opportunity to deny the accusation and did so on August 5 before the committee. With Hiss's denial, the case was on.

At the time Alger Hiss was president of the Carnegie Foundation for Peace. He had previously served in both the Roosevelt and Truman administrations. He was a prominent New Dealer who had been at Yalta in a minor capacity, had served as temporary secretary general of the United Nations, and had delivered the original U.N. charter to President Truman in a widely publicized photograph. In other words, he was the perfect symbol to bind up so many frustrations, resentments, and fears that were beginning to explode in 1948. Since the 1930s there had been rumors about his political affiliations. However, they had remained neatly within the private circles of Washington. When Chambers made his accusation, they came out in the open. Naming Hiss as a communist had symbolic political ramifications far exceeding the case itself. It put a whole generation of politicians on trial, a whole period of American–Soviet diplomacy in question, and eventually provided the basis for suspecting anyone who deviated from the emerging anticommunist consensus of being less than totally loyal to the United States.

When Hiss appeared before HUAC and denied he was a communist, many members of the committee wanted to drop the investigation. Richard Nixon dissented. He said the credibility of the committee was at stake and it had to see who was telling the truth, Chambers or Hiss, regardless of what answer they might eventually get. (Actually, Nixon had been extensively briefed before Chambers made his initial accusations and therefore he had considerable more background information than he revealed to the committee at the time or later admitted to in his first memoir. *Six Crises*.) He sought a confrontation between Chambers and Hiss which took place in the committee hearing room. During the course of the hearings, Hiss challenged Chambers to make his accusations in public where he would not enjoy immunity from slander. When

Chambers complied and Hiss sued, the case moved from the hearing rooms to the courtroom. However, the grand jury chose to indict Alger Hiss for perjury rather than indict Whittaker Chambers.

Alger Hiss was tried twice. The first trial ended in a hung jury; the second in conviction on two counts of perjury for which Hiss served forty-four months in prison. The case turned on purloined official papers Chambers dramatically turned up (part of which were the infamous "Pumpkin Papers"), the now familiar Woodstock typewriter allegedly used to type copies of some of these papers, Chambers's knowledge of Hiss's birdwatching hobby (especially the sighting of a prothonotary warbler), an oriental rug, and a variety of other details that suggested Hiss had indeed engaged in espionage of one sort or another with Chambers. Although only convicted of perjury, Hiss came to symbolize communist subversion at the very highest levels of government, an aristocratic New Dealer who had sold his country out to the communists.

Two days after Chambers fingered Hiss, Senator Alexander Wiley inserted into the *Congressional Record* a statement he had issued about communists in government. In his statement he charged that "the present administration, in spite of its pious protests against communism, has served as a fertile breeding ground for Reds during the past 16 years."[53] These charges would rise as a constant drumbeat of criticism both in that election year and in the years to come.

But the hysteria surrounding the Hiss case extended beyond the partisan ramifications of the case. When the first trial ended in an 8–4 hung jury, Nixon and others were enraged. Nixon stated: "I think the entire Truman administration was extremely anxious that nothing bad happen to Mr. Hiss. Members of the administration feared that an adverse verdict would prove that there was a great deal of foundation to all the reports of Communist infiltration into the government during the New Deal days."[54] The U.S. judicial system, from the anticommunist vantage point, had failed, and Nixon thought there were sinister reasons for the failure. The California representative wanted the jury foreman investigated because he seemed to have made up his mind about Hiss before the trial, because he had "played an active part in the Madison Square Rally for Henry A. Wallace," and because his wife was a member of the "left-wing" League of Women Voters.[55] Nixon accused Judge Kaufman, who presided in the trial, of being prejudiced for Hiss and requested an investigation into his fitness to serve as a judge.[56]

The accusations against Alger Hiss, his trials, and eventual conviction in his second trial spurred other investigations of members of both the Roosevelt and Truman administrations. Republicans cited the fact that Hiss had been at Yalta, albeit in a minor role, for the failures of administration policy in central Europe after the war. Mistakes in judgments, actual circumstances, or differences in interpretations of agreements would not account for what many saw as the closing of the iron curtain over eastern Europe. Instead, these true believers in the insidious nature of domestic communism proclaimed that disloyal Americans, such as Alger Hiss, had sabotaged U.S. peace efforts in the world and handed nations over to the communist bloc. With the accusations against Hiss, the search for subversives in government and scapegoats for U.S. policy setbacks was underway with a fury. HUAC had long been involved in this search, Truman had given it legitimacy with his Loyalty Board, Nixon had made his career out of it, and Hiss became the proof that such a search was necessary.

The China Lobby: Extending the Truman Doctrine to Asia

The China Lobby, the popular name for the American China Policy Association (CPA) and other loosely knit supporters of Nationalist China, was headed by William Loeb and Henry Luce and included among its ardent supporters Alfred Kohlberg, Representative Walter Judd, Clare Boothe Luce, and Senators Styles Bridges, William Knowland, and Pat McCarran. But the China Lobby was more than the CPA. Most of those in the China Lobby were Republicans who, like Senator Taft, had long believed Asia was more important to U.S. national security than Europe. In the early cold war period, they posed a simple question: If the Truman Doctrine were indeed a universal program to stop communism in the world, why not apply it to Asia as well as Europe? And they concentrated their attention on China where Jiang's Nationalist government was engaged in a bitter civil war with Mao Zedong's communist guerrillas. The China Lobby was not so much an advocate of the early cold war policies as a critic of the limited way in which the anticommunist crusade was applied. They took the Truman Doctrine literally and demanded that it be extended to Asia.

American attitudes toward the Chinese mirrored in one respect the attitudes toward the Soviet Union, a love-hate relationship. Robert Newman pointed out: "In our perceptual ambiguity, the sinister and repulsive Fu Manchu turns overnight into the smiling and canny Charlie Chan. The endearing peasant created by Pearl Buck metamorphoses into the Communist devil painted by Joe McCarthy and Pat McCarran."[57] However, the debates over U.S. policy toward China in the years between 1945 and 1949 proceeded somewhat differently from those over American–Soviet relations.

First, the Truman administration appeared to believe as early as 1946 that Jiang's government could not sustain itself in China. General Marshall's attempt to negotiate between the Nationalists and the communists failed and aid to Jiang was suspended in late 1946. Although the Truman Doctrine was announced as a universal program of anticommunism, the administration carefully avoided any commitment to Nationalist China in its direct conflict with communism, albeit of the Asian variety. At this point in 1947 Truman was caught between a rock and a hard place. The rhetoric proclaimed a universal crusade but the policy toward China belied that crusade. Advocates for Jiang immediately began asking about China.[58] When testifying about aid to Greece and Turkey before congressional committees, Acting Secretary of State Acheson had an opportunity to distinguish between the communist threat in Europe, as he saw it, and the civil war in China. In other words, he had the opportunity to reel in the universal rhetoric. But he did not. Instead, Acheson denied any need for aid to the Nationalists at that time because the threat of a communist takeover was not imminent. When asked directly if there were any difference between the State Department's policy toward Greece and its policy toward the Nationalists, Acheson replied, "I did not attempt to say there is a difference in policy."[59] The only difference implied by the answer was that Jiang's situation did not require the aid that the Greek and Turkish situations demanded. Thus, the administration opened the door to future demands for aid and indeed for future criticism when Jiang's armies began to lose the war. In other words, the anticommunist rhetoric justifying aid in Europe had to be maintained even to the point of not drawing limits publicly that the administration was drawing privately.

Second, the assumptions that guided the China Lobby were somewhat different from those that guided the arguments about U.S. policy toward the Soviet Union. A set of "China myths" animated the debate and later expanded from both the debate and conclusion of the civil war. The central myths, as Newman described them, held that Jiang was China's true and popular leader, that he was a western-style democrat and his government was humane and enlightened, and that the atheistic Chinese communists were aggressive, bent on conquering China to make it subservient to the Soviet Union in the world communist movement.[60] Using much of the rhetoric that had been applied to conflicts with the Soviet Union, a conflict between the Free World and the Communist World, the China Lobby demanded the Truman administration extend aid to Jiang, the Christian savior of China. The president reluctantly agreed and approved the China Aid Act of 1948.[61]

Third, the specific methods for arguing support for Jiang's government differed significantly from those the Truman administration had used in urging aid to western Europe. Thomas E. Lifka noted that the "image of European nations binding together in a democratic crusade to halt a totalitarian menace, whether Nazi or Soviet, could simply not be transferred to Asian affairs with the same effectiveness."[62] Instead of "antitotalitarianism," advocates for support for Jiang used "anticommunism" as the central concept. Several reasons accounted for this change. By the time the China Lobby began its campaign for Jiang in 1948, the anticommunist theme had begun to replace the antitotalitarian theme. Although Truman had only mentioned "communists" once in his March 12, 1947 address and had stressed that U.S. aid to Greece and Turkey was aiming at preventing "totalitarian" expansion, journalists began using the two words interchangeably with the more specific "Communist" gradually taking precedence. Another reason for this rhetorical shift came from the problem policymakers had in justifying continued good relations with fascist nations like Spain and Argentina. Lifka remarked that "[i]deological problems with these nations were avoided by characterizing U.S. goals as anti-communist or anti-Soviet rather than anti-totalitarian."[63] Equally important, many believed the communist movement was monolithic. Mao's communism was only an extension of Soviet communism. In his first speech in Congress, Representative Walter Judd proclaimed: "I am convinced now [that] the primary allegiance of the Chinese Communists is to Russia . . . and [that] their purpose is to make Russia overwhelmingly the strongest power in Asia as well as Europe."[64] It was to the China Lobby's rhetorical benefit to link the two because it strengthened its argument for applying the Truman Doctrine to Asia as well as Europe. Chinese communism and Soviet communism were only two sides of the same coin. If the government were intent on containing communism in Europe, it should also be as eager about containing it in Asia.

However, a shift in the rhetorical emphasis from totalitarianism to anticommunism meant a shift in analogy and metaphor. Comparison with Hitler's aggression seemed inappropriate to the civil war in China. Therefore, the analogy shifted to the Soviet Union and its conquest from within during the Bolshevik Revolution. In addition, supporters of Nationalist China tried to find an Asian equivalent for the iron curtain. At various times they tried the silken curtain or the bamboo curtain, but both metaphors proved too flimsy to excite the images that Churchill's metaphor excited. Therefore, a new metaphor was created that supported the notion of Mao's subservience to Stalin. The Chinese communists were characterized as "puppets" of the Soviet communists. The new metaphor fitted nicely with the China Lobby's insistence on aid to Jiang as a means not only for defending the Nationalist government but now for combating Soviet communism in a different area of the world. By 1950 viewing Mao and his new government merely as "puppets" of the Soviets had become commonplace so that when the North Koreans attacked the South, they were viewed as just another "puppet" whose strings Stalin pulled. And, of course, the metaphor spread to describe the countries of eastern Europe that the Soviet Union controlled, and eventually included any nation that allied itself with or seemed to be friendly toward the Soviet Union.

The most significant difference in the debate over China from the debates over Europe was that rhetorical positions were reversed. In arguing for containment of Soviet communism in Europe, policymakers from Truman through Acheson and Forrestal argued a universal policy that attributed melodramatic motives of inherent evil and aggression to the Soviets. Critics of that program and of particular policies argued against universalism and sought to make distinctions between ideological systems and nationalistic security concerns. In making these arguments, they relied on presenting facts and information contrary to the administration's arguments from principle. The critics sought to uncover different and more complex motives than the simple good/evil motives the administration argued from. In sum, they attempted to portray a more complex adversary than the one luridly painted by Truman, Acheson, and the others. For the most part, the critics failed. The images and fears conjured up by the anticommunist rhetoric overwhelmed them.

In the case of China, the Truman administration found itself in the critics' rhetorical position. It had to argue against an explicit application of the universal anticommunist reality to China. It decided to marshall the facts about the circumstances unique to the Chinese situation and the history of the civil war to account for the defeat of the Nationalist government by Mao in terms other than the insidious expansionism of communism. The China White Paper was designed to present compelling evidence that "Jiang, not the Truman administration, 'lost' China."[65] Dean Acheson wrote in his memoirs that he was intellectually naive in thinking that people could be persuaded by careful presentations of evidence and reason to see that the fall of Nationalist China was due to the corruption and incompetence of its leaders, not to failures of U.S. policy.[66] That statement was ironic given that two years before Acheson had recognized that Marshall's presentation of evidence and reason about Greece and Turkey had left senators unmoved and he had leapt to the rescue with his impassioned and hyperbolic recitation about the impending fall of Western civilization if they did not act. Part of that rhetoric had created the very reality that he would now marshal "evidence and reason" to argue against. In so doing, he would find himself as frustrated as Henry Wallace had been in trying to refute the original rhetoric.

When Jiang's army faltered and its defeat seemed imminent, the administration decided to release its White Paper on China in August 1949. The White Paper, formally entitled *U.S. Relations With China, With Special Reference to the Period 1944–1949*, was 1,054 pages long of which 412 pages were the State Department's narrative of events and 642 pages were supporting documents. Few people other than political elites read it. Nonetheless, supporters of Jiang began charging that important documents had been omitted; that the writers of the Paper were biased, at best, or pro-communist, at worst; and that the Paper was a coverup of the failure to come to the aid of a democratic ally besieged by communists.[67] Representative Judd made many of these charges and they were widely publicized in U.S. newspapers, notably the *New York Times*.[68] In all, the White Paper raised more suspicions than it put to rest. But it did more than that.

To gain a public audience, a Letter of Transmittal accompanied the narrative and documents. The White Paper attempted to put the Chinese civil war in perspective, to place the blame for the Nationalist loss on the incompetence of Jiang's government, and to absolve U.S. policymakers of responsibility for the fall of China to Mao. The argument was presented in excruciating detail with accompanying documents. However, the last several pages of the Letter undercut the argument in disastrous ways. Newman called these pages "incendiary in effect" containing "most of the apocalyptic rhetoric . . . which called down upon the Truman administration all the outrage of the right-wing China lobby in the United States."[69] Several paragraphs are worth quoting at length.

It must be admitted frankly that the American policy of assisting the Chinese people in resisting domination by any foreign power or powers is now confronted with the gravest difficulties. The heart of China is in Communist hands. The Communist leaders have foresworn their Chinese heritage and have publicly announced their subservience to a foreign power, Russia, which during the last 50 years, under czars and Communists alike, has been most assiduous in its efforts to extend its control in the Far East. In the recent past, attempts at foreign domination have appeared quite clearly to the Chinese people as external aggression and as such have been bitterly and in the long run successfully resisted. Our aid and encouragement have helped them to resist. In this case, however, the foreign domination has been masked behind the facade of a vast crusading movement which apparently has seemed to many Chinese to be wholly indigenous and national. Under these circumstances, our aid has been unavailing. . . .

We continue to believe that, however tragic may be the immediate future of China and however ruthlessly a major portion of this great people may be exploited by a party in the interest of a foreign imperialism, ultimately the profound civilization and the democratic individualism of China will reassert themselves and she will throw off the foreign yoke. . . .

In the immediate future, however, the implementation of our historic policy of friendship for China must be profoundly affected by current developments. It will necessarily be influenced by the degree to which the Chinese people come to recognize that the Communist regime serves not their interests but those of Soviet Russia and the manner in which, having become aware of the facts, they react to this foreign domination.[70]

These deadly words did not refute the anticipated charges from the China Lobby, but instead spurred them on. In the early pages of the

Letter Acheson argued that nothing the United States could have done could have "saved" China because the Jiang regime was ineffective. These last paragraphs suggested that Mao had triumphed because the Soviet communists had linked up with Mao to insure victory. By stating that China was under control of a "foreign power, Russia," Acheson appeared to confirm that the communist threat was worldwide and China only the latest country to fall under its dominion. Furthermore, Acheson suggested that the Chinese had been duped into believing that Mao and his followers were nationalists rather than agents of the communist conspiracy, thereby giving official sanction to the belief in an international conspiracy. All of these premises fit easily and directly within the anticommunist reality and served to reinforce it, even as the total document was intended to do just the opposite. Finally, in voicing hopes that the "democratic" Chinese would eventually rise up and throw off the "foreign yoke," Acheson encouraged the China Lobby to call for unleashing Jiang from Formosa to liberate the mainland, a theme that would resonate throughout the Korean War and the decade to follow. In sum, the White Paper on China was a rhetorical fiasco.

Two lessons need to be drawn. First, the administration could not extricate itself from its own anticommunist rhetoric. Being unable to argue from outside that rhetoric, the administration found itself reinforcing the fundamental premises of its opponents, premises it had originally used to justify its policies in Europe and therefore could not fully repudiate. Second, the administration learned how deeply the anticommunist reality had become embedded in the American psyche. The White Paper had been an attempt to bring evidence and reason to a particular international problem. The effort was futile, as futile as the efforts of some critics of the administration. Evidence and reason no longer changed reality. Evidence—specific facts and incidents—became examples of the new reality, and reason was employed as a weapon not to question, but to reaffirm faith in that all-pervasive anticommunist reality.

CONCLUSION

Prominent critics and advocates of the new reality of anticommunism reinforced the basic premises of that reality. They did this in various ways. Walter Lippmann criticized specific foreign policies of the administration, but he did so from within the basic beliefs that created those policies. By popularizing the description, cold war, Lippmann confirmed that the United States was in a deadly contest with the Soviet Union. Subsequent historians and others have labeled him as one of the realists as opposed to the universalists, but his realism was limited to means to achieve similar ends to the most adamant of cold warriors. To the observer, the appellation, "realistic," gained greater currency for Lippmann and other critics who argued from within the prevailing beliefs of anticommunism for that very reason: they did not challenge the basic intellectual assumptions upon which it was based. They accepted the new reality but only argued that the United States was overextending itself or was using an inappropriate messianic rhetoric to gain public support.[71]

Senator Taft's criticism fell on deaf ears. He was accused of isolationism, of being a political relic from the past who longed for the old days rather than facing the new "realities" of the postwar world. Furthermore, Taft's own anticommunism undermined his criticism. How could one be as adamantly opposed to communism or "creeping socialism" as Taft was and refuse to support policies aimed at containing communism? Taft never adequately answered this question because he was caught up, as so many others were, in the contradictions between his rhetoric and his policies.

Advocates of the new reality chafed at limitations placed on the universality of anticommunism. Those who sought to expose domestic communists wanted it extended beyond investigations into the loyalty of government employees. Even before the Truman Loyalty Program, Republicans on the House UnAmerican Activities Committee (and we use this name for the committee because we believe it was un-American) had attempted to show that American movies had been infiltrated by communists and communist propaganda. But they hit paydirt with the Hiss case, the most important domestic investigation of the entire early years. In investigating Alger Hiss, Republicans put an entire generation on trial.[72] He was an icon for the era. If someone as prominent as Hiss was a communist, many reasoned, and was able to rise in government without discovery for so long, how many others in influential or menial positions in American life were communists dedicated to furthering Soviet aims? The Hiss case aroused suspicions that were to be unleashed in full fury in the next decade. Beyond that, why had he remained undiscovered for so long? Conspiracy theories abounded to the point that when his first trial ended in a hung jury, Representative Richard Nixon and others condemned the judge and members of the jury for appearing to continue the cover-up of communist influence in American society. The search for domestic communists extended with force because of the Hiss case.

The China Lobby wanted the Truman Doctrine extended to Asia. If the United States was really committed to fighting an ideological battle against communism, why wasn't it fighting Mao's communists in China? The China Lobby took the basic premises of the rationale for aid to Greece and Turkey and applied them to Asia. The universal reality of anticommunism would not be complete, they argued, if a major part of the world were omitted from it. The arguments came more from the Truman Doctrine and the subsequent rhetoric used to justify commitments in Europe than from the antitotalitarian tradition. In fact, the disputes over Asia did as much as any other event to solidify the anticommunist universalism. The Truman administration found itself in the uncomfortable role of Henry Wallace in attempting to bring facts and reason to the debate. The administration was as notably unsuccessful as Wallace had been. The universal rhetoric of anticommunism overwhelmed them, setting the stage for U.S. commitment to Korea.

And finally there was Henry Wallace, the most persistent and outspoken critic of the new reality. Although Wallace mounted a frontal assault upon the premises of anticommunism, in a peculiar way, he strengthened them. His arguments were so far outside prevailing beliefs that they required an alternative explanation for his daring to present them. Journalists and others eagerly provided this explanation. They portrayed him as a dupe for communist propaganda. In picturing him in this fashion, they seemed to convince people that even a former vice president could be taken in by the insidious conspiracy threatening the United States and the world. The explanation was so believable that it remained for decades as the conventional understanding of Wallace's postwar career. Even Wallace himself finally gave in and repudiated his previous contentions. By 1950 anticommunism was firmly entrenched as the prevailing and pervasive reality of American political culture.

NOTES

1. Quoted in William E. Leuchtenburg, *In the Shadow of FDR*, rev. ed. (Ithaca, NY: Cornell University Press, 1985), p. 26.

2. On Wallace, see Norman D. Markowitz, *The Rise and Fall of the People's Century: Henry A. Wallace and American Liberalism, 1941–1948* (New York: Free Press, 1973), esp. pp. 160–303; J. Samuel Walker, *Henry A. Wallace and American Foreign Policy* (Westport, CT: Greenwood, 1976); Richard J. Walton, *Henry Wallace, Harry Truman, and the Cold War* (New York: Viking, 1976); Ronald Radosh and Leonard P. Liggio, "Henry A. Wallace and the Open Door," in *Cold War Critics*, ed. Thomas G. Patterson (Chicago: Quadrangle, 1971), pp. 76–113.

3. All quotations are from the complete text recorded in Wallace's diary as published by John Morton Blum, ed., *The Price of Vision: The Diary of Henry A. Wallace, 1942–1946* (Boston: Houghton Mifflin, 1973), pp. 589–601. The text of this private letter was released prior to his being fired in September 1946.

4. All quotations are from the version of Wallace's speech printed in Walton, *Henry Wallace, Harry Truman and the Cold War*, pp. 100–8.

5. For recounting of the events that followed the speech and Wallace's subsequent dismissal from his cabinet post, see Walton, *Henry Wallace, Harry Truman and the Cold War*, pp. 98–117.

6. Quoted in Walton, *Henry Wallace, Harry Truman and the Cold War*, p. 148. Emphasis in the original.

7. Quoted in ibid., p. 151.

8. Robert L. Ivie, "Metaphor and the Rhetorical Invention of Cold War 'Idealists,' *Communication Monographs* 54 (June 1987), p. 172.

9. Quoted from Margaret Truman, *Harry S. Truman* (New York: Pocket Books, 1974), pp. 347–48.

10. Cited in Joseph Jones, *Fifteen Weeks* (New York: Viking, 1955), p. 179.

11. Dean Acheson, *Present at the Creation* (New York: W. W. Norton, 1969), p. 224.

12. Quoted in Walton, *Henry Wallace*, p. 300.

13. Quoted in James Aronson, *The Press and the Cold War* (Boston: Beacon Press, 1970), p. 41. For the most extensive history of the Wallace presidential campaign, see Curtis D. MacDougall, *Gideon's Army*, 3 vols. (New York: Marzani and Munsell, 1965).

14. *Time* (August 9, 1948), p. 18.

15. Bert Cochran, *Harry Truman and the Crisis Presidency* (New York: Funk and Wagnalls, 1973), pp. 238–39. For a detailed description of the red-baiting of Wallace in that campaign, see Allen Yarnell, *Democrats and Progressives: The 1948 Presidential Election as a Test of Postwar Liberalism* (Berkeley: University of California Press, 1974).

16. That is not to say that Truman completely refrained from attacking Wallace's support from American communists and socialists. See the president's St. Patrick's Day speech and his speech in Los Angeles on September 23, 1948.

17. Quoted in Robert J. Donovan, *Conflict and Crisis: The Presidency of Harry S. Truman, 1945–1948* (New York: W. W. Norton, 1977), p. 360.

18. Henry Wallace, "The State Department's Case," *New Republic* (April 7, 1947), p. 12.

19. See, for example, Henry A. Wallace, "Where I Was Wrong," *This Week* (September 7, 1952).

20. See Kenneth W. Thompson, *Interpreters and Critics of the Cold War* (Washington, DC: University Press of America, 1978).

21. See Ronald Steel's excellent intellectual as well as personal biography, *Walter Lippmann and the American Century* (Boston: Atlantic-Little, Brown, 1980).

22. On Lippmann's acceptance of the division of the world, see his *U.S. War Aims* (Boston: Little, Brown, 1944), pp. 131–56 and his *U.S. Foreign Policy: Shield of the Republic* (Boston: Little, Brown, 1943), pp. 137–54 and later his *The Communist World and Ours* (Boston: Little, Brown, 1958). On Lippmann's linking of communism and fascism as two forms of totalitarianism, see his *The Good Society* (New York: Grosset and Dunlap, 1943), pp. 54–90. The other topics are generally considered within the framework of these writings by Lippmann.

23. Barton J. Bernstein, "Walter Lippmann and the Early Cold War," *Cold War Critics*, p. 19.

24. Steel, *Walter Lippmann and the American Century*, pp. 439–40.

25. Walter Lippmann, *The Cold War: A Study in American Foreign Policy* (New York: Harper and Brothers, 1947). All quotations from Lippmann are from this source rather than the *Herald Tribune*.

26. These three are specified and developed by Lippmann's biographer Ronald Steel, *Walter Lippmann and the American Century*, pp. 443–46.

27. Bernstein, "Walter Lippmann and the Early Cold War," p. 41.

28. Quoted in Steel, *Walter Lippmann and the American Century*, p. 449.

29. William Safire, *Safire's Political Dictionary* (New York: Ballantine, 1978), pp. 127–28. Originally, the coinage had been minted by Herbert Bayard Swope, speechwriter for Bernard Baruch who used the phrase in a draft of a speech in 1946 and then included it in an address in 1947.

30. Even such a distinguished historian as William L. O'Neill could not escape this psychological attitude and these embedded language structures. See his *A Better World* (New York: Simon and Schuster, 1982).

31. Theodore C. Sorensen, *Kennedy* (New York: Harper and Row, 1965), p. 243.

32. Ronald Radosh, *Prophets on the Right* (New York: Simon and Schuster, 1975), p. 149.

33. On Taft's attitudes toward foreign policy, see John P. Armstrong, "The Enigma of Senator Taft and American Foreign Policy," *Review of Politics* 17 (April 1955), pp. 206–31; Robert A. Taft, *A Foreign Policy for Americans* (Garden City: Doubleday, 1951). On Taft's critique of the cold war, see Radosh, "Robert A. Taft and the Emergence of the Cold War," *Prophets on the Right*, pp. 147–95; Henry W. Berger, "Senator Robert A. Taft Dissents from Military Escalation," *Cold War Critics*, pp. 167–204; Henry W. Berger, "A Conservative Critique of Containment: Senator Taft on the Early Cold War Program," in David Horowitz, ed., *Containment and Revolution* (Boston: Beacon Press, 1967), pp. 132–39; David Green, *Shaping Political Consciousness* (Ithaca, NY: Cornell University Press, 1983), pp. 164–206. On the fall of isolationism, see Selig Adler, *The Isolationist Impulse: Its Twentieth Century Reaction* (New York: Free Press, 1957), pp. 250–370.

34. Quoted in Radosh, *Prophets on the Right*, p. 138. See also his speech at Grove City College, May 22, 1943, and his speech at the American Bar Association, August 26, 1943 cited in Radosh, pp. 139–42.

35. Quoted in Walter LaFeber, *America, Russia, and the Cold War 1945–1975* (New York: John Wiley, 1976), p. 56.

36. See Berger, "Senator Robert A. Taft Dissents," pp. 170–77.

37. Quoted in ibid., pp. 181–82.

38. Quoted in Radosh, *Prophets on the Right*, p. 168. On his opposition to NATO, see pp. 167–71.

39. Ibid., pp. 124–26.

40. Quoted in ibid., p. 153.

41. Ibid.

42. For additional aspects of Taft's criticism in this respect, see Radosh, *Prophets on the Right*, pp. 174–88.

43. Ibid., p. 166.

44. Quoted in ibid., p. 170.

45. Quoted in ibid., p. 140.

46. Quoted in Joseph C. Goulden, *The Best Years: 1945–1950* (New York: Atheneum, 1976), p. 239.

47. David Green, *Shaping Political Consciousness: The Language of Politics in America from McKinley to Reagan* (Ithaca, NY: Cornell University Press, 1987), p. 196.

48. See Taft NBC radio address (November 17, 1947) cited in Radosh, *Prophets on the Right*, p. 160.

49. Berger, "Senator Robert A. Taft Dissents," p. 195.

50. Allen Weinstein, *Perjury: The Hiss-Chambers Case* (New York: Alfred A. Knopf, 1978), p. 510.

51. Richard M. Fried, *Nightmare in Red* (New York: Oxford University Press, 1990), p. 93.

52. Writings on the Hiss case occupy a large shelf or two in any bookcase on the cold war. However, several volumes require mention. Whittaker Chambers presented his version in *Witness* (Chicago: Henry Regnery, 1952). Hiss presented his version in *In the Court of Public Opinion* (New York: Alfred A. Knopf, 1957). He summarized it later in *Recollections of a Life* (New York: Henry Holt, 1988), pp. 149–60. The chief defense of Hiss was published by John Chabot Smith, *Alger Hiss: The True Story* (New York: Holt, Rinehart and Winston, 1976). Weinstein's *Perjury* is by all accounts the most exhaustive, if not conclusive, study of the case. On Richard Nixon's role in the case, see, in addition to the already listed books, Richard Nixon, *Six Crises* (Garden City, NY: Doubleday, 1962), pp. 1–72; Morton Levitt and Michael Levitt, *A Tissue of Lies: Nixon vs. Hiss* (New York: McGraw-Hill, 1979).

53. "Extension of Remarks of Hon. Alexander Wiley," *Appendix to the Congressional Record*, 80th Cong., 2d sess. (August 5, 1948), p. A4867.

54. Cited in Levitt and Levitt, *A Tissue of Lies*, pp. 147–48.

55. Ibid., p. 116.

56. Ibid., pp. 147–48.

57. Robert P. Newman, *The Cold War Romance of Lillian Hellman and John Melby* (Chapel Hill, NC: University of North Carolina Press, 1989), pp. 79–80.

58. See Richard M. Freeland, *The Truman Doctrine and the Origins of McCarthyism* (New York: Alfred A. Knopf, 1972), pp. 109–14.

59. Quoted in ibid., p. 112.

60. Robert P. Newman, "Lethal Rhetoric: The Selling of the China Myths," *Quarterly Journal of Speech* 61 (April 1975), pp. 114–16.

61. See "The China Aid Act of 1948" in *A Decade of American Foreign Policy: Basic Documents 1941–1949* (Washington: Government Printing Office, 1950), pp. 713–15.

62. Thomas E. Lifka, *The Concept of "Totalitarianism" and American Foreign Policy*, vol. 2 (New York: Garland Publishing, 1988), p. 724.

63. Ibid., p. 720.

64. Quoted in Lewis McCarroll Purifoy, *Harry Truman's China Policy: McCarthyism and the Diplomacy of Hysteria, 1947–1951* (New York: New Viewpoints, 1976), p. 53.

65. Robert P. Newman, "The Self-Inflicted Wound: The China White Paper of 1949," *Prologue* 14 (Fall 1982), p. 141. Our analysis of the debate over the White Paper is derived from Newman's invaluable article.

66. Dean Acheson, *Present at the Creation*, p. 302.

67. Ibid., p. 148. See also Ross Y. Koen, *The China Lobby in American Politics* (New York: Harper and Row, 1974), p. 169.

68. Ibid., p. 148.

69. Ibid., p. 146.

70. Dean Acheson, "A Summary of American-Chinese Relations: Letter From the Secretary of State to the President, July 30, 1949, Transmitting 'United States Relations With China With Special Reference to the Period 1944–1949,' " *A Decade of American Foreign Policy*, pp. 725–26.

71. See, for example, Thompson, *Interpreters and Critics of the Cold War*, pp. 65–96.

72. See Alister Cooke, *A Generation on Trial: U.S.A. v. Alger Hiss* (New York: Alfred A. Knopf, 1952).

Chapter Nine

The Final Proofs and Conclusion

The year 1950 was a dramatic one in U.S. history. To some, it was the turning point in the cold war. To others, it was only the culmination of all that had gone before. In rhetorical terms, the events of that fateful year—important as they were on their own terms—provided the final proofs of the American cold war rhetoric.

Every political rhetoric must have symbolic "proofs" to give it legitimacy as confirming accounts about the nature of the political world. Neither literary nor philosophic rhetorics require such proofs. They exist unto themselves. But political rhetoric is different. The diverse events of 1950 provided those symbolic proofs. Since the meaning of the cold war had already been fixed, these proofs became self-fulfilling of that meaning. The political and military explosions of the mid-century year came from a chain reaction of incidents and the meaning attached to them of the previous two and a half years. A brief chronology of those events may serve as a preface to the shocks of 1950.

The Soviets formally joined the rhetorical cold war with the creation of the new Cominform in September 1947. In his speech at the founding conference, Andrei Zhdanov recast Soviet postwar policy in light of the growing tensions between East and West. Zhdanov divided the world into two antagonistic camps:

the imperialist and anti-democratic [American camp] having as its basic aim the establishment of world domination of American imperialism and the smashing of democracy, and the anti-imperialist and democratic camp [of the Soviet Union] having as its basic aim the undermining of imperialism, the consolidation of democracy and the eradication of the remnants of fascism.[1]

He castigated the Truman Doctrine for bearing a "frankly aggressive character" designed to support all "reactionary regimes" and to oppose "democratic peoples."[2] Both the doctrine and the Marshall Plan, he said, were "an embodiment of the American design to enslave Europe."[3] In contrast, the Soviet Union "indefatigably and consistently upholds the principles of real equality and protection of sovereign rights of all nations, big and small."[4] Zhdanov predicted that the United States was preparing to unleash a war to achieve its goals. He attacked the rhetoric of anticommunism that had been developing since 1946 as the ideological prelude for that war. In response to it, Zhdanov called upon communist parties in western European countries to work against the Marshall Plan and to unite against U.S. aggression. His speech was a rhetorical mirror image of the anticommunist rhetoric that had been growing in the United States since early 1946. On the rhetorical level, the cold war was now completely joined.[5]

A tripartite conference on Germany opened on February 23, 1948. This was the first postwar conference of the allied powers that excluded the Soviet Union from participation. At this conference the Americans, French, and British agreed in principle to consolidate their zones in western Germany. Two days later the Soviets engineered a coup in Czechoslovakia ousting noncommunists from power and effectively making it a satellite of the Soviet Union. Western leaders immediately drew a parallel to the Munich Pact of 1938: "Because of the obviousness of the parallel with the past, the 1948 Czech coup induced in the West an almost hysterical certainty that unless decisive action were taken to prevent Stalin from making any further moves, the Soviet Union would soon have all of Western Europe under its control."[6] Once again the Munich analogy jumped to the forefront of American political thinking to provide an instantaneous meaning to the events in Czechoslovakia. The meaning attached to the coup had a profound effect. In March, Congress quickly appropriated 17 billion dollars to fund the Marshall Plan that had been lingering in Congress since June and to put it into operation. At about the same time the tripartite powers announced that they intended to integrate western Germany into the European economic community. The Soviet leadership, seeing these ominous changes, launched a "peace offensive" in May signaling their willingness to negotiate outstanding issues.[7] The offers were dismissed as propaganda, and in June, agreement by the tripartite powers was reached to unify western zones of Germany. In retaliation Stalin imposed the land blockade of Berlin, and Truman responded with the Berlin airlift. From that event it was only a short step the following year to the formation of NATO, a military bloc intended to thwart Soviet advances in Europe.

At the end of 1949 two seismographic shocks hit the political world. In September the Soviets broke the American monopoly on atomic power by exploding their first atomic bomb. That was followed by Mao Zedong's triumph in China and the proclamation of the People's Republic of China. The year 1950, then, opened on foreboding notes that intensified American fears of communism.

THE FINAL PROOFS

To believers in the anticommunist reality, three major sets of events provided the final proofs of the validity of rhetoric that had been developing over the previous four years.

In January 1950, Alger Hiss was convicted of perjury which meant treason to most people. Richard M. Fried noted that Alger Hiss "was the central symbol in America's struggle over domestic communism."[8] But he was not the only symbol. Thirteen days after his conviction, Klaus Fuchs confessed in England to passing top secret information to a communist courier while working at Los Alamos in 1944–45. Harry Gold, a Philadelphia chemist, was arrested two months later and subsequently Julius and Ethel Rosenberg were arrested in connection with atomic spying. Each of these played their role in the hysteria of domestic anticommunism. Hiss became a symbol of treachery and treason at the highest levels of government. The Rosenbergs became symbols of domestic traitors who sold the United States out and contrived to give the USSR the atomic bomb "years before our best scientists predicted Russia would perfect the bomb."[9] Quite simply, there were spies and traitors everywhere.

Into the midst of this turmoil—in fact, only shortly after Hiss's conviction—Senator Joseph McCarthy formally launched the era that bears his name. In Wheeling, West Virginia on February 9, 1950 McCarthy charged that he had a list of 205 (or 57 or some such number) communists who were working in the State Department.[10] That speech provided the springboard for McCarthy's reign of terror. But the era had its origins in the preceding years and McCarthy only stamped his heavy-handed and sinister imprint on the growing inquisition. Had it not been for Truman's Loyalty Program, for the conviction of Hiss, the confession of Fuchs, and the trials of the Rosenbergs, the terror might not have had the potency it had. In different ways each was a dramatic symbol and proof of previous charges and proof that greater vigilance was needed, even at the expense of civil liberties and traditional notions of American fair play.

The second event was even more devastating. On June 25, 1950 North

Korea invaded South Korea. The invasion was less important in actual strategic terms than in what it symbolized: a confirmation of the aggressive nature of Soviet communism. President Truman attached this symbolism immediately to the war. In his statement issued on June 27 the president declared: "The attack upon Korea makes it plain beyond all doubt that communism has passed beyond the use of subversion to conquer independent nations and will now use armed invasion and war."[11] In response he ordered the Seventh Fleet to protect Formosa, sought U.N. condemnation of the North's aggression, and eventually committed U.S. military forces under the auspices of the United Nations to fight the Korean War. The cold war had suddenly turned into a hot war. But it was a hot war of a peculiar kind. In fact, it was the new face of war in the postwar world.

The Korean War was a proxy war fought in Korea but symbolizing the worldwide struggle between the free world and the communist world. If the North Korean invasion symbolized communists' intentions to dominate the world, the U.S. response symbolized the resolve of the United States to resist Soviet domination. It was a critical moment. Metaphysical symbolism replaced tangible objectives as the focal point of war. Such a transcendental transformation had its roots in the original request of economic aid to Greece and Turkey, but it was to have consequences that would reach to the rice paddies of Vietnam.

After defending the Pusan and then executing the Inchon landing, the U.N. armies drove the North Koreans back to the Yalu River in the farthest reaches of the North. But that had severe consequences. In November China, feeling threatened by the proximity of U.S. forces, entered the war and smashed the Eighth Army, sending it reeling back and into the stalemate that lasted for the next three years. The Chinese involvement became another confirming proof of the worldwide solidarity of the communist menace. From the beginning to its end the war was rarely interpreted as an invasion by the North against the South, but rather as symbol of the universal warfare between the free world and the communist world.[12]

The anticommunism rhetoric was now pervasive and complete. Politicians and people interpreted the meaning of each of these three sets of events—the Hiss conviction and the other charges of domestic communist activities, the invasion of South Korea by the North, and the Chinese intervention into that war—by the standards of that rhetoric and at the same time used these events as proof that the rhetoric was correct in the first place. It was a classic tautology. Understanding and proving arose simultaneously and led to action. And action confirmed the understanding and proof. The Korean War was the linchpin of these final proofs. John Lewis Gaddis remarked that the widely shared but erroneous impression that the invasion of South Korea was the first military step in the Soviet Union's plan to conquer the world had three important consequences: (1) the transformation of NATO from "a traditional mutual defense alliance into a[n] integrated military structure" that led to the appointment of a U.S. supreme commander of NATO and the stationing of U.S. troops in Europe; (2) the rearming of West Germany and the signing of a peace treaty with Japan, thus making alliances with old enemies to fight a new enemy; and (3) the approval of National Security Memorandum No. 68, better known as NSC–68. It is to this final consequence that we now turn.

NSC–68 developed over a period of time, between late 1949 and early 1950. When the Soviet Union tested its first atomic weapon, American confidence in its military superiority and its policy of containment were shaken. America's monopoly on the bomb had been Truman's ace in the hole against direct Soviet aggression against the United States or Europe. Once this advantage was offset, the president first ordered work on the development of a "super" bomb and then instructed his new chief of policy planning, Paul Nitze, to review U.S. foreign and defense policy. That review conducted under the auspices of a joint State-Defense reassessment produced "The Report By The Secretaries Of State and Defense On 'United States Objectives And Programs For National Security,' April 7, 1950" (NSC–68).[13]

NSC–68 combined both a continuation of past policy with radical departures deemed necessary by new circumstances. The document reiterated the dire threat Soviet communism posed to the world:

The Soviet Union, unlike previous aspirants to hegemony, is animated by a new fanatic faith, antithetical to our own, and seeks to impose its absolute authority over the rest of the world. Conflict has, therefore, become endemic and is waged, on the part of the Soviet Union, by violent or non-violent methods in accordance with the dictates of expediency.[14]

The causes given for the Soviet drive for conquest were bluntly put: the Soviets' inescapable militancy "is inescapably militant because it possesses and is possessed by a world-wide revolutionary movement, because it is the inheritor of Russian imperialism and because it is a totalitarian dictatorship."[15] To meet this military threat required an enormous and speedy U.S. military build-up including dramatic increases in both conventional and nuclear forces. Thus, the relatively defensive policy of containment was transformed into a militant and military containment or, as Jerry Sanders termed it, "containment militarism." The threat was so great that the United States had to adopt the methods of its adversary, the very methods it so abhorred. NSC–68 stated this plainly: "In other words, [the new policy] would be the current Soviet cold war technique used against the Soviet Union."[16] What this signified, according to Sanders, was that four new premises guided American strategic thinking for the future in contrast to the old premises of containment:

First, its zero-sum calculus greatly increased the purview of "vital interests," a logic which . . . led away from diplomacy and negotiation toward militancy and rollback. Second, as NSC–68 pointed out, the quintessential goal of rollback— the retrogression of Soviet power up to and including collapse of the Soviet government—is nothing more than bluff unless it is backed by the threat of armed force and the appearance of readiness to unleash it. . . . Third, Containment Militarism would necessitate a corresponding increase in military spending, breaking with the economic orthodoxy that had been accepted in containment's earlier version. Finally, while Containment Militarism as outlined in NSC–68 was constructed upon the same ideological foundations that had inspired Kennan's thesis of the Soviet Threat, its reinterpretation as specifically a military threat was the fourth point of departure from the original formulation. It was also the key to the acceptance of the first three points.[17]

In conception and argument, NSC–68 actually ventured little from previous American anticommunist statements, especially the Clifford-Elsey Report. Nitze divided the world into two mutually exclusive antagonists, the one motivated by a fanatical ideology to conquer the world; the other motivated solely by defensive measures necessary to protect and extend freedom. These had been rhetorical commonplaces since the time of Churchill's "Iron Curtain" speech. The document was as heavy handedly blunt as the Truman Doctrine. Where Truman had declared a universal policy in reaction to the British pullout in Greece, NSC–68 formalized this policy in explicit language: "The assault on free institutions is world-wide now, and in the context of the present polarization of power *a defeat of free institutions anywhere is a defeat everywhere*."[18] Where it departed from previous statements was in its emphasis on the military threat and the development of a military response to the virtual exclusion of economic and diplomatic responses. Equally important, NSC–68 advocated adopting the enemy's methods to fight the enemy. Part of this may have been exaggerated. Secretary of State Acheson remarked that its purpose was to "bludgeon the mass mind of 'top government' [so] that not only could the President make a decision but that the decision could be carried out."[19] To achieve this effect, the Soviet military threat was exaggerated. (Adam Ulam quotes from N. A. Voznesensky's book, *The Soviet Economy During the Second World War*, to demonstrate the devastating Soviet losses during the war: 31,850 factories, mills, and other industrial enterprises destroyed; 1,865 state farms, 2,890 machine tractor stations, and 98,000 of 200,000 collective farms "completely devastated." As Ulam pointed out, Americans surely must have read the book and recognized that believing the Soviet Union intended to make war against the West "verged on the preposterous." Voznesensky's book was published in 1948 and translated into English in 1949. Stalin had him shot and killed in 1950.)[20] These exaggerations, however, served a rhetorical purpose in that at least part of NSC–68 was originally intended to be released to the public. In his examination of NSC–68 Paul Y. Hammond stated that the document had been constructed for just such a purpose:

What Nitze did with his original ranking of Soviet objectives, it is evident, was to set them in an order which would make the portion of the study paper where they appeared carry as much of the burden of the argument as he could give it. . . . [Nitze] adopted and defended a particular order for its persuasive impact: If his argument could begin with a convincing statement which maximized the nature of the Soviet threat, the burden of proof of the rest of his case would be reduced.[21]

But Nitze had only followed a rhetorical pattern long since developed of magnifying the Soviet or communist or Bolshevik threat to create a fear so great that not only would the burden of proof be reduced, but would make the wildest speculation about domestic or foreign enemies plausible and the most militant policies to confront them seem reasonable. The invocation of such ideological fears made reasonable assessments of fact and pragmatic appraisals for policy difficult.

NSC–68 was the culmination in foreign policy of rhetorical efforts to explain the new world order and the place and responsibilities of the United States in that order. Although President Truman approved the document in April 1950, he did not order it implemented because he wanted to study how much it would cost. However, in June, North Korea invaded South Korea and that seemed to prove the prescience of NSC–68 and the worst fears of the previous four years of strategic thinking. The president and most of his advisers agreed that the invasion had been ordered by Stalin as part of his master plan to conquer the world, the first in a series of military actions in small countries designed to achieve this ultimate goal.[22] Shortly thereafter Truman directed that NSC–68 be implemented beginning with enormous increases in the military budget, a decision that led to the national security state and the rampant anticommunism of the early 1950s. But NSC–68 was stamped Top Secret and not declassified until 1975. The administration had no need in 1950 of a public rationale for increasing the defense budget. The Korean War and the other major events of the year, understood by the public within the prevailing anticommunist mentality of the times, provided more than ample proof for such spending. The country had changed since 1945. The United States was now fully committed to vast military expenditures and a national security state, abroad and at home.

CONCLUSION

At the end of World War II the consensus that had held the allies together shattered. They had been bound together by their mutual resolve to defeat fascism. When Germany and Japan surrendered, the bonding elements that held the allies together dissolved. A new world was in the making, but few knew what kind of world it would be. On the American side, resolve to defeat the fascists quickly changed to fear about what the Soviets were doing in eastern Europe. No doubt the Soviets were not returning immediately to their own borders. But what were they up to? Were they imposing their system on other countries by creating "socialism in one zone" of Europe? And what did it mean if they did? Were they acting defensively by building up a buffer zone against some future attack from the West? What did that portend? Or were they consolidating their new empire in preparation for conquering the world or at least western Europe? If that were so, how would it be best for the United States to respond before that attack took place? How could the United States be prepared? Equally important, on what bases could the United States, a nation that had deliberately removed itself from European power struggles in the past, now claim intimate vital interests in those same affairs? These were urgent questions that President Truman and his advisers, as well as members of Congress, sought to answer in those anxious postwar years. Facts were facts. But they carried no intrinsic meaning with them.

In attempting to understand and assign meaning to the confusing events of the early postwar period, American policymakers drew upon their recent experiences with Nazi Germany as well as their historic antipathy toward communism as central guides to their thinking. This was not remarkable since politicians often look to the past to learn lessons from it. But it was also not inherently illuminating. The administration made choices. As events hurried on, the new Truman administration rushed to place these events in a context that would provide a rationale for its actions. In so doing it created a new reality about the world and America's place in it. That reality was rhetorically constructed. It was not constructed overnight, but through a long process, one that eventually created a universal reality that made events understandable, motives comprehensible, and actions seem compulsory. The purpose of this volume has been to bring methods of rhetorical analysis to bear in understanding the development of that new reality.

The cold war was a rhetorical war. To say that is not to say that it was strictly a figment of American imagination or that it was compelled by actions by the Soviet Union. The Red Army was in eastern Europe. The American and British armies were in western Europe. The Soviet

Union acted within the areas it controlled. So too, the United States acted within areas it controlled. But after that, events became confusing. Depending upon whom one reads, the Soviets acted and Americans reacted or vice versa. But what did such actions and reactions mean? It was at that point that rhetoric came into play. Rhetoric is the central force in interpreting events, giving meaning to life, transforming *actuality* into *reality*. The rhetoric Americans chose to describe these events and the ideas that dominated them created the cold war. They did not choose arbitrarily nor did they assign meanings without reflection.

The cold war was constructed from language and argument. But no single rhetorical effort can be said to have announced the cold war. On the Western side, the cold war was the result of a rhetorical process that began publicly in 1946 and continued through the next several years. Winston Churchill divided the postwar world into two antagonistic camps and made the division memorable through his metaphor of an iron curtain. President Harry Truman used that division to proclaim that the antagonism between the Soviet Union and the United States involved an ideological conflict between two mutually exclusive ways of life and that the United States had to assume world leadership in protecting its way of life around the world. Through the Loyalty Program Truman extended his universal foreign policy to domestic life as the administration began to search for subversives in government and the House Committee on UnAmerican Activities began to search for communists, subversives, fellow travelers or anyone they disliked in all areas of American life. The universal rhetoric of anticommunism was a melodramatic and ideological rhetoric in which political angels were engaged in mortal and moral combat with political devils. The Marshall Plan, as it was presented publicly by Secretary Marshall, demonstrated the angelic nature of the United States through its "altruistic" offer to come to the aid of devastated Europe, a motive indicative of the inherent morality of the U.S. political system. George F. Kennan's private "long telegram" convinced administration figures that the Soviet Union was up to no good and his public "Sources of Soviet Conduct" persuaded leading opinion-makers as well as much of the public that the Soviet Union was motivated by politically evil intentions. Since the administration believed it faced an ideological enemy, it constructed its own universal ideology to combat it. Only an equally potent counter-ideology could compete with the deadly ideological challenge Americans faced in the "battle for people's minds." Michael Parenti later wrote: "If America has an ideology, or a national purpose, it is anti-communism."[23] By 1947 the anticommunist rhetoric had become the all-pervasive political reality for Americans for the postwar world. By this time the major features of the anticommunist rhetoric and the mentality it created and reinforced was complete. Subsequent efforts by others only extended or refined this rhetorical conception of postwar reality, or applied it in ways the originators of it had not imagined.

The arguments anticommunists marshalled to argue for this ideology ranged from vivid metaphors to conspiratorial narratives to historical analogies with Nazi Germany. In fact, most of the metaphors and arguments were embedded in the analogy to the Nazis. It is impossible to say which of these was most important in convincing others. What can be said is that they worked together in remarkable cohesion. The principal metaphors were those of division, disease, and cold war. The metaphors of division took two forms: one dividing the world into two enemy camps (iron curtain) and the other drawing a line (containment). The metaphors of disease were made explicit in comparing Soviet actions directly to an infectious virus (cancer of communism) and to the spread of an alien ideology (poisoning the mind or military expansionism). The final and great metaphor was that of the cold war. Walter Lippmann coined this all-encompassing description of the state of Soviet–American relations and in so doing, inadvertently gave an enormous boost to the very policies—both domestically and in foreign affairs—that he opposed.

The narratives of Soviet history fit easily with the metaphors. Policymakers believed previous authorities had paid too little attention to Hitler's *Mein Kampf* and therefore had ignored the threat he posed. They went to the other extreme of believing communist dogma contained a blueprint for world conquest. Instead of concentrating on Russia's historical fears of the outside world and the even greater fears caused by two German invasions in the twentieth century, anticommunists presented ideological narratives of statements from Lenin to Stalin about revolution, the worldwide appeal of communism, the hostility toward and eventual destruction of capitalism, and the perfidious means they would use to achieve their goals. These narratives usually took the form of quotations, often stripped of context, from Soviet leaders, a rhetorical device that became commonplace in later years. More important, these "narratives" became the deductive means by which individual Soviet actions were interpreted. Philosophic analysis of Marxism replaced historical analysis of Soviet actions.

In attempting to persuade others to accept the great challenge of communism, American policymakers, like so many politicians before and after them, drew frightening comparisons to Nazi Germany as imperatives for belief and action. The analogies to Munich and appeasement, the comparisons of Stalin to Hitler, the belief Americans were engaged in a worldwide struggle like the one they had just confronted proved irresistible. The alliance was forgotten, differences between Nazi Germany and socialist Russia were minimized. The conceptual link between the fascism and communism was captured in the word, "totalitarianism." Sometimes it was stated as communist totalitarianism, sometimes as red fascism. In either case, it linked the two inextricably to convince policymakers and the public alike that they faced the same old enemy only it had a new face. To Americans only recently triumphant over Germany and Japan, the historical analogies to another enemy of the same type had special poignancy and caused them to draw lessons from the past they believed were absolutely pertinent to the present. To policymakers, World War II formed the paradigm for understanding the confusing events of the postwar world. Western nations had failed to stop Hitler in the mid–1930s but instead had "appeased" him at Munich. This appeasement "encouraged" Hitler and led to World War II. Pearl Harbor thrust the United States into this war creating, what Michael Roskin called the "Pearl Harbor" paradigm:

The interesting aspect of the Pearl Harbor paradigm, however, was its duration past World War II. The interventionist orientation had been so deeply internalized in the struggle with the isolationists that it did not lapse with the Allied victory. By that time almost all sections of the globe now "mattered" to American security, particularly as a new hostile power—the Soviet Union—seemed bent on territorial and ideological aggrandizement. In the 1930s, the fate of East Europe bothered Washington very little, but in the span of a decade East Europe became a matter of urgent American concern. Not only had the Soviets inflicted brutal, Hitler-like dictatorships upon the nations of East Europe, it was taken for granted that they were preparing to do the same to West Europe and other areas. But this time America was smarter and stood prepared to stop aggression. In the span of one decade, 1945–1955, the United States committed itself to the defense of more than seventy nations.[24]

In this paradigm Americans were once again struggling to maintain their sacred values either in explicitly religious terms ("Christian civilization") or in secular terms ("the American way of life"). Such grandiose stakes in the struggle heightened the continuing crisis and accelerated the move from economic assistance to other nations to military alliances, from defensive measures to offensive measures. The logic was inexorable once put in motion, as inexorable as Kennan's toy automobile.

One should remember that the cold war was a rhetorical war. Originally, this rhetoric had been created out of a stockpile of images and paradigms to explain certain Soviet actions and motives or to gain support from certain audiences for particular policies. The rhetoric had authority from the president, from the prophecies of Churchill, from experts. But language has a life of its own, especially when it is used to create an architectonic reality. Soon the rhetoric became an a priori explanation to which events, people, and motives were adjusted to fit the rhetoric. Critics of the new foreign policy or domestic political dissidents found that when they challenged fundamental aspects of the new reality they were consigned to political outer darkness, usually denigrated as out of touch with reality—naive, unrealistic, idealistic. As this rhetoric became a war rhetoric, dissidents were condemned as subversive, fellow travelers, or a communist fifth column. The postwar reality created by the anticommunist rhetoric was universal and therefore would admit no challenges to its fundamental assumptions. Thus, the only acceptable criticism was that which limited itself to arguing strategy and tactics, but only after paying homage to the metaphysical structure and basic premises of the anticommunist reality.

The language and arguments contained their own authority and logic. Even those who had created the rhetoric in the first place could not recall it. Kennan watched, as he said, with horror as his famous article took on a life much different than the one he had planned for it. He spent much of his subsequent career fruitlessly trying to restrain what he had once written. Dean Acheson sought in 1950 to limit the universal commitment of the Truman Doctrine by drawing another line in the Far East that excluded Korea from U.S. national interests, only to find himself viciously attacked for drawing such a line after the North Korean invasion of South Korea.[25] In his well-known letter to the executive secretary of the National Security Council in 1951, President Truman expressed his reservations about the Loyalty Program, but his concerns did little to alleviate the pains and traumas of McCarthyism which continued to roar on leaving ruined and wasted lives in its wake.

In *The Nature of Faith* Gerhard Ebeling wrote, "we do not get at the nature of words by asking what they contain, but by asking what they effect, what they set going, what future they disclose."[26] The rhetoric of anticommunism created a new political reality for Americans and thus established a new world order. Lacking a rhetorical tradition for international power politics and having dismissed the European tradition of spheres of influence, American political leaders had only the two choices available to them: withdrawal from the world or a crusade for freedom around the world. Given their experiences in World War II and their historic anticommunism, they chose a universal crusade for freedom. Some, such as Kenneth Thompson and Louis Halle, have argued that the war rhetoric of anticommunism was moderated by practical policies of realpolitik:

The paradox of the Cold War, then, is that the rhetoric in which it is publicly explained and interpreted is the language of war: victory and defeat, good and evil, utopia and anti-utopia, black and white. Cold War policy, by contrast, is shaped by realpolitik, advance and retreat, testing and probing, and salvage operations, all of which fall in the gray area of partial gains and losses, limited advances and retreats, and the balancing of power. In all this there is little which is new in the annals of statecraft.[27]

But such a division between rhetoric and policy is too sharply drawn. It presumes that the public explanation of events was one thing and the private bases for action quite a different matter. There is precious little evidence to support such a conclusion. The two arose together. Only the atomic era and cautious politicians on both sides of the iron curtain restrained the actions that came from the rhetoric. Indeed, the language Thompson uses to explain policy is the language of war (advance and retreat).

By 1950 fundamental assumptions of the new world order were rarely questioned, either in private or in public. Only specific tactics and strategy were open to debate. The goals and purposes of anticommunism were inviolate. Anticommunism had been rhetorically constructed into a universal political reality. This universal reality established a "terministic screen" by which Americans interpreted Soviet motives and actions as well as those of domestic dissidents in melodramatic and ideological form, and these people and actions served—when filtered through the same "terministic screen"—to confirm the validity of the universal reality itself. It was within the new reality that foreign policy decisions were made and the witch-hunts conducted, a reality created by rhetoric and so pervasive that it paralyzed the political thinking of a generation of Americans.

NOTES

1. Quoted in William Taubman, *Stalin's American Policy* (New York: W. W. Norton, 1982), p. 176.

2. Zhdanov, "Report on the International Situation at the founding Conference of the Communist Information Bureau in Poland, September, 1947," excerpted in *A Documentary History of Communism*, vol. 2, ed. Robert V. Daniels (New York: Vintage Russian Library, 1962), p. 159.

3. Quoted in Louis Halle, *The Cold War as History* (New York: Harper and Row, 1967), p. 151.

4. Daniels, *A Documentary History*, p. 159.

5. Others attempt to use, as we have seen, Stalin's February 1946 election speech as the rhetorical event that instigated the cold war on the Soviet side. However, few Sovietologists agree with that assessment. It should be noted that unlike Truman's speech to Congress in March 1947 or Zhdanov's September speech, Stalin's speech was devoted primarily to domestic affairs, less than a tenth of the speech concerned foreign policy.

6. Richard Whelan, *Drawing the Line: The Korean War, 1950–1953* (Boston: Little, Brown, 1990), pp. 67–68.

7. See J. Samuel Walker, " 'No More Cold War': American Foreign Policy and the 1948 Soviet Peace Offensive," *Diplomatic History* 5 (Winter 1981), pp. 75–91.

8. Richard M. Fried, *Nightmare in Red* (New York: Oxford University Press, 1990), p. 17.

9. Quoted in David Chaute, *The Great Fear* (New York: Simon and Schuster, 1978), p. 67.

10. The exact number McCarthy used is still in dispute since only reports of his speech by journalists have survived.

11. Quoted in Whelan, *Drawing the Line*, p. 115. In his *Memoirs* Truman confirmed that he saw the issue in Korea as symbolic of a larger issue, the battle between the free world and communism. See Harry S. Truman, *Memoirs: Years of Trial and Hope*, vol. 2 (Garden City, NY: Doubleday, 1956), p. 333.

12. On the rhetoric of the Korean War, see Ray E. McKerrow, "Truman and Korea: Rhetoric in the Pursuit of Victory," *Central States Speech Journal* 28 (Spring 1977), pp. 1–12.

13. The complete memorandum is published in *Naval War College Review* (May-June 1975), pp. 51–108.

14. NSC–68, p. 53.

15. Ibid., pp. 61–62.

16. Ibid., p. 71.

17. Jerry W. Sanders, *Peddlers of Crisis: The Committee on the Present Danger and the Politics of Containment* (Boston: South End Press, 1983), p. 29.

18. Quoted in Whelan, *Drawing the Line*, p. 73. (Emphasis added.)

19. Quoted in Sanders, *Peddlers of Crisis*, p. 23.

20. Adam Ulam, *Dangerous Relations: The Soviet Union in World Politics, 1970–1982* (New York: Oxford University Press, 1983), p. 9.

21. Paul Y. Hammond, "NSC–68: Prologue to Rearmament," in Warner R. Schilling, Paul Y. Hammond, and Glen H. Snyder, *Strategy, Politics, and the Defense Budget* (New York: Columbia University Press, 1962), pp. 318–19.

22. Whelan, *Drawing the Line*, p. 117.

23. Michael Parenti, *The Anti-Communist Impulse* (New York: Random House, 1969), p. 4.

24. Michael Roskin, "From Pearl Harbor to Vietnam: Shifting Generational Paradigms and Foreign Policy," *Political Science Quarterly* 89 (June 1974), p. 569.

25. See Acheson's speech on the Far East before the National Press Club, January 12, 1950 in *Ideas and Diplomacy*, ed. Norman Graebner (New York: Oxford University Press, 1964), pp. 757–60.

26. Gerhard Eberling, *The Nature of Faith*, trans. Ronald Gregor Smith (Philadelphia: Fortress Press, 1961), p. 187.

27. Kenneth W. Thompson, *Interpreters and Critics of the Cold War* (Washington, DC: University Press of America, 1978), p. xvii.

Postscript

This book has been a study of rhetoric as reality, a study in the rhetorical origins of the cold war in America. We said at the outset that the cold war between the United States and the Soviet Union is over. That seems to be true. However, if the cold war was rhetorically constructed—a political reality created by a crusading and moralistic rhetoric—it is *only* over when applied to the Soviet Union. As a political way of thinking, the cold war not only survives but thrives.

On the domestic scene the object of the current cold war has switched from communists to drug dealers and users. The war on drugs, begun by President Nixon and accelerated by Presidents Reagan and Bush, is another in a long line of domestic cold wars. Civil liberties have been suspended through the infamous "no knock" laws; foreign policy adventures, such as the invasion of Panama to capture the "drug kingpin" Noriega, issue from this war. It may be a sign of the time that loyalty oaths have been replaced with urine tests. And few venture to challenge the basic assumptions of this war without weighing the dire consequences they face.

In foreign affairs, the rhetoric surrounding Iraqi–American confrontation exhibited many of the same predispositions and arguments that originally defined the Soviet–American disputes in the late 1940s. Saddam Hussein was compared to Hitler; his invasion of Kuwait was defined as naked aggression; compromise with Iraq conjured up images of Munich and appeasement. President Bush drew a line in the sand and demanded Hussein abide by U.S. conditions for ending the conflict.

The cold war, as a rhetorically constructed political reality that conditions the way Americans think about political events both at home and abroad, lives on.

Only the names have changed.

Selected Bibliography

BOOKS

Aaron, Daniel. *Writers on the Left*. New York: Harcourt, Brace, and World, 1961.

Acheson, Dean. *Present at the Creation*. New York: W. W. Norton, 1969.

Adler, Selig. *The Isolationist Impulse: Its Twentieth Century Reaction*. New York: Free Press, 1957.

Allport, Gordon. *The Nature of Prejudice*. Garden City, NY: Anchor Books, 1958.

Alperovitz, Gar. *Atomic Diplomacy: Hiroshima and Potsdam*. New York: Penguin, 1985.

Ambrose, Stephen E. *Nixon: The Education of a Politician, 1913–1962*. New York: Simon and Schuster, 1987.

———. *Rise to Globalism: American Foreign Policy Since 1938*. New York: Penguin, 1985.

Aronson, James. *The Press and the Cold War*. Boston: Beacon Press, 1970.

Bailey, Thomas A. *America Faces Russia*. Ithaca, NY: Cornell University Press, 1950.

———. *A Diplomatic History of the United States*. 7th ed. New York: Appleton-Century-Crofts, 1974.

———. *The Marshall Plan Summer*. Stanford, CA: Hoover Institution Press, 1977.

Barnet, Richard. *The Giants: Russia and America*. New York: Simon and Schuster, 1977.

Bassow, Whitman. *The Moscow Correspondents: Reporting on Russia From the Revolution to Glasnost*. New York: William Morrow, 1988.

Bennett, David H. *The Party of Fear: From Nativist Movements to the New Right in American History*. New York: Vintage, 1990.

Bentley, Eric. *Thirty Years of Treason*. New York: Viking, 1971.

Berger, Peter L., and Thomas Luckmann. *The Social Construction of Reality*. New York: Anchor Books, 1967.

Bernstein, Barton J., and Allen J. Matusow, eds. *The Truman Administration: A Documentary History*. New York: Harper Colophon, 1966.

Biddle, Francis. *Fear of Freedom*. New York: Doubleday, 1951.

Black, Max. *Models and Metaphors*. Ithaca, NY: Cornell University Press, 1962.

Blenkinsopp, Joseph. *A History of Prophesy in Israel*. Philadelphia, PA: Westminster Press, 1983.

Blum, John Morton, ed. *The Price of Vision: The Diary of Henry A. Wallace, 1942–1946*. Boston: Houghton Mifflin, 1973.

Bohlen, Charles E. *The Transformation of American Foreign Policy*. New York: W. W. Norton, 1969.

———. *Witness to History, 1929–1969*. New York: W. W. Norton, 1973.

Bontecou, Eleanor. *The Federal Loyalty-Security Program*. Ithaca, NY: Cornell University Press, 1953.

Brockriede, Wayne E., and Robert L. Scott. *Moments in the Rhetoric of the Cold War*. New York: Random House, 1970.

Burke, Kenneth. *Language as Symbolic Action: Essays on Life, Literature and Method*. Berkeley, CA: University of California Press, 1966.

———. *Permanence and Change*. Indianapolis, IN: Bobbs-Merrill, 1977.

———. *Philosophy of Literary Form*. Baton Rouge, LA: Louisiana State University Press, 1941.

Burns, James MacGregor. *The Crosswinds of Freedom*. New York: Alfred A. Knopf, 1989.

———. *Roosevelt: Soldier of Freedom, 1940–1945*. New York: Harcourt Brace Jovanovich, 1970.

Carroll, E. Malcolm. *Soviet Communism and Western Opinion, 1919–1921*. Ed. Frederic B. M. Hollyday. Chapel Hill, NC: University of North Carolina Press, 1965.

Cerf, Christopher, and Victor Navasky. *The Experts Speak*. New York: Pantheon, 1984.

Chamberlain, William Henry. *Beyond Containment*. Chicago: Henry Regnery, 1953.

Chambers, Whittaker. *Recollections of a Life*. New York: Henry Holt, 1988.

———. *Witness*. Chicago: Henry Regnery, 1952.

Chaute, David. *The Great Fear: The Anti-Communist Purge Under Truman and Eisenhower*. New York: Simon and Schuster, 1978.

Cherwitz, Richard A., and James W. Hikins. *Communication and Knowledge: An Investigation in Rhetorical Epistemology*. Columbia, SC: University of South Carolina Press, 1986.

Church, Joseph. *Language and the Discovery of Reality*. New York: Random House, 1961.

Churchill, Winston S. *Winston S. Churchill, His Complete Speeches, 1897–1963*. Ed. Robert Rhodes James. New York: Chelsea House, 1974.

Cochran, Bert. *Harry Truman and the Crisis Presidency*. New York: Funk and Wagnalls, 1973.

Connolly, William E. *The Terms of Political Discourse*. 2d ed. Princeton, NJ: Princeton University Press, 1983.

Conquest, Robert. *The Great Terror*. New York: Macmillan, 1968.

Cooke, Alister. *A Generation on Trial: U.S.A. v. Alger Hiss.* New York: Alfred A. Knopf, 1952.

Countryman, Vern. *Un-American Activities in The State of Washington: The Work of the Canwell Committee.* Ithaca, NY: Cornell University Press, 1951.

Crabb, Cecil V., Jr. *Bipartisan Foreign Policy: Myth or Reality?* Evanston, IL: Row, Peterson, 1957.

Cragan, John F., and Donald Shields, eds. *Applied Communication: A Dramatistic Perspective.* Prospect Heights, IL: Waveland, 1981.

Dallmayr, Fred. *Language and Politics.* Notre Dame, IN: University of Notre Dame Press, 1984.

Daniels, Robert V., ed. *A Documentary History of Communism.* 2 vols. New York: Vintage Russian Library, 1962.

Davies, Joseph P. *Mission to Moscow.* New York: Simon and Schuster, 1941.

Dean, Vera Micheles. *The United States and Russia.* Cambridge, MA: Harvard University Press, 1948.

de Huszar, George B., ed. *The Intellectuals: A Controversial Portrait.* Glencoe, IL: Free Press, 1960.

Deibel, Terry L., and John Lewis Gaddis, eds. *Containment: Concept and Policy.* 2 vols. Washington, DC: National Defense University Press, 1986.

Denton, Robert E., Jr., and Gary C. Woodward. *Political Communication in America.* New York: Praeger, 1985.

Derber, Charles, William A. Schwartz, and Yale Magrass. *Power in the Highest Degree: Professionals and the Rise of a New Mandarin Order.* New York: Oxford University Press, 1990.

de Tocqueville, Alexis. *Democracy in America.* 2 vols. The Henry Reeve text, rev. Francis Bowen, ed. Phillips Bradley. New York: Vintage, 1945.

Deutscher, Issac. *Stalin: A Political Biography, 2d ed.* New York: Oxford University Press, 1967.

Diggins, John Patrick. *The Proud Decades: America in War and Peace, 1941–1960.* New York: W. W. Norton, 1988.

Djilas, Milovan. *Conversations with Stalin.* Trans. Michael B. Petrovich. New York: Harcourt, Brace, and World, 1962.

Donovan, Robert J. *Conflict and Crisis: The Presidency of Harry Truman, 1945–1948.* New York: W. W. Norton, 1977.

———. *The Tumultuous Years: The Presidency of Harry S. Truman, 1949–1953.* New York: W. W. Norton, 1982.

Draper, Theodore. *American Communism and Soviet Russia.* New York: Vintage, 1986.

———. *The Roots of American Communism.* New York: Viking, 1957.

Druks, Herbert. *Harry S. Truman and the Russians, 1945–1953.* New York: Robert Speller and Sons, 1966.

Duranty, Walter. *The Kremlin and the People.* New York: Reynal and Hitchcock, 1941.

Durkheim, Emile. *The Elemental Forms of Religious Life.* Trans. Joseph Swain. London: George Allen S. Unwin, 1915.

Eberling, Gerhard. *The Nature of Faith.* Trans. Ronald Gregor Smith. Philadelphia, PA: Fortress Press, 1961.

Edelman, Murray. *Politics as Symbolic Action.* Chicago: Markam, 1971.

————. *The Symbolic Uses of Politics.* Urbana, IL: University of Illinois Press, 1964.

Ellul, Jacques. *The Political Illusion.* New York: Alfred A. Knopf, 1967.

————. *Propaganda: The Formation of Men's Attitudes.* Trans. Konrad Kellan and Jean Lerner. New York: Alfred A. Knopf, 1965.

Feis, Herbert. *Between War and Peace: The Postdam Conference.* Princeton, NJ: Princeton University Press, 1960.

————. *Churchill, Roosevelt, Stalin: The War They Waged and the Peace They Sought.* Princeton, NJ: Princeton University Press, 1957.

————. *From Trust to Terror: The Onset of the Cold War, 1945–1950.* New York: W. W. Norton, 1970.

Filene, Peter G., ed. *American Views of the Soviet Union, 1917–1965.* Homewood, IL: Dorsey Press, 1968.

————. *Americans and the Soviet Experiment, 1917–1933.* Cambridge, MA: Harvard University Press, 1967.

Fitzgerald, Frances. *America Revised: History Schoolbooks in the Twentieth Century.* Boston: Little, Brown, 1979.

Fleming, D. F. *The Cold War and Its Origins, 1917–1960.* 2 vols. Garden City, NY: Doubleday, 1961.

Forrestal, James V. *The Forrestal Diaries.* Ed. Walter Millis. New York: Viking, 1951.

Foss, Sonja K. *Rhetorical Criticism: Exploration and Practice.* Prospect Heights, IL: Waveland, 1989.

Freeland, Richard M. *The Truman Doctrine and the Origins of McCarthyism.* New York: Alfred A. Knopf, 1972.

Fried, Richard M. *Nightmare in Red.* New York: Oxford University Press, 1990.

Funk, Robert. *Language, Hermeneutic, and the Word of God.* New York: Harper and Row, 1966.

Gaddis, John Lewis. *The Long Peace: Inquiries into the History of the Cold War.* New York: Oxford University Press, 1987.

————. *Russia, the Soviet Union and the United States: An Interpretative History.* New York: Alfred A. Knopf, 1978.

————. *Strategies of Containment.* New York: Oxford University Press, 1982.

————. *The United States and the Origins of the Cold War, 1941–1947.* New York: Columbia University Press, 1972.

Gardner, Lloyd C. *Architects of Illusion: Men and Ideas in American Foreign Policy, 1941–1949.* Chicago: Quadrangle, 1970.

Gates, John. *The Story of an American Communist.* New York: Thomas Nelson, 1958.

Gellman, Barton. *Contending with Kennan.* New York: Praeger, 1984.

Goldman, Eric F. *The Crucial Decade: America, 1945–1955.* New York: Alfred A. Knopf, 1956.

Goodman, Walter. *The Committee.* New York: Farrar, Straus and Giroux, 1968.

Gornick, Vivian. *The Romance of American Communism.* New York: Basic Books, 1977.

Goulden, Joseph C. *The Best Years: 1945–1950.* New York: Atheneum, 1976.

Graebner, Norman A., ed. *Ideas and Diplomacy.* New York: Oxford University Press, 1964.

Green, David. *Shaping Political Consciousness*. Ithaca, NY: Cornell University Press, 1983.

Halle, Louis. *The Cold War as History*. New York: Harper and Row, 1967.

Harbutt, Fraser. *The Iron Curtain: Churchill, America, and the Origins of the Cold War*. New York: Oxford University Press, 1986.

Harriman, W. Averell, and Elie Abel. *Special Envoy to Churchill and Stalin, 1941–1946*. New York: Random House, 1975.

Harris, George S. *Troubled Alliance: Turkish-American Problems in Historical Perspective, 1945–1971*. Washington, DC: American Enterprise Institute for Public Policy Research, 1972.

Hartmann, Susan M. *Truman and the 80th Congress*. New York: Columbia University Press, 1973.

Hofstadter, Richard F. *Anti-Intellectualism in American Life*. New York: Alfred A. Knopf, 1963.

Hogan, Michael J. *The Marshall Plan: America, Britain, and the Reconstruction of Western Europe, 1947–1952*. Cambridge, MA: Cambridge University Press, 1987.

Horowitz, David, ed. *Corporations and the Cold War*. New York: Modern Reader, 1969.

——. *The Free World Colossus: A Critique of American Foreign Policy in the Cold War*. New York: Hill and Wang, 1965.

Howe, Irving, and Lewis Coser. *The American Communist Party: A Critical History, 1919–1957*. Boston: Beacon Press, 1957.

Humes, James C. *Churchill, Speaker of the Century*. New York: Stein and Day, 1980.

Iatrides, John O., ed. *Greece in the 1940s: A Nation in Crisis*. Hanover, NH: University Press of New England, 1981.

Jones, Howard. *"A New Kind of War": America's Global Strategy and the Truman Doctrine*. New York: Oxford University Press, 1989.

Jones, Joseph M. *The Fifteen Weeks*. New York: Viking, 1955.

Kahn, Gordon. *Hollywood on Trial*. New York: Boni and Gaer, 1948.

Kegley, Charles W., Jr., and Pat McGowan, eds. *Foreign Policy, USA/USSR*. Beverly Hills, CA: Sage, 1982.

Kennan, George F. *Memoirs: 1925–1950*. Boston: Atlantic-Little, Brown, 1967.

——. *On Dealing with the Communist World*. New York: Harper and Row, 1964.

——. *Realities of American Foreign Policy*. Princeton, NJ: Princeton University Press, 1954.

——. *Russia and the West Under Lenin and Stalin*. Boston: Little, Brown, 1960.

——. *Russia Leaves the War*. Princeton, NJ: Princeton University Press, 1956.

——. *Soviet–American Relations, 1917–1919: The Decision to Intervene*. Princeton, NJ: Princeton University Press, 1958.

Klehr, Harvey. *The Heyday of American Communism: The Depression Decade*. New York: Basic Books, 1984.

Koen, Ross Y. *The China Lobby in American Politics*. New York: Harper and Row, 1974.

Kolko, Gabriel. *The Politics of War: The World and United States Foreign Policy, 1943–1945*. New York: Random House, 1968.

Kolko, Gabriel, and Joyce Kolko. *The Limits of Power: The World and United States Foreign Policy, 1945–1954*. New York: Harper and Row, 1972.

Krock, Arthur. *Memoirs*. New York: Funk and Wagnalls, 1968.

Kuniholm, Bruce Robellet. *The Origins of the Cold War in the Near East*. Princeton, NJ: Princeton University Press, 1980.

LaFeber, Walter. *America, Russia, and the Cold War, 1945–1975*. New York: John Wiley and Sons, 1976.

Lakoff, George, and Mark Johnson. *Metaphors We Live By*. Chicago: University of Chicago Press, 1980.

Lardner, Ring, Jr. *The Lardners: My Family Remembered*. New York: Harper Colophon, 1977.

Larson, Deborah Welch. *Origins of Containment: A Psychological Explanation*. Princeton, NJ: Princeton University Press, 1985.

Latham, Earl. *The Communist Controversy in Washington*. New York: Atheneum, 1969.

Lefebvre, Henri. *The Sociology of Marx*. Trans. Norbert Guterman. New York: Pantheon, 1968.

Leff, Michael C., and Fred J. Kauffeld, eds. *Texts in Context: Critical Dialogues on Significant Episodes in American Political Rhetoric*. Davids, CA: Hermagoras Press, 1989.

Leuchtenburg, William E. *In the Shadow of FDR*. Ithaca, NY: Cornell University Press, 1985.

Levering, Ralph. *American Opinion and the Russian Alliance, 1939–1945*. Chapel Hill, NC: University of North Carolina Press, 1976.

Levitt, Morton, and Michael Levitt. *A Tissue of Lies: Nixon vs. Hiss*. New York: McGraw-Hill, 1979.

Liebovich, Louis. *The Press and the Origins of the Cold War, 1944–1947*. New York: Praeger, 1988.

Lifka, Thomas E. *The Concept of "Totalitarianism" and American Foreign Policy*. 2 vols. New York: Garland Publishing, 1988.

Lindblom, J. *Prophecy in Ancient Israel*. Philadelphia, PA: Fortress Press, 1962.

Lippmann, Walter. *The Cold War: A Study in American Foreign Policy*. New York: Harper and Brothers, 1947.

———. *The Communist World and Ours*. Boston: Little, Brown, 1958.

———. *The Good Society*. Boston: Little, Brown, 1936.

———. *Public Opinion*. New York: Harcourt, Brace, 1922.

———. *U.S. Foreign Policy: Shield of the Republic*. Boston: Little, Brown, 1943.

———. *U.S. War Aims*. Boston: Little, Brown, 1944.

MacDougall, Curtis D. *Gideon's Army*. 3 vols. New York: Marzani and Munsell, 1965.

McElvanine, Robert. *The Great Depression: America 1929–1941*. New York: Times Books, 1984.

Manchester, William. *The Glory and the Dream*. New York: Bantam, 1975.

Markowitz, Norman D. *The Rise and Fall of the People's Century: Henry A. Wallace and American Liberalism, 1941–1948*. New York: Free Press, 1973.

Mastny, Vojtech. *Russia's Road to the Cold War*. New York: Columbia University Press, 1979.

May, Ernest R. *"Lessons" of the Past: The Use and Misuse of History in American Foreign Policy*. New York: Oxford University Press, 1973.

Mayer, Arno J. *Politics of Peacemaking: Containment and Counterrevolution at Versailles, 1918–1919*. New York: Alfred A. Knopf, 1967.

Mayers, David. *George Kennan and the Dilemmas of U.S. Foreign Policy*. New York: Oxford University Press, 1988.

Mee, Charles L., Jr. *The Marshall Plan: The Launching of Pax Americana*. New York: Simon and Schuster, 1984.

————. *Meeting at Potsdam*. New York: M. Evans, 1975.

Messer, Robert L. *The End of an Alliance: James F. Byrnes, Roosevelt, Truman and the Origins of the Cold War*. Chapel Hill, NC: University of North Carolina Press, 1982.

Mitchell, W. J. T., ed. *On Narrative*. Chicago: University of Chicago Press, 1981.

Moran, Lord. *Churchill, Taken from the Diaries of Lord Moran, The Struggle for Survival, 1940–1965*. Boston: Houghton Mifflin, 1966.

Morris, Roger. *Richard Milhous Nixon: The Rise of an American Politician*. New York: Henry Holt, 1990.

Murray, Robert K. *Red Scare: A Study in National Hysteria, 1919–1920*. New York: McGraw-Hill, 1955.

Neustadt, Richard. *Presidential Power: The Politics of Leadership*. New York: John Wiley, 1980.

Neustadt, Richard, and Ernest R. May. *Thinking in Time: The Uses of History for Decision Makers*. New York: Free Press, 1986.

Newman, Robert P. *The Cold War Romance of Lillian Hellman and John Melby*. Chapel Hill, NC: University of North Carolina Press, 1989.

Nisbet, Robert. *The Sociological Tradition*. New York: Basic Books, 1966.

Nixon, Richard. *Six Crises*. Garden City, NY: Doubleday, 1962.

Nomad, Max. *Political Heretics: From Plato to Mao Tse-tung*. Ann Arbor, MI: University of Michigan Press, 1963.

O'Neill, William L. *A Better World*. New York: Simon and Schuster, 1982.

Parenti, Michael. *The Anti-Communist Impulse*. New York: Random House, 1969.

Patterson, Thomas G. *Meeting the Communist Threat: Truman to Reagan*. Oxford: Oxford University Press, 1988.

————. *On Every Front: The Making of the Cold War*. New York: W. W. Norton, 1979.

Patterson, Thomas G., ed. *Cold War Critics*. Chicago: Quadrangle Books, 1971.

————, ed. *The Origins of the Cold War*. Lexington, MA: D. C. Heath, 1974.

Pells, Richard H. *Radical Visions and American Dreams: Culture and Social Thought in the Depression Years*. New York: Harper and Row, 1973.

Phillips, Cabell. *The Truman Presidency*. New York: Macmillan, 1966.

Pogue, Forrest C. *George C. Marshall: Statesman, 1945–1959*. New York: Penguin, 1989.

Ponomaryov, B., A. Gromyko, and V. Khvostov, eds. *History of Soviet Foreign Policy, 1945–1970*. Trans. David Skvirsky. Moscow: Progress Publishers, 1974.

Prange, Gordon W., in collaboration with Donald M. Goldstein and Katherine V. Dillon. *At Dawn We Slept: The Untold History of Pearl Harbor*. New York: Penguin, 1982.

Purifoy, Lewis McCarroll. *Harry Truman's China Policy: McCarthyism and the Diplomacy of Hysteria, 1947–1951*. New York: New Viewpoints, 1976.

Rad, Gerhard von. *Old Testament Theology*. 2 vols. New York: Harper and Row, 1965.

Radosh, Ronald. *Prophets on the Right*. New York: Simon and Schuster, 1975.

Reedy, George. *The Twilight of the Presidency*. New York: World, 1977.

Rees, David. *Korea: The Limited War*. New York: St. Martin's Press, 1964.

Ricoeur, Paul. *Hermeneutics and the Human Sciences*. Trans. John B. Thompson. Cambridge, UK: Cambridge University Press, 1981.

Robertson, James Oliver. *American Myth, American Reality*. New York: Hill and Wang, 1980.

Rowley, H. H. *Prophecy and Religion in Ancient China and Israel*. New York: Harper and Brothers, 1956.

Safire, William. *Safire's Political Dictionary*. New York: Ballantine, 1978.

Sanders, Jerry W. *Peddlers of Crisis: The Committee on the Present Danger and the Politics of Containment*. Boston: South End Press, 1983.

Schapsmeier, Edward L., and Frederick H. Schapsmeier. *Prophet in Politics: Henry A. Wallace and the War Years, 1940–1945*. Ames, IA: Iowa State University Press, 1970.

Schilling, Warner R., Paul Y. Hammond, and Glen H. Snyder. *Strategy, Politics, and the Defense Budget*. New York: Columbia University Press, 1962.

Schlesinger, Arthur M., Jr. *The Cycles of American History*. Boston: Houghton Mifflin, 1986.

———. *The Politics of Upheaval*. Boston: Houghton Mifflin, 1960.

Schoenbaum, Thomas J. *Waging Peace and War: Dean Rusk in the Truman, Kennedy and Johnson Years*. New York: Simon and Schuster, 1988.

Smith, John Chabot. *Alger Hiss: The True Story*. New York: Holt, Rinehart and Winston, 1976.

Sorensen, Theodore C. *Kennedy*. New York: Harper and Row, 1965.

Spanier, John W. *American Foreign Policy Since World War II*. New York: Holt, Rinehart and Winston, 1980.

Steel, Ronald. *Walter Lippmann and the American Century*. Boston: Atlantic-Little, Brown, 1980.

Stephanson, Anders. *Kennan and the Art of Foreign Policy*. Cambridge, MA: Harvard University Press, 1989.

Stillman, E., and W. Pfaff. *Power and Impotence: The Failure of America's Foreign Policy*. New York: Random House, 1966.

Stoessinger, John G. *Nations in Darkness*. New York: Random House, 1971.

Sumner, Charles. *Speech of Hon. Charles Sumner of Massachusetts on the Cession of Russian Alaska to the United States*. Washington, DC: Congressional Globe Office, 1867.

Swanberg, W. A. *Citizen Hearst*. New York: Charles Scribner and Sons, 1961.

Taft, Robert A. *A Foreign Policy for Americans*. Garden City, NY: Doubleday, 1951.

Taubman, William. *Stalin's American Policy: From Entente to Detente to Cold War*. New York: W. W. Norton, 1982.

Theoharis, Athan. *Seeds of Repression: Harry S. Truman and the Origins of McCarthyism*. Chicago: Quadrangle, 1971.

Thomas, Hugh. *Armed Truce: The Beginnings of the Cold War, 1945–1946.* New York: Atheneum, 1986.

Thompson, Kenneth W. *Interpreters and Critics of the Cold War.* Washington, DC: University Press of America, 1978.

Travis, Frederick F. *George Kennan and the American-Russian Relationship, 1865–1924.* Athens, OH: Ohio University Press, 1990.

Truman, Harry S. *Memoirs.* 2 vols. Garden City, NY: Doubleday, 1955, 1956.

———. *Off the Record: The Private Papers of Harry S. Truman.* Ed. Robert H. Ferrell. New York: Harper and Row, 1980.

Truman, Margaret. *Harry S. Truman.* New York: Pocket Books, 1974.

Ulam, Adam. *Dangerous Relations: The Soviet Union in World Politics, 1970–1982.* New York: Oxford University Press, 1983.

———. *Expansion and Coexistence: The History of Soviet Foreign Policy, 1917–1967.* New York: Praeger, 1968.

———. *The Rivals.* New York: Penguin, 1976.

———. *Stalin: The Man and His Era.* Boston: Beacon Press, 1989.

Vandenberg, Arthur H. *The Private Papers of Senator Vandenberg.* Ed. Arthur H. Vandenberg, Jr. Boston: Houghton Mifflin, 1973.

Vaughan, Robert. *Only Victims.* New York: G. P. Putnam's Sons, 1972.

Walker, Samuel. *Henry A. Wallace and American Foreign Policy.* Westport, CT: Greenwood, 1976.

Walton, Richard J. *Henry Wallace, Harry Truman, and the Cold War.* New York: Viking, 1976.

Weinstein, Allen. *Perjury: The Hiss-Chambers Case.* New York: Alfred A. Knopf, 1978.

Whelan, Richard. *Drawing the Line: The Korean War, 1950–1953.* Boston: Little, Brown, 1990.

Wilkie, Wendell L. *One World.* New York: Simon and Schuster, 1943.

Williams, William Appleton. *American-Russian-Relations, 1781–1947.* New York: Rinehart, 1952.

———. *The Tragedy of American Diplomacy.* New York: Delta, 1962.

Windt, Theodore Otto, Jr. *Presidents and Protesters: Political Rhetoric in the 1960s.* Tuscaloosa, AL: University of Alabama Press, 1990.

Wittner, Lawrence S. *American Intervention in Greece, 1943–1949.* New York: Columbia University Press, 1982.

Yarnell, Allen. *Democrats and Progressives: The 1948 Presidential Election as a Test of Postwar Liberalism.* Berkeley, CA: University of California Press, 1974.

Yergin, Daniel. *Shattered Peace: The Origins of the Cold War and the National Security State.* Boston: Houghton Mifflin, 1977.

ARTICLES

Alsop, Joseph. "The Strange Case of Louis Budenz," *Atlantic* (April 1952): 29–33.

Armstrong, John P. "The Enigma of Senator Taft and American Foreign Policy," *Review of Politics* 17 (April 1955): 206–31.

Blankenship, Jane, and Janette Kenner Muir. "On Imaging the Future: The

Secular Search for 'Piety.' " *Communication Quarterly* 35 (Winter 1987): 1–12.

Brummett, Barry. "A Eulogy for Epistemic Rhetoric." *Quarterly Journal of Speech* 76 (February 1990): 69–72.

Cowley, Malcolm. "Russian Turnabout." *New Republic* (June 14, 1943): 800–1.

Darcy, James. "The Legend of Eugene Debs: Prophetic *Ethos* as Radical Argument." *Quarterly Journal of Speech* 74 (November 1988): 434–52.

Ehrlich, Larry G. "Ambassador in the Yard." *Southern Speech Communication Journal* 38 (Fall 1972): 1–12.

Fisher, Walter R. "Clarifying the Narrative Paradigm." *Communication Monographs* 56 (March 1989): 55–58.

———. "Narration as a Human Communication Paradigm: The Case of Public Moral Argument." *Communication Monographs* 51 (March 1984): 1–22.

Gaddis, John Lewis. "The Emerging Post-Revisionist Synthesis on the Origins of the Cold War." *Diplomatic History* 7 (Summer 1983): 171–90.

———. "Reconsiderations: Was the Truman Doctrine a Real Turning Point?" *Foreign Affairs* 52 (January 1974): 386–402.

Goodnight, G. Thomas. "The Personal, Technical, and Public Spheres of Argument: A Speculative Inquiry into the Art of Public Deliberation." *Journal of the American Forensic Association* 18 (Spring 1982): 214–17.

Hensley, Carl Wayne. "Harry S. Truman: Fundamental Americanism in Foreign Policy Speechmaking, 1945–1946." *Southern Speech Communication Journal* 40 (Winter 1975): 180–90.

Hikins, James W. "The Rhetoric of 'Unconditional Surrender' and the Decision to Drop the Atomic Bomb." *Quarterly Journal of Speech* 69 (November 1983): 379–400.

Ivie, Robert L. "Literalizing the Metaphor of Soviet Savagery: President Truman's Plain Style." *Southern Speech Communication Journal* 51 (Winter 1986): 91–105.

———. "Metaphor and the Rhetorical Invention of Cold War 'Idealists.' " *Communication Monographs* 54 (June 1987): 165–82.

———. "Presidential Motives for War." *Quarterly Journal of Speech* 60 (October 1974): 337–45.

Kauffman, Charles. "Names and Weapons." *Communication Monographs* 56 (September 1989): 271–85.

Kennan, George F. "The Sources of Soviet Conduct." *Foreign Affairs* 25 (July 1947): 566–82.

Leff, Michael. "Topical Invention and Metaphoric Interaction." *Southern Speech Communication Journal* 48 (Spring 1983): 214–29.

Lyne, John, and Henry F. Howe. "The Rhetoric of Expertise: E. O. Wilson and Sociobiography." *Quarterly Journal of Speech* 76 (May 1990): 134–51.

McKerrow, Ray E. "Truman and Korea: Rhetoric in the Pursuit of Victory." *Central States Speech Journal* 28 (Spring 1977): 1–12.

Mark, Eduard. "Charles E. Bohlen and the Acceptable Limits of Soviet Hegemony in Eastern Europe: A Memorandum of 18 October 1945." *Diplomatic History* 3 (Spring 1979): 201–13.

———. "The Question of Containment: A Reply to John Lewis Gaddis." *Foreign Affairs* 56 (January 1978): 430–40.

Messer, Robert L. "Paths Not Taken: The United States Department of State and Alternatives to Containment, 1945–1946." *Diplomatic History* 1 (Fall 1977): 297–319.

Newman, Robert P. "Lethal Rhetoric: The Selling of the China Myths." *Quarterly Journal of Speech* 61 (April 1975): 113–28.

———. "The Self-Inflicted Wound: The China White Paper of 1949." *Prologue* 14 (Fall 1982): 141–56.

Oravec, Christine. " 'Observation' in Aristotle's Theory of Epideictic." *Philosophy and Rhetoric* 9 (Summer 1976): 162–74.

Pegler, Westbrook. "What Strange Bedfellows." *American Legion Magazine* (April 1939): 10–11.

Poulakos, Takis. "Isocrates's Use of Narrative in the Evagoras: Epideictic Rhetoric and Moral Action." *Quarterly Journal of Speech* 73 (August 1987): 317–28.

Procter, David E. "The Dynamic Spectacle: Transforming Experience into Social Forms of Community." *Quarterly Journal of Speech* 76 (May 1990): 117–33.

Roskin, Michael. "From Pearl Harbor to Vietnam: Shifting Generational Paradigms and Foreign Policy." *Political Science Quarterly* 89 (Fall 1974): 563–88.

Ryan, Henry Butterfield, Jr. "The American Intellectual Tradition Reflected in the Truman Doctrine." *American Scholar* 42 (Spring 1973): 294–307.

Scott, Robert L. "Epistemic Rhetoric and Criticism: Where Barry Brummett Goes Wrong." *Quarterly Journal of Speech* 76 (November 1990): 300–3.

———. "On Viewing Rhetoric as Epistemic." *Central States Speech Journal* 18 (February 1967): 9–17.

Towner, W. Sibley. "On Calling People 'Prophets' in 1970." *Interpretation* 24 (October 1970): 134–51.

Trout, B. Thomas. "Rhetoric Revisited: Political Legitimation and the Cold War." *International Studies Quarterly* 19 (September 1979): 251–84.

U.S. National Security Council. "NSC–68: A Report to the National Security Council, April 14, 1950." *Naval War College Review* (May-June 1975): 51–107.

Walker, J. Samuel. " 'No More Cold War': American Foreign Policy and the Soviet Peace Offensive." *Diplomatic History* 5 (Winter 1981): 75–91.

Wander, Philip. "The Rhetoric of Foreign Policy." *Quarterly Journal of Speech* 70 (November 1984): 339–61.

Wharton, James A. "The Occasion of the Word of God." *Austin Seminary Bulletin* (September 1968): 22–34.

Windt, Theodore O., Jr. "The Evolution of Soviet Diplomacy." *Pennsylvania Speech Annual* 23 (September 1966): 58–64.

UNPUBLISHED MATERIALS: DOCTORAL DISSERTATIONS AND PAPERS

Carl, William Joseph III. "Old Testament Prophecy and the Question of Prophetic Preaching: A Perspective on Ecclesiastical Protest to the Vietnam War and the Participation of William Sloane Coffin, Jr." University of Pittsburgh, 1977.

Hinds, Lynn Boyd. "The Social Construction of the Cold War Reality." University of Pittsburgh, 1977.

Ingold, Beth. "The Committee on the Present Danger: A Study of Elite and Public Influence, 1976–1980." University of Pittsburgh, 1989.

Iselin, John J. "The Truman Doctrine: A Study in the Relationship Between Crisis and Foreign Policy-Making." Harvard University, 1964.

Sirgiovanni, George. "An Undercurrent of Suspicion: Anti-Communist and Anti-Soviet Opinion in World War II America." Rutgers University, 1988.

Weiner, Bernard. "The Truman Doctrine: Background and Presentation." Claremont Graduate School, 1967.

Windt, Theodore O., Jr. "The Rhetoric of Peaceful Coexistence: A Criticism of Nikita Khrushchev's American Speeches, 1959." Ohio State University, 1965.

———. "The Rhetoric of Politics." University of Pittsburgh, 1970.

Young, Marilyn. "The Rhetorical Origins of American Anti-Communism." University of Pittsburgh, 1970.

Index

ABOUT THE AUTHORS

LYNN BOYD HINDS is Associate Professor of Broadcast Journalism at the Perley Isaac Reed School of Journalism at West Virginia University. He is both an academic and a professional journalist.

Dr. Hinds spent 20 years in radio and television with ABC, Group W., and Hearst Broadcasting companies. In addition to his academic duties, he is currently producer and host of "The Pennsylvania Game" for the Pennsylvania Public Television Network

THEODORE OTTO WINDT, JR., is Professor of Political Rhetoric at the University of Pittsburgh. He is one of the Chancellor's Distinguished Teachers of the University. Dr. Windt is the author of two previous books, *Presidents and Protesters: Political Rhetoric in the 1960s* and *Rhetoric as a Human Adventure: A Biography of Everett Lee Hunt*. He is the editor of *Presidential Rhetoric: 1961 to the Present* (now in its 4th edition) and co-editor with his wife, Dr. Beth Ingold, of *Essays in Presidential Rhetoric* (now in its 3rd edition).

Dr. Windt is also a political consultant and professional journalist. He served on the Harvard Commission on Presidential News Conferences that issued its report, *Reviving the Presidential News Conference*, in 1988. He is political commentator on national politics for "Weekend Magazine" on KDKA-TV and for KQV radio in Pittsburgh.